KASHI PRASAD JAYASWAL
The Making of a 'Nationalist' Historian

KASHI PRASAD JAYASWAL
The Making of a 'Nationalist' Historian

Ratan Lal

AAKAR

Kashi Prasad Jayaswal: The Making of a 'Nationalist' Historian
Ratan Lal

First Published 2018

ISBN 978-93-5002-528-4

Published by
AAKAR BOOKS
28 E Pocket IV, Mayur Vihar Phase I
Delhi 110 091 India
aakarbooks@gmail.com

Laser Typeset at
Arpit Printographers, Delhi 110 032

Printed at
Mudrak, 30 A, Patparganj, Delhi 110 091

Foreword

Kashi Prasad Jayaswal was a leading intellectual of India during the early 20th century. He was born in 1881 and died in 1937 and lived a very eventful life. Educated in both India and England, he got involved in nationalist politics early in life which profoundly influenced his writings. He wrote prolifically on ancient Indian history and social issues of the time in Hindi as well as in English. His writings, like those of other nationalist historians, posed a major challenge to imperialist perception of Indian society. Inspired by a strong feeling of nationalism, Jayaswal produced many works, of which his *Hindu Polity* became very popular. It provided an ideological weapon to the nationalist movement and has continued to influence many Indians in independent India.

In this study, Dr. Ratan Lal has discussed at length the relevance of Jayaswal's writings during the period of India's freedom movement and has situated them in the changing context of nationalist discourse in recent years. He is fully aware that in post-colonial India Jayaswal's ideas about ancient India have lost much of their relevance, but their importance in the history of ideas in modern period cannot be minimized. It is from this point of view that Dr. Lal has presented a thorough analysis of Jayaswal's writings. This comprehensive study, based on several years of labour with meticulous attention to details, is a pioneering analysis of the ideas about the past in an important phase of India's history. It will be of great value not only to those who are interested in the development of Indian historiography but also to those who wish to investigate the intellectual dimensions of India's anti-imperialist struggle.

Going beyond Jayaswal's writings on history, Dr. Lal has explored his immense contribution to Hindi language and literature. A prolific writer in Hindi, Jayaswal penned travelogues, biographies, poetry and articles on an astounding range of themes including history, social issues, domestic and international politics, language and script. Of particular interest is Lal's detailed exposition of Jayaswal's position on the contentious issue of 'national' language and script—an issue that provoked heated debates and agitations in the pre-independence period and the immediate post-independence years and still refuses to die away.

Jayaswal, besides being a towering scholar and indefatigable writer and speaker, was an efficient institution builder. It is to this another remarkable aspect of his persona that Dr. Lal draws attention to. Not only did Jayaswal play a key role as the founder-member of two institutions, viz. Bihar Oriental Research Society and Patna Museum, but he was also associated with the Patna University in various academic and administrative capacities for almost two decades. His multidirectional initiatives were chiefly aimed at building the human and material resources of these institutions and establishing their pre-eminence as centres of excellence. I am full of praise for Ratan Lal's work in bringing to the fore a multifaceted public intellectual of modern India relegated to oblivion, and wish him greater success in his future academic ventures. I commend his work to scholars and students of history.

D.N. Jha
Professor of History (Retired)
University of Delhi.

Contents

Note on Transliteration

Sanskrit personal names, titles of texts and other terms appear in the book both with and without italics and diacritical marks, as well as with different diacritical marks. Further, compound names and titles appear both with and without hyphenation. Some instances are Bhāraśivas/Bhāra-Śivas, *Arthaśāstra*/ Arthaśāstra/ Artha-Śāstra, *Devīcandraguptam/Devī-Chandraguptam*, *Mudrārākṣasa/ Mudrā-Rākshasa*, Bindusāra/Bindusara, Candragupta Maurya/ Chandra Gupta Maurya, etc. Such discrepancies are due to differences in the way KPJ used them and the way in which they are rendered as per the current international system of Sanskrit transliteration. Further, it appears that he used diacritical marks in his academic writings but sparingly so in his popular writings. No attempt has made to standardize the use of diacritical marks and hyphens in the words, since the purpose has been to retain them in the way they appear in the excerpts from KPJ's works and at the same time follow the modern system of transliteration in the rest of the book.

Acknowledgements

I have incurred a lot of debt during the course of the journey of my research and it would be impossible to acknowledge the contributions made by all my teachers, friends, and family members. Still, the occasion demands it, and my gratitude to all of them is heartfelt.

Being busy teaching and participating in diverse areas of political and social activism, I had given up all hope of getting into any kind of serious research. And then, Dr. Pradeep Kant Choudhary, my first teacher in the Delhi University academic world, took me to Prof. K.M. Shrimali and requested him to take me under his wings. Prof. Shrimali threw a serious, penetrative glance at me, saying, "Fine, but hope you understand what you are getting into. You will have to give up on all your activism, and distractions." I was prepared and made a promise to that effect. He gave me the *K.P. Jayaswal Commemoration Volume* and asked me to write a proposal. That is how the process of my knowing Kashi Prasad Jayaswal began. My sincere thanks to Prof. Shrimali for holding my hand through the entire process of research and writing. His numerous visits to my house during which he spent several hours on each occasion to correct, reframe, and raise serious questions have polished this work. Words would fail me in expressing my indebtedness to him for all his inputs.

After the retirement of Prof. Shrimali in September 2012, Dr. Shalini Shah became my formal supervisor. Though Prof. Shrimali continued to guide me althrough, she took an active interest in my work, and enriched it with her invaluable suggestions and corrections. "Thank You", Dr. Shah!

My M.Phil. supervisor and Guru, Prof. D.N. Jha, has been a permanent source of inspiration and wisdom. I will always remember him as somebody who taught me how to search and find books in the library. I hope he can, in this work, find some echoes of the training he imparted to me.

Prof. R.C. Thakran, the then Head of the History Department, offered sagacious and practical advice, always with an assuring smile. "Sir, I know it is not the final word." The two Kants in my life—Pradeep and Ravi—were responsible for my academic baptism at Deshbandhu College, and have been constant sources of encouragement and intellectual insights since my graduation days. A special thanks to both of them.

Raman Kumar, Asim Kumarji (Bihar Vidhan Sabha), Advocate Aditya P. Sahay (Patna), Advocate Aditya Kumar Choudhary (Delhi), Sujit Kumar Singh, (IPS, J&K Cadre), Uttam Prakash, Rakesh Ranjan, P.K. Bhagat, Amit Chamaria, Praveen Sonkar, Geetanjali Kumar and Satish Kumar Singh (Banaras) not only provided me infrastructural support and comfortable stay in different parts of the country during the field work, but also helped provide financial support when required. Rohit Parmar, Niraj Kumar, Samir Kumar, and Rudrani have always taken care of the confirmation of my train tickets so that I could reach my destinations on time. Dr. Atul Agarwal and Dr. Chandrashekhar have taken care of the health of my family, especially our kids, during my hectic field work and research. A big thanks to all of them.

Akash Sethi and Dr. Poonam Sethi have drilled into my research a sense of balance between material collection and its analysis and made me a disciplined researcher. My friend Sanjeev Dutt Sharma, Librarian (Hindu College), unearthed for me some invaluable manuscripts. Late Dr. D.N. Gupta and Mrs. Suchitra Gupta, my colleagues at Hindu College, were always ready with their suggestions and support. The grandson of Kashi Prasad Jayaswal, Advocate Anil Jayaswal (Patna High Court) gave me some rare books and photographs of Kashi Prasad Jayaswal and his family members. Ved Kumar Jayaswal (Delhi) provided me one of the rarest speeches of Kashi Prasad Jayaswal (at the Jabalpur Akhil Bharatavarshiya Haihay Kshatriya Mahasabha). Prof. Ramniranjan Parimalendu (Gaya) shared with me a rare manuscript of *Sapt-Suman* (written by Mohanlal Mahato Viyogi) on seven distinguished scholars of Bihar and Uttar Pradesh that is dedicated to Kashi Prasad Jayaswal. My former student Dipankar

Das helped me in correcting proofs and preparing the index. My sincere thanks to all of them.

My heartfelt thanks to my long-standing friends—Saumya Gupta, Prabhat Kumar Jha, Naresh Mohan Jha, Anumeha Jha, Mahesh Kumar Singh, Prof. Manoj Kumar Jha, Joseph Mathai, Satish Kumar, and Prof. Ajay Ghosh (Bhopal), Rajendra Verma (Lucknow), Dr. Shankar Kumar (Maharaja Agrasen College), Advocate Sanjay Paswan, and social activist Sanjay Yadav, Dr. Anupam Kumar and Shailendra Singh (Delhi)—for all their support and cooperation. The young researchers Kundan Raj, Rajesh Gautam (Delhi), Niraj Kumar (Banaras), and Amit Kumar (Patna) extended invaluable support in the collection of research material. My best wishes and thanks to all of them.

Dr. Sanjay Paswan (Patna University and former Minister of State, HRD, GoI) not only gave invaluable ideas but always encouraged me by giving moral support like an elder brother, whenever I felt exhausted and frustrated.

Ismail *Chacha* of my village provided me shelter and food for a month when I first came to Delhi in 1991, and leaving his work he took me to the different colleges of Delhi University and Jawaharlal Nehru University. I learnt a basic lesson in secularism from him and a big *salam* to him.

I do not think I can ever repay the *matri-pitri rina*. *Mai* and *Babuji* tolerated my early misadventures and kept faith in me. They never allowed the social and economic challenges of an extremely hierarchical society to affect me. I salute them once again. My late *Dada* and *Dadi* (Etwari Ram and Mahajani Devi)—illiterate jute mill workers in Calcutta—laid the foundations of education in my family way back in 1950s, which enabled me to reach this stage. All my academic achievements are dedicated to them.

Jaswant, Pushpa, Geeta and Gorakhnathji—the support staff at home—and my *grambhai* Balendra Mallah kept me absolutely free from all the household worries. Without their support, my research would not have been so smooth. Sincere thanks to them from the bottom of my heart.

During the course of research, my wife, Shalini, son Ishaan and the little '*badmash*' daughter Aadya have quietly put up with my *ekantwas*. I never took them out; they never demanded anything. When I started my work Aadya was just born and now she is going to school. How has time flown! I am very lucky to have such a mature and understanding family. I promise, I will make myself available to all of you now.

Libraries are the backbone of any research; without them no research would be completed. Therefore, huge thanks are due also to the librarians, officials and other staff members of the following libraries and research institutes: Hindu College Library; History Department Library, University of Delhi; Central Reference Library, University of Delhi; CSDS Library, Delhi; Indian Council of Historical Research, New Delhi; National Museum, New Delhi; National Archives of India, New Delhi; Nehru Memorial Museum and Library, New Delhi; Natrang Pratishthan, New Delhi; Central Reference Library, Allahabad; Hindi Sahitya Sammelan Library, Allahabad; Nagari Pracharini Sabha Library, Banaras; Central Reference Library, BHU; Bharat Kala Bhawan, BHU; History Department Library, BHU; Bihar State Archives, Patna; Bihar Research Institute, Patna; Kashi Prasad Jayaswal Research Institute, Patna; Patna Museum; Sachchidanand Sinha Institute, Patna; and Madhav Rao Sapre Library, Bhopal.

I am also grateful to Hindu College for granting me study leave from 2010 to 2013 and the non-teaching staff of the college for all their support and cooperation.

Finally, I thank all my 'critics' from Bihar to Delhi, whose challenges forced me to reinvent myself again and again.

Ratan Lal

Abbreviations

ARPM - *Annual Report of the Patna Museum*
ARPU - *Annual Report of the Patna University*
BORS - Bihar and Orissa Research Society
BORI - Bhandarkar Oriental Research Institute
BSA - Bihar State Archives
EI - *Epigraphia Indica*
GOS - *Gaekwad Oriental Series*
IA - *Indian Antiquary*
KPJ - Kashi Prasad Jayaswal
JASB - *Journal of the Asiatic Society of Bengal*
JRAS - *Journal of the Royal Asiatic Society of Great Britain and Ireland*
JBORS - *Journal of the Bihar and Orissa Research Society*
JOR - *Journal of Oriental Research*
JISOA - *Journal of the Indian Society of Oriental Art*
JA - *Jaina Antiquary*
KPJRI - Kashi Prasad Jayaswal Research Institute
KPJCV - *Kashi Prasad Jayaswal Commemoration Volume*
MR - *Modern Review*
NPP - *Nagari Pracharini Patrika*

Introduction

The modern history-writing in India was initiated by the British administrator-historians whose primary interest, of course, was the consolidation of their empire, and hence, it was no surprise they interpreted India's historical evolution to justify their rule. However, very soon, we find the presence of a group of Indian scholars who took upon themselves the responsibility of defending Indian history, culture, and polity against the vigorous attacks of the imperialist historians. The most prominent among such Indian scholars were—R.G. Bhandarkar, V.K. Rajwade, P.V. Kane, D.R. Bhandarkar, H.C. Raychaudhuri, R.C. Majumdar, and K.A. Nilakanta Sastri, etc., who were later on designated as 'nationalist' historians. Kashi Prasad Jayaswal (hereinafter KPJ) (1881-1937) belonged to the same age and creed.

KPJ was one of the earliest historians who challenged the ideological foundations of the British empire through his research work and innovative interpretations of ancient Indian history. He was the first multifaceted intellectual coming from the backward Kalwar community. Since his young days, KPJ was in close association with people like Mahavir Prasad Dwivedi, Kedar Nath Pathak, Acharya Ramchandra Shukla and so on. Later on, his house in Patna also became the *adda* (shelter) for the intellectuals coming from different parts of India and abroad. Scholars like Ramdhari Singh 'Dinkar', and Rahul Sankrityayan considered him *'pitatulya'* (like father) and *'agraj'* (elder brother) respectively. It is interesting to note that a number of Ph.Ds and M.Phils were awarded by different universities of independent India to the above-mentioned scholars, along with the publications of their collected writings and speeches. But KPJ—who was then considered as Jayaswal 'the international'—was denied such honours, which certainly showed the casteist mindset of the academia of independent India. Except a few obituaries and research articles and two doctoral theses,[1] no serious attempt has yet been made to contextualize and assess the writings and speeches of KPJ.

The present work is a modest beginning in the direction of an assessment of KPJ's life and his works. The work is divided into five chapters entitled: (1) KPJ: A Biographical Sketch, (2) Player in the Field of 'Hindi Nationalism', (3) The Fourth Estate Emerges: KPJ and the *Pataliputra*, (4) Conformist and Confrontationist: The Multifaceted Historian, and (5) Pedestalling Bihar's Intellectual Identity: KPJ as an Institution Builder. Our major sources have been both archival and published contributions of KPJ in Hindi and English. These include not only about a dozen monographs (authored and edited) but also more than 200 articles lying scattered in journals, magazines, and newspapers.

The work begins with a brief biographical sketch of KPJ in the first chapter. His early childhood was full of adventures and whatever little details we have, show him to have been a brave child. He passed the high school examination in 1899 and joined the Queen's College in Banaras. His father had a thriving business in shellac, which made it possible for him to send KPJ to England to study for the degree of Barrister. KPJ's marriage took place quite early according to the practice of the then time and when he went to England in August 1906, he left behind his wife Malati Devi and two children for four years. During this period, KPJ acquired several degrees such as M.A. in History and was also called to the Bar at Lincoln's Inn, London. However, he could not keep himself aloof from politics and his sincerity brought him to the notice of the Indian revolutionaries exiled in Europe. After coming back to India, KPJ was desirous of entering the University of Calcutta as a teacher but his appointment was thwarted by a suspicious British administration. Having been denied an opportunity in the academic domain, he decided to establish himself in the legal profession and started practising at the Patna High Court. KPJ's rehabilitation in Patna from 1914 onwards marked the next innings of his life. KPJ lived an eventful life. He lived for only 56 years of which nearly four decades were spent in serious academic writings. Despite his hectic professional and family life, he established himself as a literary critic and historian of international repute. Apart from writing numerous monographs and articles, he also edited several journals and weeklies.

The second chapter discusses the immense contributions made by KPJ to the Hindi language and literature. KPJ was a multilingual scholar and he knew several languages such as Sanskrit, Hindi, Pali, English, Chinese, French, German, and possibly Bengali. However, he wrote extensively in two languages, viz., Hindi and English. Essentially, he was one of the players in the field of 'Hindi Nationalism'—at least until the first decade of the twentieth century. From his initial years, KPJ was writing in Hindi and advocated the use of Hindi throughout his life. KPJ wrote several articles in reputed Hindi journals of the time, such as the *Saraswati*, *Hindi Pradeep*, *Nagari Pracharini Patrika*, *Kalwar Gazette* and *Hindi Kesari*. We can identify three distinct phases of KPJ's contributions to Hindi writings: (i) from 1898 to 1912, (ii) 1914-15 as the editor of the Hindi weekly *Pataliputra* and (iii) from 1928 to the last days of his life. Most of his original writings in Hindi belong to the first phase. If we do a content-wise analysis of KPJ's writings in Hindi, it could be categorised under several categories: (A) Hindi language and literature, (B)Travelogues, (C) Biographies, (D) Social Issues (E) Poetry, (F) Translated articles and (G) Miscellaneous articles.

The period in which KPJ started writing in Hindi is known as the period of 'Hindi Renaissance' in the region corresponding to the present-day Uttar Pradesh. In that period, there was a sustained movement under the leadership of Bharatendu Harishchandra to secure official recognition for Hindi language and Nagari script. By and large, KPJ took a position which was much closer to the position of Bharatendu Harishchandra, the doyen of the Hindi intelligentsia in the second half of the nineteenth century and early decades of the twentieth century. KPJ wrote on many themes and one of the important segments of his writings and speeches in Hindi was focused on the question of Hindi language, including its grammar, purity, antiquity, and importance. His speeches were remarkable intellectual exercises in philological exposition and polemics grounded in solid evidence. As far as the standard of Hindi language was concerned, KPJ always advocated the use of simple Hindi, which could be understood by common people including women and children. He was a very enthusiastic proponent of history-writing in Hindi language, so that the masses could be made aware about the cultural and political heritage of India. Travelogues also constitute an important segment of KPJ's

Hindi oeuvre. There are two categories of his writings in this genre: first, his travels within Britain during student days, and second, stories of his return journey from Britain to India after the completion of his studies. KPJ was of the opinion that the political profiles and biographies should be considered a part of the history-writing traditions. He wrote and published four biographies in the *Saraswati* related to A.F. Rudolf Hoernle, F.S. Grouse, Maheshcharan Singh, and John Beams.

From the available records, KPJ's writings on social issues are almost negligible. However, his Presidential Speech at the 4th Annual Conference of the Akhil Bharatavarshiya Haihay Kshatriya Mahasabha in Jabalpur in April 1927 is remarkable. In this speech, he questioned the very foundation of caste as being divine; he also highlighted the importance of the modern/English education. By no stretch of imagination was KPJ a prolific poet. We have been able to lay our hands on only two poems of his early days that were published in the *Saraswati*. Later, his friend Rahul Sankrityayan identified, located and reproduced eight additional poems from KPJ's diary. Most of the poems are sarcastic pieces on the existence of God. KPJ also translated material of historical importance from 1900 onwards. KPJ's Hindi writings can be considered in the category of what Mahavir Prasad Dwivedi called 'useful' literature.

The third chapter on KPJ's stint as the editor of the Hindi weekly *Pataliputra* could have been a part of the second chapter, but we have preferred to discuss it separately because (a) this facet of KPJ's life is almost unknown, and (b) apart from several other issues of the language, literature, history, gender and caste, the *Pataliputra* is the only source available through which we can understand the political posture of KPJ *vis-à-vis* the British rule and the national movement.

The multifaceted persona of KPJ is truly reflected in his journalistic pursuits. KPJ started writing for Hindi journals in 1898, but his formal journalistic career began in 1905. In January 1906, Kalwar Mahato Sabha of Mirzapur published a Hindi monthly *Kalwar Gazette* with KPJ as its editor. The second innings of KPJ, the journalist, started in the middle of 1914, when a weekly named *Pataliputra* was published from Patna. The contents of the weekly are quite rich. However, our study is based largely on the readings of the editorials and some other articles, which had significant ideological tones on the then relevant issues. The broader complexion of the *Pataliputra* should be comprehended on the basis of its exposition on such issues as: (i) its political posturing, (ii) its stand on language and script, (iii) its descriptions of class and caste relations, and (iv) its attitude towards newly emerging questions about women in society. The work tries to explore the transformation of a radical intellectual who was once considered a 'revolutionist' and the 'cleverest Indian of the present time' by colonial administrators, into the pro-British editor of the weekly. The question of loyalty to the British Crown (*rajbhakti*) was so important for him that he was at that point of time in favour of suspending all the contentious and divisive issues—regional, national, and international. For example, unlike his contributions to the *Saraswati, Hindi Pradeep, Nagari Pracharini Patrika,* etc. KPJ's pieces in the *Pataliputra* take a fairly flexible and fluid position on the question of languages and scripts.

The fourth chapter is an exploration of KPJ's contributions in the field of history-writing. In this chapter, we have analysed his contributions to history-writing. We have divided his contribution into three segments: (A) Monographs: *Hindu Polity; Manu and Yājñavalkya: A Comparison and Contrast; History of India 150-350 A.D.; An Imperial History of India (700 B.C. to c 770 A.D.),* and *Chronology and History of Nepal,* (B) Edited and translated works such as: *The Rājanīti-Ratnākara by Chaṇḍeśvara;* Bhaṭṭa-Svāmin's Commentary on Kauṭilya's Arthaśāstra; *Descriptive Catalogue of Manuscripts in Mithila,* Vol. I., *Smṛiti Manuscripts* (with A.P. Sastri); *Descriptive Catalogue of Manuscripts in Mithila,* Vol. II: Literature, Prosody; *Adhyarddhaśataka* by Mātṛcetā, and *Vigrahavyāvarttanī* by Ācārya Nāgārjuna (with Rahul Sankrityayan), *Lassen*'s *History of Indian Commerce,* (Co-translated with A.P. Banerji Sastri) and (C) Research articles, further divided into several segments: epigraphy, numismatics, writings on Indian arts, polity, etc.

KPJ started writing articles of historical importance in Hindi at the age of 17. In 1924 the publication of his English monograph *Hindu Polity,* made him truly eminent. *Hindu Polity* consists of two parts: the first part deals with the republics, and the second deals with the monarchy. There are 39 chapters and four appendices. The whole book is divided into ten segments the last of which deals with the decay and revival of what he considered Hindu constitutional tradition (650-1650 A.D.). The story takes off from the Vedic period and goes on to the middle of the fourth century A.D. to the Gupta imperial system and further on till the seventeenth century. He began with a brief discussion on the varieties of sources: indigenous, religious and non-religious, foreign (Greek), inscriptions, as well as numismatic evidences. On the basis of these sources, KPJ demonstrated the existence of eighty-two republics in different parts of the sub-continent from the post-Vedic times to the Gupta period.

Manu and Yājñavalkya: A Comparison and Contrast was published in 1929 from Patna. It is a collection of KPJ's Tagore Law Lectures delivered in 1917 at and under the auspices of the University of Calcutta. The monograph is a comparison and contrast of the two treatises on the basic 'Hindu' law by Manu and Yājñavalkya. KPJ applied the historical method and used a variety of other sources, both literary and epigraphic, to establish the continuity and change in the 'Hindu' legal system over several centuries.

The most widely read and discussed book of KPJ on political history is *History of India c. 150 A.D. to 350 A.D.* He christened the period as Nāga-Vākāṭaka imperial period. This appeared first in the volume IX of the *Journal of Bihar and Orissa Research Society* (hereafter *JBORS*) and was published as a monograph in 1933. The period 150-350 A.D., from the fall of the Kuṣāṇas to the rise of the 'Imperial' Guptas, was dubbed as the 'Dark Age' in Indian history. Looking at the contents of the monograph, it appears that this monograph is an anti-thesis to V.A. Smith's *Early History of India* (1924 edition), who had characterised it as the 'Dark Age'.

An Imperial History of India (c. 700 B.C. - c. 770 A.D.) is another important monograph by KPJ, published in 1934. This monograph is based on the Tibetan version of *Mañjuśī Mūlakalpa,* which was edited in collaboration with Rahul Sankrityayan. This monograph is enriched with KPJ's comments, and contains new information about the political and cultural history of the country, particularly with regard to the Gupta and the later Gupta history. If KPJ's *History of India* was a rebuttal of V.A. Smith's work on the post-Mauryan centuries, *An Imperial History of India* was similarly a rejoinder to the colonial administrators' understanding of the post-Gupta centuries in North India.

KPJ made an invaluable contribution to the Indian epigraphic studies. He wrote 34 articles on epigraphy and published them in several journals. We have classified these articles broadly into three categories: Hathigumpha inscription, Aśokan inscriptions and epigraphs of miscellaneous variety. Many of these articles, written almost a century ago, continue to inspire scholars till this day. KPJ was also quite aware of the importance of the numismatic studies for the reconstruction of the Indian history and made several important contributions.

KPJ's contributions towards the study of ancient Indian art are also remarkable. He wrote extensively on varied subjects concerning monuments, sculpture, paintings, etc., which range from the pre-Mauryan times to the medieval period. KPJ's contributions in this category can be divided in two phases: in the first phase (1898-1919), he published only three articles in Hindi and in the second phase from 1919 onwards, he published articles only in English. Monuments and their conservation also drew KPJ's attention. He reads quite futuristic on this issue. On the basis of *Śilpaśāstras*, the origin of the Nāgara and Vesara styles of temple architecture was underlined:

(i) Unlike the Dravida and Kaliṅga styles, the Nāgara and Vesara were not territorial appellations, (ii) the Nāgara meant a building on a square plan, and the Vesara meant an 'ornamental' voluptuous style having a round plan; both of them may be *śikhara* or non-*śikhara* edifices, (iii) the Nāgara is derived from Nāga, the dynastic name of the Nava Nāga kings, who drove the Kuṣāṇas out of Āryāvarta, (iv) the Draviḍa and Kaliṅga are ethnic or territorial, but that does not necessarily mean that the other two terms must be similarly ethnic. The Nāgara might be an ethnic expression, but the Vesara cannot be so regarded. Throughout this short article, the accent is on crediting the Nāgas with the origin of the two styles—Nāgara and Vesara. Obliquely, it was also argued that the Guptas were recipients of this legacy. KPJ wrote numerous articles on political developments as well and defined several terms in inscriptions and Sanskrit literature, identifying places, persons, events, and geographical and topographical boundaries, the use of eras, etc.

The fifth and the last chapter deals with the contributions of KPJ as an efficient institution builder. In 1912 a new province of Bihar and Orissa was carved out of the Bengal province. As a result, several new institutions were created, namely, the Patna High Court, the Bihar and Orissa Research Society (hereafter BORS), the Patna Museum, and the Patna University, etc. KPJ was closely associated with all these institutions from their very beginning. His organisational skills were seen at an early age when he organised Chapra Sabha in Mirzapur and later when he edited the Hindi weekly *Pataliputra*. KPJ made tremendous contributions as the founder member of BORS, and remained closely and intimately associated with the Society for more than two decades, till his death on the 4 August 1937. He was one of the founding members of another historic institution, the Patna Museum. He served as its president for almost a decade. He also served as an advisor, as a member of its managing committee, and a donor of antiquities and artefacts. The BORS and the Patna Museum were twin institutions, in the sense of a shared moment of their birth, but their life histories also remained interconnected in several important ways. While the Society represented the theoretical work of research and criticism, as evidenced by the learned articles in its journal on subjects of historical and archaeological interest, the Museum sought to source and preserve these artefacts. Thus, functioning together, each institution complemented the other. The Museum also presented a popular, living, material interface for historical artefacts. Another abiding institution of great repute with which KPJ worked for several years, was the Patna University. KPJ's association with the Patna University began in 1918, and lasted till his death. He worked hard in various academic and administrative capacities and finally it was the Patna University which returned the favour by conferring on him an honorary doctoral degree in 1936. KPJ's engagements with historical discussions and controversies found expression in his vision of establishing the Bharatiya Itihas Parishad, an organisation dedicated to Indian history-writing by Indians of all hues.

Through a contextual and an analytical assessment of such heterogeneous and rich contributions of KPJ, we have, in this work, also attempted to reflect upon the validity and limitations of labelling him as a 'nationalist' historian.

NOTES

1. The first doctoral thesis was done by Anil Kumar: *Bihar ke Rajnitik Utthan mein Kashi Prasad Jayaswal ka Yogdan aur Unka Itihaslekhan*, KPJRI, Magadh University, 2001. The second doctoral thesis was done by Babita Kumari: *Dr. Kashi Prasad Jayaswal ka Itihas Darshan: Ek Adhyayan*, Patna University, 2009 (This research was sponsored by ICHR, New Delhi). Both theses are unpublished.

1

Kashi Prasad Jayaswal: A Biographical Sketch

This work is not an attempt to write a complete biography of KPJ. It is an endeavour to understand his intellectual contributions to the national life. However, a brief biographical sketch would help us to visualise the milieu in which this scholar worked. After the death of KPJ, Rahul Sankrityayan planned to write his biography and for that he visited KPJ's birth-place, Mirzapur, and met his relatives, friends, and teachers and collected considerable background material. But unfortunately he lost all that material on the railway platform and after that he never found enough time for that project.[1] Since no comprehensive account of the life of KPJ is available anywhere, we have to depend on the articles and memoirs written by his friends, relatives and well wishers, which are scattered in various journals, magazines, newspapers as well as his History-Sheet prepared by the C.I.D. of the colonial government.[2]

KPJ has been described and perceived in various ways by his contemporaries, friends and scholars. Pandit Mahavir Prasad Dwivedi called him 'घमंडाचार्य', (an egoist) and 'barrister saheb'[3], while Acharya Ramachandra Shukla labeled him as 'kotadhish' कोटाधीश (lord of the *Courtghat*),[4] and Rajendra Prasad as a 'social reformer.'[5] The British administration marked him as 'dangerous revolutionary' and the 'cleverest Indian' of the present time,[6] and mentioned his name in the "Politico-Criminal Who's Who" in the colonial records.[7] He was also known as a 'vocal caricaturist' and 'Jayaswal the International' by his friends and colleagues at Bar,[8] and 'विद्यामहोदधि' (Vidyāmahodadhi or the 'great ocean of knowledge') and 'पुण्यश्लोक'[9] (Puṇyaśloka or 'well spoken of') by his well-wisher. He sometimes used a pseudonym 'बाबा अग्निगिरी' (Baba Agnigiri) for himself and sometimes sarcastically as 'महाब्राह्मण', (Mahābrāhmaṇa or the 'Great Brahmin') while writing some controversial and sarcastic material. The intellectuals of later generations remember him as a 'nationalist historian.' In the post-independence era, the Government of Bihar established a research institute,[10] commemorating his name, and the purpose was to encourage and promote scientific research in Indian history. The Government of India, celebrating his 100th birth anniversary in 1981, issued a 'postal stamp' in his honour.[11] However, the irony is that KPJ's life, his literary and intellectual contributions and the context in which he grew up and wrote have not been analysed properly till date.

Childhood and Early Days

Around Jhalda, a small town in Bengal Presidency, were forests where *dhak* or *palash* (Latin name: *butea monosperma*) grew in abundance. This tree was home to the insects whose resinous secretions were used for making lac. The raw material gathered from the forests around Jhalda was taken to Mirzapur for refining and converting it into lac. Mahadev Prasad was the main player of this trade in Mirzapur and his other two brothers—Sahu Mata Badalji and Sahu Sheetal Prasad Ji—were also involved in this trade.

KPJ was born on 27 November 1881 in Jhalda, where his father, Sahu Mahadev Prasad, had built a *kothi* (mansion) to stay while supervising the lac collection operations. Very soon, after his birth, KPJ was brought to Mirzapur, a district town on the south bank of the Ganges in Uttar Pradesh.[12] KPJ was born in a family of the backward caste of Kalwar.[13] His father Sahu Mahadeo Prasad had two wives, Somaro Devi and Janaki Devi, and eight children: two children, KPJ and Govind Prasad Jayaswal, were from the elder wife Somaro Devi, and six children, four sons and two daughters, were from Janaki Devi. KPJ was the eldest among all of his siblings.[14]

Sahu Mahadeo Prasad was a small businessman who made it big. He took loans to expand his business. We read of him taking a loan of Rs. 5000 from his friend Sitaram and using it to successfully expand his business.[15] Later on, KPJ's father became a big merchant of Mirzapur and owned a firm called Kashi Prasad Mahadeo Prasad & Co., which dealt in shellac and carpets. Sahu Mahadeo Prasad was a self-made man; he did not have any ancestral property; whatever property he had, was earned by him. Though he was a supporter of the cow protection movement and was a sympathiser of the Arya Samaj, Sahu Mahadeo Prasad did not take any interest in politics.[16] He was influenced by the reform movements of the ninteenth century and concerned about the low position of his caste. In 1904, he came into contact with Sh. Sitaram Batham, a social activist of Kanpur belonging to his caste. Inspired by him, Mahadev Prasad established Kalwar Sabha in Mirzapur and encouraged his caste brethren to work for the welfare and the progress of their caste. Mahadev Prasad was also instrumental in establishing Kalwar Mahato Sabha in 1905 in Mirzapur. Throughout his life, Mahadev Prasad worked for the betterment of the people of his caste. Mahadev Prasad's views influenced the young KPJ.[17]

Mahadev Prasad took keen interest in the education of his children. This enabled KPJ to get the best education available at that time. The early education of KPJ began under a private tutor. Private tuition at home continued till he was seven (1888). After that, KPJ pursued his studies at London Mission High School in Mirzapur.

All through his childhood, KPJ was fond of fun and frolic. In his neighborhood, people would offer sweets and occasionally live goats to the ghost deity installed beneath a banyan tree. KPJ, with a bunch of friends, would go to the site, pick up the sweets scattered on the deity's pedestal, and share them amongst themselves. They once even rode on the back of a sacrificial goat. This group of small boys used to spend a lot of time around the deity's shrine and roam around the adjacent sites. KPJ also learnt a lot of things from his family barber who used to narrate stories connected with the events occurring in daily life. KPJ treated his family barber as one of his teachers. The seeds of challenging religious practice were thus being planted in his head and heart from the early days. Later, it grew to a belief in the need for social and religious reform and the countering of superstitions.

KPJ studied Sanskrit at home from Handiababa, a *sadhu* known by that name because he cooked his meals in a *handia* or earthen pot. Handiababa made a big impression on the young KPJ because of his character and the depth of his knowledge and the learning he imparted. KPJ remembered Handiababa with reverence even to the last days of his life. KPJ always recalled with gratitude the debt he owed to Handiababa, and how the learning imparted by Handiababa stood him in good stead throughout his career as an Indologist, making him feel much surer of his ground in Sanskrit than other scholars who had got their knowledge of Sanskrit from formal learning as imparted in colleges.

After passing the high school examination in 1899, KPJ joined Queen's College in Banaras and came in contact with the leading Hindi intellectuals of Banaras and Allahabad. However, his father called upon KPJ to return home and assist him in the expanding business. KPJ obeyed his father and contributed to the family business with zest and remarkable success. In leisure time, he used to engage himself in studies and writings.

At this point in his life, KPJ's public spirit found three different outlets. In the first place, he organised the Chapra Sabha (Shellac Association) for the protection of the economic interests of shellac traders of varying strata. It was an important step in the direction of a trade association of which indigenous merchants were members. It also served as a forum for discussion for promoting the interests of Indian traders who had to bear the brunt of unfair competition from British traders and monopolists. As a second outlet, KPJ was also associated with the Kalwar Sabha, an association of people of his caste for the purpose of social reform. The Kalwar community in the Hindi-speaking area of the Gangetic valley had emerged as a significant community that produced business magnates in a much higher number than other caste communities outside the traditional trading castes. Like many other communities, the Kalwar community looked for ways in which they could modernise. They wanted to work against superstitions, the practice of taking dowry and drinking. Through the Kalwar Sabha, KPJ launched a fight against orthodoxy and superstition. He advocated the cause of widow re-marriage and vehemently opposed the practice of child marriage, which was rampant in the Kalwar community. He encouraged the community to educate both sons and daughters. And finally, KPJ began to write. He contributed articles in leading Hindi journals such as the *Hindi Pradeep*, *Nagari Pracharini Patrika* and *Saraswati*. Around 1906, he was also editing the monthly Hindi Journal, *Kalwar Gazette,* for some time.[18] His writings in Hindi soon attracted the attention of Hindi intelligentsia of northern India.

Though KPJ's life would seem fulfilling to many, as it had

numerous dimensions to it, the world of knowledge never lost its appeal for him. He would return to the world of letters giving up his father's various businesses. In August 1906, KPJ left his wife, Malati Devi, two children and the extended family to pursue higher studies in England.

England Years (1906-10): The Making of a Barrister

Why did KPJ give up the family business and once again turn towards studies? There is an interesting anecdote about this change of mind. In a meeting of traders one day, KPJ presented his views regarding the trade. KPJ used to speak a lot and was in the habit of presenting forceful arguments. A trader said something about the shellac trade, which KPJ strongly refuted. The senior traders felt slighted at KPJ's strong arguments and one of them was said to have commented, "Will you teach us how to do trade? Just because you have passed matriculation, you think that you have become a barrister." KPJ felt offended, and showed it by refusing to join dinner at home. When his mother wanted to know what had happened, he replied, "Now I have to become a barrister."[19]

To gain social prestige and recognition within and outside his community was, perhaps, one of the incentives for KPJ to go to London to pursue studies and attain the degree of a barrister. In those days, orthodoxy still ruled the society and foreign travel was looked down upon. However, KPJ was permitted to go to England on the condition that he would not eat food touched by anyone there, except his Brahmin cook who accompanied him, and that he would remain a vegetarian. His cook was sent with all sorts of food supplies and even charcoal from India! Arrangements were made thereafter to send weekly consignments of these articles for the entire duration of his stay in England. He went to England to study Law, but along with that he also pursued other courses. He kept writing in Hindi for the *Saraswati* and other magazines as well. He joined and graduated from Jesus College, Oxford, where he was also awarded the Davis Chinese Scholarship for studying Chinese language in 1909. He did his M.A. in History. And he was called to the Bar at Lincoln's Inn and became a Barrister-at-Law.

There were diverse reactions in Mirzapur and Banaras to KPJ's studies in London. Pandit Mahavir Prasad Dwivedi wrote several editorial notes on him and also published his photograph in the *Saraswati*. He observed, "Nowadays Babu Kashi Prasad is in

London. Last August he went to England from Mirzapur. There is a seaport called Marseilles in southern France. When he reached there he remembered '*Saraswati*' and took a photograph of the painting by the world-famous painter Raphael. This is a painting of St. John and it is being published in this issue."[20] In another editorial, Pandit Mahavir Prasad Dwivedi noted, "The readers of *Saraswati* obviously are familiar with Babu Kashi Prasad. Till date, a number of his articles have been published in *Saraswati*. Even in this issue his small article on 'Shakespeare' is being published. In these days he is engaged in his studies in England. On the one hand, he is studying to get a degree from Oxford, and on the other he is working to pass the examination of Barrister-at-Law from London. Till date, he has appeared in three examinations and has passed all these successfully. After looking at the papers of the first examination, we get to know that he got the 13th position among 100 students. It is only the result of two months. It appears that other Indian youth are not properly utilising their time there. It is not an easy task to get two different types of education from two Colleges and to clear both successfully. We congratulate the lover and admirer of Hindi on his success and publish his photograph too in this issue".[21] In another issue, he promised "...the articles of Babu Kashi Prasad Jayaswal will be published regularly. Hopefully, these articles will be more useful and entertaining in comparison to the previous ones".[22] When Dwivedi heard the news that KPJ had got the Davis Scholarship to study Chinese language, he wrote a full article on him titled 'Babu Kashi Prasad Jayaswal'. He wrote, "... Almost two years ago, you went to England. Apart from the education of Barristership, you are also pursuing other degrees. The Chinese language is very difficult. But Mr. Jayaswal has acquired a good qualification within a short span of time. This reflects his hard work for studies. There is an examination at Oxford for persons who wish to learn Chinese language and those who are most eligible receive a scholarship of Rs. 1500, which was fixed by Davis Saheb. This year the scholarship is awarded to Babu Kashi Prasad... It is a matter of pride for us that person from our region (प्रांतवासी), Babu Kashi Prasadji has got such honour in the reputed University of Oxford. To get a scholarship in the University is a matter of pride in England. Therefore, in whatever College Mr. Jayaswal is getting education, the College feels proud about his scholarship. They have chosen you as an 'honorary scholar'. On that occasion, to honour Jayaswalji, a meeting was organised in Oxford. You are, perhaps, the first Indian whom the Oxford University has made a 'scholar' in a non-Sanskrit language. India is a land where scholars like Kumarajiva went to China in ancient times, to learn Chinese language and translated a number of Sanskrit texts into the Chinese. Hopefully, after learning Chinese language Babu Kashi Prasadji will utilise it."[23]

There was not only admiration for KPJ, but also criticism directed at him and jealousy towards him. It is well known that there was some tension between him and Acharya Ramachandra Shukla even before he went to England. It was about some articles published in *Bangabasi* and *Mohini*. Shukla had written number of letters to Kedar Nath Pathak regarding the strained relations.[24] When KPJ proceeded to England, Shukla wrote another letter to Pathak, "...कोटाधीष विलायत में बैरिस्टरी भी पढ़ेगें और व्यापार भी सम्भालेंगे, वेंकटेश्वर समाचार में हिन्दी लेखक का विलायत गमन देखा।"[25]

While in England, KPJ, who till then was known as Kashi Prasad, started using the caste surname. Before KPJ's leaving for England, i.e, till 1906, he called himself his first name—Kashi Prasad. KPJ's ancestors used 'Sahu' as their surname. In fact KPJ is said to be the first in his community, to use his caste title, Jayaswal.[26] It has been stated that it was because of KPJ, the title — Jayaswal got its recognition.[27] Why did KPJ assert his caste identity when he was in England? The answer is not clear. It was, perhaps, his tense relations with the people belonging to upper castes. Kalwar, the caste community he belonged to, was a backward community. He wrote an article titled 'Jati' in the *Kalwar Gazette* and Bal Krishna Bhatt's aggressive reaction against it might have led KPJ to take such stand.[28] As mentioned above, KPJ had strained relations with Ramachandra Shukla (a Brahmin scholar). In 1905, Ramachandra Shukla wrote several articles in English magazines such as the *Indian People* and the *Advocate* criticising plagiarism in Hindi from other languages. In that series he also wrote in the Hindi magazine *Mohini* attacking KPJ and using harsh words against him. This incident created a sensation amongst the Hindi intelligentsia of Banaras and Allahabad, and Mahavir Prasad Dwivedi had to intervene in the matter and write editorial comments in the *Saraswati*. Finally, Shukla had to apologise to KPJ.[29] Later on, KPJ also had tense relations with other Brahmin writers including Kedar Nath Pathak, Pandit Mahavir Prasad Dwivedi and others.[30] An anonymous and sarcastic article about KPJ was published in the *Shri Venkateshwar Samachar* titled 'Hindi Lekhak ka Vilayat Gaman'.[31] It was in England that KPJ started writing under the name Kashi Prasad Jayaswal.

During his stay in England between 1906 and 1910, KPJ travelled a lot,[32] but could not keep himself aloof from the politics of the extraordinarily stirring times. His intelligence and sincerity brought him to the notice of Indian revolutionaries exiled in Europe, who had just then formed a centre in London for recruitment of their countrymen who had gone to that country for higher studies. He was actively associated with this group which had its secret cell in the India House, London.

The story of KPJ's involvement with the Indian nationalists living in London and centred around the India House comes to us from the history sheet prepared by the criminal intelligence office of the colonial police. The record states:

> Kashi Prasad also present at a large gathering of Indians held at Cadby Hall, Kensington, on the 6th October 1908; among those present were Har Dayal, Harnam Singh, and B.C. Pal, the first two making speeches in favour of the revolutionary movement. [KPJ] was residing at 17 Camden Garden, Shepherd's Bush, and Har Dayal who occupied rooms at the India House stayed with Kashi Prasad for a few nights. His photograph appeared in a group taken probably about July 1908, which includes amongst others, V.V.S. Aiyar, M.A. Rashid, Madan Lal Dhingra (the assassin), W.V. Padke, U.L. Joshi, Devendran, and Govin Amin.[33]

> Kashi Prasad was first mentioned as having accompanied Bipin Chandra Pal from Paris to London on 26th August 1909. He seems to have acted as the representative of the Paris section and at the Sunday meetings of the "India House" held on the 27th September 1909. Kashi Prasad proposed that a deputation should be formed to approach Bipin Chandra Pal with a view to dissuade him from playing into the hands of Government, and if he refused, to disown him publicly and declare that like Gokhale, he had turned a 'traitor' to the Nationalist cause. Kashi Prasad was one of those elected to form the deputation which included B.K. Das, Bar-al-Islam, Ali Khan, V.D. Savarkar, and Har Dayal.[34]

> Kashi Prasad apparently soon after this went to Oxford to continue his studies, his address being 14 St John's Street, where some other Indians were residing. He no doubt kept in touch with the movement

> in London, for it is reported on the 28th May 1909, that he was one of the many helpmates of Savarkar and V.V.S. Aiyar in their propaganda. Soon after Savarkar's arrest, Kashi Prasad went to London and was seen in the vicinity of the Court during the hearing of the case. He was said to intend returning to India for the purpose of defending Savarkar in the case of his surrender and is known to have visited Savarkar in jail on the 17th and 18th May, 1910.[35]

The record indicates that KPJ played a supporting role to the revolutionaries centred around the India House. KPJ was influenced by nationalist feelings. In fact, it was the nationalist fervour kindled by the contact with the revolutionaries that drove KPJ into the study of India's past and sustained him in his intellectual pursuits throughout life.

Another potent factor which left a very deep impression upon KPJ's mind was his contact in England with Don Martino De Zilva Wickremsinghe, an eminent Sinhalese scholar of Indology. KPJ received his first lessons in Indian epigraphy and archaeology from Wickremsinghe. KPJ accepted him as *guru* (teacher) and felt the same reverence for Wickremsinghe that he felt for Handiababa. Indeed, it was Wickremsinghe who turned KPJ's mind from Hindi journalism to the study of India's past, and it would be no exaggeration to say that the KPJ, whom we generally know as the author of *Hindu Polity* and *History of India (150 A.D. to 350 A.D.)*, is one of the gifts of Wickremsinghe to modern India.[36]

Return to India and Hardships of a Suspected Radical

KPJ, while returning to India after finishing his studies in England, was worried about his arrest because of his revolutionary linkage in England with the Indian revolutionaries. When he realised that he would not be arrested, he returned to India, passing through Turkey, Hungary, and Colombo and finally reached home in July 1910. He wrote a travelogue of this journey which was published in the *Modern Review* titled 'The Man in Turkey' in two parts and as a detailed story in four parts in the *Saraswati* titled 'Meri Yatra' in 1912. In this travelogue KPJ gave out, very interesting information regarding the history, culture, religious beliefs, political system and also drew interesting parallels between the East and the West.[37]

When he returned to India his reputation had already travelled ahead of him, thanks to his columns and writings in Indian journals, and he had different classes of friends and admirers. First, there were the Hindi writers and readers who admired him for his courage and sagacity and his love for his mother tongue and hoped that he would continue enriching the growing corpus of Hindi literature by his writings. Secondly, there were scholars and historians who expected much from him and whose hopes were amply fulfilled in the course of time by his researches and he began to contribute articles to research journals devoted to Indology. In England, he came in contact with scholars like George A. Grierson. There were his near and dear ones who naturally hoped that his talent would bring honour and fame and also money from his practice at the Bar. Lastly, there was a special kind of 'friends' waiting for him: the police and the government. He had a handicap to overcome on account of his political views and activities in England which made the police and the government suspicious.[38] The government had special interest in him.

He returned to India in mid-1910. On account of his past association, his movements were closely watched. A note on his history was sent to the Registrar with a view to prevent, if possible, his being enrolled as an advocate. He was, however, enrolled as lawyer in January 1911. The judge, before whom the past history of KPJ was laid, refused to act on the information supplied by the CID. At the end of August 1910 he took his family to Mirzapur and returned to Calcutta in October.[39]

The History Sheet says that in February 1911, "Kashi Prasad attended the meeting of the Bengal Branch of the All India Hindu Association and was elected a member of the Provincial Executive Committee." However, no other sources speak about such association. In May of the same year he was reported to have been appointed as one of the examiners of the Final Law Examination to be held in the following June. In the Weekly Report dated 17 May 1911, the Commissioner of the Police reported that he interviewed KPJ who said that, "he had severed his political association with his political friends". In the Commissioner's opinion, "Kashi Prasad had thrown up his political connection with the party of unrest and desired to advance himself in the profession as a Barrister-at-Law". In August, KPJ was reported to be very friendly with the Japanese Research Scholar, Yama Kami, who was attached to the University of Calcutta.[40] The History Sheet also mentions that since his enrolment as an advocate of the Calcutta

High Court, KPJ associated with many 'undesirable political suspects', such as Shyam Sundar Chakrabarty, Ranjan Nath Ray, Aghore Nath Chatterji, C.R. Das, etc. He attended several political meetings at the Town Hall and other places and was considered a dangerous extremist.

After settling down in Calcutta, KPJ was desirous of entering the University of Calcutta, whose Vice-Chancellor, Sir Asutosh Mookerji (Ashutosh Mukherjee), had a sharp eye to pick out brilliant young scholars. It was, therefore, not difficult for him to be selected for an appointment at the University of Calcutta. Had this materialised, the field of Indological research might have been more enriched by KPJ, who nevertheless made lasting and pioneering contributions in different fields of research in ancient Indian history. But this 'dangerous revolutionist' could not be tolerated by the colonial masters. In those days, the universities were not really free enough to make appointments of their choice. When the University of Calcutta appointed some young lecturers on the basis of their academic distinctions, the government refused to sanction the appointment of those who were, in the government's view, 'seditionist'. KPJ was one of them; the other two were; A. Suhrawardy and Abdul Rasool, the President of the historic Barisal Conference of 1906, which inaugurated the anti-partition movement in Bengal. This action of the government created a sensation in the country in 1913, but made no impression on the imperialist ruling class.[41]

The rejection, however, did not in the least affect KPJ's cordial relations with Sir Asutosh Mookerji. It rather raised him in the eyes of that nation-builder, who as the sequel will show, invited him again as the Tagore Law Lecturer in 1917. When the Carmichael Chair for Ancient Indian History was founded in the University of Calcutta, Sir Asutosh offered it to KPJ. However, KPJ did not accept it as by that time he had a lucrative legal practice at the Patna High Court; therefore, he had entirely given up the idea of teaching profession again.[42]

The unjust and suspicious attitude of the government was really uncalled for. KPJ was not an active political agitationist. He was a brilliant intellectual anxious to serve the goddess of learning, and undertake research to illuminate the dark corners of the country's ancient history. He was anxious to make the best use of the academic training and tools that he had acquired in England.

KPJ repeatedly tried to impress upon the government that whatever his political activities in England may have been, on return to his country he had ceased to take part in political movements and should not therefore be under suspicion.[43]

After being thwarted in his attempts to join the University of Calcutta as a lecturer, he decided to establish himself in the legal profession. However, circumstances in Calcutta were not conducive even to his legal profession and the continuous police surveillance must have affected his profession and also his peace of mind necessary for the pursuit of academic activities. Even in these inhospitable circumstances, he made his debut in the domain of history-writing. Before his migration to Patna he wrote a series of articles of historical importance in *Indian Antiquary* and in the *Modern Review*.

After separation of Bihar and Orissa from Bengal in 1912, KPJ settled in Patna and stayed there till the last days of his life. He transferred his practice to the Patna High Court and he was on the rolls of the court from its inception. But even here, he was allowed no peace. It appears that he was constantly harassed by the government, directly or indirectly and at one point of time KPJ even wished to migrate abroad. He continued to be a suspect in the administration's eyes. The government was so scared of his movement that when he shifted to Patna, the Bengal Intelligence Branch (Copy of D.O. No. 101 I.B. dated 5.1.14) reported to the Bihar Special Branch, "Kashi Prasad Jayaswal, a well known suspect and advocate of the Calcutta High Court, came to see me the other day and said that he intends going to Bihar early next year and asked me to give him a letter to you regarding his conduct here. I promised I would write to you about him... He talked about himself and said that he might have associated with wrong people in England, but he had given up any ideas he may have imbibed there and that he was fully convinced in the maintenance of British rule being beneficial to India. He said that he had led a quiet life since his return to India, but this is not quite so according to the report received regarding him and he is still viewed with considerable suspicion."[44]

KPJ appears to have tried on many occasions to impress upon the authorities the honourability of his intentions. Charles Cleveland was satisfied and on 4 June 1914 he (from Criminal Intelligence Office, Shimla) wrote to the Lieutenant Governor of

Bihar and Orissa,

> But I am particularly anxious not to drive him abroad. He is a man of exceptional talents with a special taste for historical research, and I believe that the time has come when it would be wise thing to let him settle down quietly and make the best possible of life in India. I have introduced him to Sir Reginald Craddock who I think agrees with me. Neither of us is at all willing that any whitewashing of Jayaswal now should throw the least doubt on the propriety or justice of his disqualification as a lecturer of Calcutta University. That punishment was richly deserved as at the time Jayaswal was to the public eye an unrepentant seditionist with a bad record in Europe. At the same time, so far as my department is concerned we now accept Jayaswal's repentance. We think he has had sufficient punishment and we believe that the best way of treating him will be to let him start afresh with as little handicap as possible. We think that this treatment will not only be the best for Jayaswal but also for ourselves and for the Government. If then this case comes up before you in any way, I venture to hope that you will consider the point of view that I have given in this letter.[45]

The matter, therefore, was considered in the Council of the Governor and it was decided that, "The ban on him should be suspended and that he should be given a chance of rehabilitating himself. The officers should receive him when he calls and all suspicious supervision or police surveillance should be dropped. The District Magistrate and the Superintendent of Police should, however, keep themselves thoroughly acquainted with his doings and connections, so that when—as will assuredly—he begins to ask Government for briefs, posts or other favours, they may know whether to advise that he should be given them" (vide McPherson's confidential letter to C.E.A.W. Oldham, I.C.S., dated Ranchi 12 June 1914).[46] The ban was lifted, even though he continued to be suspect in the administration's eyes. He was a threat that the colonial government wanted to tame and guide into creative channels by a push here and a nudge there. They were watching with great interest and apprehension every move of his in terms of location, profession and the people and organisations he befriended.

Rehabilitation in Patna

KPJ's rehabilitation in Patna from 1914 onwards marked the next innings of his life. Here he diversified his energy on a multilevel basis. Professionally, he established himself as a lawyer at the Patna

High Court.[47] He was the founder editor of the Hindi weekly *Pataliputra* and served it for almost a year.[48] He had been associated with the BORS and the Patna Museum since its inception and also served the Patna University in various capacities.[49] Rajendra Prasad wrote, "By the time the Patna High Court was opened, he had established a position at the Bar and had already acquired a great reputation as a historian and research worker. He came to Patna and continued his activities in both directions. Till the last days of his life he retained his double love."[50]

British Loyalist

It appears that once settled in Patna, KPJ started playing a hide and seek game with the government's law enforcing and intelligence agencies. In his public gestures, he showed loyalty to the Crown and the government by denouncing his past linkages, connections and activities; on the other hand he had started countering the notion of white man's burden through his historical writings. There are instances when he showed loyalty to the colonial government. For instance, 1914 was a period of great global turmoil because of the First World War. In Patna too, as elsewhere, a number of voluntary meetings were organised by the people to help the British empire. KPJ gave a suggestion as a volunteer by writing a letter to the editor of a newspaper, "Sir, Motor cars have a great utility in modern warfare. May I suggest through your paper that owners of private motor-cars ought to volunteer the loan of their cars to our Army Department?"[51] However, it is not clear whether he himself loaned his personal car!

There was a rush among the elite of Patna—both Hindu and Muslim—to help out the British empire in the war. A meeting of loyal Hindus was held in Patna to express deep and sincere loyalty to the British empire and to form a committee in order to realise subscriptions for the Imperial War Relief Fund on Sunday, 30 August 1914. It was presided over by Rai Saheb Radha Krishna Jalan (a well-known wealthy man of Patna). KPJ not only played an active role in the framing of several pro-government resolutions but also moved the vote of thanks. The meeting was considered a great success.[52] As an editor of the *Pataliputra*, KPJ took an extremely pro-British position and the *Pataliputra* was one of the earliest who announced that the Indians should support England in the First World War.[53]

Landmarks in KPJ's Life

In 1917, KPJ started one of the most ambitious projects of his life: reading of the Hathigumpha inscription. This inscription came to notice in 1817 and Father Sterling discussed it about 1825. James Prinsep had tried to read it but he did not succeed and rather did a meaningless reading of the text. After that in 1880, Rajendra Lal Mitra published another interpretation of the text, in which even the name of the king was not deciphered properly. In 1885, Bhagwanlal Indraji published another reading through which a part of its importance came to light. But till then no estampage of this inscription was taken by anyone and it was understood that it could not be done. The major portion of the inscription could not be read and in whatever was read, there were a number of mistakes. With the help of his friend R.D. Banerji, KPJ started deciphering this inscription in 1917 and it took almost ten years to render possible the full reading of the text. During this period, KPJ revised his reading several times and published these in a series in the volumes of *JBORS*, *EI*, etc.

Presenting the Annual Report of 1920, Sir Edward Gait said,

> Our Society has now been in existence for five years and has continued to show vigorous growth and development. When the Society was inaugurated there were many who doubted whether Bihar and Orissa contained a sufficient number of persons interested in the subjects which it deals with to ensure its survival for any considerable time. Those doubts have now, I hope, been dispelled. Each year has been a steady improvement in the variety and value of the papers published in the journal, the reputation of which continues to grow both in this country and in Europe. This gratifying result is largely due to the researches of Mr. K.P. Jayaswal, who is rapidly acquiring a European reputation and whose successful work in deciphering the Kharavela inscription in the Hathigumpha cave at Udayagiri has aroused the widest interest.[54]

V.A Smith described KPJ's editing of the great inscription of Khāravela as the most notable work of BORS.[55]

The year 1924 was an important for KPJ for two reasons: His first monograph titled *Hindu Polity* was published and he became one of the members of Bodh-Gaya Temple Inquiry Committee. For a long time, the Buddhists of India, Burma and Sri Lanka were engaged in a movement demanding that the shrines of Bodh-Gaya be placed under Buddhist control.[56] There was a controversy between the Buddhists and the Hindus regarding the control of the shrine. The matter was discussed in Gaya and Cocanada sessions of the Congress. Mahatma Gandhi asked Rajendra Prasad to inquire into the matter and make a report to the Congress.

On the Bodh-Gaya Temple controversy, Rajendra Prasad wrote,

> Soon after returning to Bihar from Belgaum. I set up a committee, consisting of Braj Kishore Prasad, Dr. Kashi Prasad Jayaswal and Damodar Das, who later became Bhikkhu Rahul Sankrityayan. A Ceylonese Buddhist, Gunasinha, came to Bihar to help the committee in its work and stayed with us for some time. In order to assess the views of the Hindus. I convened two meetings in Patna, but the attendance was poor and could not take decision.

Rajendra Prasad further wrote,

> At that time, a Hindu Mahasabha session was being held in Muzaffarpur under Lala Lajpat Rai's presidentship. I attended the session to which also came some representatives of the Mahant of the Bodh Gaya temple. The Hindu Mahasabha adopted the resolution recommending the management of the temple by a joint committee of Hindu and Buddhists but suggested that the question should be studied further and that a committee should be set up enlist the support of the Mahant. So, on the committee I had already set up and which the Hindu Mahasabha also adopted as its own the Mahant was co-opted as a member. When it started work, however, the Mahant stayed away from the meetings. So the committee of four prepared a detailed report on behalf of the Congress and the Hindu Mahasabha.[57]

The management of the Bodh-Gaya Temple, the principal place of pilgrimage for the Buddhists, was in the hands of a Śaiva Mahant. The committee recommended that the management of the Bodh-Gaya temple be handed over to a joint committee of Hindus and Buddhists and that religious ceremonies in the temple be performed according to Buddhist rites, without depriving the Hindus of the right to worship and offer *puja* there. The Hindus consider Lord Buddha as one of the ten *avatara*s (incarnations), although the Buddha *puja* is not current among the Hindus. The arrangements regarding *puja* and worship in vogue in the temple were hardly in keeping with the dignity and importance of the great shrine. The committee thought that there was substance in the complaint of the Buddhists and recommended that if the ceremonies were to be improved they must be conducted by the Buddhists themselves. The committee met the Mahant and tried to persuade him, but in vain. The report was submitted to the next A.I.C.C. session and was accepted. However, the problem was not resolved till 1939.[58]

There is another interesting dimension to the story. In Ceylon there was a famous temple known as Katargama. The Hindus claimed that it was theirs but the Buddhists had taken possession of it. When the committee was inquiring into the Bodh-Gaya temple dispute, it received a number of telegrams and letters from the Hindus in Ceylon pleading that the Hindus should not give up any right to the Buddhists in the Gaya temple as long as the Buddhists did not concede the right of Hindus to the Katargama temple.[59]

Honours and Awards Given to KPJ

During his lifetime, KPJ got all possible honours, positions, and awards and, above all, respect and prestige from the people as a whole. In 1926-27, he was awarded the Baroda Golden Jubilee Prize for which the ceremony was inaugurated by the Gaekwad ruler himself. The prize was considered to be the Nobel Prize of the Baroda State of that time. Rai Brij Raj Krishna, while making a speech on the occasion of the conferment of Ph.D. to KPJ, remarked,

> The condition attached to the prize is that His Highness, himself a most enlightened ruler, invites persons of established reputation in the field of scholarship to go to Baroda and lecture before His Highness. Mr. Jayaswal was the second out of the three persons so far invited, the other two being Dr. Rabindranath Tagore and C.V. Raman. So we see that Mr. Jayaswal has been honoured everywhere and we would be failing in our duty if we did not confer on him this degree even at this late stage.[60]

KPJ was invited by several learned societies to deliver his enlightening speeches. He gave a brief speech on 'A Voussoir from Patna' at the second All India Oriental Conference.[61] He represented the BORS, as the editor of its journal, at the fifth All India Oriental Conference held in Lahore in November 1928 and on behalf of the Society, by a communication, invited the assembled Orientalists to hold their sixth session in Patna. The invitation was placed before a general meeting of the conference and was unanimously accepted.

Accordingly, the sixth All India Oriental Conference was held in Patna in 1930. KPJ was elected as the President of the Reception Committee. He was also elected as the member of the Executive Committee as well as the member of the Entertainment and Accommodation Committee.[62] He gave a long welcome address at the opening ceremony of the conference.[63] He gave a full description of the contributions made by Pāṭaliputra and felt proud about that, and at the same time he was also concerned about the reviving the ancient tradition of Pāṭaliputra.[64] Further, he enumerated the contributions made by the modern scholars such as Rai Bahadur Hira Lal, Haraprasad Sastri, George A. Grierson, Alexander Cunningham, Georg Būhler, Franz Kielhorn, J.F. Fleet, Bhagwanlal, R.G. Bhandarkar, Rajendra Lal Mitra, R.D. Banerji, Ramavatar Sharma, Jadunath Sarkar, etc., in the field of history, historical linguistics, numismatics, epigraphy, philosophy, etc.[65] He also expressed his gratitude to the government for the financial help given to the institutions and also hoped for the same in the future.[66] He also thanked the Maharaja of Darbhanga, because of whom a chair in Maithili was established at the University.[67] This was the time when Hindi nationalists, by and large, were abhorrent of their own mother tongue. They had privatised their own languages, for conversation in domestic/rural settings, etc. One can even argue that they had chosen to sacrifice a part of their own selves for the greater cause of Hindi, which was also seen as a weapon against colonialism. The case of Maithili is significant in the context, as we shall see later.

KPJ also gave a description of the progress made by such institutions as the BORS, Patna University, the Patna Museum, the Bihar and Orissa Sanskrit Association, Khudabaksh Oriental Library, Sanskrit Colleges, Ayurvedic College and a Tibbia College, and the generous contributions made by the government. In his eyes, Nalanda was the 'Oxford of Hindu India'[68] and the Khudabaksh Oriental Library of Patna was the 'Bodleian of India'.[69] In this address, KPJ weaves in every bit of significant local history with a sense of regional pride, a regional pride that is not exclusivist but inclusivist, and is humble and non-aggressive. He himself said, "Pataliputra is already known to you; in fact it is as much your heritage as mine."[70] He emerges as an propagator *par excellence*, but not as mere salesman, trying to sell the wealth of Patna's history. While glorifying the possessions and the buildings that house those possessions, he does not forget to refer to the contributions of his ancestors in the field of diverse disciplines of scholarship. And one actually wonders how fluid the disciplinary boundaries were at that time. We also get no hint of the sectarian divide that came to characterise the Ancient-Medieval-Modern periodisation in the post-independence India. Like a true scholar, he also draws the gathering's attention to the new areas of research demanding urgent attention.

In 1933, KPJ made a Presidential speech at Bihar Provincial Hindi Conference, Bhagalpur, on 21 October.[71] One of his major contributions to the Hindi literature was his participation in the debate on the date of Hindi literature. In the beginning of the speech he refuted the opinion of Rai Bahadur Shyam Sunder Das that the beginning of Hindi was believed to be from Chand Bardai, i.e., 1000 A.D. an opinion voiced at the sixth All India Oriental Conference in Patna in 1930. KPJ said that this opinion was misleading. He enumerated the contribution of Tulsidas, Vidyāpati, and Jayasi, but most importantly he believed that nobody had the right to say that there was no evidence of the history of Hindi before Jayasi. In the secondary (*gauṇa*) language of India the oldest one is the Eastern Hindi which was only written in the centres of Vikramaśilā near Bhagalpur and Nālandā near Patna.

KPJ was elected the President of the seventh All India Oriental Conference held in Baroda on 27 December 1933.[72] Rahul Sankrityayan has given a vivid description of this journey in which KPJ travelled to Ajanta-Ellora with his family members and retinue and presided over the seventh All India Oriental Conference in Baroda.[73] It was at this conference that KPJ canvassed support for the scheme of writing a comprehensive history of India. In the honour of KPJ a long *khutba* was read at the beginning of the procceding which was in a mixed language—Hindustani would be the best way to describe it.[74] KPJ opened his address with a brief but joyous expression of felicitation at the Conference under the patronage of His Highness the Maharaja of Gaekwad, describing him as the "modern Bhoja".[75] Turning to the field of Indology proper, KPJ observed: Our Indian scholars, if they aspire to the glory of interpreting history from this wider stand-point, will have to acquire knowledge of the science of Elamite, Mesopotamian and Western Asian archaeology. States and universities ought to send out and train special students for the task."[76] As an ardent conservationist, KPJ praised those who had taken keen interest in the preservation of the monuments and criticised those who had neglected it. Historical and artistic remains are so widely scattered all over India that unless the public take a dutiful interest in their preservation, they cannot be effectively protected from vandalism and natural decay. An Indian State is especially expected to protect its ancient temples and objects of art.[77] KPJ also highlighted the role of non-professionals in the writing of history.[78]

KPJ expressed his satisfaction on the materialisation of a critical edition of the *Mahābhārata* through the efforts of V.S. Sukthankar; he pointed out the necessity of an early analysis of a critical edition of the *Rāmāyaṇa* on the basis of its four recensions lately established by Harichand Shastri at the Oxford session of the Oriental Congress.[79] KPJ also emphasised the importance of Sanskrit education and expressed his displeasure over the deteriorating condition of Sanskrit,[80] Again, on retirement of Hirananda Sastri from the post of the Government Epigraphist and the editorship of *Epigraphia Indica*, KPJ expressed profound regret at this undeserving end of so useful a career with which men like Būhler, Burgess, Bhagwanlal Indraji, R.G. Bhandarkar, Fleet, Sir Richard Temple, etc., were so closely associated.[81] KPJ concluded his speech with a forceful presentation of the imperative necessity for undertaking the preparation of a history of India written from the Indian point of view.[82] He said there was a fundamental difference between the Indian point of view and that of others and to begin Indian history at 600 BC was to present a headless body. Imagine an ancient history of Egypt which begins with the Ptolemies and leaves out the Pharaohs! According to an Indian historian, they had to record fully the Dynasty of Manu.[83] But within a short span of time KPJ passed away (August 1937) and he did not fulfil his dream of writing a comprehensive history of India during his lifetime.

In April 1935, he delivered the Presidential Speech at the History Section of the Hindi Sahitya Sammelan,[84] Indore, and in June he delivered a lecture at the Royal Asiatic Society in London. He also delivered the Presidential Speech for two consecutive terms at the Numismatic Society of India, one at the 25th session in Mysore (December 1935), and another at the 26th session in Udaipur (November 1936).[85] In the month of November, he was conferred an honorary Ph.D. degree by the Patna University[86] and in the same year he visited Nepal.

In Indore, KPJ started his speech with deep regret at the apathy of Indians towards their history. He invokes the past for showing the importance of history, "In that situation having a history section in the Conference is an appropriate subject. Hopefully, the voice of the *Itihasa Parishad* will not be a failure." KPJ expressed his pleasure at writing and teaching history in Hindi and encouraged the audience to take up the cause of history-writing, "If some gentleman amongst you stands up with courage and spends some money for history-writing, then it is possible to write the history chronologically by establishing a group of historians. If you do not think it necessary, then the matter is finished, and the world will go on. Then, why not the Hindus could live without history?" There were diverse reactions to KPJ's speech. One the one hand, in the general Presidential speech in the same conference Gandhi said, "I have no hesitation in accepting, whatever Jayaswalji has said".[87] On the other hand, the editor of *Veena* wrote in his editorial, "The Chairperson of the History-Council has been thinking of the Comprehensive History of India, but is there any concrete proposal about that? The speech of the Chairperson of the History Council throws light on the depth of his literary love. You have attracted the attention in the absence of the true history of India."[88] The complaint was addressed in 1936, when KPJ established Bharatiya Itihas Parishad.

In June 1935, he visited England to lecture at the Royal Asiatic Society in London.[89] The Society's Secretary, C.E.A.W. Oldham, who was present at the lecture, made appreciative remarks and drew a comparison between KPJ and Cunningham, "Mr. Jayaswal's work and that of another pioneer, Sir Alexander Cunningham, whose views, not always accepted at the time, have since been mostly justified."[90] He was, perhaps, the first Indian scholar to receive the honour of an invitation to lecture at the learned Society. He also placed the discovery of the coinage of the Mauryas before the Society. B.P. Sinha remarked, "His views were naturally not endorsed by the learned assembly, but the President prophetically warned the members that like the theories of Sir Alexander Cunningham, those of Jayaswal were criticised by his contemporaries, but might find acceptance afterwards." P.L. Gupta, a noted numismatist, assigned a particular series of punch-marked coins to the Nandas and the Mauryas.[91] The thesis presented to the Royal Asiatic Society in London was further developed by KPJ with additional evidence and fresh data and presented at the Annual Conference of the Numismatic Society of India, Mysore, in December 1935.[92] He was the General President of the conference. In November 1936, KPJ gave another Presidential Speech in Udaipur. D.R. Negmi, one of his disciples, who had accompanied him to Udaipur, has given a vivid description of the journey.[93] While explaining the general development of numismatic studies, KPJ highlighted the importance of Yaudheya coins in the history of Rajputana.[94]

In mid-1936, KPJ was invited by the Government of Nepal to visit that country. Before that he had unsucessfully tried to visit Nepal in 1932. He had written a letter to the Political Secretary of the Nepal government on 8 April 1932, "...necessary permission to visit and reside at Kathmandu for two and half months for the purpose of studying Sanskrit and Prakrit manuscripts in the State Library and private libraries in Nepal (e.g. the library of the Junior Rajguru). My interest is purely archaeological and historical. I desire to accompany my family members (wife, daughter, and children) who would like to live with me there and visit the sacred shrine of Sri Pashupati."[95] However, after several correspondences, KPJ was denied permission. Later on, it was through the efforts of Rahul Sankrityayan that he was able to visit Nepal in 1936.[96] However, his Nepal visit led to a tense relationship between the Rajguru of Nepal and the King of Nepal on one side and KPJ and Sankrityayan on the other.[97]

In November 1936, KPJ was awarded an honorary Ph.D. by the Patna University. The resolution was passed in the Senate meeting held on 28 March 1936. On that occasion, a number of people spoke including the Vice-Chancellor, praising the contribution made by KPJ in Indology and other branches of knowledge.[98] This was the last important event of his life. Just like the other great Indologist D.D. Kosambi, KPJ too never actually acquired any doctoral degree. And if Kosambi was a mathematician by training, KPJ was a lawyer by profession. And yet the contributions of these two savants to Indology and ancient Indian history have been truly seminal.

KPJ was diabetic and had to be careful about his diet and exercise. He walked two miles daily to take an early morning bath in the Ganges. This he did throughout the year and this was the only physical exercise he took. He could not, however, get rid of his disease and passed away from this world on 4 August 1937, after an illness of two months, due to a virulent type of carbuncle. During his last illness, there appeared a remarkable equanimity on his face, which was doubtless due to his feeling that he had done his best in his life and that his mission had been taken up by his successors.[99]

Political World View of KPJ

As far as KPJ's political views are concerned, diverse opinions are held by his contemporaries and friends. It should be noted here that KPJ was never a member of any political party. Even in England he was a sympathiser of the Indian revolutionary group and after returning to India he gave up those sympathies. His closest friend and the intellectual partner Sankrityayan wrote, "He was a staunch nationalist. But because Jayaswal had an opportunity to get in touch with the Communist ideas earlier, he could not be a blind nationalist. Although he knew that Communism would have to begin with our own nation, his idea about history was generally revolutionary."[100] He further wrote, "His political ideas were of radical Communism. In some ways, he had suppressed this idea after returning to India."[101] However, such a characterisation of KPJ never matched his self-image; he never expressed anything about Communism or Socialism, either in writing or in any speech. On the other hand, at several places he took an absolutely pro-British position and expressed his happiness and gratitude for the progress India made during the British regime.[102]

Ramdhari Singh Dinkar has narrated a story of a public meeting of Gandhi at the Patna Maidan and wrote, "He was a firm believer in the National Movement, although he was critical of the idea of non-violence, he had great respect for Gandhi. One day I went to his place little late in the evening. When I was asked why I was late, I said that I was listening to the speech of Gandhi, and then I narrated his speech in brief. I saw that he was getting emotional, although there was nothing in it to cry. Jayaswalji got emotional by thinking that our motherland has produced a great warrior."[103]

One of KPJ's admirers and disciples, Mohanlal Mahato Viyogi gave an interesting and, perhaps, a realistic narrative of KPJ, "It was obvious that he wanted to satisfy both the Government and the public (सरकार और जनता). Such a weakness could be found in every person, who lives in the situation in which Jayaswalji lived.

He never supported openly either the Government or the people. He was obsessed with the glamour of the Government but also shed tears on the misery of the people. That was a strange attitude, but it could obviously be said that in the major part of his times, he was more on the side of the people and kept his distance from the Government. I cannot say what the reason was for that. Was it a result of the purification of the heart or an outcome of frustration? Whatever could be the reason, it has happened."[104] He further narrated, "Jayaswalji was a supporter of Gandhiji, but he did not believe in the idea of the 'emancipation of the country through Khaddar'. ...The small industry and the *charkha-khaddar* will push back India to the middle ages; on the other hand the world is progressing through diverse scientific means... will there be establishment of 'sutrayuga' or 'stone age' in India? Jayaswalji was worshipper of Power... he thanked Italy that they established the supremacy of power over Africa."[105] Looking at the narrative of Viyogi, it appears that KPJ believed that people should be progressive and powerful.

In the provincial assembly election of 1937, KPJ's political views were clearly reflected. In 1937, the Congress secured an extraordinary victory in the election and KPJ was very happy about it. He was happy not only because the sycophants of the British got defeated but also because the feudal lords were wiped out in the election. After the election, KPJ wrote an article, which was published in the *Modern Review*.[106] It was a piece of literature pregnant with its revolutionary feelings and enthusiasm of the general public that had swept away the misdeeds-mongering Zamindars in that election. He had also translated every local song in that article in which anti-landlord feelings were obvious and prevalent and he equated those songs with the revolutionary song of France, "The village masses composed songs in their local dialects which were sung with the fervour of *La Marseillaise* on their march to the voting booths."[107] Those days Swami Sahajanand was the leader of the farmers, not only in Bihar but also at the national level. In that election, a number of songs were written, praising Swami Sahajanand and KPJ also praised him. The landlords of Bihar got very angry with KPJ after the publication of that article. One of the Zamindars wrote a letter to KPJ saying that he was getting his bread and butter from them and and yet he was trying to cut their roots. KPJ replied, "You are giving money to me not because you are kind towards me but because you are not getting any advocate of my calibre." After that, the Zamindars got silenced.[108]

In KPJ's opinion, the election of February, 1937 marked a definite landmark in social history of India. He wrote, *L'ancient regime* is closed. Old age is left behind. Praising Gandhi and the Congress he further wrote, "Mahatma Gandhi might say today with satisfaction that when he announced to the world that he and the Congress represented the villages of India, he spoke nothing but the bare truth. The Congress has proved today to be the accredited agent of the seven hundred thousand villages."[109] However, he was also aware of the class character and internal contradictions of the Congress Party, "While the Congress leaders have been vacillating in their decision—many of them are themselves landlords and most of them do not wish to abolish the old-age institution of the agrarian middleman, their principles have decided their duty for them in the meantime. The situation is this: that while the Congress will wait for the day of *Swaraj* to remove the misery of the real Indian, the cultivator says, 'No, do it at once; do it now'."[110]

KPJ further wrote, "The party which will retain the confidence of the masses must be the party which undertakes to remove the capitalist from the land, effectively in spirit if not in form. The Congress or any other party which strives to possess the allegiance of the voter will have to create peasant proprietors in India in the near future. If the Congress fails in this, Socialists will come in."[111] Citing his experience of legal practice over twenty-five years, he wrote,

> I have come across only two cases where the landlord was well-spoken of by the tenants. The normal tale is the one of extreme dissatisfaction and suffering. The age-old position between the cultivator and the landlord had been that the landlord was the *raja* (sovereign) and the tenant his *praja* (subject). The Tenancy Law has been cutting at the root of this old theory. The arm-chair revenue administration of the Moguls never touched the tenant; it dealt with him through the machinery called *Zamindar* to collect revenue. Estates were farmed out to him and the Mogul State dealt with him as the middleman who stood between the State and the producer. Virtually he was the *raja* to the Indian villagers; and the latter was his serf or *praja*. The Tenancy Acts changed the theory and turned the latter into a freeman possessed of rights of defence enforceable against his so-called *raja*.

> The franchise of voting has now converted him into a full citizen with rights of self-determination. The revolution in the status of the villagers is now complete.

He also expressed his pleasure over the fact that everyone saw the landlord going from door to door, begging his tenants for votes.

KPJ also analysed the economic dimension of the election,

> It is the economics which rules citizens. It is the economic policy of a party which will determine its life as the ruling party in the country. That economic policy must be such as will reduce the suffering of the Indian who makes the mass. The economic policy must be one which would remove the capitalist middlemen from the land, whereby it will not only bring more food and clothing to the cultivator, but will also release capital from indolence and land for investments in activity and industry. Land is the easiest investment, bringing ease plus social dignity to the investor and depression to the fellow beings under him. It creates a class of indolent lotus-eaters. If you remove the landlord middleman who unnecessarily intervenes between the Cultivator and the State, you not only liberate your countrymen from the relic of serfdom - both economic and social—you not only make him a full citizen without a middleman between the Indian and the State—you also turn an indolent class into an active and earning part of the society. You benefit thereby both agriculture and industry, in addition to adding largely to public revenue. The key of the economic policy of the Indian Government should be the removal of this unhealthy incubus. And in this behalf the policy has to be in spirit socialistic, whether we like it or not.[112]

KPJ here comes through as a 'progressive liberal'. His views about the agrarian class configuration were certainly radical, which might have alienated his Zamindar clientele and perhaps cost him many a brief. But that was KPJ, as fearless publicist as he was an advocate. Convention and convenience mattered little to him; convictions mattered most. On the query of Viyogi about this article, KPJ said, "Now, I have nurtured the hobby of speaking truth. If life remains, then I will speak more dangerous truth than this." In a letter written to him on 24 April 1937 KPJ wrote, "Now Baba Agnigiri has developed the habit of speaking truth." However, very soon his desire for speaking truth came to an end as he died on 4 August 1937.

Religious World View of KPJ

KPJ's religious ideas or his beliefs are not very clear from his writings or speeches, although he picked up his symbols and metaphors from the 'Hindu' scriptures/texts/beliefs. It is not clear whether he was a believer in God or not. Once, when he was trying to get a no objection certificate to visit Nepal for academic purposes, he wrote a letter to Wilcock, Under Secretary to the Political Department, Government of Bihar and Orissa, Patna, "Being a Hindu, I can adjust myself with any arrangements possible there."[113] This is, perhaps, one of his remarkable statements as far as his religious beliefs are concerned, Hinduism for him was not a monolithic religion, but an amorphous way of life in which there was space for everything.

There are a number of instances when KPJ made fun of God. One can find some expression of this view in his conversation with one of his disciples, Ramdhari Singh Dinkar. Dinkar recalls that he was not able to understand KPJ's ideas about the existence of God. He once asked, 'You believe in Yoga, in tantra-mantra and even in the existence of Ghosts, then how come you are an atheist? You should have been a theist.' KPJ replied, 'My teacher in my childhood was an atheist. When I went to England, my landlady was free from the burden of God. When I returned to India I got the company of Pandit Ramavatar Sharma. Now in old age, when there was a possibility of securing God's shelter, Rahulwa (Rahul Sankrityayan) has come in the way.'[114] In other words, he wanted and kept finding excuses for remaining a non-believer.

Dinkar narrated another instance,

> There was no rain even in the rainy season in Patna. People became scared and started seeking God's refuge. The Hindus of Patna started worshiping Indra and offering rituals to God, but nothing happened. Now it was the turn of the Muslims; they started assembling and collectively offered prayer (*Namaz*). And the coincidence was that after one or two *Namazs* the sky became heavily cloudy and there was heavy rain throughout the night. Next day when Jayaswal reached the High Court, his friend Barrister Younis (who was the interim Chief Minister of Bihar in 1937) cracked a joke, "See Jayaswal, you wasted your butter and barley, while God was waiting for a collective *Namaz*. We offered *Namaz* and the land is full of water because of heavy rain. KPJ quietly replied, "What can I do Younis, your Allahatala has also became a communalist.[115]

KPJ did not even spare Allah.

KPJ wanted to make the youth liberal in terms of their food habits. He gave a variety of arguments in its favour. He used say, "The *Shastras* mention that the ancestors of those cry even in the heaven, from whose house the smell of flesh does not come." He lamented that "By leaving flesh eating, Buddhadeva made the Hindus fools." Another argument was that "Your body will not resist the onset of old-age because you have survived only on milk." One evening, when Dinkar went to his place, he said, "Well, return to the roadside." He could not understand. Again he said, "Well not to the roadside, go to that flower." Dinkar returned to that flower. Then KPJ said, "Well return" and I return to him." Now KPJ asked, "Well, tell me is it meritable or a sin?" Dinkar smiled and replied, "Is it a question to be asked? It is neither meritable nor sinful." Then Jayaswalji, pretending to be serious, replied, "Then flesh eating is neither a merit nor a sin, it is only food."[116]

On another occasion, KPJ made his wife speechless. He had recently returned from the mountains. He narrated the story like this:

> This time we went to see Renuka Mai on the mountain. You have to cover several miles by bus. In the bus we saw that everyone was travelling with either a pigeon or a hen in his hand. When we reached the sacred place (*dham*), another drama awaited us. There were hen sellers all over. I thought this might not be a Renuka-*dham*; perhaps, this might be a shrine of a saint (*pir*). But when we enquired, we got to know that indeed it was the Renuka-*Dham* and there was a tradition to sacrifice a hen or pigeon here. Then I said to my wife, Take a look, Renuka Mai ate hen and pigeon regularly and, therefore, could give birth to Parashuram. And since you eat only pumpkin and bitter gourd, you gave birth to Chet Singh and Chaturbhuj Singh (sons of KPJ), instead of Parashuram.[117]

KPJ was also humorous by nature and he often made sarcastic comments on Gods and Brahmans. Dinkar narrated a story of gossiping under moonlight,

> All of a sudden Jayaswalji asked, "Have you heard of Baba Agnigiri's take on God?" I replied, "If Baba Agnigiri permits it, I am ready to listen to it." Jayaswalji continued, "Baba Agnigiri once asked Munshi Ajmeri if he knew something." Ajmeri replied, "Which thing, Sir?" Agnigiri then explained that God said, "I will become a fish; I will become a tortoise; I will become a pig, but I will never become a

> Brahmin." Ajmeri had doubts, "Why, Parashuram was after all a Brahmin." Agnigiri said, "Absolutely wrong; when the incarnation of Ram is available, then how come the incarnation of Parashuram? At a time it is very difficult to have one incarnation. Then at the same time, how come two incarnations? And if you remember, there was fight between Ram and Parashuram. God incarnates to fight each other God? No brother, Parashuram was a pretender." But Ajmeriji was not convinced. When he realised that the argument of Parashuram was not convincing, he said, "Sir, will you believe Vaman as an incarnation?" Now Agnigiri lost his temper. He said, "Ajmeri now you have got the point. When God realised that now we have to cheat, betray and the generous have to be shown the Netherworld. Then, he agreed that for this calamity there is no greater garb than that of the Brahmin.[118]

KPJ's friend and colleague at the Bar, P.C. Manuk recalled,

> His attitude to religion was worthy of the man. His wide reading and deep thinking gave him a breadth of vision in matters religious. He saw good in all the great religions of the civilised world, respected the teachers and founders of each and scoffed at the precepts and tenets of none. He may have adopted, perhaps, unconsciously, a doctrine of Stoicism: Not only are we all brethren, but also the "children of one Father". In a more serious mood, he compared the lives of the great teachers and emphasised how environment and circumstances had influenced their teachings. In a lighter mood, he humorously exposed the cant and hypocrisy of avowed followers of all religions. Flashes of humour, however, always illumined even his most serious talks.[119]

KPJ was far removed from the idea of the existence of God and most of the stories he used to recount contained sarcastic references to God. Rahul Sankrityayan has collected number of such Hindi poems written by him such as, 'नर और नारायण', 'तथ्य गीता', 'अग्निगिरी का बेढब उलहना', 'देवों का भारत गीत'।[120] At a point of time, KPJ thought of embracing Buddhism as Sankrityayan recalled, "When I returned from Europe and Lanka in 1933, he wrote to me, "I am also fed-up with the world and want to become a follower of the Buddha"[121]

On the one hand, KPJ was scientific in his approach, and on the other he also believed in palmistry and astronomy. Sankrityayan felt that this was, perhaps, due to the financial crisis he was facing.[122] Viyogi also wrote, "He had blind faith in the forecasts of the astrologers. He, generally, asked the astrologers about himself. An astrologer with recommendations from several high officials, was asked by KPJ about the future of his daughter—whether she would become a judge of the High Court. When the astrologer predicted favourably, the father exulted like a child."[123]

At another instance, when KPJ was suffering from fever and Viyogi went to see him, KPJ said, "Son, do not think that I am a complete atheist. It is not only the gods and goddesses, but I also believe in ghosts. However, because of the current fashion I have to oppose *Shradha*, etc. I myself want to perform *Shradha. Shradha* should be performed for the ancestors. Recently, whatever is happening in the family, perhaps, is because of the curse of the ancestors. I will come to Gaya in the coming *Pitra Paksha*—make arrangements for a learned Brahman. I will stay in the kothi of the Maharaja of Tikari and you will be with me during the *Shradha Karma*." After that he said, "My problems will not wither away without performing *pinda* at the Vishnucharan." Viyogi continued, "After that a painful incident happened in the family of Doctor Saheb. His younger brother died at a very early age. Scarred by this painful incident, he wrote to me, "What has happened? I wanted to free myself from the *pitririna*, but this is the thunder of *Anujrina*. Has God desired this?"[124]

Was KPJ an atheist or a complete theist? Viyogi has the following narrative on this,

> He opposes God either to tease the theists or out of fun. Once he narrated a story to me: there was a person who was absolutely devoted to his Emperor. He worshipped him. Kept *Vrata* on his birthday. He always recited the *Samrat-charita*, after taking bath; muttered his name regularly, but he never followed the rules of the government of the King and always disobeyed these rules. On other hand, there was a person, who was not devoted to the King but always obeyed the rules of the government and behaved accordingly. Could you tell me, who was the better patriot? Those who performed acts of devotion to God, day and night, but disobeyed the things made by God like truth, love, mercy, non-violence and so on? Such a person is not only an atheist, but an animal in the garb of a man. Such was the atheism of Jayaswalji.[125]

Social and Family Life of KPJ

KPJ never wrote anything about himself. It is only through the writings of his friends and relatives that we are able to decipher something about KPJ's social life. Deeply steeped in the age-old culture of India KPJ too held that, "There is no God other than your parents; that was his principle", as his daughter Sushila Jayaswal recalled.[126]

As far as his life style is concerned, Viyogi wrote, "By appearance he was looking like an appropriate 'Saheb' but his heart was pure Indian."[127] He had great pride in Indian culture, as Rahul Sankrityayan observed, "His western dress might have led someone to believe that he was a blind follower of the European culture. This was also possible because of his minute knowledge of European dress, courtesies, and manners. But anyone who had seen his work, and had the opportunity to have discussions with him or live with him would have no doubt that he was not an imitator of the West - but a staunch nationalist."[128]

KPJ was a person of great wit and humour both in his private and professional space and he made use of this wit and humour even in serious debates. KPJ's daughter, Sushila Jayaswal wrote, "Once, one of my father's personal servants could not tolerate the fact that my mother ordered him to work. He went straight to my father, while he was engrossed in his studies and when my father looked at him and asked What has happened? He said, 'Saheb am I your servant or servant of Mem Saheb?' My father smiled and replied that he was also a servant of Mem Saheb. The face of the servant was worth watching. When we heard the story we laughed a great deal. However, he never passed any comment on anyone nor did he ever hurt anybody's sentiments."[129]

Even in literary and historical discussions his humoir was *par excellence*. Ramdhari Singh Dinkar and Maithilisharan Gupt have mentioned some such instances. Dinkar narrates a story: "One night we came out after dinner, and then Jayaswalji said, 'Well, come Son! Let's have some literary gossip.' After sitting on the chair I said, 'Let's start.' Jayaswalji said, 'There were only two poets in Hindi.' I asked, 'Who were they?' He replied, 'One is Chand and the second one is this Harichand.' I straightaway asked, him 'And Tulasidas?' Jayaswalji immediately said, 'अरे तुलसिया भी कौनो कवि रहा? उसकी तो बंदरवा न सुधार देता रहा जैसे गुप्तवा की महावीरवा मिलाओ हाथ.' After that he started laughing uncontrollally. There is a story that the incomplete poems of Tulasidas were completed by Hanuman. And it is well known that the poems of Maithilisharan were edited by Pt. Mahavir Prasad Dwivedi."[130] Then what a combination of Mahāvīra and Hanumāna!

Here is one more instance, "There was a rumour that a scholar of Kashi has been successful in deciphering an inscription. Once KPJ was in Kashi and he invited the scholar and asked, 'How do you read the inscription? I also want to see that.' The photograph of the inscription was taken before him. But after having a look at the his reading style of the text he said, 'Sir, if that is the case then when you return from here you will find inscription even on the jalebi kept in the shop'."[131]

Manuk also recalled such stories from the court premises, "Interruptions from the bench never flustered him—interruptions by his opponents, he was less tolerant of. Generally he met such interruptions with a pithy remark, short, terse and to the point, which would cover the interrupter with ridicule. With a strong sense of dry humor, ridicule was a facile and effective weapon in his hand."[132] Manuk further narrates,

> In the Bar Library and especially in the luncheon room, during the luncheon interval, the humorist *par excellence* was always Jayaswal—no matter what the topic under discussion was—from the idiosyncrasies of a learned judge to the foibles of his colleagues. Being an excellent mimic, he punctuated his sallies with a by-play of face, voice, and manner in imitation of the subject of his story. No one was immune from it, if the occasion arose; but it was all done with such complete good humour that resentment was out of the question. One had to laugh at oneself as seen in the mirror of Jayaswal's creation. A vocal caricaturist of no mean order was this placid scholarly gentleman in his middle age.[133]

Manuk recalled another instance of his wittiness, "One day he told us the following story; a client came to him and said his master had a case but wanted to know whether Jayaswal was a Mohammedan or a Bengali. 'Why does he want to know?' queried Jayaswal. 'Because they say that Mohammedans are good cross-examiners, while Bengalis are good speakers', replied the client. 'Then tell your master that I am a Bengalee Mohammedan', said Jayaswal quite seriously. He added, 'That satisfied the fools and they engaged me. Now they know that I am a Hindu from the United Provinces, God knows what they will do.' A wag replied, 'Report you to the Bar Council of course-you had better run to Bengal and turn Mohammedan!"[134]

KPJ was a man of conviction and helpful by nature. Sometimes, his personal bond with a person appears more powerful than anything else. That is why in personal discourse Rahul for him was Rahulwa, Maithilisharan Gupt was Guptwa, and Mahavir Prasad Dwivedi Mahavirwa and even Rabindranath became Budda.

There are a number of incidents of KPJ's life which show his considerate nature. His Nepalese cook Lakshman repeated a mistake twice or thrice. KPJ snubbed him for that. Lakshman disappeared from the house for a day. Next day in the morning KPJ called him and made him understand that he treated him like his younger brother. KPJ said, "Lakshman, see, I got angry with you and snubbed you, but then I was also deprived of food for twenty-four hours. So, both of us have got punishment. Now go, and bring some food."[135]

KPJ was extravagant by nature and generous to the core. He did not know how to save money. If sometimes his wife objected, KPJ had a quick reply, अरे तू बनिये की बेटी है न![136] He used to help budding scholars and poor students cutting across caste lines. Once, a young sadhu came to meet Rahul Sankrityayan at KPJ's place. This sadhu wanted to go abroad for the study of Pali. Rahul Sankrityayan suggested Burma or Sri Lanka for this purpose. KPJ was quite impressed by the talent of this young man and motivated him. He stayed there for a week with Rahul. KPJ brought some clothes and a blanket for him. One day when KPJ returned from the High Court, he gave some money silently to this *brahmachari*—perhaps Mrs. Jayaswal would not have liked it. The name of the *brahmchari* was Vigyanmartanda and he went to Ceylon for his studies.[137]

Rahul Sankrityayan has given us a number of such instances from his personal experiences: "I had been facing financial problems in my travelling. It was not enough to have only a look at the hand-written manuscripts; there was the need to take photographs of those. Jayaswalji gave me a camera, some photo material and some money and I went on my tour."[138] In one of his letters to Anand, Rahul wrote, "जायसवाल जी बड़े उदार हैं, और मालूम होने पर वह रुपए पैसे के लिए संकोच नहीं करेंगे। और उनका संकोच न करना ही मुझे मजबूर करता है, कि ऐसे फुटकर खर्चे की भनक तक उनके कान तक न पहुँचने पावे।"[139]

Remembering his experiences Viyogi has written,

> People get punishment for their extra-expenditure and Jayaswalji was repeatedly punished for this 'crime'. There was enough income and no account for expenditure. It is very difficult to say how many poor

students and families were surviving on his donations. And no one was to know about the donations. Once he gave me 300 rupees and said, "Give it to that person, silently. His son is ill. I have earned lot of money from his father. Now, bad days have come for him. Tell him that there is nothing to worry; I will take care of him." He further wrote, "He never discloses these things even with his private secretary. I have seen with my eyes a number of people belonging the upper strata, who were victims of circumstances and whom he secretly helped. He felt relaxed after distributing his earnings. He occasionally said, "When my hands are empty and someone comes for help and I have to face a problem for fulfilling their demands, then my heart becomes the happiest. Then I think I did something.[140]

KPJ was a man of dignity and he never compromised on that issue. Viyogi narrates,

One of our friends was Raja Saheb. He was rich and having a big estate. He was also an intellectual and was very keen to meet Jayaswalji. With my ordinary intelligence, I thought that Jayaswalji would obviously visit Raja Saheb at his palace, because he is a Barrister and he must be used to fawning over the rich. But at that time the inadequacy of my intelligence became clear, when Jayaswalji emphatically said, "Never." I will never go to a Raja to salute first. If he wishes, he can come to my house and meet me." I went blank. How could I forget that Jayaswalji came to my house, after crossing the dirty gutters of Gaya, even without my invitation? Finally, Jayaswalji's stance prevailed. Raja Saheb came to Jayaswalji's place very happily and then both of them became very close friends.[141]

Describing KPJ's attitude, Viyogi further narrates,

Jayaswalji did not receive any honours from the Government. He was alienated from these honors because of his roughness and extreme self-respect (अक्खड़पन और अत्यधिक आत्मसम्मान). This is an era of sycophancy and propaganda. He considered sycophancy as 'suicide' (आत्मघात) and propaganda for self as 'mean' (नीचता). Any university would have raised its stature by honouring him and any government would have proved the importance of their titles by honouring him, but Jayaswalji never paid any attention towards it. He was convinced that he did not need any showy honour. 'Knighthood' or 'Doctorate' held no significance for him. The world respects and will continue to respect his scholarship. The honour given by Saraswati was enough for him. Here, the Raja-Maharajas are conferred with the D.Litt degrees and there is no importance given to the scholars. But then no

> one can hope for more than this in this enslaved country.[142]

KPJ's narcissism and an acute sense of what was his due as a scholar ('the international') and barrister of eminence could be so fierce and implacable at times that he would not spare even Rabindranath Tagore and the close associates of Gandhi and Rajendra Prasad. Dinkar recalled two such instances:

> One evening Sh. J.C. Kumarappa and Sh. Mathura Prasadji (Secretary of Rajendra Babu) came to meet him. When they came, Jayaswalji turned them back by saying, 'I am busy right now, come tomorrow morning at 9.30'. Next day unfortunately they came fifteen minutes late. Jayaswalji was ready to leave for the court and if he wanted he could have spared them a few minutes. He looked at his watch and said, 'We cannot have any discussion right now, come some other time.' I felt bad about it. After they went back, I asked Jayaswalji, 'Even you know who Kumarappaji is'? He is one of the closest associates of Gandhiji.' Jayaswalji started laughing and said, 'Oh I could not recognize them! I thought that one is Mathura and the one is Mathuri.' I felt ashamed. Jayaswalji did not like Mathura Babu and perhaps he did not meet Kumarappa because he came along with him.[143]

There was one more instance:

> Perhaps not vanity exactly, but one more time I saw the exposition of his rude dignity, when Rabindranath came to Patna with his team to generate funds for Shantiniketan. I came to Patna during my transit leave and I stayed with Jayaswalji. When I met him, very excitedly he said, 'Rabindranath is coming to Patna and you take leave and come to Patna on 13 April. I will make Rabindranath listen to your poem and ask him how these poems are' I accepted his order with pleasure and asked, 'Is he going to stay with you?' Jayaswalji said, 'Nothing is sure now, if you wish, you can see his letter.' In that letter Rabindranathji had written to Jayaswal about his programme in Patna and asked for his help in the success of the programme. I thought Gurudeva will stay with Jayaswalji only and Jayaswalji did not refute my assumption. On 13 April, I reached Patna with great expectations. But all my excitement was in vain when I saw the unpleasant face of Jayaswalji. There was no laughter, no happiness, not even any indication of poetry recitation. He was angry and my visit might have added to his anger. At night, I asked his younger brother Umesh Prasad, an engineer, 'What's the matter?' He replied, I think Bhai Saheb is angry with Gurudeva. He might have thought that Gurudeva

> would stay with him, but he has reached the house of Barrister P.R. Das's who is not in town. Because of this Bhai Saheb is feeling slighted.

Dinkar continued:

> There was a call from Gurudeva. On the other side of the phone was Barrister Sh. Gopal Prasad, 'Now Gurudeva is free and he wants to have some discussion with you'. Jayaswalji's replied, 'I have no time' and put down the receiver. When Umesh (KPJ's younger brother) said, 'Gurudeva is very old. If he did not come to meet you, then it was not a matter of crime, but you should not have replied like that.' KPJ lost all his patience and exploded, 'In this city is there any person of international reputation like me? After coming to Patna it was Rabindranath's first responsibility to visit me. For a person who has not maintained this minimum courtesy, why should I run after him and that also on Gopal's invitation? He could have also called me personally? I am feeling bad that I invited this boy (Dinkar) for this purpose. And what is special in Rabindranath? He has become famous because he writes in English. Let's see I am going to write the biography of the Buddha in style. And you are a fan of poetry, then, you will see how much poetic this writing will be.' When things settled down KPJ said, that the heat of Baba Agnigiri has to be tolerated by everyone.
>
> On the same day, in the evening, the team of Rabindranath played Chitrangada. Rabindranath was sitting at a corner of the stage. At the end of the play, KPJ came to Rabindranath in a royal style and said, "Poet, you have made it a Gupta thing" and came out from the hall. At 10 pm, there was a phone call from Gurudeva. Again Gopal Babu was on the phone. He said, 'Gurudeva has been getting excited. He has said several times that Jayaswalji has summarised my art in one word.' Obviously, Chitrangada was a Gupta art work, that thing I was not aware till that time. When Dinkar asked, KPJ replied, "You poets need praise every day. It is your only food. Go and see the Oldie (बुड्ढा) who would be dancing.[144]

Looking at the entire Rabindranath episode, it appears that to some extent KPJ was a narcissist in his behaviour.

Dinkar considered KPJ a father-like figure and kept him at par with God and he took several personal favours from him and used his house as his transit camp as well. KPJ was from Kalwar community, which did not matter for Dinkar. But in one of his letters written to Shiv Kumar, when he was posted in Darbhanga and in need a helper, he wrote, "ऐसी संभावना है कि मुझे यहाँ कुछ दिनों तक

रहना पड़ेगा। इसलिए एक नौकर की जरूरत है। कोई ऐसा स्वजातीय लड़का हो जो रसोई भी बनावे और सानी-वानी भी लावे। मेरा विचार है कि मेरे यहाँ का बाबूलाल (बौधा) इस काम के लायक होगा।''[145]

Dinkar has been considered a revolutionary poet and later became a Member of Parliament and was proclaimed the 'National Poet' later on. However, it appears somewhat ironical that unlike a person of his stature was accepting personal favours from a person belonging to a backward caste, even considered him a father figure, but in private space he was perpetuating the age-old practice of the oppressive caste system! What kind of a 'nationalist' and revolutionary was he?

The time and milieu in which KPJ lived and worked was extremely caste-ridden and the intelligentsia was largely dominated by upper-caste Hindus, especially the Brahmins. KPJ must have also faced such problems in his personal and professional life, which is evident from the letters written by Mahavir Prasad Dwivedi and Ramachandra Shukla. Except one article titled 'Jati' and numerous sarcastic jokes on Brahmins, KPJ never wrote anything on caste. Contrarily he defended the Varṇa system in his historical writings. However, he was associated with his caste association and extended help from time to time and encouraged the young boys of his caste to love their caste.[146] KPJ also presided over the fourth session of Akhil Bharatavarshiya Haihay Khsatriya Mahasabha in Jabalpur in 1927.[147]

KPJ, however, cannot be branded as sectarian or casteist; as Rahul Sankrityayan, Mohanlal Mahato Viyogi and Ramdhari Singh Dinkar wrote several times that KPJ extended help to the people cutting across caste and religious lines. His daughter Sushila Jayaswal also wrote, ''मैंने उन्हें प्राय: संस्कृत के निर्धन विद्यार्थियों को आर्थिक सहायता देते हुए देखा है। स्वजातीय गरीब विद्यार्थियों को भी वे सब तरह की सहायता देकर आगे बढ़ने में प्रोत्साहित करते थे। उनके बनाए हुए अनेक जन उच्च पदस्थ अधिकारी बने।''[148]

Rahul narrated another such story, when KPJ was the President of Patna Museum:

> Jayaswal was fearless person and above casteism and regionalism. One of his close friends and associates was Shri Kshiroda Rai. He was a very talented person and interested in historical and archaeological activities. He was living in Patna along with his family. He used to meet Jayaswal everyday and when he was on history-writing tours, Rai used to go along with him. After the death of the

> curator of Patna Museum, Babu Manoranjan Ghosh, Jayaswalji tried to get him as a curator. But there arose the controversy of Bengali-Bihari. If he would have been a Bihari then there may have been the question of Bhumihar-Kayastha. People have not accepted the opinion of the President of the Patna Museum. Kshirod Babu could not get appointed and because of that Jayaswal became very sad.[149]

KPJ, however, did not make even his caste brethren quite happy and he did not come up to their expectations. Once a delegation went to KPJ's place for some help but they did not find him up to the mark, therefore, wrote a sarcastic article in *Kalwar Kesari*:

> कलवार-कुल तिलक श्रीयुत बाबू काशी प्रसाद जायसवाल एम.ए., बार-एट-लॉ, पटना ने जो सहायता की है, उसके लिए जाति चाहे तो उसे धन्यवाद दे और उनके प्रति कृतज्ञता का प्रकाश करे। मैं तो समझता हूँ, जायसवाल साहब ने अपने उचित कर्त्तव्य का पालन मात्र किया हैं। हाँ, मैं इस बात के लिए अवश्य उन्हें धन्यवाद दिए बना नहीं रह सकता कि उन्होंने 15 दिनों तक हमें खूब बढ़िया बढ़िया माल खिलाएं और हमारी अति प्रेम और मानपूर्वक मेहमाननवाजी की। हमारे जैसे अकिंचन आदमी की इतने बड़े आदमी के द्वारा खातिरदारी होना निःसंदेह उस बड़े आदमी के जाति प्रेम का परिचायक है।[150]

In another instance,

> ता. 6.8.24 को बाँकी पुर पहुँचा। यहाँ बाबू यमुना लाल जी से भेंट नहीं हुई। श्रीमान बाबू काशी प्रसाद जी जायसवाल, बैरिस्टर साहब से भेंट हुई, परंतु आप साहब, 'आप सुखी संसार सुखी' का बर्ताव रखते हैं।[151]

KPJ also created tension and controversy amongst his caste brethren about the origin of Kalwars, on which the editor of *Kalwar Kesari*, Chandrika Prasad Jigyasu wrote:

> भगवन्, जब से आपने मोतिहारी के भाषण में कहा है कि हम लोग वैश्य हैं, जहाँ तक ज्ञात हुआ है, तभी से जाति में एक ऐसा दल बन गया जो अपने को वैश्य ही कहना चाहता है। वैश्यत्व के विचार लोगों में पहले से भी थे, पर आपके भाषण से उनको उतेजना अवश्य मिली और वे हिम्मत करके खुल्लम खुल्ला अपने पक्ष का समर्थन करने लगे हैं। आप से यह भी छिपा नहीं है कि जाति में एक बहुत बड़ा भाग ऐसा भी है जो अंत तक अपने को क्षत्रिय ही कहने पर तुला हुआ है। गत वर्ष की महासभा में जाति इसी झगड़े में पड़कर दो भिन्न भिन्न दलों में विभक्त हुआ चाहती थी। पर बहुत यत्न से छः महीने का समय देकर जाति को दो दलों में विभक्त होने से बचाया गया। अब आगामी वर्ष के सम्मलेन में फिर वही प्रश्न सामने है। आपने कृपा करके जो व्यवस्था दिलाई, उससे यह सिद्ध हो गया है कि यह जाति उत्पत्ति से क्षत्रिय है और वैश्यवृति द्वारा अपना निर्वाह करती है। अब आप कृपा करके अपनी निज की स्पष्ट

> सम्मति भी प्रकाश कर दीजिए की क्या इस जाति को अपनी उत्पति को बलवान मान कर 'क्षत्रिय' नाम से अपना परिचय देना चाहिए अथवा कर्म को प्रधानता देकर अपने को वैश्य कहना चाहिए? जाति के लाखों मनुष्य आपके श्रीमुख की ओर टकटकी लगाए निहार रहे हैं, अतएव आपसे हाथ जोड़ कर विनती है कि आप कृपा करके जो पक्ष श्रेयष्कर हो, उसकी स्पष्ट घोषणा कर दीजिए। आप जैसे सर्वविद विद्वान से और अधिक क्या निवेदन किया जाए।[152]

On the women's question, KPJ appears a complex man. Although, he spoke about women's reservation in the Patna University Senate and respected women in general, he was in favour of the eastern, 'ideal' Indian women.[153] When KPJ's married son, Chet Singh went to England for his Law studies and got engaged and married an English woman, KPJ got extremely annoyed with Chet Singh and refused to extend any help to him.[154] Rahul writes that KPJ himself was married, but when he was coming back after finishing his studies he also got married to an English woman, although he did not take her to India.[155] However, the story of KPJ's second marriage is not corroborated by any other source. Remembering her early days, KPJ's daughter Sushila Jayaswal wrote:

> मेरे दादा जी पुराने समय के विचार के थे। अत: जब मैं आठवें में गर्ल्स हाई स्कूल बांकीपुर में पढ़ थी, तभी उन्होंने मुझे मिर्जापुर घर प बुला लिया। उनका कहना था, लड़की सयानी हो गई है, नौकर-चाकर घर में आता है, वहाँ नहीं रहेगी, उसे यहाँ भेजो। पिता जी बिना एक शब्द भी व्यय किए मेरी पढ़ाई छुड़ाकर मिर्जापुर भेज दिए। यह तो बाद में शादी के बाद मेरी माँ जी की इच्छानुसार पुन: घर पर ही संस्कृत के धुरंधर विद्वान पंडित रंगनाथ जी से मैंने शिक्षा प्राप्त की।[156]

There is another story,

> कभी भी मेरी माँ के इच्छा के विपरीत कोई भी शब्द उन्होंने नहीं निकाला। परिवार की प्रतिष्ठा उनके लिए बहुत महत्व की चीज थी। बात मेरे सबसे छोटे चाचा के ब्याह की है। 1930 की। बारात लखनऊ गई थी। फेरे पर चुकाने के बाद ज्ञात हुआ कि लड़की वालों ने धोखा दिया है। जो लड़की दिखाई गई थी, उससे शादी नहीं किए हैं। मेरे चाचा लोग बारात वापस लाने पर अमादा थे। पिता जी को पता चला तो वे सख्त नाराज़ हुए। कहा कि 'जैसी भी लड़की है, मेरे घर की बहू हो गई, अब वह घर में रहेगी', और सम्मानपूर्वक बहू को घर लाए।[157]

KPJ's life was full of events: from education to business, from business to education, from Mirazapur to London, from London to Patna via Calcutta. He lived only for 56 years and worked for only 25 or 26 years. Despite his hectic family life with a wife and eight children, KPJ not only established himself as a successful professional lawyer but also well-known literary critic and a historian of international reputation. He wrote more than 200 articles in Hindi and English dealing with various subjects, wrote and edited nearly a dozen books, and edited several journals and weeklies. Looking at his prolific contributions, it is very difficult to say in which of these KPJ ranks first: a numismatist, epigraphist, historian, linguist, lawyer, or a journalist. On several issues KPJ contradicts himself, which is evident from his writings and speeches. However, no one is perfect and everyone evolves over a period of time.

Rahul Sankrityayan lamented his death in his diary on 5 August 1937:

> हा मित्र! हा बंधु! हा गुरो! अब तुम मना करने वाले नहीं हो, इसलिए हमें ऐसा सम्बोधन करने से कौन रोक सकता है? हो सकता है, तुम कहते– हमने भी तो आपसे सीखा है, किन्तु तुम नहीं जानते (कि) मैंने कितना तुमसे सीखा है। इतनी जल्दी प्रयाण! अभी तो अवसर आया था, अभी तो तुम्हारी सेवाओं की इस देश को बहुत जरूरत थी। आह! सभी आशाएं खाक में मिल गईं! जायसवाल! ओः ऐसा! दुनिया के लिए (कुछ) करना ही होगा, तुम्हारे बहुत-से स्नेहभाजन थे, मैं भी उनमें से एक था। समय दूसरों के दिल से वियोग के दुःख को क्षीण भले ही करता जायगा, किन्तु स्मृति उसे दिन-पर-दिन ताजा कराती जायगी। तुम्हारा वह सांगोपांग भारत का इतिहास तैयार करने और साम्यवाद के लिए मैदान में कूदने का ख्याल!!! हा, वंचित श्रमिक वर्ग, सहृदय मानव! निर्भीक, अप्रतिम मनीषी, दुनिया ने तुम्हारी कदर न की!!![158]

Commenting on the statement, Vishwanath Tripathi wrote:

> समूचे राहुल वाङ्मय में ऐसे भावुक उदगार और किसी के प्रति न मिलेंगे। राहुल की यह भावुकता पिर्फ जायसवाल के लिए है। यह मार्क्स-एंगेल्स की मित्रता की कोटि की मित्रता है। इसे पढ़कर तथागत के वे शब्द याद आते हैं जो उन्होंने मौदगल्यायन की मृत्यु पर कहे थे– भिक्षुओ, मुझे आज यह परिषद् शून्य-सी लग रही है।[159]

Remembering the contributions of KPJ, President of the ninth All India Oriental Conference, F.W. Thomas said:

> There are still two matters of a personal character which you would not, I think, permit me to pass over. Ripe in years, as in wisdom, most of my predecessors have attained a well earned rest: they were *krita-kritya* and they have left us the heritage of their good deeds. But concerning one, recently taken from us, we cannot but feel that an obscure destiny has forestalled the fruition of his strenuous labours.

Already at Patna Conference in 1930, a main factor—as President of the Reception Committee—in the success of the gathering, Dr. Kashi Prasad Jayaswal was judged worthy of election to the Presidency of the Baroda Conference held in 1933; and well did he, the youngest in the series of Presidents, by his eloquent, comprehensive and learned address as well as his vigorous discharge of the other duties of his office, sustain the dignity and efficiency of the Conference. His extensive published researches, which, as we know, were seconded by personal labours in the archaeological field and by active stimulus of, and participation in, enterprises carried on by his Society and by the Government of Bihar and Orissa, might encourage in an outsider the thought he had done enough. That that was not his own view is evident from the increasing output of his latest years: and those who had followed his scholarly career from his earliest brilliant papers in the *Modern Review*, and had marked the increasing gravity and sense of reality apparent in his methods and deportment during those last years, will share the conviction that the outcome of his exceptional vigour and insight would have been crowned by a ripe master-piece of enduring value. In sympathy with the relatives and friends of Dr. Kashi Prasad Jayaswal and with the Bihar and Orissa Society, which proposes to commemorate him in a special volume, and also in gratitude for his personal services to the Conference, I invite you to pay him the tribute of rising for a moment from our seats.[160]

NOTES

1. Sankrityayan, Kamla (ed.), *Rahul Vangmaya*, Vol. II, Part I, Radhakrishna Prakashan, New Delhi, 1994 p. 679.
2. For his biographical references see; Mohanlal Mahato Viyogi, 'Vidya Mahodadhi K.P. Jayaswal', in Mohanlal Mahato Viyogi, *Sapt-Suman*, Sahitya Nikunja, Saran 1935, pp. 141-48, Viyogi, Mohanlal Mahato , 'Doctor Jayaswal' , *Saraswati*, October 1937, Part 38, No. 4, pp. 330-40, G.P. Ambastha, 'Dr. K.P. Jayaswal - A Memoir', in K.P. Jayaswal, *Hindu Polity* (2nd enlarged ed.), Bangalore Printing and Publishing Co., Bangalore City, 1943, pp. xxiii-xxxii, Rahul Sankrityayan, 'Dr. Kashi Prasad Jayaswal' in J.S. Jha (ed.), *K.P. Jayaswal Commemoration Volume* (*KPJVC*), K.P. Jayaswal Research Institute (KPJRI), Patna, 1981, pp. 1-12 (first published in Vishal Bharat, 1937), Ramdhari Singh Dinkar, 'Punyashlok Jayaswalji', *KPJCV*, pp. 13-22, (first published in Ramdhari Singh Dinkar, *Sansmaran aur Shraddhanjaliyan*, Udayachal, Rajendranagar, Patna, 1969), Umashankar, 'Kashi Prasad Jayaswal' 1881-1937, *KPJCV*, pp. 23-26, Sachchidananda Sinha, 'Kashi Prasad Jayaswal', *KPJCV*, pp. 27-30,

(first published in Sachchidananda Sinha's, *Some Eminent Bihar Contemporaries*, Himalaya Publication, Patna 1944), Sinha, B.P., 'Kashi Prasad Jayaswal', *KPJCV*, pp. 31-43, (first published in S.P. Sen (ed.), *Historians and Historiography in Modern India*, Institute of Historical Studies, Calcutta, 1976), first published in Dr. Rajendra Prasad, 'Kashi Prasad Jayaswal', *KPJCV*, pp. 44-45, (first published in *JBORS*, Vol. XXIII, Part IV, 1937, pp. 399-402), P.C. Manuk, 'Dr. K.P. Jayaswal–The Barrister and Man–A Character Sketch', *KPJCV*, pp. 46-53, (first published in *JBORS*, Vol. XXIII, Part IV, 1937, pp. 403-17, Rahul Sankritayayan, 'Dr. Kashi Prasad Jayaswal' *KPJCV*, pp. 54-55, (first published in *JBORS*, Vol. XXXVII, 1952), Sushila Jayaswal, 'Mere Pujya Pita Shri Kashi Prasad Jayaswal', *KPJCV*, pp. 56-58, Rajendra Ram, 'Life and Works of Kashi Prasad Jayaswal', *KPJCV*, pp. 59-72, Rahul Sankrityayan, 'Dr. Kashi Prasad Jayaswal', *Rahul Vangmaya*, Vol. II, Part I, pp. 672-80, Baijnath Singh 'Vinod', 'Ve Din: Ve Log, Janmshati Shraddhanjali: Dr. Kashi Prasad Jayaswal, *Nai Dhara*, 1981, pp. 20-27, Vinod, Bhagawan Chandra, *Dr. Kashi Prasad Jayaswal (Mahaan Jivan-Laghu Parichay)* Bateshwar-Priya Shodh Sansthan, Madhepura, 1983, Diwakar (ed.), *Itihas Purush Dr. Kashi Prasad Jayaswal* (*Sansmaran evam Shraddhanjali*), Drishti Prakashan, Nawada, 2003, Kesari, Arjun Das, 'Jayaswal: Ek Apritam Pratibha, Anokha Vyaktitv', *Dharmyug*, 15 November 1981, pp. 43-44, Chaturbhuj Singh Jayaswal, 'Dr. Kashi Prasad Jayaswal: Bikhari Smritiyan', *Aaj*, Patna, 1 December, 1981, History-Sheet of KPJ prepared by the I.B. of Bengal, Bihar State Archives, File No. 118 C, File No. 137, Political Special, File No. 178/1914, File No. XIIIE-41/36, File Nos. 83, 2N-1 of 32, 42/102(1), 4036 P. 42/102(3), Bihar State Archives, Patna, Verma, Mathura Prasad, *Jayaswal Jati Parichay*, H.K. Jayaswal Sabha, Prayag, 1978, Verma, Mathura Prasad and Jayaswal, Mishrilal, *Vishwavikhyat Itihaskar Dr. Kashi Prasad Jayaswal*, H.K. Jayaswal Sabha, Prayag, 1985.

3. Yayavar, Bharat, *Mahavir Prasad Dwivedi Rachanawali*, Vol. XIV, Kitab Ghar, New Delhi, 1995, p. 216, also see, Sharma, Ramvilas, *Mahavir Prasad Dwivedi aur Hindi Navajagaran*, Rajkamal Prakashan, New Delhi, 1977, pp. 361-62.
4. Singh, Om Prakash, *Acharya Ram Chandra Shukla Granthavali*, Vol. VIII, Prakashan Sansthan, New Delhi, 2007, p. 221. (Courtghat is a residential place of KPJ in Mirzapur and during my field survey I visited the place).
5. Rajendra Prasad, op. cit., p. 45.
6. History Sheet of K.P. Jayaswal, File No. 118c, Bihar State Archives.
7. Criminal Intelligence Office, Shimla, Letter dated 04.6.1914, See, File No. 137, Bihar State Archives.
8. P.C. Manuk, op. cit., p. 46.

9. Ramdhari Singh 'Dinakar', op. cit., p. 13.
10. For the entire official proceedings, See, Chitaranjan Sinha, *K.P. Jayaswal Research Institute: An Introductory Glimpse*, KPJRI, Patna, 1985.
11. For entire proceedings of the event, See, *Prajña-Bhārati*, Vol. 3, Part I, KPJRI, Patna, 1983, pp. 1-19.
12. Chronological summary of KPJ's life and some of the photographs of KPJ and his family members are given in Appendix A.
13. Describing the origin of Kalwars, Harivansh Rai Bacchan wrote "मुट्ठीगंज मोदियों की, बनियों की बस्ती होगी। अब भी बनिए बड़ी संख्या में वहाँ बसते हैं, उनके बाद शायद कलवार हैं। उनका पेशा मदिरा बनाना बेचना था। बंदरगाहों पर उतरने-चढ़नेवाले यात्री कलवारिया–हौली, मयखाना, मधुशाला के तलाश में रहते होंगे ही। कभी हल्के मूड में मैं सोचता हूँ की उस भूमि पर मधुशाला की कल्पना अतीत की किसी कलवारिया के संस्कार से तो नहीं उठी थी। मिट्टी बड़ी रहस्यमयी होती है। मुमकिन है मेरा कयास गलत न हो। पहले कलवार अपने को कलवार ही लिखते थे, अगर नाम के आगे कुछ जोड़ते थे। जब डॉ. काशी प्रसाद जायसवाल प्रसिद्ध हुए– वे भी कलवार थे – तो पेशे वाला नामांश त्याग कर उन्होंने मूलस्थान वाला नामांश अपनाया था– जयस से जायसवाल, जैसे जयस से जायसी– मलिक मुहम्मद जायसी। बाद को बहुतों ने गुप्त अपनाया। अब कुछ अपने को हैहय क्षत्रिय कहते हैं।" (हरिवंश राय बच्चन की आत्मकथा, *नीड़ का निर्माण फिर*, राजपाल एंड संस, दिल्ली, 1970, पृ. 126)
14. For, KPJ dynastic cycle of three generations, see, Verma, Mathura Prasad, Jayaswal, Mishrilal, op. cit., pp. 23-30.
15. Mohanlal Mahato Viyogi, 'Doctor Jayaswal', *Saraswati*, October 1937, Part 38, No.4, pp. 330-40, Verma, Mathura Prasad, Jayaswal, Mishrilal, op. cit., pp. 17-18.
16. History-Sheet of KPJ, op. cit.
17. Verma, Mathura Prasad, Jayaswal, Mishrilal, op. cit., p. 32.
18. I have tried to find out the copies of *Kalwar Gazette* in different libraries of Northern India, but these could not be located anywhere.
19. *Rahul Vangmaya*, Vol. II, Part I, p. 679, also see Arjun Das Kesari, *Dharmayuga*, 15th Nov. 1981, p. 43.
20. Editorial, *Saraswati*, November, 1906.
21. Editorial, *Saraswati*, February, 1907.
22. Editorial, *Saraswati*, December, 1907.
23. *Saraswati*, No. IV, Part X, April 1909, p. 146.
24. *Acharya Ramachandra Shukla Granthavali* Vol. VIII, pp. 219-20.
25. Ibid., p. 221 (the article is not traceable).
26. Verma, Mathura Prasad, Jayaswal, Mishrilal, op. cit., p. 14, KPJ traced the origin of the surname Jayaswal from the village Jayas in Rae Bareli and argued, "......before Tulasi there is a continuous literature (Hindi) till Vidyapati and my village brother (*Gaon bhai*) Jayasi" (See, KPJ speech at Prantiya Hindi Sahitya Sammelan, Bhagalpur, 1933).
27. Verma, Mathura Prasad and Jayaswal, Mishrilal, op. cit., pp. 14-15.

28. This issue will be discussed in the next chapter on Player in the field of 'Hindi Nationalism'.
29. *Mahavir Prasad Dwivedi Rachanawali*, Vol. 15, pp. 11-12 & 109.
30. See, Mahavir Prasad's letter to Maithilisharan Gupt, *Mahavir Prasad Dwivedi Rachanawali*, Vol. 14, pp. 214-16.
31. See, Ramachandra Shukla's letter to Kedar Nath Pathak, *Acharya Ramachandra Shukla Granthawali*, Vol. 8, pp. 210-20.
32. These travelogues will be discussed in the next Chapter on 'Hindi Nationalism'.
33. *History-Sheet* of K.P. Jayaswal, File No. 118c, Bihar State Archives.
34. Ibid.
35. Ibid.
36. G.P. Ambastha, op. cit., p. xxiv.
37. For a detailed description of the content, see the next chapter on 'Hindi Nationalism'.
38. Rajendra Prasad, op. cit, p. 44.
39. History-Sheet, op. cit.
40. Ibid.
41. G.P. Ambashta, op. cit., p. xxv.
42. Ibid., p. xxv.
43. B.P. Sinha, op. cit., pp. 31-32.
44. File No. 137, Bihar State Archives, p. 2.
45. History Sheet, File No. 137, Bihar State Archives.
46. History Sheet, File No. 118c, Bihar State Archives.
47. He practised for more than three decades and must have fought a number of important cases, having very high-profile clients like the Maharaja of Darbhanga, and the Maharaja of Hathuwa. He also used go to London for his cases. His legal profession is a domain fit for separate research.
48. The content of the *Pataliputra* will be discussed in Chapter No. 3.
49. KPJ's contribution to the Institutional Building of Patna will be discussed in Chapter No. 5.
50. Rajendra Prasad, op. cit. p. 44.
51. *The Express*, Saturday, 8 August 1914.
52. *The Express*, 1 September 1914.
53. The detailed discussion of the issue will be done in the Chapter No. 3.
54. *JBORS*, Vol. VI, Part I, p. 1.
55. Quoted in Manuk's speech on the occasion of the inauguration of the new building of the Museum, *ARPM*, 1929, p. 13.
56. For the entire representation and communication regarding the issue, see, File No. 28 of 1923 of Government of Bihar and Orissa, Bihar State Archives, also see, Prasad, Rajendra, *Autobiography*, Asia Publishing House, Bombay, 1957, pp. 232-34.

57. Prasad, Rajendra, *Autobiography,* Asia Publishing House, Bombay, 1957, pp. 232-33.
58. Ibid., p. 233-34.
59. Ibid., p. 234.
60. I have tried to find out a copy of the lecture in several libraries even in Gujarat, but it was not available. An extract from the recorded speech made by Rai Brij Raj Krishna on the eve of tributes paid by members of the Patna University Senate to K.P. Jayaswal, File No. XIIIE-41/36, also quoted in *Hindu Polity,* p. xliii.
61. *Proceedings and Transactions of the Second All India Oriental Conference,* Arch Stone, 1922, pp. 271-74.
62. *Proceedings and Transactions of the Sixth All India Oriental Conference,* Patna, December, 1930, pp. x-xi.
63. Ibid., pp. xxvi-xxxiii.
64. Ibid., pp. xxvi-xxvii.
65. Ibid., pp. xxviii-xxix.
66. Ibid., p. xxviii.
67. Ibid., pp. xxvii-xxviii.
68. Ibid., p.xxx.
69. Ibid., p. xxxi.
70. Ibid, p. xxxii.
71. For entire Speech see, Verma, Brajshankar, *Bihar ki Sahityik Pragati,* Bihar Hindi Sahity Sammelan, Patna, 1956, pp. 245-56.
72. *Proceedings and Transactions of the Seventh All India Oriental Conference,* Baroda, December, 1933, Oriental Institute, Baroda 1935, pp. lix-lxxxii.
73. *Rahul Vangmay* Vol. II, Part I, .p. 674.
74. See, Appendix B, This *Khutba* is available in Vinod, Bhagawan Chandra, op. cit, and also in Diwakar, op. cit.
75. *Proceedings and Transactions of the Seventh All-India Oriental Conference,* Baroda, December 1933, Oriental Institute, Baroda, 1935, p. lix.
76. Ibid., pp. lxii-lxiv.
77. Ibid., pp. lxvi-lxvii.
78. Ibid., pp. lxxii-lxxiii.
79. Ibid., p. lxxvii.
80. Ibid., p. lxxviii.
81. Ibid., pp. lxx-lxxi.
82. Ibid., pp. lxxix-lxxxi.
83. Ibid., p. lxxxi.
84. *Veena,* May 1935, p. 521-23.
85. Gupta, P.L., *Sixty Years of the Numismatic Society of India* (1910-71), History and Presidential Addresses, Numismatics Society of India, Banaras, 1973, pp. 128-48
86. For entire proceedings see, File No. XIII E-41/36 of Bihar State

Archives.

87. *Veena*, May 1935, p. 530.
88. Ibid., pp. 561-62.
89. For the entire Speech see, *JRAS* (London), No. 4, October 1935, pp. 788-796.
90. Ibid., p. 791.
91. B.P. Sinha, op. cit., pp. 35-36.
92. Gupta, P.L., op. cit., p. 142.
93. See, *Prajña-Bhārati*, Vol. 3, Part 1, KPJRI, Patna, 1983, pp. 49-53.
94. Gupta, P.L., op. cit., pp. 144-45.
95. For the entire Correspondence, File Nos. 83, 2N-1 of 32, 42/102(1), 4036 P., 42/102(3), Bihar State Archives.
96. *Rahul Vangmay*, op. cit., pp. 675-76, also see, D. R. Negmi, 'K.P. Jayaswal: Reminiscence', *Prajna-Bharati*, Vol. 3, Part 1, Patna , 1983 pp. 49-53.
97. KPJ wrote an article 'An Muhammadan Invasion of Nepal' which led to this tense relationship (the details will be discussed in the Chapter on History, Chapter No. 4).
98. For the entire proceedings see, the Senate meeting held on 28 March 1936, File No. XIII E-41/36 of Bihar State Archives, also *Hindu Polity*, pp. xxxvii-xlvii.
99. G.P. Ambastha, op. cit, pp. xxxi-xxxii.
100. Rahul Sankrityayan, 'Dr. Kashi Prasad Jayaswal', *KPJCV*, p. 2.
101. Ibid., p. 11.
102. This issue will be discussed in the Chapter 3 on *Pataliputra*.
103. Ramdhari Singh Dinkar, op. cit., p. 21.
104. Mohanlal Mahato Viyogi, 'Doctor Jayaswal', *Saraswati*, Oct.1937, Part 38, No. 4, pp. 335-36.
105. Ibid.
106. Jayaswal, K.P., 'Self- Assertion of the Masses Inevitable', *Modern Review*, Vol. LXI, April 1937, pp. 387-88.
107. Ibid., p. 387.
108. Rahul Sankrityayan, 'Dr. Kashi Prasad Jayaswal', *KPJCV*, p. 6.
109. K.P. Jayaswal, 'Self-Assertion of the Masses Inevitable', *MR*, Vol. LXI, April 1937 p. 387.
110. Ibid.
111. Ibid.
112. Ibid., p. 388.
113. File No. 2N/32, Bihar State Archives.
114. Ramdhari Singh Dinkar, op. cit., p. 19.
115. Ibid., p. 19.
116. Ibid., pp. 20-21.
117. Ibid., p. 21.
118. Ibid., p. 18, also see, Paliwal, Krishndutt, *Maithilisharan Gupta*

Granthavali, vol. XII, Vani Prakashan, New Delhi, 2008, pp. 515-16.

119. P.C. Manuk, op. cit, pp. 50-51.
120. Rahul Sankrityayan, 'Dr. Kashi Prasad Jayaswal' *KPJCV*, pp. 7-11, (will be discussed in chapter 2 on 'Hindi Nationalism').
121. *Rahul Vangmay*, op. cit., p. 673.
122. Ibid., p. 676.
123. Mohanlal Mahato Viyogi, 'Doctor Jayaswal' , *Saraswati*, October 1937, Part 38, No. 4, p. 335.
124. Ibid., pp. 334-35.
125. Ibid., p. 335.
126. Sushila Jayaswal, op. cit., p. 57.
127. Mohanlal Mahato Viyogi, 'Doctor Jayaswal', *Saraswati*, October 1937, Part 38, No. 4, p. 336.
128. Rahul Sankrityayan, 'Dr. Kashi Prasad Jayaswal', *KPJCV*, pp. 1-2.
129. Sushila Jayaswal, op. cit., pp. 56-57.
130. Ramdhari Singh Dinkar, op. cit., pp. 18-19, *Maithilisharan Gupta Granthavali,* op. cit., p. 515.
131. Ramdhari Singh Dinkar, op. cit., p. 20.
132. P.C. Manuk, op. cit, p. 48.
133. Ibid., pp. 48.
134. Ibid., p. 49.
135. Rahul Sankrityayan, 'Dr. Kashi Prasad Jayaswal' *KPJCV*, p. 2.
136. Ibid., p. 3.
137. Rahul Sankrityayan, 'Dr. Kashi Prasad Jayaswal', *KPJCV*, p. 54.
138. *Rahul Vangmaya*, op. cit., p. 674.
139. Mishra, Shiv Gopal, *Rahul Ji ke Agyat Patra*, Hindustan Academy, Allahabad, 2010, p. 55.
140. Mohanlal Mahato Viyogi, 'Doctor Jayaswal', *Saraswati*, October 1937, Part 38, No. 4, p. 338.
141. Ibid., p. 338.
142. Ibid., pp. 338-39.
143. Ramdhari Singh Dinkar, op. cit, pp. 15-16.
144. Ibid., pp. 16-17.
145. Naval, Nand Kishore; Kumar, Tarun (ed.), *Dinkar Rachnawali*, Vol. 14, Lok Bharati Prakashan, Allahabad, 2011, p. 288.
146. For such association see, Verma, Mathura Prasad, *Jayaswal Jati Parichay*, also see, Verma, Mathura Prasad, Jayaswal, Mishrilal, *Vishwavikhyat Itihaskar Dr. Kashi Prasad Jayaswal*; Jigyasu, Chandrika Prasad (ed,) *Kalwar Kesari*, Sampadakiya Tippaniyan, Vol. 2, No. 2, Āśvina-Śukla, Saṁvat 1981, pp. 122-23.
147. *Proceedings of the Akhil Bharatavarshiya Haihay Kshatriya Mahasabha*, Jabalpur, 1927, also see, Verma, Mathura Prasad, op. cit., p. 12.
148. Sushila Jayaswal, op. cit., p. 58.
149. *Rahul Vangmay*, op. cit., p. 676.

150. *Kalwar Kesari*, Sampadakiya Tippaniyan, Vol. 2, No. 2, Āśvina-Śukla, Saṁvat 1981, pp. 122-23.
151. Ibid., p. 90.
152. Ibid., pp. 123-24.
153. This issue has been discussed in the Chapter 3.
154. *Rahul Vangmaya*, op. cit., p. 673.
155. Ibid.
156. Sushila Jayaswal, op. cit., p. 57.
157. Ibid., p. 58.
158. *Rahul Vangmaya*, op. cit., p. 679.
159. Ibid., p. 16.
160. *Proceedings and Transactions of the Ninth All India Oriental Conference*, Trivandrum, Decembe 20-22, 1937, pp. 20-21.

2

Player in the Field of 'Hindi Nationalism'

KPJ was a multilingual scholar. He knew several languages-Sanskrit, Hindi, Pali, English, Chinese, French, German, and possibly Bengali. However, he wrote extensively in two languages, viz., Hindi and English. English for KPJ was the language of the world and Hindi, the language of the region to address the local masses. Facility with more than one tongue was a matter not just of skill but also of sensibility. The writer, his work, and his audience, all benefited from the fact that that the person in question was in command of more than one linguistic and cultural universe. He comes quite close to Ramchandra Guha's description of the 'linguidextrous' intellectual.[1] Perhaps, the desire to connect with the masses in the vernacular was part of the agenda to spread anti-colonial/nationalist feelings amongst pre-independence intellectuals, leaders and scholars for the purpose of spreading anti-colonial/ nationalist feeling amongst the people.

KPJ was educated in the English system, yet right from his initial years he wrote in Hindi and advocated the use of Hindi throughout his life. Writing and reading Hindi at that time could mean different things to people with different *saṁskāras*,

> For Brahmin Pandits it meant entering a modern public sphere and accepting a wider medium. For the Urdu-educated it meant espousing a sense of identification with a broad Hindi-Hindu community and accessing a larger and growing public. For the English-educated it could mean adhering to the nationalist project, the desire to communicate with a wider public and possibly to act as interpreters between the local and outside worlds. For women it was a public voice they had hitherto lacked. In any case, Hindi was an acquired, sometimes a chosen, public voice which, required some rearticulation of identity.[2]

KPJ is better known to the world as a 'nationalist historian'. However, he had an equally prolific career as a Hindi writer. KPJ got his intellectual training in Hindi under the leadership of noted Hindi laureate Chaudhari Badrinarayan Upadhyaya Premghan, who started the Hindi Magazine *Anand Kadambini* from Mirzapur in 1881. KPJ was associated with it and got intellectual inspiration from it.[3] He started writing at the age of 17 and his first article was published in *Hindi Pradeep* in 1898. However, most of his early writings in Hindi appeared in the *Saraswati*. This pioneering journal had acquired a premier stature among the intellectuals at that time and led an almost renaissance-type movement. Noted Hindi litterateur Ramvilas Sharma has observed,

> हिंदी में सरस्वती से पहले, उसके साथ साथ और उसके बाद बहुत सी पत्रिकाएं निकलीं और निकलती रहीं पर किसी भी पत्रिका में हिंदी लेखक अपनी रचनाएँ छपाने के लिए ऐसे आतुर और उत्सुक नहीं दिखाई दिये जैसे सरस्वती में।...सरस्वती सबसे पहले ज्ञान की पत्रिका थी, वह हिंदी नवजागरण का मुख पत्र थी, और हिंदी भाषी जनता की सर्वमान्य जातीय पत्रिका थी। ज्ञान की पत्रिका होने के अलावा वह कलात्मक साहित्य की पत्रिका थी, ऐसे साहित्य की जो रीतिवादी रूढ़ियों का नाश करके नवीन सामाजिक सांस्कृतिक आवश्यकतों के अनुरूप रचा जा रहा था। इसलिये उसने हिंदी साहित्य में, और उसके बाहर व्यापक स्तर पर भारतीय साहित्य में, वह प्रतिष्ठा प्राप्त की जो बीसवीं सदी में अन्य किसी पत्रिका को प्राप्त नहीं हुई।[4]

More recently, Francesca Orisini, too, has echoed almost similar ideas and highlighted the role of Pandit Mahavir Prasad Dwivedi in setting the agenda of this *patrika*,[5] which had a distinctive impact on KPJ's early writings in Hindi.

Apart from KPJ's contributions in *Saraswati* (25 articles), his writings could be found in the other noted magazines of his times such as *Hindi Pradeep* (3 articles), *Nagari Pracharini Patrika* (7 articles), *Kalwar Gazette* (which he edited in his early days), *Hindi Kesari*, and the Hindi weekly *Pataliputra* (the contents of the *Pataliputra* will be discussed in the next chapter). However, the files of the *Kalwar Gazette* and *Hindi Kesari* are not available anywhere, except for a few pages of *Hindi Kesari* in the Madhavrao Sapre Library in Bhopal, Madhya Pradesh, which does not contain any writing by KPJ. As far as the *Kalwar Gazette* is concerned, we get an indirect reference to his editorial titled 'Jati' in the magazine, inferred from the writing of Pandit Bal Krishna Bhatt.[6] KPJ also wrote two Hindi poems, published in the *Saraswati* and some of the poems were collected by Rahul Sankrityayan from his personal diary. During his lifetime, KPJ also gave four important speeches in Hindi; first, at the third Hindi Sahitya Sammelan in Calcutta in 1912 on 'Hindu Rajyashastra', when his intellectual guru Chaudhari Badrinarayan Upadhyaya Premghan was the General President of the Sammelan. This speech in Hindi on Hindu polity was later translated into English, serialised and published in the *Modern Review* with several titles[7] and finally as a monograph titled *Hindu Polity* in 1924. The concept highlighted in the 'Hindu Rajyashastra' soon became a tool and a template for nationalist mobilisation and raised the morale of the freedom fighters and for whom the monograph became the second *Gita*[8] and the Bible, "Meet any educated old man; he knows about Hindu Polity."[9] He delivered the second speech as the President of the 4th Conference of the Akhil Bharatavarsiya Haihay Kshatriya Mahasabha in Jabalpur in April 1927. This is the only available speech of KPJ, in which he addressed the issues and problems of the Kalwar caste.[10] The third speech was delivered at the Prantiya Hindi Sahitya Sammelan in Bhagalpur in 1933, in which KPJ highlighted the antiquity of Hindi. And, he dlivered the fourth speech as the Sectional President of History at the All India Hindi Conference, Indore, in 1935, when Gandhi was its General President. In this lecture, KPJ visualised the idea of writing a comprehensive history of India.

One can identify three distinct phases of KPJ's contributions to Hindi: (i) from 1898 to 1912, (ii) 1914-15 as the editor of Hindi weekly *Pataliputra* and (iii) from 1928 to last days of his life. Most of his original writings in Hindi belong to the first phase. In the long gap of almost 14 years between the second and the third phases, he concentrated on establishing himself as a successful lawyer and also made notable contributions to history-writing in English. Most of his writings in Hindi in the last phase are translations of his own contributions in English from the preceding phase. Content-wise, KPJ's writings in Hindi could be categorised under; (A) Hindi language and literature, (B) Travelogues and memoirs, (C) Biographies, (D) Social Issues, (E) Poetry, (F) Translated articles, and (G) Miscellaneous articles.

(A) Hindi Language and Literature

The period in which KPJ started writing in Hindi is known as the period of 'Hindi Renaissance' in the region designated as North-West Province in the nineteenth century, i.e., present-day Uttar Pradesh.[11] In that period there was a sustained movement under the leadership of Bharatendu Harishchandra and Pandit Bal Krishna Bhatt and others to get official recognition for Hindi language and Nagari script. The period also witnessed the 'communalisation of language' as well. Under the aegis of Nagri Pracharini Sabha and later, Hindi Sahitya Sammelan, there was an emphasis on inventing a new, Sanskritised Hindi from which Urdu and Persian words had to be thrown out. It resulted in the process of identification of Hindi as the language of the Hindus, and Urdu as the language of the Muslims.

The concept of a national language was initially introduced by the British and applied to the Indian situation. They found no single language which could claim a national status. However, under the Mughals, it was a composite language, which went by the name of Hindavi or Hindustani, which was understood in some measure across the length and breadth of the subcontinent. In the complex linguistic situation of the country, the British policies and institutions initiated the process which quickly led to a split in Hindustani and the creation of Hindi and Urdu as the national languages of Hindus and Muslims respectively, and to their subsequent development as two autonomous print language spheres. However, the concept of Hindi as the language of the Hindus, with vast territorial and ideological aspirations, was appropriated by nationalists and thenceforth developed almost exclusively by them. It was here that Banaras played a larger role, and as the merchant spokesman of the newly forming middle class, which claimed to speak for the whole nation, Harishchandra occupied a special position.[12] It should be noted here that KPJ also belonged to a rich middle class of business family of Mirzapur, 70 kms away from Banaras and was in dialogue with the Hindi scholars of the region.

Vasudha Dalmia has argued,

> The development of Hindi was, then, not to be separated from its cultural and religious identification with Hindus at a supra-regional, and later, at a national level. The evolution of Hindi as the language of the Hindus continued through the nineteenth century. It can be viewed as threefold: (1) It was first and foremost a process of dichotomisation, that is, separation from Urdu, coupled with the claim of absolute autonomy for Hindi, (2) The language thus separated was standardised by means of grammars, dictionaries and school primers, which not only represented autonomy but also cultivated and

> increased it, by introducing new vocabulary and stressing those phonological and grammatical alternatives that were different from those of Urdu, the contrast language which most threatened its autonomy, and (3) Along with the standardisation came a historicisation, that is, the process of establishing historical links with literary works connected with great ideological movements of the past. Speech communities create myths and genealogies concerning the origin and development of standard varieties of language. The archaisation thus constructed provides for respectable ancestry. The origin of Hindi from Sanskrit as the ancient mother tongue of the Aryans was supported by the nineteenth century discovery of historical regularity. The great ideological movement, which Hindi came to be associated with, was offered by the devotional Bhakti movement, which came to be seen as the Hindu response to the threat posed by Islam.[13]

By the 1860s and 1870s, the stage was set for a full-fledged campaign for Hindi as the national language of the Hindus, for in the meantime the language had been codified and thus ideologically fortified in a series of increasingly sophisticated grammars and dictionaries. The agitation for the use of Nagari script in the courts was to forge further uniformity and to bring forth a literature which was fit for the expression of new aspirations. Bharatendu Harishchandra was one of the crucial leaders for this campaign.

One important segment of KPJ's writings and speeches in Hindi was focused on the question of Hindi language, including its grammar, purity, antiquity, and importance. However, KPJ's position on the question of language was somewhat fluid and imbibed several influences over the years. In his earliest piece, 'Nagari Pracharini Sabha ke Prashnon ke Uttar', the influence of Bharatendu is clearly visible.[14] The purpose of the article was to show how to write good Hindi. He argued, "Bharatendu had made a distinction between *Sadhu Bhasha* (pure language) and *Prachalit Bhasha* (colloquial language) and in both cases there is no use of the Persian words. Therefore, one should not write in a Persian mixed language."[15] KPJ further elaborated on what genres of text should be written and in what linguistic registers, "The language of novels, biographies, philosophy, articles on special issues, the texts on literature, etc. should be *Sadhu Bhasha* and for ordinary history, newspapers, etc. the popular language would be more appropriate."[16] On the question of the language of prose and poetry,

KPJ reiterated the opinion of Bharatendu that the language of prose and the poetry could not be one. He argued that it was an established fact that the language of poetry of the North-West Province is Brajbhasha and from ancient times people had been using this language for poetry. KPJ himself, however, tried his hand at writing poetry in *Khari Boli* but the results did not satisfy him, and therefore, he argued that writing poetry in Brajbhasha was the best option.[17]

KPJ was very serious about the purity of language, grammar and even the use of hyphen, "One should use the case in both noun and pronoun while writing, because in speech the case is not separated. It is good to use hyphen while using foreign words with the Hindi words."[18] Continuing with the idea of linguistic purity, he wrote, "One must use Sanskrit in *Sadhu Bhasha* and *Apabhramsha* in *Prachalit Bhasha*. One cannot write an *Apabhramsha* word with Sanskrit combination, like; *madandh hathi* or *matwala hasti* but *matwala hathi* and *madandh hasti*. If the meaning changes with adoption of *Apabhramsha* words while sanskritising them, then leave them as it is."[19]

On the question of Persian script and English he wrote, "I do not know the script of Persian and that is why I cannot say anything about it, but the use of the punctuation marks makes English language very easy and one cannot write English without it."[20] KPJ was very particular about writing Hindi: its technicality, grammar, syntax, sentence formation, use of gender, and the proper use of the word and branded Urdu as *Narini* (effeminate). There was no question that Hindi could be written in a script other than the Nagari. As Ramvilas Sharma has pointed out, "Erthrington thoroughly sanskritised the language. The kind of sanitisation which had taken place in Urdu in the late Mughal period began to take place in Hindi now."[21] Therefore, one finds here some hints of linguistic chauvinism in KPJ's writing. However, on the question of the gender of the languages, KPJ had a different option to offer, "लिंग का प्रयोग लोक व्यवहार पर निर्भर है। व्याकरण उसके लिए– संस्कृत, प्राकृत, या हिंदी में– मेढ़ नहीं बाँध सका और न कभी बाँध सकेगा।"[22] So, while laying down certain normative terms in response to Bharatendu, he could also see language as a social practice, and as something that was continually constructed by everyday use.

Similarly, on the question of the simplistic identification being advocated those days between languages and communities, KPJ had a completely different take on the issue. In the following extended comment he satirised those fiction writers of Hindi who were trying to vitiate the cultural atmosphere by reading Indian history and society in naive, essentialist, and communal terms:

> दो चार को छोड़कर प्राय: सभी बंग भाषा से अनुवादित उपन्यासों में एक प्रायिक या सामान्य दोष हैं– और उसी दोष के लिए हमारा उलहना है। वह महादोष यह है– मुसलमानों के चरित्र का ऐसा चित्र खींचना कि जिससे यह भाव होने लगे कि संसार के मनुष्य जाति भर में सबसे नीच, दुष्ट, अत्याचारी, विश्वासघातक ये ही होते हैं– सभी अवगुण और पापों के मुसलमान अवतार हैं!! पृथ्वी तल पर किसी विशेष जाति व सम्प्रदाय के जनमात्र दुष्ट या पापी नहीं हो सकते– सबों में अच्छे और बुरे होते हैं। हिन्दू मुसलमानों में मेल करना तो दूर रहा, इस प्रकार दिन-दिन दोनों में घृणा और द्वेष बढ़ाया जा रहा है! देश के अहित करने वालों में यों उपन्यास लेखकों का भी साझा है!
>
> हमारे उपन्यास लेखक जी! आप समझते होंगे कि बुझे बुझाए हिंदुओं में आप जोश डालकर बड़ा उपकार कर रहे हैं! किन्तु तनिक ध्यान देने से आप जान जाएँगे कि आप कैसा बड़ा उपकार कर रहे हैं। आपके जोश दिलाने से कुछ भी लाभ है? लाभ होना तो दूर रहे उलटी हानि है! आप जोश दिलाइए और हिन्दू अपना ही लोहू पिया करैं!!! ...दोनों दलों में बड़े परिश्रम से यदि प्रीति भाव जमाया भी जाय तो आप उसे लवण सदृश्य हो फाड़कर अलग कर देते हैं। शाबाश! देश हितैषियों शाबाश! – साधु! विचारशील उपन्यास लेखकों साधू!! तुम धन्य, हम जी धन्य हैं क्योंकि हम आपके देश भाई कहलाने का 'गौरव रखते हैं'–
>
> भाइयों! यदि एक दल के लोग अपने दूसरे दल के प्रति घृणा करने की बुरी प्रकृति को छोड़ दें तो कुछ दिनों में दूसरे दल वाले भी उनके तरफ स्वच्छ हृदय हो जाय– एक हाथ से ताली नहीं बजती– ...हमारे देश हितैषी उपन्यास लेखकों! आपसे यह हाथ जोड़ कर प्रार्थना है कि ऐसी चेष्टा किया कीजिए जिसमें हिन्दू मुसलमान दोनों मिल जाएँ– आपकी लेखनी में बड़ी शक्ति है-- आप जो चाहें कर सकते हैं।
>
> उपन्यास लिखना कोई बुरी बात नहीं है– यदि 'उपन्यास लिखा जाए तो– उपन्यास से संसार का जितना हित और उपकार साधन हो सकता है उतना और किसी प्रकार की पुस्तक से होना कठिन है– इससे मनुष्य घोर पापी से देवता में परिणत हो सकता है– और तुर्रा यह कि बिना कोई कठिन परिश्रम के ही।[23]

This essay, written at the impressionable age of eighteen, betrays an uncharacteristically mature thought process in KPJ. Like so many others of his time, he recognised the great transformative role novels could play, but he also castigated the incessant demonisation of Muslims in Hindi fiction writing. He argued that if judiciously written, novels could ignite the imagination of their readers, so could the use of language, "It is only the language which differentiates the human being from the animal and without language, the human being is even inferior to the animal. It is through the language that we enter into a new world, formulate new ideas, make continuous speeches, and pass on our ideas to the next generation, perform our worldly and other worldly duties, and transmit our priceless heritage."[24] KPJ argued that command over language made human being the king of the entire world and criticised those who did not value the importance of language:

> सारांश यह कि भाषा से ही मनुष्य, पशु से पहचाना जाता है, भाषा से ही मनुष्य अपने को पहचानता है, भाषा के ही द्वारा वह ऐहिक और पारलौकिक कर्तव्यों का साधन करता है। भाषा ही उसकी अमूल्य पैतृक संपत्ति है; भाषा से ही वह समस्त सृष्टि का महाराज है; अधिक क्या, भाषा ही से मनुष्य 'मनुष्य' है। सो उसी भाषा को, उसी भाषा के शास्त्र को, न जानना, उसी भाषा के मर्मों को न समझना, उसी भाषा की अवहेलना करना, क्या मनुष्य जाति के लिए लज्जा-शतवार, सहस्त्रवार लज्जा– का कारण नहीं है? जन्म लेना और भाषा के महत्त्व को बिना पहचाने मर जाना, क्या जीवन में बहुत ही बड़ी भूल नहीं है?[25]

This heartfelt comment was characteristic of all Hindi intellectuals born after Bhartendu's much publicised and commented upon Balia proclamation: 'nij bhasha unnati ahai'.

As pointed out earlier, the authenticity of a language was attested to by its antiquity, and also by its divinity. The rationalist KPJ would entertain no such illusions about Hindi, "Hindi originated from Prakrit and Prakrit from Sanskrit, but Sanskrit? Sanskrit is the language of the God; this was the general belief of all countries. In other words, the language has originated from the heaven and the human being had picked it up."[26] However, KPJ saw human craftsmanship in the origin of the language and made a departure from several other nationalists of nineteenth century. Describing the benefits of language, KPJ wrote,

> भाषा के लाभ अनंत हैं। भाषा की घनिष्ठता अद्भुत है। भाषा का सम्बन्ध लोकोत्तर है। लोगों कि समझ में रुधिर का सम्बन्ध बड़ा घनिष्ठ और सबल है। पर हम दोनों भुजा उठाकर ललकारते हैं कि भाषा का सम्बन्ध, संसार के यावत सम्बन्धों से कहीं ज़ोरावर है। यदि आप चीन में जावें जहाँ लम्बी चोटीवाले पीले मनुष्य की किड़विड़ाहट में एक आपका बांधव मिले जो चीन ही में पला हो और चीनी ही बोलता हो। और एक दूसरा चीनी ही हो, जो टूटी फूटी भी आपकी भाषा बोल लेता हो और समझ सकता हो तो बतलाइए आपका मन किसकी ओर झुकेगा। रुधिर की एकता भाषा की एकता के बिना, व्यर्थ है और भाषा की एकता रुधिर की विभिन्नता रहते भी एकता संपादन करने वाली है। हमारे प्रभु अंग्रेज़ों की यह उन्नति कदापि न हो सकती यदि

उन सभों की भाषा एक न होती। जर्मनी सा छिन्न-भिन्न देश भाषा की एकता सूत्र में गठित होकर राष्ट्र को दृढ़ करता है। भाषा की एकता सब एकताओं की जननी है। भारतवर्ष और अंग्रेज़ों में भाषा शास्त्र ने ऐसी कड़ी लगाकर उनके राज्य को ऐसी दृढ़ता प्रदान की है कि जिसके संपादन में करोड़ों सैनिक कृतार्थ न हो सकते।[27]

To paraphrase, KPJ was of the opinion that language was an ultimately intimate entity and the supreme one amongst all the relationships, even above that of blood (*rudhir*). The unity of blood was useless without the unity of language and the unity of language could deliver unity despite the difference in blood. Our British rulers could not have progressed so much without their linguistic unity. A splintered Germany could emerge as a nation, because of the unity of the language. The unity of the language was the mother of all unities. And the bond that philology had struck Britain and India could not have been accomplished even by battalions of forces.

When the relationship was established between Sanskrit and the European languages, KPJ termed it as an earthquake and argued, "It has turned the world upside down. This earthquake was the miraculous invention of the philologists. They have proved that the primeval language, Sanskrit is the sister, elder sister of the Greek, Latin, German, etc. of the Westerns. *Maatar* of this land is equal to their Mother and our *Bhratar* is equal to their Brother. Both of them are from the same source. Both of them are equal to two children of the same father. Therefore, philology has created unprecedented love between both of them."[28] It was the question of language in the writings of Shakespeare, which attracted KPJ most. In a piece entitled 'Shakespeare' he wrote, "This poet was fabulously proud of his language and his nation. The example of this is his "Richard the Second", which makes every lover of his language and country emotional."[29] Forcing someone to give up one's own language was seen as equivalent of an exile. It was in tune with the voices of Hindi intellectuals of the nineteenth and early twentieth centuries.

Coming back to the issue of the origins of Hindi, Rai Shyam Sundar Das had in his Presidential Speech at the sixth All India Oriental Conference held in Patna in 1930, argued that the 'Adikala' of Hindi started in c. 1000 CE or around the time of Chand Bardai. However, KPJ refuted this argument and considered it misleading. On the basis of the reading of the Jaina manuscripts and other historical texts, KPJ tried to show that Hindi was as old as the early medieval period. In this context, he wrote, 'The Beginning of Old Hindi'[30] and 'Purani Hindi ka Janm-Kal'.[31] The arguments given in the aforesaid articles were further elaborated by him in his Presidential Speech at 11th Hindi Prantiya Adhiveshan, Bhagalpur, in 1933.[32] Briefly, he did not see the genesis of Hindi from Sanskrit or any *devavani*, but on the basis of the linguistic evidence available from the non-Sanskritic texts.

At the conference, KPJ also shed light on the poetry of the 84 Siddhas, and explicated several poetic compositions of Sarojvajra Siddhācārya (750 CE). He was trying to find the ancient origin of Hindi. He said:

> You might have given me your attention when I said that whatever examples I have given from 750 AD to Vidyapati (1450 AD), in all of them *kriya-rupa* and *shabda-rupa* Magadhi, Shurseni etc. are different from Prakrit. Their grammar is different and this grammar is completely similar to the grammar of Old Hindi. That is why I call it Old Hindi. Today, I have given all examples from eastern Hindi because Sir George Grierson had written to me with sorrow that the texts of the eastern language, which has connection with Bihar, have not been found and there has not been any study of their ancient form, although, there are some previous forms of western Hindi in the Jaina literature. When I saw them in chronological order, I found that the history and examples of the old eastern Hindi are available from c. 750 AD to till date. The history of this goes back to 600 AD because Bana, along with other poets of Prakrit and *Desh-bhasha*, used to show acting skills in the public. The poet of Deshbhasha—*desbhasha* of Bana—which became different from Prakrit, and became distorted, —there must have been a poet of *Poorvi Hindi*. He was the resident of his village. When Saraha—who was intellectual and residents of Magadha—wrote in Doha, then he was not the first to write in *chhanda*. Here we remember Devasena when in 990 AD he wrote Jaina religion in Doha, then his disciple stopped him because at that time the language of the Jaina religion was Prakrit and they used to write *gatha* in Prakrit *chhanda*. It proves that Doha was the *chhanda* of *desbhasha* only. Doha has never been found in original Prakrit. Same is true of *chaupai* as well. Long before Jayasi there was a system to write stories that were interspersed with *chaupai* and *dohas*. This is proved by the texts like *Nagakumaracharita* of Pushpadanta. *Chappaya, Rola, Kundaliya* etc. all of them belonged to *desbhasha*.
>
> The meaning of the word apabhramsha has been changing from

> time to time. Ordinary or colloquial Prakrit has been termed apabhramsha by Patanjali and in support of them he has given 'gavi', 'goni', 'gopitalika'. There are a number of inscriptions in that language. For example, the copper plate of Sohagaura. But till the time of Bhoja, Prakrit had become an old classical language. Irrespective of whether one calls it apabhramsha or Hindi or even just *bhasha*; the style of the poetry written in *deshbhasha* and from Tirhut and Bihar and from doab and Rajaputana, was indeed the ancient Hindi kavya. Vidyapati has called Hindi as *apabhrashta bhasha* and *desil bhasha*. But the language which was called *apabhrashta* by the medieval people was the *deshbhasha* only. That *deshabhasha* was called '*bhasha*' by Jayasi and Vidyapati had said that the language of his Kirtilata, was *deshabhasha*, and *apabhrashta*. It implies that it was the language which was separated from Prakrit and used by the common people. The Chinese traveller Huen-Tsang had found people speaking that language.[33]

KPJ further argued, "Looking at this history, nobody has the right to say that there is no evidence of history of Hindi before Jayasi. In the secondary (*gauṇa*) language of India, the oldest is the eastern Hindi only. And it was written in the centres of Vikramashila near Bhagalpur and Nalanda near Patna."[34]

Commenting on the modern Hindi *kāvya chanda* system (prosody), KPJ wrote,

> The language is becoming Sanskritised and because of that it is becoming difficult for the women and the common men to understand. The vocabulary of the pure (*nichhakki*) Hindi is quite large. We must not leave that treasure. Lavani and other mean *chhanda* does not suit Hindi. The popular poems have been composed in Gujarati, Marathi, and Nepali. If Hindi follows that pattern, then it will become readable to the entire country and the prestige and glory of Hindi will be maintained. One must not leave the old *chhanda* completely because it is our linguistic heritage (*bapauti*) for the last 1200 years. A number of beautiful Hindi *chhandas* have been given in the Prakrit pingal. They must be reinforced and on the basis of that a new *chhanda* must be created, as it was happening in the past as well. The seven-eight forms of *doha* were created by the older people of Hindi which is given in Prakrit pingal.[35]

This speech was a remarkable intellectual exercise in philological exposition and polemics grounded in the evidence offered by some rare texts and their translations that could not have been available to Hindi writers such as Shyam Sundar Das. What is equally remarkable is that KPJ was very conscious of Hindi's literary heritage – for which he used an effective term, *bapauti*. While recognising that innovation was very much part of any work of literary creativity, past or present, he stressed that Hindi litterateurs must not abandon the musicality achieved by centuries of poetic praxis, examples of which could still be found in oral/folk performances.

The historian's eye of KPJ also underlined the continuity of Hindi language through the ages by analysing more 'hard' sources: coins. In collaboration with Pandit Mahavir Prasad Dwivedi, he wrote an interesting article, 'Pathani Sikko par Nagari,' which was published in *Saraswati*.[36] After analysing dozens of coins of the Slave Dynasty, they argued, "The Nagari script has been engraved on the Royal coinage from Muhammad bin Sam to Pathan chief Ibrahim Lodi. After the decline of the Pathans and the arrival of Babur and during the reign of the Mughals, a new kind of Hindi called Urdu was developed. It was only then that Nagari ceased to be engraved on the coins."[37] They lamented the fact that the imperial government used Persian, instead of Nagari script, on the new one rupee coin. They asked for its immediate rectification arguing that in all the provinces the number of people knowing Nagari script outnumbered those who knew Persian script.[38]

As far as the standard of Hindi language in concerned, KPJ always advocated the use of simple Hindi, which could be understood by common people including women and children. He cited examples from the Buddha's sermons, which were always in the language of common people rather than in *chandas* that is Vedic or Upaniṣadic Sanskrit. He went on to compare obsoleteness of *chandas* with that of the Brajbhasha of his own times and cited the examples of contemporary poets such as Pandit Shridhar Pathak and Babu Maithilisharan Gupt who preferred to write in spoken Hindi (*Khari Boli*) instead of archaic Brajbhasha, "Those who care that their composition should reach, and become popular, with the populace and be not being confined to the learned few, will give up the shackles of classics, cast off the artificiality of learnedness, and appear in the homely, intimate language of the public".[39] A disciple of his, Mohanlal Mahato Viyogi wrote in an obituary that whenever he got an opportunity to speak to KPJ regarding language, he always heard him advocating the use of simple 'homely' Hindi (*gharau-Hindi*):

> Jayaswalji's thoughts on Hindi were progressive and he felt proud about accepting Hindi as a national language. Except under extreme necessity, he used to work in Hindi. Once a Prof. Saheb came to meet him and started speaking in English. Jayaswalji replied in Hindi, notwithstanding the fact that the professor had spoken in English. Then, his roughness (*akkharata*) got stirred and he started speaking in French. Prof. Saheb got surprised. He said sarcastically, 'Gentleman, if you want to speak in a foreign language, French is more melodious and cultured than English. Let's talk in that. This is the proof of utmost love for Hindi. He even wrote addresses on the envelopes in Hindi, at least, the letters sent to me. He never liked the use of English words, while speaking in Hindi. In his opinion that was the effort of the stupidity.[40]

History-Writing in Hindi

In 1935, at the All India Hindi Sammelan in Indore, KPJ was the President of Bharatiya Itihas Parishad of the Sammelan and gave a long speech, in which he highlighted the importance of history-writing in general and history-writing in Hindi in particular. He said:

> It is a matter of pleasure that the system of the study of history has begun once again and there are good teachers of it available in Hindi at present. In the Rajaputana, Honorable Mahamahopadhyaya Gaurishankar-Hirachand Ojha, in Antarveda my disciple Pandit Jayachandra Vidyalankar and in the Etaddesh Kumar Saheb, Pandit Reuji, Pandit Rameshwar Ojha, etc. in the field of history; and my friends Muni Jinavijayji, Muni Kalyanavijayaji, Mahapandit Rahul Sankrityayan have done wonderful work in the field of religious history. In the field of Indian art and history, Dr. Hiranand Shastri and Shri Chaman Lal Mehta and in the study of the history of the Indian literature, Rai Bahadur Shyamsundar Das, all of them have done their studies in Hindi in such a fashion which has not been done in any other foreign language. Hindi appears specially privileged, for, several prominent Indian scholars are writing both in English and Hindi. The frontrunner in this field was Dr. Hira Lal Saheb, who passed away recently. If he were alive, obviously he would have been amongst us in Indore. There are famous pandits like Dr. Hiranand Shastri, Dr. Laxman Swarupa, who take great pleasure in writing in Hindi. Similarly, there are several scholars, who had knowledge of several treatises, and authors and speakers of Hindi,

> are alive with the blessings of Saraswati. There are scholars, who are experts in the different branches of studies, like Dr. Gorakh Prasad and Pandit Suryanarayana Vyasa in the Indian astronomy, Dr. Motichandra and Rai Krishna Das in the Indian painting, and above all, my friend Dr. Ganganath Jha, who is modern scholar of literature and the *Dharmashastra*.[41]

At that time, history was written largely in English. KPJ was of the opinion that the history of India should be available in Hindi so that the masses would be made aware about the cultural and political heritage of India. He was also of the opinion that non-availability of history books in Hindi was a matter of shame because in his eyes Hindi was the language of Āryāvarta and the position of Hindi was similar to that of Sanskrit at the time of *Māhābhārata* and Māgadhī at the time of the Buddha and Mahāvīra. This identification of Hindi with the geography of Āryāvarta is interesting as is his invocation of Etaddesha, Antarveda and Rajputana. Quite clearly, KPJ was looking for denominational continuities in cartographic imagination here as much as he was looking for the same in his philological exegesis discussed above. His historian's vision remains vast with scope of proliferating disciplines and sub-disciplines. But the ideal here is that of a bilingual, informed vernacular historian of India who could assimilate knowledge from several language resources to write meaningfully and purposefully, and in Hindi.

(B) Travelogues

Travel-writing in Hindi was a relatively novel venture. Like every other genre it was an area in which content was sought to be generated with a great degree of enthusiasm. The editors of information-hungry newspapers and magazines made constant demands on writers travelling to far-off places and countries. So, the transmission of basic information about these strange places was the prime drive. If comparison and evaluation were the two key modes of organising the information gathered and observations made, difference and sometimes similarity were the primary impulses. It was also a process through which the travel writer and his reader became conscious of certain regional, cultural, or national senses of the self. So, the journey was made and reported like an encounter with difference. The confrontation with difference often began in the first leg—the train—itself. Railway travelling also meant much discomfort and inevitably the native traveller experienced racial arrogance and discrimination. Arriving at his destination, the traveller encountered strange landscapes, peoples, and cultures and described these with wonder and a certain sense of adventure. The journey meant, then, a mapping of the country in that the traveller took an experimental and cultural view of it. It meant a new awareness of a cultural identity constructed in commonality and difference.[42]

Travelogues constitute an important segment of KPJ's Hindi oeuvre. There are two categories of his writings in this genre: (a) his travels within Britain during his student days,[43] and (b) narratives of his return journey from Britain to India after the completion of his studies. After finishing his studies in England, he anticipated some kind of arrest, due to his links with the revolutionaries in England. Therefore, he avoided the obvious direct route and chose to return to India via Hungry, Turkey, and Sri Lanka. In the course of this journey, he used road, rail, and sea routes. The reflections on this journey were published in *Saraswati* in four parts as 'Meri Yatra'.[44] Later, in 'The Man in Turkey' he abbreviated all of these in two parts for the *Modern Review*.[45]

(a) Travels within Britain: Four essays of KPJ, published in *Saraswati* between 1907 and 1908, fall in this category. These pieces fulfil the objectives of the *Saraswati*, i.e., to make its readers aware of things that were useful for people. In the first of these viz., 'Bank of England', KPJ gave a history of the establishment of the Bank and all the descriptive accounts of the functioning of the Bank of England: the printing of the currency-notes, debit-credit transactions, its relationship with the government, parliament, and the Emperor, the role of Comptroller and the Auditor General and also the exchange value with gold and the Indian rupee. In the second part of the article, KPJ shares the details of his personal visit and gives every detail of his journeys in the city of London: colonies, buildings, and even about the staff of the bank. There is also a detailed description of the new mode of travelling in England: the London Underground rail.

Another informative article is, 'London ka Kew Namak Shahi Baag' (लंदन का क्यू नामक शाही बाग़), in which every detail—its history, geography, landscape, climate, museums and building inside the garden, painting gallery, plants, ponds, behaviour of the visitors etc.—is narrated by KPJ. He was so impressed by this botanical garden that he wrote, "The mind is surprised to see the hygiene, management, wonderful trees, flowers, and the fruits of the garden." He visited the place on the occasion of Easter by tram and gave a rich description of the journey: "The scene was similar to some of our fairs. The only difference was that there was no noise. No one was shouting or laughing. People making disorder or engaging themselves in frivolous arguments were not to be seen. And, in our country the young lovers could not be seen holding each other and having romantic chit-chat. But here in the shade of every tree, every plant, couples were gazing at each other and expressing the feelings of their heart by holding each other's soft hands." This is a remarkable description in as much as it notes the difference in decibel levels, but interestingly, does not edit out the intimacy between young couples in public places. A young KPJ's own desire and fascination for the Western Women comes through clearly in between the lines. He celebrated what he liked.

Writing another interesting travelogue, 'England ki Jatiya Chitrashala' (इंग्लैंड की जातीय चित्रशाला), KPJ noted, "This lively community has also developed its arts like poetry, painting, music etc." Immediately he switches back to his learned memories of the ancient glory of India, "In the days of yore, when our Hindu community was completely alive, we exhibited great love for painting. In our royal families, there were big painting galleries, the proof of which has been given in the Sanskrit plays. Sometime ago, I was in a village here, I saw that the fair complexioned wife of a Lieutenant was sitting and painting a scene of nature, I instantly remembered our civilisation depicted in the play *Ratnavali.* How quickly had Sagarika drawn the picture of Vatsaraj; and her friend—*Parshvavartini of Mahisi* too had drawn a picture of Sagarika near that painting. It showed that every young girl was familiar with the art of painting." However, KPJ was quick to express his sorrow over the present condition, "But now, how many of us are aware of even the name of the painting gallery—how many women of ours have seen paintings! With the degradation of our lively life—after subjugation, our love for painting has withered away."

Clearly, this is a subjugated historian's mind taking huge spatial and temporal leaps. He was unable to concentrate on the world he is watching and describing. His restless mind often meandered to the pre-colonial, in fact, pre-Mughal (there was no difference between the two in his reckoning) mythical-utopian golden age, when arts prospered and all was well. So, the travelogue is as much about Indian history as it is about contemporary England.

KPJ's mind also meandered into another comparative hierarchy within arts, between the poet and painter in the East and the West. In his opinion, "In our country, the position of painting comes next [to poets]. Although poets like Kalidasa and Ashvagosha gave reference of pictures while explaining their poems, however, we have not preserved the names and contributions of our painters, as the names of Kalidasa and Ashvagosha are still surviving in our community. However, in Europe the names of their painters became equally famous." KPJ realises the importance of painting gallery and the tradition of sketching and wrote, "When the modern European communities emerged, they bought a number of paintings from Italy. The painters of other countries got stimulated to see their paintings. They sketched their paintings but the painting of Italy is still the best. After independence, Italy has made a law that any painting could not be sold to the foreigners till the time the government is not willing to take that." These early musings are crucial for understanding the making of the future KPJ—the aesthete, the writer, the historian, the institution builder, and the museum curator.

In the second part of the article KPJ gave every detail; history, landscape, donation, paintings, departments, price of the paintings of the 'National Gallery' of England, including the Royal Academy where paintings of every year were being preserved. KPJ informs that in Europe more precious pictures are kept in the capital; however, the National Gallery houses the paintings by the artists of every place.

The religious significance of the paintings is quickly taken care of and KPJ informs that 50% old paintings are religious in nature: the subject is Son-Mother—Mary and Christ. He also explains the reason for that; the old creations were made from the heart and with the feeling of devotion. But now, there is deterioration of the feeling of devotion everywhere. People are painting now for fame and money. KPJ also tried to establish an emotional relation between India and Europe and wrote, "There was a feeling of devotion among the old Christians. That is why they were idol worshippers like us." Again, citing the opinion of the German and other historians, he wrote, "They have proved with great endeavour that near the place which is shown as the birth-place of Christ, there was a Buddhist colony, for which there is historical proof. They say that on the basis of the stories of the Buddhist texts, the birth of the imaginative Christ is believed and it was on the basis of the sermons of the Buddha, Christ's sermons were written. They have also shown that the rituals of the Christian religion are absolutely taken from the Buddhist religion. No scholar has challenged these opinions yet. Acceptance or non-acceptance of these arguments is left to individual judgement. It is my personal belief that the research of these scholars is right." However, KPJ was conscious of the nature of information he was giving to the readers of *Saraswati*, "I have to show the example of the craftsmanship of the fine art. I do not have to give the religious sermon."

'England ke Dehat mein Maharaja Banaras ka Kuan' (इंग्लैंड के देहात में महाराजा बनारस का कुंआ) is KPJ's last article from his stay in England. This is an interesting account of his visit to West Manestar—a village (about 20 miles/32 kms from Oxford) of novelist Reed whose brother had been an employee of the East India Company. On the request of Reed's brother, Raja Ishwari Prasad Narayan Singh, 'the Maharaja of Banaras' got a 346 feet deep well dug in that village between 1763 and 1827 and it took 64 years to complete this work, at a cost of over Rupees ten thousand. KPJ was struck by the memories of the Raja, seen in the engravings of 'Maharaja of Banaras' on the canopy and his royal emblem and a complex named 'Ishwari terrace'. A pasture land meant exclusively for cows, where even KPJ was not allowed to enter, pleased the author.

(b) Narratives of the Return Journey: The four-part 'Meri Yatra' published in the *Saraswati* in 1912 takes us through KPJ's return journey from Britain to India, after the completion of his studies. He undertook travel by rail, road, and sea. In the first article of the series of four, 'Hungary se Turk Desh' (हंगरी से तुर्क देश), KPJ wrote about the history, culture, language, etc. of Hungary: "Hungary is a country of eastern-Asian community in the west. There has been one-upmanship between Europe and Asia for a long time, which has been considered natural by the Europeans. The old Paras (Persia) had invaded Greece with their 'Parsi and Hindu' soldiers; under the leadership of Alexander, Greece invaded Persia and India. The Asian Huns and the Tatars had invaded Europe. The Huns had won that area from the Slav, which is now called Hungary". It is obvious that KPJ was excited about this Asia-Europe encounter and wrote, "Hungary is the indelible imprint of that event— a flag pillar of the Asian effort, power, and valour in Europe." The meaning is that even the Asians could invade Europe." Is this a 'clash of civilisation' theory in the making?

Throughout this article on Hungary, KPJ underlines (a) its 'eastern-ness' (*poorvipan*) and Asian-ness, (b) its antagonism to 'Āryan' Germans, (c) its anti-absolutism [we can find echoes of early Indian 'republics' (*gaṇa*)], (d) people's love for their language and literature (which KPJ was eager to portray as inspirational for Indian). Beauty of the gorgeous Budapest, the capital of Hungary, and its Parliament House building ('man amongst monuments') as well as the university were specially praised by him. Notwithstanding all this, he felt saddened that lively life of the Western Europe was conspicuously absent there.

The second part of the same article, 'Hungary se Turk Desh' (हंगरी से तुर्क देश), takes us to the land of Serbia and Bulgaria—into the Balkans. The chief markers, as mentioned above, get further underlined—specially the 'eastern-ness' of the people of the area. To take one distinctive example, during his conversation with a German speaking Serb and a French-speaking Bulgarian in a train, KPJ felt that their religious persuasions were comparable with those of the 'Satyamargis' back home, "They were the believers of the ideas that the human being was the maker of his own fate, not overwhelmed by hate or love of a God. They believed that to work for the welfare of the human being was the religion and to believe in nationalism was the appropriate worship of the people. Their opinion was European, but the physique and nature was like ours i.e. the Eastern." The sight of a buffalo, a *dhenki*, (a water-drawing contraption/ mortar to pound grains), waterman selling water for money, and stray dogs on railway stations, fruit-sellers, tiled roofs of houses, practice of 2/3 year conscription, etc. often reminded KPJ of his homeland and Nepal. Another notable element in this narrative is his allusion to "Hamare Turki Bhai" (Our Turkish Brothers) echoing the contemporary milieu of pan-Islamism, perhaps, anticipating by several years Gandhi's support for the Khilafat Movement. KPJ's sympathy for 'Asian-ness' could perhaps also be indicative of his anti-imperialist posture.

The two-part narrative on Turkey and Constantinople starts off with a graphic account of a big rail accident, highlighting the lackadaisical handling by the officials. KPJ had to identify himself as a "Hindu" to escape the wrath of these officials who were perhaps taking him to be an Arab on account of his dark complexion (*kṛṣṇavarṇa*)—Arabs were not too welcome, even then.

Throughout these narratives, the emphasis on Asia vs Europe (East and West antagonism) comes through. The fall of Constantinople on the 29 May 1453 is specially taken up for an analogy of the emergence of an Asian power. The sight of the fluttering of an 'eastern flag' (*poorvi jhanda*) over Constantinople gave special solace to KPJ. He does not miss the opportunity to hint that not many Indians had been privileged to see that - indeed, prior to his own visit only three or four 'Hindus' may have visited Turkey.

Apart from providing vignettes of KPJ's sense of history [descriptions of the Byzantine empire, Justinian and his contribution in the making of the Church at Sophia and its later day conversion into a mosque by the addition of minarets (Ayya-Sophia), flight of science and philosophy from Constantinople to Europe giving rise to a new enlightened Europe, and so on], these narratives are also marked by: (a) quite frequent comparisons between Indian cities (Banaras, Jaipur, Lucknow) and Istanbul and lives of people therein, (b) attribution of laziness and lethargy (*alasya* and *laudharpan*) to the east contrasted with the liveliness of Europe, (c) dirt, filth, poverty of old Turkey not only reminded KPJ of his own country but also presented contrasts with cleanliness healthy and hygiene of Europe.

In Sophia, KPJ saw a lively form of Islam. He wrote,

> I was moving with my Turkish friend having tied the Masjidi clothes on my shoes; then a Mullah having tied a green turban on his head, which was the symbol of being a Sayyid, came to me and asked, "Are you a 'Hindu?' When I said 'Yes', he again asked, 'if I was a Muslim or Christian' I said 'Barahmani'. After that he took me around the library. I said 'Show me the oldest book.' Mullah Saheb, who was himself the librarian, brought a manuscript of the Quran and said in Turkish– "It is written by the son-in-law Ali'." KPJ took the book in his hands and felt obliged about the kindness of the Mullah. KPJ further narrates, "Afterwards, I was taken to a coffee shop. The discussion there was wonderful. A debate got initiated about the need of my becoming a Muslim. When I made them understand that I could not feel the necessity thereof, then the Mullah asked, 'How many

> Gods do you have?' I said "One." He felt relieved that unlike the Christians I did not have three Gods; 'The Christians are the only Kafirs of the world'. When I raised the topic of politics, he showed acquaintance with not only the Quran and the Shariat, but also with the world around—specially the count of the Muslims in India, Russia, and China.

KPJ concludes his narrative with these words:

> Turkey is changing before our eyes. This is an education for Asia. They are not distant from us. Turkey is our Asian *pushta* (edge) in Europe. We must be inquisitive about happenings there. It is a matter of regret that even the English newspapers are not aware of the affairs of Turkey. There is not even a single Muslim in India who is aware of any event of this country. Perhaps, there is not even a single Indian who knows the Turkish language. Hope this condition will not be permanent.

This last observation forms part of the statement of promise that KPJ made, viz; there would be subsequent write-ups on the museum, army, newspapers, political upheavals, parliament, manners and customs etc. Apparently, he does not seem to have fulfilled this promise.

On the whole, looking at the contents of these articles, it may be said that it was perhaps an expression of KPJ's cosmopolitan desire—people must not be narrow or inward-looking at all. KPJ was a keen observer of things he saw and he always made comparative notes. He also feels about the degradation and subjugation of his country—so his mind was not free even when he was roaming free. It was an important work insofar as it introduced the Hindi-speaking people to the neighbouring countries as well as European countries. There are a number of instances where KPJ tried to establish Asian supremacy and dominance over Europe and that was important because it must have tangentially infused confidence and pride amongst his Hindi readers.

Critique of the Prevalent Indian Thought

On numerous occasions, KPJ wrote about the ancient glories of India. However, he does not seem to have lived in the past. His international exposure led him to develop a comparative and critical analysis of the ideas and behaviour of the people prevalent in Europe and India. He wrote, 'Europe aur Hamare Vichar', published in the *Saraswati* in two parts[46] where he gave point-wise details of similarities and differences between India and Europe:

1. Europe looks forward. They believe that the present is better than the ancient times. Humanity is always developing by the day. They believe that the present day philosophy is better than the ancient philosophy... We look backward. We believe that the ancient time was good, old philosophy was flawless and believe that all questions had been solved by it. We want to go back to the ancient times. We respect the older values. In the Western world there is respect for 'new' values. There is a fundamental difference in the ideas. We do not believe that the human being would do better in all respects in the future in comparison to the past, but they believe so.
2. The European concept of the 'ultimate truth' is completely opposed to ours. We are too other worldly and are only too eager to indulge in good acts such as gift-making and donations in order to ensure good life in that world. Unlike us, the Europeans live in this world and concentrate on making this life more enjoyable and fruitful not only for themselves but for other fellows of the society as well.
3. The foundation of our society is individual-centred—we think about our family, lineage, the other world, and self salvation. Europeans believe that they are part of the crowd called the society or the nation; they are mere parts of that whole. Whatever they do, they are related to the society. Therefore, the fundamentals of European courtesies are hinged on the idea that nobody should be inconvenienced or hurt by their actions. To illustrate, they never speak loudly in the restaurant or in the railway trains because they feel that this will disturb the comfort of the others. They never shout even in their own house; they do not cry loudly even on the death of their near and dear ones. The soldiers work for the nation, not for the salary, and the political intellectuals work for the society not for the self.
4. Our aim is life after death, but they believe in the present life.
5. We, the Hindu community, are believers in the existence of the God. We believe that even the leaves move by His direction. Human being is the puppet in His hand. The Europeans do not believe in the existence of God. They offer and explore the causal relation of every event. They believe that the human being is not a puppet in anybody's hand. They are the makers of their own destiny. Human being is everything, he is independent, and there is no God above him. They believe in religion not because of anyone's threat, but because they consider it as a duty. While discussing the European concept of atheism, Jayaswal notes that he was reminded of an article

written by Pandit Balkrishna Bhatt in *Hindi Pradeep*, in which he had written that in the living community there had always been atheism and for that he gave examples from the Sanskrit texts.

6. Endorsing Aristotle's view that 'the human being is a political animal', Jayaswal underlines that it was especially true of the Europeans. Nationality is their religion. In contrast, the Indians are the familial/domestic animals.
7. We believe in the 'unseen' (*a-drishtavadi*). The European does not do so.
8. Being highly ambitious is a virtue for the Europeans but a sin amongst Indians. When Curzon was studying at Oxford, he was known to have freely expressed his ambition of becoming the 'Viceroy' of India. While people in Europe consider ambition to be necessary for progress, we condemn it as thirst. For us satisfaction is the highest pleasure (संतोष परम सुख है).
9. Youthfulness is not a pride for us. People above the age of 40 would start considering themselves as old. Europeans do not entertain such negative thoughts. Views of the young are not overlooked nor are the young apologetic about expressing their views openly and freely.
10. They have great respect for the people adept in politics (*rajnitikushal*) rather than intellectuals. Therefore, there is no sculpture of Shakespeare in London, but they have a huge sculpture of a third grade commander Havelock. In Germany, busts of Bismarck can be seen very often, but that of Goethe is rarely found. It could be said that patriotism is considered the greatest of all the virtues. Bravery and patriotism are not separate things; they are the same. Patriotism is considered even above the worship of God.
11. All human beings are considered equal there. There is no hierarchy in the country. Even the poor are not considered inferior because it is considered as the weakness of the nation. Human beings are equal by birth - this theory is given only by the new Europe and America. Independent America and Germany, victorious France, powerful Japan and lively Turkey are the contributions of this theory only. Nationalism, community feelings, and equality of human beings have created a new Europe. Europe should be called *dwijanma* (one who has got the second birth). In our country human beings are not equal; there is hierarchy and even untouchability. Although, there have been several sects that have been consistently opposed to such inequalities, but somehow these traits have persisted.

Notwithstanding this enumeration of the distinctive traits of the Europeans and the Indians, KPJ made an important disclaimer: "I have merely noted these features without making qualitative any judgement about one being right and the other being wrong. Further, I have only highlighted such ideas that seem to be more pronounced and perhaps believed in by a large number of people—both in Europe and India. There are exceptions everywhere. The atheistic Europe has the presence of several religious missionaries engaged in propagating religions of the Christ and the Jews. Similarly, in our land, too, there are people who are not self-centred and work for larger society."

This is a very cautious remark, especially in the light of the sharp binary created in the long quote above. Actually this is where we should take a special note of his subjectivity in the context of his understanding of caste. His critique of the caste system in India is profoundly manifested in his praise of the 'new modern man' of Europe, whom he considers a true '*dwijanma*', unlike the perennial birth-defined *dwijas* of his own country. He also critiques the state of mental attitude vis-à-vis age, other-worldliness, lack of political consciousness, lack of a sense of nation, idealism rather than materialism, backward-looking disposition, etc. in the inverted mirror of Western Europe. His tame disclaimer and the fact that he has to cite Bal Krishna Bhatt is proof of his own lack of surefootedness about how his travelogue would be received in a Brahmin-dominated print public sphere of editors, writers, and readers.

(C) Biographies

Political profiles and biographies are very much a part of the art of history-writing. These traditions, however, followed the path of eulogy and portrayed the British rulers and administrators in the most admirable light. During the editorship of Mahavir Prasad Dwivedi, the *Saraswati* published several biographies. However, most of the biographies published were those of the British administrators and the Indian feudal lords. The writers, scientists, the Indian political leaders, and the Indologists came later.[47] Publishing biographies of people, who had contributed to the development of the language and literature, particularly Hindi, had been one of the major concerns of the *Saraswati*. Describing such a policy decision of the *Saraswati*, KPJ wrote, "*Saraswati* is a magazine of Hindi literature; it has very close relation with the Hindi language. Therefore, it believes that the biographies of the writers of Hindi are the best thing to produce. The biographies of the frontrunners amongst such gentlemen, viz., Babu Harishchandra, Raja Lakshaman Singh, etc., had already been published by this magazine."[48] KPJ himself published five biographies in the *Saraswati*.[49]

(i) 'Panditwar Dr. A.F. Rudolf Hoernle', C.I.E: Of these five biographies, four dealt with colonial administrators. In an introductory remark in his first biography, 'Dr. Augustus Frederick Rudolf Hoernle', KPJ provides the following explanation for choosing his subject, "If we write something for the cause of Hindi, it would only be carrying out our dharma, for, it is our mother-tongue. Savants coming from abroad have wide fields of Sanskrit, Arabic, Chinese and Hebrew languages to fly the flag of the glories of their fame and have the full capability to achieve such victory targets. Yet, when they give up such urges and prefer to serve the interest of our poor mother-tongue, then writing about their lives and works for the Hindi speakers/readers become our duties".[50]

Notwithstanding Mahavir Prasad Dwivedi's reservations about the non-Indian scholars of Hindi,[51] KPJ went ahead with his venture. The biography of Hoernle is an exhaustive account of his life and works, which takes us through his birth (in 1841) in a family of German origin, settled in Sikandara, near Agra. His father was a priest of long standing in India. His early education was in Germany, and went to England to learn Sanskrit under the renowned Prof. Goldstucker. At a young age of 24, he was appointed as a teacher of Sanskrit and Philosophy in 1865 in the Jainarayan College in Kashi.

Hoernle's early writing entitled *Essays in Aid* of *Comparative Grammar of Gowdian (Gaudian) Languages* was a provocative subject. Following Collwell's use of the nomenclature of 'Dravidian' for non-Sanskritic languages such as Tamil, Hoernle coined 'Gaudian' for a group of languages that included Hindi, Bengali, Oriya, Marathi, Gujarati, Sindhi, and Kashmiri. KPJ pointed out how the exponent himself gave up this usage, for, scholars did not accept it. Instead, the most favoured nomenclature 'Modern Indian Languages of North India' was invoked by Hoernle in later years.

KPJ highlighted the importance of Hoernle's grammatical writings that showed great familiarity with the linguistic intricacies of Sanskrit, Prakrit and Hindi. In an appreciative tone he also underlined the impact of these contributions on the vexed question of the origin of Hindi and roots of its grammar. While the expert opinions were vertically split—one group favouring non-Āryan origin of Hindi located in either Dravidian or Semitic sources and the other group standing for tracing its origin from Sanskrit. Hoernle had different ideas on these issues. His 'thoughts' on Hindi Grammar located the roots of Hindi in Prakrit.[52] Several Prakrit grammar books were written by Hemacandra, Vararuci, Kramadīśvara, Mārkaṇḍeya, Trivikrama, Śubhacandra—most of these were unpublished works. These and allied contributions "established his fame throughout Europe as a philologist of the first rank."[53] No wonder, the famous Institut de France honoured him with the famous Volney Prize in 1882—this Gold medal was given every year to the best work on an eastern language.

Apart from this pathbreaking work impacting the understanding of the roots of Hindi, KPJ was careful to point out that there were numerous other 'scientific' articles and monographs produced by his 'Dr. Saheb'. In addition to scattered contributions in the pages of the *Indian Antiquary* and the *Journal of the Asiatic Society of Bengal*, KPJ drew attention to the following:

i. *A Comparative Dictionary of the Bihari Language* (in collaboration with George A. Grierson—who later went on to produce the monumental *Linguistic Survey of India*).
ii. Starting the work of editing the *Prithviraj Raso* of 'Chand Barḍai'. As soon as 'Dr. Saheb' realised that the ascription of its authorship to 'Chand' was suspect, he decided to stop the work.
iii. The publication (in two volumes) of the *Uvāsagadāso*, the seventh *Aṅga* of the Jainas. This work established Hoernle as an authority on the religion of the Jainas.
iv. The editing of 'Bower Manuscript' of possibly Buddhist authorship. This was recognised as the earliest Sanskrit manuscript that was found in the relic chamber of a Buddhist stupa in Turkestan.

Hoernle's services in various capacities in the Asiatic Society: his headship of the Calcutta Madrsa College (the oldest government college in India) and teaching in the renowned Presidency College, his archaeological explorations in Central Asia, and continuing with his love for Hindi in a sustained manner have been duly recalled by KPJ. On his recommendation, the Nagari Pracharini Sabha elected Hoernle as its Honorary Member in 1902. 'It is as a numismatist, as an archaeologist and as an epigraphist that Dr. Hoernle has been best known to the scientific world..."[54] KPJ's translation of this assessment is reflective of his ornamental style of writing Hindi, "डॉ. साहब का बहुकार्य्यकर जीवन सार्थक है, शिक्षाप्रद है। मनुष्य होकर उसी का जन्म सफल है जिसका नाम गुणियों कि गणना के आरंभ में लिखा जाय। डॉ. साहब कि भाषातत्वोदघाटिनी, प्राचीन-मुद्रा-रहस्य-भेदिनी, प्राचीन-निर्माणवर्णन-कारिणी और पुरात्व-ज्ञान-दायिनी कलाओं से उनकी कीर्त्तिचंद्रिका आज कल के वैज्ञानिक लोक को आलोक प्रदान कर रही है।"[55]

(ii) Buddhwar Mr. F.S. Grouse' C.I.E: In 1906, KPJ wrote another biographic article on Frederick Solomon Grouse (an M.A. from Oxford), who served most of his time as a Collector in the Agra Province. Grouse's attraction towards 'Hindu' religion and his contributions to Hindi were the reasons for KPJ's interest in him. He wrote,

> He was a great lover of the old monuments of the Hindus. Wherever he was the Officer-in-charge, one would find the renovated temples, newly constructed markets, bridges, schools etc. by Grouse Saheb. It is only because of him that the famous Govind Deva Temple of Vrindavana and the numerous ancient structures of Mathura got renovated.

Grouse was also interested in the studies of language and literature (the study of the vernacular of the Upper India). In the court language debate, he strongly opposed the Persian mixed language and advocated the use of the easily understandable language (*sarva-sugam*). But, like many others he had to abandon that debate, because of the obduracy. KPJ also informs us about his contributions on Raso of Chand, critiquing Hoernle's early translations and Beams' views on the text, transliteration of Indian Alphabets in the Roman characters, and his monograph *'Mathura: A District Memoir'*. However, in KPJ's opinion it was his translation of Tulsidas' *Ramacharitmanas* (mostly in prose) which made him famous because before him this *Rāmāyaṇa* remained almost sealed for the English people. It was because of his translation that *Rāmāyaṇa* was popularised amongst the Europeans. The preface of the *Rāmāyaṇa* was published by him in the *Journal of the Asiatic Society* in 1876. KPJ enumerated numerous examples of beautiful translations of several verses and also drew the conclusion that perhaps Grouse's utter devotion to the text accounts for such involvement. KPJ wrote, "Although, the Ramayana was known earlier too, but because of his beautiful writing it has got attractive power which proves his belief in the Ramayana".

Significantly, KPJ also drew our attention to the marginal notes of Grouse on Cunningham's *Archaeological Reports* stocked in the Collector's Office Library in Fatehpur. The editor of the *Saraswati* added that he had himself seen numerous notes of Grouse (in pencil) in the left and right margins of the work of Hunter, Cunningham, and Prinsep pointing out their mistakes. KPJ also informs us that his 'Grouse Saheb' was also a member of the Committee of the Asiatic Society of Bengal and a Fellow of the University of Calcutta.

(iii) 'Shriyut Maheshcharan Singh', B.A., M.S. (Master of Science): Maheshcharan Singh was responsible for the discovery of the content analysis of coffee. After giving details of his family background, his education in Japan and then in America, KPJ also gave an account of the newspaper reports in America and England about the achievements of Maheshcharan Singh.

KPJ wrote, "In America, the Japanese boys from both the rich and the ordinary families, earn their livelihood and learn the craft and artisanship. There is no loss of respect for physical labour as compared to education. Our brothers will feel surprised (although it is not a matter of surprise) that there the salary of the munshi is higher than their judge because the munshi had to perform more labour. The meaning is that earning livelihood by work and honesty and then to get education is a matter of pride in the western world (Mr. John Burn, who is one of the Ministers of England at this time and considered a leader of the country, himself survived on a labour work. America at this time has hundred times better democracy than England). Mr. Singh has also performed varieties of work (big and small) and got education and made us proud."

KPJ further worte, "Maheshcharan Singhji had acquired good knowledge of agricultural science in America. He had knowledge of agriculture and craft by experience. He had done a number of experiments in science. He had done a good study and analysis of the education system of Japan and America and what kind of education system was required in India. His political ideas were very independent. He had also completed military training for one year in America and had praised for this as well. If any Princely State were to take him, then we would consider them fortunate.

Mr. Singh was a big supporter of Hindi language and Nagari script. He had written a book on chemistry and wanted to print it out in Nagari. He was planning to come back to his motherland."

(iv) 'Parlok-vasi Mr. John Beams': After giving details of the family background, education, and professional life as a bureaucrat of John Beams, the most important thing KPJ narrated was his contribution towards the development of Hindi language and literature. He informed his readers that because of his stay in the Punjab and Bengal, Beams acquired a good knowledge of local languages and the sub-languages (*upbhasha*). Beams' first article, 'Should the Arabic words be used in the Court Urdu or not', was published in *JASB* in 1866. However, his most important work "Outlines of Indian Philology" was published in 1867 and this was the first text on the origin of the Indian languages. Before that no one had written any book on the Indo-Aryan family of lanugages. Although much of his thesis was rejected by the later philologists (Hoernle, Grierson etc.), KPJ thought highly about Beams' contributions.

KPJ also remembered Beams' contributions to the languages of Nepal and Bhojpur that were published in the *Journal of the Royal Asiatic Society of Great Britain and Ireland* (hereafter *JRAS*). This was the first article on these sub-languages. However, KPJ's special attention was on his contributions to the poems of Chand Bardai. KPJ also enumerated his scholarly contributions such as, 'Indian Geography at the Time of Akbar', 'The Comparative Grammar of the Aryan Languages of India', etc. KPJ's concluding observation in the form of an appeal, for, 'Archaeology of Hindi Grammar' provides an indication of a larger vision about linguistic developments. He expected that someone should undertake such a venture on the bases of the works of Hoernle, Beams and Grierson.

(v) Finally, within the broad genres of biography, one may also include a short 'Preface' that KPJ contributed to the *Festschrift* on Ayodhya Singh Upadhyaya 'Hariaudh.'[56] This renowned poet, known for popularising Hindi language with his simple but pure Hindi, attracted KPJ, whose acquaintance of the poet went back to his childhood days. Recalling the contributions of stalwarts such as the late Bal Krishna Bhatt, late Balmukund Gupt, Hiralal,, Babu Gopal Ram Gahmari and Pandit Mohanlal Mahato to the making of *gharau-Hindi* (Hindi for the common household), KPJ was keen to give credit to 'Hariaudh' for taking this simple language to great heights—an achievement that KPJ calls 'embroidery of pen' (कलम की सूईकारी)।

After reading Hariaudh's *Priya-Pravas*, KPJ became so happy that he wrote:

प्रसाद है, भाव भरा हुआ है,
रसमता है, रमणीयता है।
गिरारथ, गौरिशिवा, साथ-साथ हैं,
सुपद्य साहित्य यही सही है।

(D) Social Issues

From the available records, KPJ's writings on social issues are almost negligible. As the editor of the Hindi monthly *Kalwar Gazette*, KPJ might have written on such issues.[57] Since the issues of the *Kalwar Gazette* are not traceable, it has not been possible to undertake any detailed analysis of its contents. Nonetheless, the impact of KPJ's writings in the monthly seems to have been quite significant. An illustration in point would be Bal Krishna Bhatt's rejoinder to his article 'Jati' (perhaps in April 1905). Judging from the contents of this rejoinder published in the *Hindi Pradeep* in May 1905, it appears that KPJ must have unleashed an unrestrained attack on the Brahmin caste. Bhatt, therefore, underlines: (i) the necessity of retaining 'purity of blood' (possibly also of semen (रजवीर्य की शुद्धता) to maintain the purity of race, (ii) fundamental difference with the Musalman *jati* which functions like a cat-like mentality, (iii) his opposition to 'inter-religious marriage' between the Hindus and the Muslims as advocated by the Gaekwads of Baroda, (iv) his sarcasm about KPJ's conceit, and finally (v) the not so veiled threat to the *Kalwar Gazette* that it should not be publishing such absurd pieces (as that of KPJ)."[58] It should be noted here that most of the Brahmin writers had the tendency to present history in a way that gave centrality to the Brahmin's role in Hindu society.[59]

After a long gap of twenty-two years, KPJ delivered a long Presidential Speech at the 4th Annual Conference of the Akhil Bharatavarshiya Haihay Kshatriya Mahasabha in Jabalpur in April 1927.[60] The name of the Mahasabha was decided in the same conference and all the monthly magazines were requested to use 'Haihay' instead of Kalwar. KPJ was appointed the President of the Mahasabha. Some of the major issues addressed by KPJ are as follows:

1. शायद अब दिन नज़दीक आता जाता है कि जब जाति की सभाओं की ज़रूरत न रह जायगी। जाति की संस्था उठा देने के कानून बन रहे हैं और एकता सम्पादन के अनेक साधन प्रस्तुत हो रहे हैं। मेरी सहानुभूति उसी विचार से है। जाति मनुष्यकृत है ईश्वरकृत नहीं, ईश्वरकृत देश–जातियाँ हैं, जाति–जातियाँ नहीं। मनुष्य ने जाति जमाई है और मनुष्य जब उसकी जरूरत न समझे तो उठा दे और उठा देता है। जितने बड़े बुद्धि–विधाता हुए प्रायः सब ने इसे बुरा और निरर्थक कहा ...इसे हानिकारक कहा।
2. सब देशों में शुरू और आदिम अवस्था में जातियाँ होती हैं और उन्नति, सभ्यता, ज्ञान–प्रसार के साथ जातियाँ टूट जाती हैं। इतिहास इसका गवाह है। ...पर भारत में हिन्दुओं ने बहुत बातों में उन्नति की पर जाति अभी तक न तोड़ी। ...अस्तु, अभी अपना देश बीमारी की अवस्था में है। ऐसी अवस्था में जातियाँ हैं और जब तक जातियाँ हैं तब तक जाति सभाओं की सार्थकता है। पर हम लोग भूल न करें और जाति को अमर न मान बैठें। जाति और जाति–सभाओं को सामयिक और अस्थायी चीज़ मानकर उनकी सेवा करें।
3. नये प्रवाह की दृष्टि से और जातिहित की दृष्टि से यह जरूर है कि वर्ग के बाहर, जाति के भीतर, जहाँ कहीं हो रोटी बेटी का सम्बन्ध बढ़ाया जाय। फिर चातुर्वर्ण्य का इतिहास ऐसा नहीं है कि उसकी नितान्त अटलत समझी जाय। ...चातुर्वर्ण्य को एक पक्का सिद्धान्त मानना और उसे एक पक्की चीज़ मान उत्पत्ति खोजना बिलकुल व्यर्थ परिश्रम है। ...जन्म से हम क्षत्रिय और कर्म से वैश्य हमारा उत्पत्ति–इतिहास है। ...मध्य काल में बिरादरी के बहुत से राज्यकर्ता थे। ...पर 'बीती ताहि बिसारि देए आगे की सुध लेय।'
4. हर एक को चाहिए कि अपनी अपनी उन्नति करे। इस उन्नति की जड़ शिक्षा है और शिक्षाओं में राजशिक्षा का आदर सब देश सब काल में अधिक रहा है, और रहेगा। इसमे जो चुकता है वह पिछड़ता है। मुसलमानी राज्य में कायस्थों ने मध्य हिन्दुस्तान में और ब्राह्मणों ने बंगाल में राज–भाषा और राज शिक्षा को पकड़ा जिससे आज भी वह आगे है। जो अँग्रेज़ी शिक्षा का आज तिरस्कार करेगा पीछे पड़ा रहेगा और पददलित रहेगा। ...संस्कृत उतने ही जानने की जरूरत है कि शास्त्र दूसरे के द्वारा न जानना पड़े। जो विद्या 10,000 या 5,000 वर्ष पहले ठीक थी वह आज काम नहीं दे सकती। दुनिया आगे चलती है, आप भी आगे चलें। यहाँ शिक्षा के सम्बन्ध में यह कह देना चाहता हूँ कि जाति के लिए अलग बोर्डिंगहौस या स्कूल कालेज बनाने की भूल हम लोग न करें। जो सर्वसाधारण के लिए संस्थाएँ मौजूद हैं उन्हीं से काम चला लेना चाहिए, नहीं तो कट कर अलग होने के बुरे परिणाम झेलने के अलावा व्यर्थ खर्च करने की भूल होगी। जो खर्च हम कर सकें उससे स्कालरशिप आदि रूप से पात्रों की मदद कीजिए।
5. हमारी सुरीतियाँ– पंच पंचायत की आज्ञा मानना, जाति भाई की सेवा करना, अमीर–गरीब भाई को बराबर समझना, पंचों के सामने विवाह या नियोग करना, भाई के हाथों का पका अन्न खाना, लड़की वाले से दहेज न ठहराना, नौकरी न करके छोटा–मोटा रोजगार करना, किसी और की दासता न करना उन्नति की निशानी है द्विजता की

निसेनी पर चढ़ने वाले लोलुप भाई जो इन सुरीतियों को तोड़ेंगे उनका व्यवहार घृणित समझ जायेगा।

One of the crucial agenda points of the Conference was to determine the origin of the Kalwar community. For a long time, there were two groups amongst the Kalwars: one who believed in the Kṣatriya origin and the other the Vaiśya origin of the Kalwars. In 1924, KPJ spoke in the favour of the Vaiśhya origin of the Kalwars, which created tension and controversy amongst the Kalwars.[61] Even at the Jabalpur Conference, this issue was debated and most of the delegates were in favour of Kṣatriya origin. KPJ also spoke that by profession the Kalwars are Vaiśhyas and by birth they are Kṣatriya. However, finally he was successful in getting a resolution passed in the favour of the Kṣatriya origin and for this KPJ cited the studies of Babu Narayan Chandra Shah and Haraprasad Sastri. KPJ also obtained a vow from the delegates that they would not follow the issue of sub-caste in inter-dining and marriage (रोटी-बेटी) functions. And finally he donated Rs. 100 to the Prantiya Vidya Pracharak Kosh.

It is significant that KPJ positioned himself in agreement with the Ambedkarite radical view that caste had to be gotten rid of in the long run. Even more interesting, perhaps, was his counter-positioning of caste as human-made against that of the community called nation (देश-जातीय), which was divinely ordained. As we know, *jati* was being interchangably used for both caste and nation, alongside the Urdu *qaum* in those days. But in the heyday of anti-colonial nationalism, its status could be nothing less than divine. The implication was that if humans did not create something, they had no right to dissolve it. *Jati* as caste, on the other hand, was seen as a state of continued sickness of Hindu society that it had not done away with so far. The role of all the other societies was worth emulating in this regard, as this type of primordial affiliation and loyalty did not belong to this day and age. It was a residual affliction calling for a permanent cure. In consonance with his theory of caste being human-made, and therefore, always mutable, KPJ questioned the alleged inviolable status of the concept of *chaturvarnya* (fourfold division).

Another notable similarity between KPJ and B.R. Ambedkar is that both emphasised English education as the key to progress, especially for the depressed castes. He aligned education with power and cited historical examples of Brahmins and Kayasthas in the medieval period to underline the necessity to flow with time. Like his progressive position on education of women in the context of Patna University, KPJ also put forward common schooling and boarding for all castes, and found caste-based segregation abominable and financially unviable. He also advocated scholarship for weaker sections.

His last point in this presidential address was a forceful argument against Sanskritisation, against those who wanted to use the ladder of *dvijtva* (the state of being *dvija* or twice born) to climb up in social hierarchy. In this context, he also identified some progressive features in the 'backward' caste practices of the time, and was thus not in favour of throwing the baby out with the bathwater. These signs of progress included: obeying the authority of the *panchas*, fraternal equality in dining and marriage, not asking for dowry, and not depending on and slaving for government or taking up private jobs but setting up independent businesses.

Quite clearly, his history-writing might be aligned with the dominant Hindu nationalist view of the times, but his reflections on caste, including on its history were far more radical than those of the leading upper-caste intellectuals of the time. From the slender evidence of this speech, we can surmise that KJP was thinking broadly on lines that were to be underlined by Ambedkar several decades later.

(E) Poetry

The production of poetry had been one of the main concerns of the Hindi intelligentsia since the time of Bharatendu and there was also a debate on the preferred language for prose and poetry. On that question KPJ in his first article, 'काशी नागरी सभा के प्रश्नों के उत्तर', reiterated the opinion of Bharatendu that the language of prose and poetry could not be one. It is an established fact that the language of poetry in the Paschimottar Prant is Brajbhasha and from the ancient times people had been using this language for poetry. KPJ himself tried several times in vain to write poetry in *Khari Boli* and, therefore, argued that writing poetry in Brajbhasha was the best.

Mahavir Prasad Dwivedi changed the entire understanding of the language and content of the prose and poetry. He exercised strict screening and censorship of the material to be published in terms of both language and content. He was famous for the stinging sarcasm he directed at works that did not meet his standards, and he could be equally harsh against Brajbhasha poetry and *Chayavad*, which he rejected as being 'useless' and harmful to Hindi literature. Dwivedi thus embodied the figure of the editor-arbiter before the figure of the professional critic existed, and used the *Saraswati* as a means to spread 'standard' norms and values in the Hindi public sphere.[62]

By no stretch of imagination was KPJ a prolific poet. We have been able to lay our hands on only two poems of his early days that were published in the *Saraswati*, viz. 'Swarna'[63] and 'Kavi-Kirti'.[64] Later, his friend Rahul Sankrityayan identified, located and reproduced eight additional poems from KPJ's diary.[65] Taken together, these poems represent an impressive range in terms of form, language, as well as content.

Of the two poems mentioned above, 'Swarna', is a *chandobaddha* poem, bound by ancient/medieval metres then prevalent in Hindi at the turn of the century. The mixed language (Brajbhasha and *Khari Boli*) of the poem is an interesting feature. Does this represent a more flexible position of KPJ on the question of preferred poetic language? Is it a marker of a transitory phase? Perhaps both. Another remarkable formal quality of the poem is its referencing pattern. Providing footnotes and references to English poets and thinkers must have been a rare poetic practice in those days, as indeed it is even now. It needs underlining that the poet is not an ordinary literary poet, but a historian, philosopher and a critic—all combined into one. And since his references came from obscure global and local historical events, he made sure to elaborate them in the footnotes. The second poem, 'Kavi-Kirti', written in a metre different from the first, is also a historian's poem extolling the virtues of poetry as an immortal source of history. He contrasted the virtue of poetic evidence of Sanskrit poets such as Vālmīki, Kālidāsa and Bāṇabhaṭṭa with the material ones like buildings, towers and other perishable monuments built by the patron kings such as Vikramāditya and Harṣavardhana. It seems that KPJ, the poet, was privileging the literary source as a living archive in the context of the destructible materiality of physical objects the kings were fond of building for imperial glory and for posterity.

Commenting on the later poems, the collector Sankrityayan wrote that these poems represented a lighter side of KPJ. He remembered numerous poems, jokes and humorous stories, loved relating them, and these poems, written in the same vein, and are making fun of gods from all religions. In the first untitled poem he ridicules the power of God by citing disasters in Quetta and Bihar and even holds Him responsible for the historical defeat in Panipat. The next poem, a conversation between a human being and God, puts the latter in the dock for betraying the cause of the motherland.

The *Bhagavadgītā* became an inspiration for many leaders of the national movement, including Gandhi. KPJ's 'Tathya-Gītā' has an interesting and a challenging take on this famed text. The poem reads:

प्रभु बोले।

न साथ देना उनका कभी नरो!
पड़े भरोसे मम आस जो रहे।
लड़ूँ कड़े सैनिक ओर ही सदा
कदापि भूले अ कदर्य-साथ हूँ।

किया हमारा इतिहास देख लो।
भगे जभी क्रिशचन सेंट सोफिआ
किया विजेता महमूद तुर्क को,
हलाल नि:शंक हुए वहाँ कई।

सहस्त्र नारी नर पुत्र पुत्रिका।
छिपे पड़े, देवल जान, सुस्थ थे
दिया न मैंने शरणगतत्व भी।
दिया किया साथ समर्थक सदा।

दिया न सांगा नृप संग सीकरी,
लड़ा किया बाबर-तोप आड़ में।
पुकार सूलीपर कि सुनी परन्
न ईसु-आंसू तक पोंछने उठा।

लड़े, करें, जो निज कार्य-साधना,
करें वही, मैं कुछ भी करूँ नहीं–
तटस्थ निष्कर्म टिका रहूँ सदा–
सुनो, यही प्रांजल तथ्य-गीतिका।

माया मिटी, नयन– ओट हटी, प्रभु की–
वाणी रहस्य-गहरी सुन तथ्य गीतिका।
मुझे मिली नाथ बड़ी विभूतियाँ
तथापि मांगू यदि तू कृपा करे

स्वतंत्रता का वर दे स्वहिन्द को
हिमाद्रि मेरा घर हो निहंगका।
धरा तुम्हारी प्रभु पींजरा बनी
गृहस्थ चारा बिन हो रहा जहाँ
निरीह निर्मोह निहंग मस्करी
तदापि रोया वह देख अग्नि भी।

The poem seems to be a critique of the *Bhagavadgītā*—a sort of an anti-thesis. Insofar as it reinterprets the theory of *karman* as a theory of *inaction* (rather than action) and in demanding the boon of freedom from Lord Kṛṣṇa, it represents a complete inversion of the generally held understanding of this text.

The poem titled 'Agnigiri ka Bedhab Ulahana' is a satirical complaint by KPJ, written under his pseudonym (Agnigiri), especially reserved for such literary occasions, accuses God of giving him birth in an unfree godless country (न ब्रह्म ही रहा, न रहा रहीम ही) afflicted by the scourge of untouchability, a general decline of religion and the Vedas; a country so materially impoverished that everybody was crying out for a mere 'job'; in short, 'a country which had been reduced to a cage': तपी तुम्हारी सब भू हरी जली/धरा धरित्री पर पींजरा बनी। The poem ends with a call to Hari to spare the poet's country, as he had no hopes from him. Similarly, the 'God's Song for India' (देवों का भारत गीत), a wonderful poem by any standard, extols the virtues of great humans born in India and hopes for a non-divine, i.e., human life, because gods had not really helped the cause of this country:

जहाँ जन्म बहुवार पुरुष का धारण कर कर
रूप नाम हीनता हीनकर उसने जाकर
भारत अभिजन प्राप्त किया, भगवान कहाया।
अपने भी कर वीर्य दया वा, पाप कटाया।
कृष्ण तथागत आदि देह से मोक्ष चुकाया।
भारत की श्रीकला कर्मभू फलद मोक्षदा
ली उसने अपना, भारतमय हुआ कर्महा।
क्यों नचले मन हम अमरों का देखो ह्वां पंर
हमसे बढ़कर हुए गुप्त सम्राट कई नर
शङ्कर सम शंकराचार्य आचार्य आर्यभट
दयानन्द तिलकादि मालवी हमसे वर बढ़
रामकृष्ण गाँधी विवेकानंद चितरंजन

कृत्यु सुंकृत जिनके निहार डोले इन्द्रासन
भेजो हमको नाथ नाम तेरा हम लेंगे
होंगे ब्रह्मभिखार भूमि भारत में देंगे
देह नेह, तज जाति अछूतों साथ रहेंगे
देवपना हम नहीं चाहते, यह कच्चा है
हमको भारतभूमि चूमने की इच्छा है।

Creating an idyllic image of India, the poet doesn't aspire to achieve fragile 'godliness' (*devapanaa*) and expresses his desire to kiss the motherland called 'Bharatabhumi'. It reminds us of Makhan Lal Chaturvedi's poem, 'Pushp ki Abhilasha', 'मुझे तोड़ लेना वनमाली, उस पथ पर देना तुम फेंक, मातृभूमि पर शीश चढ़ाने, जिस पथ पर जायें वीर अनेक' (*mujhe tor lena vanmali, us path par dena tum phenk, matribhumi par sheesh charhane, jis path jayein veer anek*) which was famously recited by generations of freedom fighters and nationalists, and which is also commonly found in the textbooks produced in the independent North India.

Crossing over the religious divide, he wrote a few lines in *Saṁvat* 1992 (=1935) visualising a close hug from his Muslim friend Munshi Ajmeri:

अजमेरी मम मीत, जब गायें हरि के भजन।
आयें अज तब नीत, नेह डोर में, मिलन हित।
अजमेरी मेरा हुआ अजमली चिरगाँव
चिर गाया रघुनाथ जस, पाया प्रभु का पाँव।।
(रोला) हुआ खुदाखुद शुद्ध, गले मिल मम अजमेरी।
हरी अजामिल-मेल "सीट" अजमेरी तेरी।
(दो.) नहि आये मम गाँव चिर, बसे बहुत चिरगाँव।
जन्मभूमि यद्यपि वहाँ "हरि मंदिर" इस ठाँव।।

Citing his intimate relationship with Ajmeri in a poem addressed to the nationalist poet Maithilisharan Gupt, he said, although he read *namaz* with Ajmeri and received the divine blessings in the mosque he also told his dear friend not to go for *Hajj* as it amounted to loss of religion (धरम का हज है धक्का।)–

सखे मैथिलीशरण। तू मत होना छनमान।
खिन्न; मैथिलीशरण को मोह हनन "हरि" जान।।
सुख दुःख की हुंडी चुके, घुंडी भव की टूट
खोख हरीके हाथ दे रहे न लूट न कूट।।

अजमेरी के साथ पढ़ी मैंने नमाज नत
मन मसजिद में मिलाप मुझे वाहिद प्रकाश तत
बोला, जायसवाल, न जाना हज करने को
काबा तेरा कलब बास मेरा पक्का वह
हृदय हूक तेरे में पक्का मेरा मक्का
वही अरब की भूमि धरम का हज है धक्का।

One may not agree with Sankrityayan's characterisation of KPJ as a 'radical Communist' but it is clear in these public and private poems that he was a non-believer and a committed patriot and perhaps also a non-sectarian, if not completely a secularist. If we look at the internal evidence of these poems written over several decades, we can see a certain evolution in his style, terminology, and poetics. His early poems are laden with Sanskrit-*tatsam* words, written very much in a Sanskritic mode. The composition of his later poems is simpler, homely ('धराऊ') and bending towards a *tadbhav*/Hindustani register.

It is curious that, a prolific writer like KPJ only produced a few poems; perhaps, this could have been due to his other literary and professional engagements. However, he was a great lover of poetry. When Ramdhari Singh 'Dinkar' went to the Bhagalpur Conference (Prantiya Hindi Sammelan, 1935) to recite his poems, he was deeply impressed by KPJ's sincerity and sensitivity towards poetry — indeed; he found it to be greater than the blessings from several divinities. Further, he also felt that only such poems were worthy enough that received KPJ's appreciation.

(F) Translated Articles

Given the geo-political and cultural importance of what is today known as the 'Hindi Belt', the British seem to have made a definitive decision, i.e., establishing a link between their two missions—propagation of Christianity and espousal of the cause of Hindi language and Devanagari script. It was, therefore, considered essential that important works available in such languages as English, Sanskrit, Bengali, and Urdu were translated into Hindi. Recent contributions on the role of Bharatendu Harishchandra in this direction in the late nineteenth century are worth noting in this context.[66]

A point has been made above about the influence of Pandit Mahvir Prasad Dwivedi and Bharatendu Harishchandra on the mind of KPJ. Recognising the merits of the aforesaid movement of the introduction of translation work, KPJ also started producing translated material of historical importance from 1900 onwards. His first translated material of historical importance, 'भारतवर्ष' की पुरानी इमारतें' ('Bharatavarsha ki Purani Imaraten') was published in the April issue of the *Saraswati*.[67] It was a translation of Lord Curzon's speech on Indian's old monumental structures given at the Annual Conference of Asiatic Society of Bengal in February 1900. KPJ's second translated article was a piece of V.A. Smith on '*Kaushambi*', which was published in the *Nagari Pracharini Patrika*.[68] KPJ himself translated his several articles of historical importance published in the *Nagari Pracharini Patrika*.[69] KPJ also supervised the translation of his pioneering work *Hindu Polity*.[70] Describing the purpose of the publication of the translation he himself wrote in one of his articles on Hathigumpha inscription,

> It was the opinion of the Jain Scholars like Pandit Nathuram, Shrimuni Jinvijayji Prabhriti that I must also publish the translation, and meaning of this article in Hindi. My reading of this inscription has been introduced in the syllabi of the several Universities. Following the order of the Jain Scholars and for the purpose of making available to the students, I publish the article in Hindi with its meaning in the journal of the Sabha.[71]

By publishing, therefore, the translation work in Hindi, KPJ was serving the larger agenda of Hindi readers and intelligentsia.

(G) Miscellaneous Articles

In the genre of 'useful' literature, two other articles of KPJ need to be mentioned: 'जलवर्षक वृक्ष' 'Jalvarshak Vriksha'[72] and मार कर लौट आने वाला अस्त्र' 'Mar Kar Laut Aane Wala Astra'.[73] In 'Jalvarshak Vriksha' (Rainy Tree), he highlighted the water problem and its solution in the Phero Island of the Atlantic Ocean. KPJ wrote, "In the ancient times, there was no rain or the source of water in the Phero Island of the Atlantic Ocean. It is understandable that in this situation, it was impossible for any living being to survive. But the Creator had to nurture the beings even in this part of the world. There was a category of a tree there, which was called the rain tree. The people got abundant water from this tree and the whole requirement of water was fulfilled from it". Further KPJ mentioned the description of the tree and its capacity to release water by quoting the account of traveller Louis Jackson. KPJ also suggested that wherever there was drought, this tree must be planted for the benefit of agriculture.

In another article, KPJ tried to locate the history of the weapon called 'Boomerang', which was the chief weapon of the people of the jungles of the Australian island and tries to relate its use to the Indian context. While writing this article, KPJ took assistance from an English writer J.W. Wood's *Man and His Handiworks* and argued, "It appears that before the coming of the Aryans, the use of boomerang was prevalent among the non-Aryans, like the Australians who used it before the coming of the British. The Aryans had learned the use of it from the non-Aryans because in the *Niti-Prakashika* of Praneet it is described as 'आस्तर' (Aastar)."

Describing the use of boomerang, KPJ argued that the long held view of the British that it was known only to the Australians was not correct. It was found in India and Africa too. The African boomerang did not come back, but the Indian boomerang had all the knwon features. The Dravidians used it in hunting. In the museum of Madras there were two boomerangs of ivory, which had been brought from the armoury of Tanjore. Dr. Opert of Madras also had an iron and four black-wood boomerangs from Pudukottai. In the armoury of Pudukottai there was a big collection of it. In the local language it was called 'Balai Tadi' i.e., the bent wood. The 'Madrasees' knew its features and ways of using it. Although it lost its importance after the coming of the bow and arrow, but there was no doubt that it was used by the Āryans at some point of time; otherwise it would not have counted as a weapon in Sanskrit texts. The making and the use of the bow and arrow was easier than the boomerang; therefore, it was natural that the boomerang lost its importance.

The overall Hindi writings of KPJ are quite heterogeneous. Perhaps it was influenced by the nationalist call of Dwivedi and other advocates of Hindi at that time. In this context, we remember the call made by Dwivedi; echoing Harishchandra he said in 1903, "The progress of dharma and of the country rests on propagating the mother tongue and on the growth and enrichment of national literature. To strive and work for the progress of Hindi is at present the foremost duty of every patriot and right-thinking man."[74] And later on, "We request all scholars of English to grant us the favour, to write articles about the condition of their society and country in their own language. If they do not know how to write it, they need not feel ashamed: if they really do not know, they only have to learn! Please fulfil your duty!"[75]

NOTES

1. Ramchandra Guha has shown in his article 'The Rise and Fall of the Bilingual Intellectual', that between (roughly) the 1920s and 1970s, the intellectual universe of India was 'linguidextrous'. With few exceptions, the major political thinkers, scholars, and creative writers and many of the minor ones too thought and acted and wrote with equal facility in English and at least one other language (*EPW*, 23 January 2010).
2. Orsini, Francesca, *The Hindi Public Sphere* (1920-1940), Oxford University Press, New Delhi, 2011, p. 46.
3. Cf. Brajadev Pandeya, in Vibhuti Mishra, ed. *Hindi ki Vikas Yatra aur Hindi Sewi Sansthayen*, Hindi Sahity Sammelan, Allahabad, 2011, pp. 1017-19.
4. Sharma, Ramvilas, *Mahavir Prasad Dwivedi aur Hindi Navajagran*, Rajkamal Prakashan, New Delhi, 2010, p. 360.
5. Orsini, Francesca, op. cit., p. 54.
6. *Hindi Pradeep*, May 1905, Editorial Note, pp. 4-5.
7. 'Ritual at Hindu Coronation: Their Constitutional Aspects', Vol. XI, January 1912, pp. 97-106, 2. 'An Introduction to Hindu Polity', Vol. XIII, May, pp. 535-41, 1913, 3.' An Introduction to Hindu Polity', Vol. XIII, June 1913, pp. 664-68, 4. 'An Introduction to Hindu Polity', Vol. XIV, July, pp. 77-83, 1913, 5. 'An Introduction to Hindu Polity', Vol. XIV, pp. August 1913, 201-06, 6. 'An Introduction to Hindu Polity', Vol. XIV, September 1913, pp. 288-91, 7. 'The Hindu Parliament: Paura-Janapada', April 1920, pp. 466-68, 8. 'The Hindu Parliament under Hindu Monarchy', Vol. XXVII, Feb. 1920, pp. 121-39.
8. A.R. Kidwai, Governor of Bihar, speaking on the occasion of KPJ's 100th Birth Anniversary, see *Prajna- Bharati*, Vo. 3, Part I, 1983, p. 14.
9. Sharma, R.S., *Rethinking India's Past*, Oxford University Press, New Delhi, 2009, p. 66.
10. For KPJ's speech see, *Proceedings of the Akhil Bharatavarshiya Haihay Kshatriya Mahasabha*, Jabalpur, 1927, pp. 21-25.
11. In the nineteenth century the 'Paschimottar Prant' meant regions including Agra, Meerut, Rohilkhand, Kanpur, Allahabad, Banaras, Balia-Gorakhpur, etc. In 1857, after the inclusion of Avadh Prant it was called Paschimottar and Avadh; after that Sanyukta or Yukta Prant and after 1947 it got the name of Uttar Pradesh, See, Talwar, Veer Bharat, *Rassakashi: Unnisavi Sadi ka Navjagaran aur Paschimottar*

Prant, (2nd edn.), Saransh Prakashan, New Delhi, 2006.

12. Dalmia, Vasudha, *The Nationalization of Hindu Traditions*,Oxford University Press, New Delhi, 1999, pp. 146-47.
13. Ibid., p. 148.
14. 'Kashi Nagari Sabha ke Prashnon ke Uttar', *Hindi Pradeep*, 30 June 1898, pp. 10-15. As we know, there was a whole debate raging over in North India at the turn of the century about which of the two languages is better suited for poetry. For detailed discussion on the issue, see Rai, Alok, *Hindi Nationalism*, Orient Blackswan, New Delhi, 2001 and Talwar, Veer Bharat, op. cit.
15. 'Kashi Nagari Sabha ke Prashnon ke Uttar', *Hindi Pradeep*, 30 June, 1898, p. 11.
16. Ibid., p. 11.
17. Ibid.
18. Ibid., pp. 11-12.
19. Ibid.
20. Ibid.
21. Quoted in Dalmia, op.cit.
22. Kashi Prasad Jayaswal, 'Vayu aur Agni Striling kyon Hai' *Hindi Pradeep*, Vol. 25, No. 58, May-August, 1903.
23. 'Hindi-Upanyas Lekhakon ko Ulhana', *Hindi Pradeep*, January 1899. KPJ also exhorted Hindi writers to write original texts and chastised them for plagiarising from Bangla: सम्प्रति हिंदी भाषा में उपन्यासों की बड़ी भरती देख पड़ती है–इनमें से अधिकांश बंग भाषा के उपन्यासों के अनुवाद हैं–हिंदी के मूल उपन्यासों की गणना थोड़े ही है–उन अनुवादित उपन्यासों में भी कुछ ऐसे घिनौने हैं कि उनका गंगाजी में प्रवाह कर देना ही श्रेय है–केवल नागरी अक्षरों में उपन्यास (या कोई पुस्तक) लिखे जाने से वह 'हिंदी उपन्यास' या 'हिंदी पुस्तक' नहीं कहा जा सकता–एकाध हिंदी उपन्यास लेखक विद्वान रेनाल्ड्स साहेब की बराबरी करना चाहते हैं और उन्हीं के पुस्तकों से खींच-खींच चोरी/चमारी कर बड़े-बड़े पोथे रंग डालते हैं किन्तु उनका करतब ही उनको रेनाल्ड्स–उपन्यासों का समझने वाला बतला देता है!!! ...बंगदेशीय लेखक अपने उपन्यासों में भारतवर्षीय पात्र और स्थान रखते हैं और उनमें विलायती रीति नीति भर कर हिमालय और सहारा के दृश्यों को एक में मिला कर एक अद्भुत दृश्य रच डालते हैं और जब उन्हीं पुस्तकों पर हमारे हिंदी लेखकों की लेखनी फिरती है तो फिर क्या पूछना है एक और भी अनोखी छवि खिंच जाती है। 'एक तो तित लौकी दूसरे चढ़ी नीम।'
24. Kashi Prasad Jayaswal, 'Bhasha ka Mahattva', *Saraswati*, No. 6, Part 4, 1903, p. 209.
25. Ibid., pp. 209-10.
26. Ibid., p. 210.
27. Ibid., p. 210.
28. Ibid., p. 210.
29. Kashi Prasad Jayaswal, 'Shakespeare', *Saraswati*, No. 2, Part 8, Feb. 1907, pp. 70-71.
30. *MR*, Vol. XLII, July-Dec, 1927, pp. 270-72.

31. *Nagari Pracharini Patrika*, Part-8, 1928, pp. 219-27.
32. For entire speech see, Verma, Brajshankar, *Bihar Ki Sahityik Pragati*, Bihar Hindi Sahitya Sammelan, Patna, 1956, pp. 245-56.
33. KPJ argued that the metres used in Chand Bardai had been used at least 300 years before him. He cited the examples from the *Padmavat* of his '*gram-bhai*' Jayasi (Malik Muhammad) to say that he could not have imagined those *dohas* and *chaupais* from nowhere. He further argued that Jayasi himself mentioned several Hindi texts that got lost in time. KPJ also sourced Tibetan translations of Siddha poems procured by his friend Rahul Sankrityayan to underline the existence of a *Sandhya Bhasha* in which poems were written in ulatbansi style. These examples were shown by him to have been in existence from 750 to 100 A.D.
34. Ibid.
35. Ibid.
36. *Saraswati*, No.11, Part 5, November 1904, pp. 380-85 (The editor - Bharat Yayavar - of *Mahavir Prasad Dwivedi Rachnavali* has not mentioned the name of the joint writer KPJ).
37. Ibid.
38. Ibid., (The question of Nagari script is also discussed in the Chapter 3 on *Pataliputra*, KPJ wrote several articles and editorial comments over the question of Hindi language and Nagari script).
39. Kashi Prasad Jayaswal, 'Purani Hindi ka Janm Kaal', *Nagari Pracharini Patrika*, Saṁvat 1984, Part 8, p. 224, and, 'The Beginning of Old Hindi', *MR*, Vol. XLII, July-Dec, 1927, pp. 270-72.
40. Mohanlal Mahato Viyogi, 'Doctor Jayaswal', *Saraswati*, October 1937, Part 38, No. 4, p. 337.
41. For the full text of the Address, see *Veena*, May 1935, pp. 521-23.
42. For reference to some early travelogues, see Dalmia, op. cit., pp. 322-28, and Ramvilas Sharma, op. cit., pp. 59-60.
43. All these articles were published in the *Saraswati*: 'Englishtan ka Bank' ('Bank of England'), No. 5, Part 8, May 1907 pp. 202-05, 'London ka Kew namak Shahi Bag', No.7, Part 8, July 1907, pp. 287-89, 'England ki Jatiya Chitrashala', No.12, Part 8, December 1907, pp. 496-99, 'England ke Dehat mein Maharaja Banaras ka Kuan', No. 7, Part-9, 1908, pp. 299-302.
44. 'Hungary se Turk Desh', *Saraswati*, No.1, Part 13, January 1912, pp. 1-5, 'Hungary se Turk Desh', *Saraswati*, No.3, Part 13, March 1912, pp. 121-25, 'Turkey-Kustuntuniya ki Rah', *Saraswati*, No.5, Part 13, May 1912, pp. 233-36, 'The Turk Rajdhani Constantinople', *Saraswati*, No.7, Part 13, July 1912, pp. 345-53.
45. 'The Man in Turkey', *MR*, Vol. X, August 1911, pp. 139-41, 'The Man in Turkey', *MR*, Vol. X, October 1911, pp. 386-92. However, I have only used the original version published in the *Saraswati*.

46. *Saraswati*, No. 11, Part 11, November 1910, pp. 483-84, and No. 1, Part 12, January 1911, pp. 36-37.
47. Haraprakash Gaur, *Saraswati' aur Rashtriya Jagran*, National Publishing House, New Delhi, 1983, p. 3.
48. Kashi Prasad Jayaswal, 'Dr. Rudolf Hoernle', C.I.E, No. 10, Part 4, October 1903, p. 337.
49. 'Panditwar Dr. A.F. Rudolf Hoernle', *Saraswati*, C.I.E, No. 10, Part 4, October 1903, pp. 337-45, ' Buddhwar Mr. F.S. Grouse' C.I.E., *Saraswati*, No.1, Part 7, January 1906, pp. 5-10, 'Shriyut Maheshcharan Singh', B.A., M.S. (Master of Science), *Saraswati*, No. 3, Part 8, March 1907, pp. 119-22, 'The Late Mr. John Beems', *Saraswati*, No.4, Part 8, April 1907, pp. 134-37.
50. 'Panditwar Dr. A.F. Rudolf Hoernle', C.I.E, Part 4, No. 10, October 1903. pp. 337-38.
51. He was little bit critical about them, 'बीम्स हार्नली और ग्राउज साहब आदि हिंदी के बहुत बड़े जानने वाले माने जाते हैं परन्तु हिंदी में उन्होंने कितनी किताबें लिखी हैं? जो कुछ हिंदी के विषय में उन्होंने लिखा है प्राय: सभी अंग्रेजी में, quoted in Ramvilas Sharma, op. cit., p. 202.
52. Several treatises on Prakrit grammar were written by Hemacandra, Vararuchi, Kramadīśvara, Mārkaṇḍeya, Trivikrama, Śubhacandra - most of these were unpublished works.
53. From the *Proceedings*, Asiatic Society of Bengal for January 1899.
54. Ibid.
55. 'Panditwar 'Dr. A.F. Rudolf Hoernle', C.I.E, No. 10, Part 4, October 1903, p. 345.
56. 'Preface' *Hariaudh-Abhinandan-Granth*, Nagari Pracharini Sabha, Arrah, 1937.
57. In January 1906, Kalwar Mahato Sabha of Mirzapur published a Hindi monthly *Kalwar Gazette* with KPJ was the founded editor for some time. See, Vijaydatta Shreedhar, *Bharatiya Patrakarita Kosh*, Vol. 2, New Delhi, 2010, pp. 663-64.
58. *Hindi Pradeep*, May 1905, editorial note, pp. 4-5. This was KPJ's first and last article on the issue of caste conflict. It appears that there must have been two reasons for that: (i) after lifting the police surveillance in 1914, KPJ might have consciously restrained himself from writing any controversial piece, either social or political, (ii) the world in which KPJ lived professional, intellectual and personal was surrounded by the people from upper caste/class, his friends, clients, intellectual partners, sponsors—all of them were coming from that background only. Therefore, there might have been a threat perception also, as seen in his last phase of life, when he wrote a piece for the newspaper in favour of the farmer and his clients threatened him of boycotting him, although KPJ snubbed them by saying, "You are hiring me because of my talent, not on charity".

59. Patel, Hitendra, *Communalism and Intelligentsia in Bihar*, 1870-1930, Orient Blackswan, New, Delhi, 2011. p. 132.
60. *Proceedings of the Fourth Annual Conference of the Akhil Bharatavarshiya Haihay Kshatriya Mahasabha*, Jabalpur, April 1927.
61. *Kalwar Kesari*, Sampadakiya Tippaniyan, Vol. 2, No. 2, Āśvina-Śukla, Saṁvat 1981, pp. 122-23, (The issue has already been discussed in Chapter 1).
62. Orsini, op. cit., p. 54.
63. *Saraswati*, No. 6, Part 4, 1903, pp. 198-99.
64. *Saraswati*, No. 23, Part-4, 1903, pp. 51-52.
65. See, Rahul Sankrityayan, *KPJCV*, pp. 7-11.
66. The real agenda for the utility of translation and production of knowledge in Hindi with Nagari script was set under the leadership of Bharatendu Harishchandra, which he propagated in his Balia speech. For detailed discussion, see Vashuda Dalmia, op. cit, 202-05.
67. Saraswati, No. 3, Part. 3, April 1900, pp. 96-105.
68. 'Kausambi' *Nagari Pracharini Patrika*, Part. 4, 1900, pp. 75-95.
69. 'Purani Hindi ka Janmkal' Vol. 8, 1927, pp. 219-27, 'Kalinga Chakrabarti Maharaja Kharavela ke Shilalekha ka Vivaran', 1928, Vol. 8, pp. 301-22, 'Shri Kharavela Prashasti aur Jain Dharm ki Prachinata, Vol. 10, 1929, pp. 499-502, 'Jyotisha Granth Garg-Samhita mein Bharatiya Itihas, Vol. 10, 1929, pp. 1-14, 'Bhāraśiva Rājvaṇśa' Vol. 13, 1932, pp. 1-6.(the content of these articles will be discussed in the Chapter 4).
70. Verma, Ramchandra, *Hindu Rajya-Tantra*, p. xi.
71. Kashi Prasad Jayaswal, 'Kalinga Chakrabarti Maharaja Kharavela ke Shilalekha ka Vivaran, *Nagari Pracharini Patrika*', 1928, Vol. 8, pp. 301-22.
72. *Saraswati*, No. 2, Part 5, 1903, pp. 66-67.
73. *Saraswati*, No. 11, Part 4, May 1903, pp. 386-89.
74. Mahavir Prasad Dwivedi, 'Deshvyapak Bhasha, *Saraswati*', November 1903.
75. Mahavir Prasad Dwivedi, 'Hindustaniyon ki Angrezi Lekh', *Saraswati* September 1914.

3

The Fourth Estate Emerges: KPJ and the *Pataliputra*

"Nothing less than Hindustan ought to be given away to the English in a grateful reward for introducing the art of printing, which is emancipating thousands of minds from the yoke of a superstition that held us brutes for centuries."[1] Making a small allowance for some exaggeration in this assertion, it should nonetheless be recognised that the press provided the scope for articulation by educated people and thereby enabled them to emerge as social leaders. Keshavram Bhatt was the man who single-handedly heralded modern journalism in Bihar. He started *Bihar Bandhu*, the first Hindi weekly newspaper of Bihar in Calcutta. After gaining adequate experience, he shifted the base of the paper to Bankipur (Patna). However, the overall growth of the press in Bihar was considerably slower than in Bengal.[2]

The multifaceted persona of KPJ is reflected in his journalistic pursuits. Apart from being the editor of the short-lived monthly the *Kalwar Gazette* (1906) published from Mirzapur and the weekly *Pataliputra* published from Patna, he also wrote articles for important newspapers of Patna. However, in this chapter we shall evaluate his journalistic career based on the contents of the *Pataliputra* alone, of which he was the editor for about a year 1914-15. The weekly continued, though somewhat irregularly, till 1924.

KPJ had started writing for Hindi journals in 1898, but his formal journalistic career began in 1906. In January 1906, Kalwar Mahato Sabha of Mirzapur published a Hindi monthly *Kalwar Gazette* with KPJ as its editor.[3] KPJ had to leave for England for higher studies in the middle of 1906. Therefore, it is possible that the monthly's publication was discontinued after a few issues. While he was in London, he continued to write articles on various subjects in the most reputed Hindi journal of the time viz., the *Saraswati* (see, Chapter 2). He also wrote a few articles for the *Hindi Kesari*, a weekly published from Nagpur, but the files of the weekly are not available anywhere, except for a few pages in the Madhavrao Sapre Library in Bhopal, Madhya Pradesh. A persual of these showed that they did not contain any contributions of KPJ.

The second innings of KPJ as a journalist started in the middle of 1914, when the weekly named *Pataliputra* was published from Patna. The *Pataliputra* was started by a company called 'The Bihar Printing and Publishing Syndicate Ltd', which had already been publishing the *Express* in English. The entire expenses of the *Pataliputra* and the *Express* were borne by the Maharaja of Hathuwa directly and by the Maharaja of Darbhanga indirectly, as the latter did not want to make himself conspicuous. Babu Ram Gopal Chaudhuri, Managing Director, was the financial front.[4] The *Pataliputra* was the sister concern and before the publication of its first issue, *The Express* announced in June 1914,

> It gives us very great pleasure to announce that we have completed our arrangements for bringing out our new Hindi Weekly, *Pataliputra*, on the 27th instant. Mr. Kashi Prasad Jayaswal, M.A. (Oxon.), Barrister-at-Law, who is a well known Hindi writer, will have complete editorial control of the journal. The services of competent Hindi writers have also been secured, and, altogether, it is hoped that the new journal will be a useful addition to the vernacular journalism of the land. As already announced, *Pataliputra* will deal largely with topics of literary, historical, social and political interest.[5]

Right from its inception, the *Pataliputra* was exempted from depositing security money under the Press Act. Such a concession may have been the result of the deal between the proprietors of the weekly and the colonial administrators involving some constraints on free expression.

Why did KPJ agree to take up the editorship of the *Pataliputra* is not clear, especially in the context when he had flourishing legal practice in the courts and he was also busy in his abiding interest in the research into Indian's ancient past? There might have been several reasons for this plunge into journalism: the experience and training and the old habit of writing in Hindi (1898-1912), conflict with Mahavir Prasad Dwivedi and others and his eagerness to continue Hindi writing and to make the Hindi readers aware about the developments in the world, and possibly also his relationship with the patrons of the *Pataliputra*—both the Maharajas of Hathuwa and Darbhanga were his clients.

The launching year of the *Pataliputra* -1914 - was very important for KPJ for many reasons: he had recently settled in Patna and the police surveillance on him was lifted, although he was still a suspect in the eyes of the colonial masters; the First World War broke out soon after the weekly's launch; the Hindi-Urdu debate was still on; the era of Gandhian nationalism had not started yet; and it was also the time of cataclysmic developments in Russia. KPJ served the *Pataliputra*, both as an editor and contributor for almost a year, i.e. from June 1914 to April 1915.

The first issue of the *Pataliputra* appeared on 27 June 1914 and its editorial ('Hamara Parichay') made its policy intentions clear:

> ...पाटलिपुत्र के संचालकों की यह अभिलाषा है कि यह पत्र देश कि सेवा में सदा अग्रसर रहे, देश के सामायिक पत्रों का बल बढ़ावे और हिंदी भाषा के साहित्य तथा सर्वोपरि हिन्दू धर्म का पोषक हो। राजनैतिक बातों में इसकी स्थिति बिलकुल स्वाधीन रहेगी। यह किसी राजनीतिक दल या सम्प्रदाय के सिद्धान्त का अनुयायी नहीं होगा। जिस बात में देश का कल्याण वह उसी का स्वन्त्रभाव से समर्थन करेगा। देश कल्याण ही उसका परम सिद्धान्त है जिसके निष्पादन के लिए सच्ची सलाह और सच्ची आलोचना में पाटलिपुत्र नि:शंक आगे रहेगा।
>
> प्रजा के सुख का बहुत बड़ा साधन राजा और प्रजा के बीच परस्पर अच्छे भाव का रहना है। 'पाटलिपुत्र' इस भाव को बनाए रखने की चिन्ता रखेगा। इसके लिए वह प्रजा और राजा के अन्योन्य विचार और भाव शुद्ध रीति से समझाएगा।
>
> 'पाटलिपुत्र' का विश्वास है कि संसारचक्र में अनेक बातें अटल और सनातन नियमों के अनुकूल घटा करती हैं। वे सब मनुष्यजाति के भले और उसकी उन्नति के लिए है। इंग्लैंड और इस देश का नाता भी इसी तरह इस देश कि भलाई के लिए है। इंग्लैंड के सम्बन्ध से इस देश की बहुत उन्नति होने वाली है, हो रही है और हो चुकी है। इसका अनुभव बड़ी आसानी से हो सकता है। हंगरी के पूरब और जापान के पश्चिम चाहे जिस देश से मिला लीजिए, भारत की वर्त्तमान उन्नति और कहीं न पाइएगा। पर साथ ही अभी उन्नति में यहाँ सूत्रपात मात्र मानना चाहिए। उन्नति की प्रफुल्लावस्था स्वायत्तशासन-प्रणाली की प्राप्ति है। जब तक ब्रिटिश साम्राज्य के और अङ्गों के समान इस देश में प्राण न आ जाय तब तक वह साम्राज्य शरीर अरोग्य-मूर्त्ति नहीं। साम्राज्य सब तरह और सर्वांग बलिष्ट तभी होगा जब भारतवर्ष सप्राण सजीव राज्य की दशा में पहुंच जायगा। सजीवता के लिए ब्रिटिश साम्राज्य के और राज्यों की तरह भारतवर्ष को स्वच्छन्दता की ऐसी ही आवश्यकता है जैसे प्राणों के लिए शुद्ध जलवायु की। अतएव भारत के लिए स्वच्छन्द, आत्मशासन-संस्था पाने के लिए चेष्टा करना 'पाटलिपुत्र' का मूल अभीष्ट है।
>
> 'पाटलिपुत्र' में देशीय और विदेशीय समाचार प्रकाशित करने का विशेष प्रबन्ध

किया गया है। इंग्लैंड से हर सप्ताह निज संवाददाता का पत्र छपा जायगा। यह आगामी मास से प्रारम्भ किया जायगा। योरोप के कुछ अन्य देशों के मुखपत्रों से उनकी मूल भाषा से हिन्दी में अनुवाद कर लेख और समाचार दिए जायंगे।

देश के विद्वान और विचार-नायकों तथा प्रसिद्ध हिंदी-लेखकों कि सहायता और सहयोगिता का 'पाटलिपुत्र' अधिकारी समझा जाय इसकी चिन्ता उसके संचालकों को बराबर रहेगी। साहित्य, इतिहास, विज्ञान को पत्र में वैसे ही स्थान दिया जायगा जैसे योरोप के मुख्य साप्ताहिक पत्रों में दिया जाता है। कृषि और व्यपार के हित की बातें भी पत्र में बराबर रहेंगी।

'पाटलिपुत्र' यद्यपि बिहार की राजधानी से निकलता है पर उसमें एकदेशीयता न रहेंगी। जैसे पुराना पाटलिपुत्र देश मात्र के ममत्त्व और देश मात्र की सार्वजनिकता का केंद्र था उसी तरह उसका नामधारी 'पाटलिपुत्र' देश मात्र का ममत्त्व-कांक्षी और देश मात्र का सेवक है।

It is the desire of the Directors of *Pataliputra* that this weekly should become a frontrunner in the service of the nation; it must enhance the strength of the contemporary publications of the country, and it should be the main nourisher of the literature of the Hindi language and above all the Hindu *dharma*. Hindi and Hindu *dharma* were interlocked here which was the common feature of the Hindi intelligentsia in Bihar and other Hindi speaking area at that time.

In the political sphere, the position of the weekly will be independent. It will not be a follower of any political party or policies of any group. It will support independently the cause of the welfare of the nation. The welfare of the nation will be its ultimate goal and for the execution of that, in taking true advice and criticism *Pataliputra* will undoubtedly be the frontrunner. The ultimate goal of the beginning is the realization of the achievement of self-governance. To make an effort to achieve the autonomous, institution of self-governance is the fundamental goal of the *Pataliputra*.

The directors have been eager to have the cooperation and participation of the famous intellectuals and scholars and Hindi writers for the *Pataliputra*. Following the lead given by the European weeklies, this weekly will also give space to literature, history and science as the European weeklies gives. There will be regular news having a bearing on the interests of agriculture and trade.[6]

Bihar was a newly created province; therefore, there were a number of expectations, questions, aspirations, etc. of the Hindi reading and Hindi-speaking people of Bihar in particular. It appears from the contents of the editorial that it tried to fulfil those expectations. During KPJ's tenure as the editor, fourty-one issues of the weekly were published between 27 June 1914 and 24 April 1915. Except for the two holidays of Dusehra and Holi, it had a continuous run, but the rest of the files are not to be found in India. The number of pages were 8 in each issue, the weekly subscription was 2 annas and the annual subscription was Rs. 2. The eight-page weekly, of which the last one-and-half pages were devoted exclusively to advertisements, was divided into several segments: Editorial, Political, Historical, Classics, and Literary, with an additional sub-section on Novels, Social Matters, Education, News (local, provincial, national and international), and the War. Most of the articles bore their authors' names but several were published anonymously. On the basis of their content and style it is not difficult to surmise that some of the anonymous pieces were written by the editor himself. From the available files, we have a range of editorials starting with the inaugural one, which is a good index of the intent and future policy of the weekly. The First World War attracted the maximum editorial attention, with as many as fourteen dealing with it and international relations in general. Not only that there was a page devoted to the War reporting, four dealt with religion, six with history, five about individuals, two on education, and another couple on the language issue, and six articles focused on the economy and polity. Debates and discussions on religious themes, especially Hindu mythology, festivals and fairs were regular features of the *Pataliputra*. The editor also wore the lawyer's hat and used his vocation and expertise to create a niche of reports on legal proceedings in important cases of the time, such as the Delhi Conspiracy Case. The weekly also carried weather reports from different regions of India and Bihar, articles about agricultural cooperatives, and so on... The editor was also aware about the resource generation for the proper running of the weekly. Therefore, separate pages were given for the commercial advertisements with the rates specified as follows: for one column, Rs. 15, half column Rs. 8, quarter column Rs. 5, per inch Rs. 1, and for the permanent advertisement for three months per column Rs. 18. Quite clearly, the weekly, although driven by its editor's own intellectual and political interests, and located in Patna, its ambition was not hemmed in by these two narrow factors. As the inaugural editorial pointed out, the name of the weekly indicated a larger role for it, like the *Pataliputra* once had in the life of the country.[7]

The colonial officials, on the other hand, saw the publication as a rival to the already existing weeklies, supported by another set of royal patrons. The C.I.D. report dated 8.8.1914 mentions that the chief aim of this paper which has been started in the office of the '*Express*' is to beat down the Hindi edition of the '*Beharee*' which is issued from the Beharee Press. These newspapers—the *Express* and the *Pataliputra*—have in reality been started by Hathuwa at the instance of the Maharaja of Darbhanga to crush down the English and Hindi editions of the *Beharee* which is supported by the Banailli Raj.[8]

After the publication of the first issue of the *Pataliputra, The Beharee* wrote, "A welcome addition to vernacular press of India is the *Pataliputra*, a local weekly, whose first issue has just been published. The editor is a graduate of an English University, and a barrister-at-law. It augurs well for the future of the vernacular of the province that such men should take to conducting newspapers in their mother tongue. The first issue contains some very interesting articles contributed by very distinguished Sanskrit scholars. It would, however, have added to the popularity of the journal with the English educated people, if it had been written in a more familiar language. Mr. Jayaswal, we hope, will rise above the ordinary level of Hindi writers, and give to the vernacular a more familiar language and an easy style."[9]

The contents of the weekly are quite rich. However, our study is based largely on the readings of the some of the editorials and some other articles, which had significant ideological tones on the contemporary relevant issues. The broader complexion of the weekly can be comprehended on the basis of its exposition of such issues as: (i) its political posturing, (ii) its stand on language and script, (iii) its descriptions of class and caste relations, and (iv) its attitude towards the newly emerging questions about women in society.

(A) Political Posturing

The editor claims in the introductory editorial: "In the political sphere, the position of the weekly will be independent. It will not follow any political party or policies of any group. The welfare of the nation will be its ultimate goal and for the execution of that, in taking true advice and criticism *Pataliputra* will undoubtedly be the frontrunner." Though it espoused the idea of 'स्वछंद आत्मशासन' ('autonomous self-governance') as its goal for India, this first editorial simultaneously underlined, "One of the biggest means of the welfare of the subjects (*praja*) is the cordial reciprocal/mutual relationship between the subjects and the king (raja). *Pataliputra* will try to foster this relationship." Throughout the tenure of KPJ's editorship, the weekly remained extremely pro-Raj.

Once considered a 'revolutionist' and the 'cleverest Indian of the present time' by the colonial administrators,[10] why did KPJ take a pro-British position as the editor of the weekly? There might be several reasons: one might be his personal reason, because after repeated endeavours, the police surveillance had been lifted and he might thus have avoided any conflict with the government. KPJ was probably looking for an opportunity to do away with his revolutionary image and show loyalty to the government. Second, his intellectual training in the early decades in the Nagari Pracharini Sabha and the Hindi Nagari movement might have shaped his literary *saṁskaras*. In the second half of the nineteenth century, especially after 1857, expressing loyalty to the British government had become an integral part of the political culture of this elite class. It was not because of any threat or without reason but because of the material interests. The colonial government had also opened up several opportunities for the educated urban gentry, which had developed vested material interests. Most of the leaders of the Nagari movement came from this background and till the 1880s, Banaras was the main centre of this class. Later on, Allahabad became such a centre. The immediate intellectual environment of KPJ was anti-Urdu/anti-Muslim and largely pro-British.[11] It should be noted here that the *Pataliputra* was patronised by the Hathuwa estate directly and the Darbhanga estate indirectly, and both of them were also pro-British.

Soon after the beginning of the *Pataliputra*, the First World War started. The way the *Pataliputra* and KPJ tried to woo the colonial regime was well reflected in the news related to *Komagata Maru* incident and several articles related to the First World War. The *Komagata Maru* was one of the three events, which brought the Ghadar movement to a head: the other two were arrest and escape of Har Dayal, and the outbreak of the First World War. These events led to the opposing world views of two erstwhile friends Har Dayal and KPJ.[12]

KPJ's pro-government position was also reflected on the *Komagata Maru* incident.[13] The editor wrote,

...अंग्रेजी प्रजा होने से यह हक़ नहीं मिल जाता कि चाहे जिस अंग्रेजी प्रजा के घर

घुस जाय। उपनिवेश स्वतंत्र राज्य हैं, वे चाहे जैसा कानून बनाएं। उनकी स्वतंत्रता कहां रही यदि उन्हें अपने मज़दूरों की रोटी छीन लेने वाले दूसरे अंग्रेजी प्रजा-कूल के लिए अपने घर का दर्वाजा खोल देना पड़े। उपनिवेशों का उलाहना दो बातों का है। एक तो यह कि उनके मज़दूर भारतीय मज़दूरों के कारण दुःख पातें हैं... फिर यहां के लोगों की रहन-सहन पसंद नहीं करते। जैसे, योरोप के लोग नाक ज़मीन पर छिनकने से बहुत घिन मानते हैं, सिक्ख लोग उनकी तरह रुमाल अपने पास नहीं रखते। और न उनका सा शिष्टाचार जानते हैं...। इस तरह से हिन्दू उपनिवेशों में रहता और कमाता हुआ हर बात में वहां की प्रजा से भिन्न और अलग रहता है। ...मनुष्य मनुष्य पहले और अंग्रेजी प्रजा उसके बाद है। अंग्रेज़ी प्रजा होने से मनुष्य कुछ पकाया हुआ घी नहीं हो जाता, उसका मानवस्वभाव, भय, प्रेम, द्रोह, रोष सब बना रहता है। गुरदत सिंह कि उपकार बुद्धि सराहनीय है पर उनका विचार बहुत निर्बल है। 'मान न मान मैं तेरा मेहमान'... वृथा के झगड़े उठाना केवल भेदबुद्धि बढ़ाना और अख़बारों की जगह छेकने के लिए ख़बर तैयार करना मात्र है... उपनिवेश यद्यपि प्रायः इंग्लैंड से गये हुए लोगों द्वारा बसे हुए हैं पर ध्यान देने कि बात है कि कोई कोई अंग्रेज़ मज़दूरों तक को नहीं आने देते। मामला जीवननिर्वाह का है। न तो कानून का है और न अंग्रेज़ी झंडे का है।[14]

Here, KPJ's emphasis is quite clear - merely being an English subject was no passport to enter another 'colony' of the British. Cultural differences apart, the economic deprivation of the Canadian labour was not acceptable. The real question for KPJ was that of 'livelihood' rather than that of 'law' or the flag.[15] Not just that, the treatment that was meted out to the violent Sikhs coming back to India was considered to be 'liberal'[16] (उदार) When a committee was constituted to enquire into the violence, KPJ expressed his thanks thus:

हमारे प्रजाप्रिय बड़े लाट लार्ड हार्डिंग ने सिखों के बजबज वाले दंगे पर खेद प्रकट किया है और उसका कारण जांचने के लिए एक कमिटी बिठाई है। प्रजा की पुकार पर ध्यान देने में आप की जो प्रसिद्धि है और जिसके के लिए प्रजा आपको हृदय से चाहती है उसकी उज्जवलता श्रीमान के इस कार्य से और भी बढ़ जाएगी।

(Our benevolent Governor-General Lord Hardinge expressed regret over the violent incident at Budge Budge. Sir, your fame of responding to the calls of people and for which the people are heartily grateful to you, would be further enhanced through this gesture [appointment of a broad-based committee]).

The news related to the First World War and international relations occupied the maximum space of the weekly. Out of the fourty one editorials, fourteen were written on the War. Not only that details and progress of the War both at the national and international levels were prominently given from the issue of the 1 August 1914 onwards. These fourteen editorials were: (1) युद्ध और हमारा कर्त्तव्य[18], (2) हमारा उत्साह[19], (3) युद्ध में भारत[20], (4) युद्ध में हमारा योग[21], (5) युद्ध को भारतीय युद्ध समझना चाहिए[22], (6) लम्बी लड़ाई की तैयारी[23], (7) शत्रुओं की हार[24], (8) फ्रांस में हिन्दुस्तानी सेना[25], (9) जर्मन जल सेना[26], (10) 'न्यूट्रलाइज़ड स्टेट्स' अथवा उदासीन बनाए हुए राज्य[27], (11) रूम की भूल[28], (12) स्विट्ज़रलैंड कि स्थिति[29], (13) इंग्लैंड और युद्ध[30], (14) डारडॉनेलेस[31] [(1) *Yudh aur Hamara kartavya,* (2) *Hamara Utsah,* (3) *Yudh mein Bharat,* (4) *Yudh mein Hamara Yog,* (5) *Yuddha ko Bharatiya Yudh Samajhana Chahiye,* (6) *Lambi Ladai ki Taiyari,* (7) *Shatruon ki Haar,* (8) *France mein Hindustani Sena,* (9) *German Jal-sena,* (10) *Neutralised State athwa Udasin banaye hue Rajya,* (11) *Room ki Bhool,* (12) *Switzerland ki Sthiti,* (13) *England aur Yuddha,* (14) *Dardanelles*].

1. युद्ध और हमारा कर्त्तव्य

> ...धीरज और विश्वास कि हमारे साम्राज्य और हमारे सम्राट की विजय होगी। काम पड़ने पर यहाँ कि सेना और देशी राज्यों की सेना से मिश्र या अन्य कहीं की रक्षा की जा सकती है। और वे और सभी प्रजा जहां कहीं हो जी जान से इस देश की भक्ति का परिचय देवेंगी। यहां के मुसलमान का भी यही देश है। हिन्दू मुसलमान सभी को एकमत एकमुख और एक देह से ब्रिटिश साम्राज्य की सेवा के लिए तैयार रहना चाहिए। इस देश की अंग्रेजी झंडे के नीचे बहुत उन्नति हुई है। उसे बहुत सुख मिला है। अंग्रेजी झंडा उसकी प्रीति और भक्ति का सदा पात्र है। सारे देश की प्रार्थना सदा विजयी इंग्लैंड की विजय के लिए ही है। इंग्लैंड धर्म और न्याय के लिए लड़ने उठा है। जहाँ धर्म है वहाँ विजय भी है, यह सनातन वचन है, सनातन सत्य है। ईश्वर इंग्लैंड और हमारे पक्ष को चकाचौंध पैदा करने वाली विजय दे... । भारत के शरीर और प्राण में जहां तक बल रहेगा वह अंग्रेजी झंडे का वैसा ही साथ देगा जैसा कि कोई भी अंग्रेज या कोई भी अंग्रेजी प्रजा। इंग्लैंड की जीत हमारी जीत है।[32]

2. हमारा उत्साह

> जैसा कि आशा और अनुमान किया जाता था इस देश ने इस अवसर पर उत्साह, वीरता और भक्ति का यथेष्ट परिचय दिया। यहाँ सभी बड़े शहरों में ब्रिटिश साम्राज्य के लिए लोग लड़ाई के मैदान में जाने के लिए कमर कस तैयार होने लगे। देशी राज्यों ने मारु दूदुम्भी का जबाब भक्ति और वीरता के हुंकार से दिया। ...स्याही सूखी न कि नेपाल का तार भारत सरकार को पहुंचा कि वहां की सारी सेना गवर्नमेंट को नज़र है। ...कलकत्ता हाई कोर्ट के सब बैरिस्टर और बहुतेरे वकील स्वयंसेवी सिपाहियों की तालिका में नाम लिखा चुके। विलायत में हिंदुस्तानी छात्रों ने भी ऐसा ही किया तथा भारतीय मुखियों ने बादशाह जॉर्ज को भक्ति संदेशा भेजा की चाहे गवर्नमेंट से हमारा घरेलू बातों में विभेद भले ही रहा हो पर इस समय हम सब ब्रिटिश प्रजा एकमुख और

एक देह हैं। ...भारतीयों का वीरभाव और वीरभक्ति जिससे इस समय सारा देश क्या सारा संसार गूंज रहा है और जिसने शत्रुओं के हृदय को विलोडित किया होगा, भारतोचित है। यह देश रण भिक्षा के भिखारियों को बिना दिए हुए कभी नहीं रहा, यहाँ रण-क्षेत्र सा पुनीत कोई दूसरा क्षेत्र नहीं माना जाता। शत्रु के ललकारने पर भारत कभी भी नहीं पिछड़ता। स्वाभाविक वीर भारत का वीर ब्रिटेन का साथ सोने में सुगंध सा मेल है। जो कोई समीप या दूर ब्रिटिश झंडे से द्रोहबुद्धि कर सर उठाना चाहेगा वह अपनी नसीहत को पहुंच जायगा। आयरलैंड के भक्ति के आचरण के कारण उसका भाग्य सुधर गया। शत्रुओं के विध्वंस करने पर उसे स्वराज्य देने में अब किसी को बाधा न होगी। भारत का भी इस भक्ति भाव से बहुत कुछ ऐसा ही भला होगा।[33]

3. युद्ध में भारत

...ब्रिटिश साम्राज्य की सेवा और रक्षा के लिए हिंदुस्तानी सेना भी योग देने जा रही है। यह भारत भक्ति पर विश्वास का तिलक स्वरूप, साम्रज्य के रक्षा-कर्म के यज्ञ में उसका भी अधिकार, और उसके बल पर इंग्लैंड के भरोसे का सूचक है। इस समाचार से देश की दाहिनी भुजा फड़क उठेगी। भारत की वीरता का नाम और भारत और अंग्रेजी झंडे की आन ये भारतीय योद्धा अवश्य रखेंगे। ...भारत इस समय अंग्रेज़ों की की हुई उस के प्रति भलाई का बदला तन मन धन से देने को तैयार है। लाट साहब की पुकार का उत्तर वीर, दानी, स्नेही और दयाशील भारत अलौकिक रूप से देगा। हम अपने योद्धाओं के कुटुंब के भरण को अपनी रोटी तक बांट कर देंगे। वे योद्धा देश और आर्य जाति के लिए कमर कस कर जा रहे हैं। वे विजय पताका लेकर लौटेंगे। जो खेत रहेंगे उनके लिए हमें दूना गर्व होगा। भारत की कोख उनसे सुफल हो जायेगी। उनके स्वर्ग जाने से देश तर जायगा। उनके कुटुम्ब के लिए हमारा छदाम और हमारी स्त्रियों की नथ तक बहार निकलेगी।[34]

4. युद्ध में हमारा योग

इस समय हमको चाहिए कि दूसरों के कहने पर बिना पूरा विचार किए हाँ में हाँ न मिलावें। मुर्खता, शरारत, और घबराहट की रची हुई खबरों के द्वारा हमारे उत्साह की ज्वाला पर पानी पड़ने का डर तो है ही, शत्रु जर्मनी और उसके गोइन्दों के द्वारा भी बहुत कुछ बदनामी और हानि हो सकती है।... गवर्नमेंट ने यहां के उत्साह का आदर हजार गुना कर दिया जब कि उन्होंने निश्चय किया कि हिन्दुस्तानी सेना रण-भूमि में जा अंगरेज़ी सेना की बराबरी में लोहा बजाए। यह ऐंसी बात थी जिसके मांगने की भी हिम्मत हिन्दुस्तानियों को नहीं पड़ सकती थी। हिन्दुस्तानी पलटन का लड़ना हिन्दुस्तान का लड़ना है। हिन्दुस्तानी योद्धा रण भूमि में भारत के प्रतिनिधि हैं।... मरहम पट्टी करने वालों की जो सेना बनने वाली थी उसमें बंगाली भाईयों ने एक ऐसा उज्र किया कि जिसका जवाब गवर्नमेण्ट क्या सब को यही देना पड़ेगा कि रहने दीजिए, तकलीफ मत कीजिए। बंगाली महाशयों ने गवर्नमेंट को लिखा की यह बात साफ कर

दी जाय की उन्हें घायलों की डोली नहीं ढोनी पड़ेगी। इसके बाद ही गवर्नमेंट से परवाना आया कि आप की पलटन हमें नहीं चाहिए। रणक्षेत्र में बाबूगिरी करने तो कोई जाता नहीं, वहां तो कमर कस कर सब कुछ आप ही करना पड़ता है। चलें हम मरहम पट्टी करने को और कहें की घायल का जूठा या उसकी थूक न छूएंगे या उसे कंधे लाद खंदकों से बाहर न निकालेंगे या पिछड़ती पलटन के साथ उन्हें कलेजे लगा मीलों न ढोयेंगे, तो मदद करने क्या चले खुद इल्लत हुए। भला वह कौन सा सैनिक विभाग है जो ऐसी शर्तें मंजूर करेगा?[35]

5. युद्ध को भारतीय युद्ध समझना चाहिए

यद्यपि युद्ध भारतभूमि के बाहर हो रहा है पर वह हम लोगों के लिए भारतीय युद्ध है, हमारा युद्ध है। ...युद्ध को हम केवल राजभक्ति की दृष्टि से नहीं देख सकते। इस युद्ध को हमें स्वार्थ दृष्टि से अपना युद्ध समझना चाहिए। जो कुछ उन्नति हुई है और हो रही है बिना अंग्रेजी सरकार के लिप पुत कर बराबर हो जायगी। हज़ारों वर्ष के लिए हम फिर पीछे फेंक दिए जायेंगे। योरप या एशिया में कोई दूसरी जाति नहीं जो अंग्रेज़ों सा उदार व्यवहार करेगी। ...युद्ध में हर तरह सरकार की सहायता करना अपनी सहायता करना है। ...जब तक युद्ध नि:शेष न हो बराबर भारत के बेटे भारत के लिए और अपने मालिक के लिए मैदान में जाते रहें। जर्मन कोई पौने पांच करोड़ हैं। पर हम तीस करोड़ हैं। वे कहां तक लड़ सकते हैं? महाराजा, राजा और जमींदार और साधारण प्रजा, संकट के समय के लिए अलग रखे धन को उसी तेजी और उत्सुकता से निकाल अर्पित करेंगे जैसे मैसूर महाराज ने 50 लाख युद्ध के खर्च के लिए निकाल बाहर किए। धन और जन दोनों से हम भिड़े रहेंगे। ...संकट के समय धैर्य रखना भारत का सनातन स्वाभाव है। धैर्यपूर्वक युद्ध में योग देना ही इस समय हमारा परम धर्म है। ...हारिए न हिम्मत बिसारिए न राम, यहाँ के मूल मन्त्रों में है।[36]

6. लम्बी लड़ाई की तैयारी

...लम्बी लड़ाई से ही हम शत्रु का नाश कर सकते हैं। इसका कारण यह है की रुपया और जन जितना हमारे पक्ष में है उतना शत्रु के पास नहीं। फिर शत्रु की नई रण–सज्जा हमें मालूम हो जायगी जिसका प्रयोग हम आगे चलकर स्वयं कर सकेंगे। लोहा को लोहा काटता है। जर्मन जर्मन नीति से नष्ट होगी। केवल घबराहट को जीतने की हमें जरूरत है, रण की जीत निश्चित है। शत्रु जर्मनी की पुरानी नीति है कि जीत के साथ ही उदार शर्तों पर सुलह का पैगाम भेजना। ऐसा ही उसने ऑस्ट्रिया के साथ किया जिसके कारण आज तक ऑस्ट्रिया उसके साथ है। शत्रु की इस समय भी कुटिल नीति होगी कि फ्रांस से पेरिस लेने के बाद कहे कि सुलह कर लो तुम लड़ाई से दूर रहो, हम सारी भूमि तुम्हें लौटा देते हैं, अल्सास– लारेन को स्वराज्य देते है आदि। पर इसका उत्तर मित्र राज्यों ने पहले ही दे दिया। उन्होंने प्रकाशित कर दिया कि इंग्लैंड, फ्रांस, और रूस शत्रु से मेल करेंगे तो साथ ही करेंगे। मित्र राज्यों में रूस की प्रजा

खेतिहर है, वह 10 वर्ष तक लड़ाई जारी रख सकती है। पर उतने दिन तक लड़ाई चलने की संभावना नहीं। दूसरे दो राज्य फ्रांस और हम, तीन चार साल आसानी से, धीरज के सहारे, वीरता पूर्वक लड़ विजय लक्ष्मी को वशीभूत कर सकते हैं और करेंगे। जहां धर्म है, वहीं जीत निश्चित है। हम लोग धर्म के लिए लड़ रहे हैं। विजय हमारे झंडे के साथ घूमती रहेगी।[37]

7. शत्रुओं की हार

...जर्मनी की इस हार (पैरिस विजय का विफल प्रयास) का मूल कारण अंग्रेजी सेना है। ...जैसे ग्राह से गज की रक्षा हुई उसी तरह पेरिस की रक्षा जर्मन सेना से अन्तिम समय हो गई। पेरिस के द्वार तक पहुंच जर्मन सेना को जर्मनी की सरहद पर वापिस जाना पड़ा। शत्रु का गर्व चूर्ण हो गया। साथ ही मित्र राज्यों में रूस ने ऑस्ट्रिया को बड़ी हार दी। ...जहां जर्मनी की एक दो हारें और हुईं कि बवेरिया तथा अन्य राज्य जो भीतर भीतर कैसर से बुरा मानते हैं अलग हो जायेंगे। साथ ही बर्लिन में भी दंगा मचेगा। शत्रु के दिन अब बुरे आ गए जान पड़ते हैं।[38]

8. फ्रांस में हिन्दुस्तानी सेना

...सिख पलटन, पंजाबी पलटन जिसमे हिन्दू मुसलमान दोनों हैं, बलूची और गुरखा पलटन, देशी राजाओं के साथ फ्रांस की भूमि पर मारु बजाती, पहुंची। फ्रांस आगत स्वागत में सदा उत्साही रहता है। इस समय उसने भारतीय सेना का, उसे अपना सहायक और रक्षक मान जो सत्कार किया उसका भागी होना इतिहास में दुर्लभ सौभाग्य है। नर नारियों ने उनपर पुष्प की वर्षा की, योद्धों के कपड़ों में अपने राज्य की झंडियां आलपिन से लगा दी। फ्रांस के इस सत्कार का उत्तर भारतीय योद्धों ने अपने मुस्कान से और रणब्रत के उत्साह भरे चेहरे से दिया। फ्रांसीसियों का कलेजा उनके मुंह पर आ गया जब कि भारतीय सेना ने फ्रांस का राष्ट्रय गीत 'ला मार-सेई' अपने जंगी बाजे के मुख सुनाना आरम्भ किया। ...मानो यह बतलाया कि फ्रांस से शत्रु की मुक्ति का उन्होंने बीड़ा उठाया है, फ्रांस को उन्होंने स्वदेश समझा है। इस पुण्यव्रत का बदला भारत को मिले न रहेगा। फ्रांस की भूमि राज्यनैतिक तीर्थ है। फ्रांस ही की बदौलत इस समय योरोप में प्रजातंत्र राज्य है। फ्रांस की रक्षा के लिए अपना रक्त गिराने वाला अपने और अपने देश को तार देने वाला होगा। ...इस समय भारतीय योद्धों पर भारत का भविष्य निर्भर है।[39]

9. जर्मन जल सेना

जर्मन जल सेना केवल 15 वर्ष के अंदर तैयार हुई है। ...यह इंग्लैंड को ललकारना था तभी से इंग्लैंड के कान खड़े हो गए। ...कहते हैं जर्मनी ने पनडुब्बी नार्वे अर्थात् छोटे छोटे जहाज जिनसे टारपीडो के महागोले पानी के अंदर से छूट सकते हैं, बहुत बनाई है। ...इन्हीं पनडुब्बी जहाजों से जर्मनी अंगरेज़ी बेड़े पर एक एक करके हमला करेगी। ऐसे पनडुब्बी जहाज़ अंगरेज़ सरकार के पास भी अनेक हैं। सब से पहले

अंगरेज़ी पन–डुब्बी ने जर्मन जंगी जहाज़ डुबाया। जो जर्मन बेड़ा इतनी मिहनत से बना है शीघ्र ही अंगरेज़ी बेड़े से नष्ट कर दिया जायगा और शैख़चिल्ली का मंसूबा जहां का तहां रह जायगा।[40]

10. 'न्यूट्रलाइज़ड स्टेट' अथवा उदासीन बनाए हुए राज्य

हिन्दू लोग पराए राज्य के तीन प्रकार मानते थे– मित्र, अमित्र, और उदासीन। उदासीन वे राज्य कहलाते जो लड़ने वालों के बीच न किसी से शत्रुता और न किसी से मित्रता दिखलाते। आजकल षाडगुण्य (international politics) अर्थात राज्यों के बीच सन्धि विग्रह की नीति में मुख्य तीन तरह के राज्य माने जाते हैं। पर इनसे भिन्न एक नए प्रकार के राज्यों की उपज योरप में हुई है जिसे 'न्यूट्रलाइज़ड' या 'मीडिएटाइज़ड' राज्य कहते हैं। ये राज्य बड़े-बड़े राज्यों की रज़ामन्दी से उदासीन बना दिए जाते हैं। ...ऐसे उदासीनी कृत राज्यों की रचना का कारण पड़ोसी राज्यों के बीच एक मेड़ होने की आवश्यकता मात्र है। जैसा हिन्दू आचार्यों ने कहा है, पड़ोसी राज्य स्वभाविक दुश्मन है। इससे पड़ोसियों के बीच एक दूसरे राज्य का होना पड़ोसी मात्र के लिए श्रेयस्कर है। और ऐसी दशा में उस बिचले राज्य का उदासीन रहना भी परमावश्यक है। ...बिचले राज्य दो मुहिए सांप होते हैं। वे मनमाने दोनों तरफ चल सकते हैं। हमेशा ध्यान लगाए रहना पड़ता है कि वे किधर चल रहे हैं, क्या कर रहे हैं। सदा सचेत रहना पड़ता है, वे या तो शत्रु या मित्र समझे जाते हैं। मित्र भाव के बिचले राज्य बड़े काम के होते हैं, जैसा कि बेल्जियम की उपयोगिता से इस समय देख पड़ा। बिचले राज्य बड़े बड़े राज्यों के आपस के बंदोबस्त से कभी कभी उनमें से एक ही के षाडयगुण्य के इलाके में कर दिए जाते हैं। ऐसी दशा इस समय अफग़ानिस्तान और स्याम की है। बनावटी राज्य में एक दोष और भी है। कभी कभी उसका राज्य मण्डलकृत बंदोबस्त वहां की प्रजा को पसंद नहीं आता और दंगा हुआ करता है। ऐसा ही अल्बानिया में देखने में आया। वहां बड़े बड़े राज्यों की ओर से चौकी बैठी हुई थी और वीड के कुमार विलियम वहां के राजा बनाए गए थे। वहां की प्रजा बिगड़ रही थी और अब मौका पाए जब बड़े राज्य युद्ध में फंसे रहे हैं, अल-बानिआ ने दूसरा राजा चुन लिया। इस तरह इस नई सृष्टि में कितनी ही कमी है, स्वयम् चिकित्सा में रोग है।[41]

11. रूम की भूल

रूम ने योरप की युद्धाग्नि में कूद कर अपने लिए बुरा किया है। वर्त्तमान युद्ध से उसका कुछ सम्बन्ध नहीं था, लड़ने वाले की जय पराजय से उसका कुछ विशेष बनता बिगड़ता नहीं था। तब उसने क्यों लड़ाई मोल ले ली। ...इसका एक मात्र कारण जर्मनी की बहकावट है। जर्मनी ने रूम को सब्ज बाग़ दिखलाया है और रूम उसकी लालच में पड़ गया है। ...हमारी सरकार ने रूम को बहुत कुछ भरोसा दिया और उसे तटस्थ रहने की बार बार सलाह दी किन्तु रूम जर्मनी के हाथ का खिलौना

बन गया। इसका परिणाम तो पीछे प्रकट होगा किन्तु रूम की दुर्बलता अभी से प्रकट हो रही है। मंत्रियों में से चार– करीब आधे ने इस्तीफ़ा दे दिया। रूम के सुलतान, युवराज और प्रधान वज़ीर आरम्भ से ही वर्त्तमान युद्ध में पड़ने के विरोधी हैं। केवल अनवर पाशा और उनके साथी नौजवान तुर्क युद्ध के पक्ष में हैं। या यों कहना चाहिए कि उन्होंने रूम के लोकमत पर लात मार कर लड़ाई ठानी है और योरप के तीन बड़े राज्यों को अपना शत्रु बनाया है। उसका आधा बल तो इस मतभेद में ही घट जायगा। दूसरे देश के मुसलमान रूम की इस भूल को समझ रहे हैं और वे इस युद्ध में उसका साथ देने को तैयार नहीं हैं। अफ्रिका के मुसलमानों के विषय में ऐसे ही तार आए हैं, हिन्दुस्तान के मुसलमान रूम की कार्यवाई पर अफ़सोस जताते हुए ब्रिटिश राजभक्ति पर अटल रहने की घोषणा कर रहे हैं। जर्मनी का कैसर जो इस ख्याल में पड़े हुए थे कि रूम को भड़का देने से संसार भर के मुसलमान बिगड़ जायेंगे। ...रूम की प्रजा भी इस लड़ाई के लिए वैसा उत्साह नहीं है जैसी जर्मनी या ऑस्ट्रिया की प्रजा में है। फ्रांस, इंग्लैंड, या रूम के राज्य में पड़े हुए किसी जर्मन या ऑस्ट्रियाई को आज तक यह कहते नहीं सुना कि हमें अपने कैसर की प्रजा कहलाना स्वीकार नहीं है। ...किन्तु रूम से युद्ध छिड़ते ही बर्मा और कलकत्ते में बसी हुई उसकी कितनी ही प्रजा ने ब्रिटिश गवर्नमेंट से प्रार्थना की है कि हम ब्रिटिश प्रजा समझे जायें और हमे ब्रिटिश प्रजा के अधिकार मिलें। इससे स्पष्ट है कि दूसरे देशों में बसी हुई रूम की प्रजा भी वर्त्तमान युद्ध में अपनी सरकार के विरुद्ध है। सो रूम ने भारी भूल की है और इसका प्रायश्चित उसको करना पड़ेगा।[42]

KPJ was quite sarcastic about the defeat of Turkey and in one of the editorial comments he wrote,

तुर्कों पर छिपकली चढ़ी है। जिधर चलते हैं उधर ही पिटते हैं। हिन्दुस्तानी सेना ने इधर बगदाद के पास अधिकार छीन लिया। उधर रूस ने सेना कैद कर ली। जिहाद का झंडा उठाने का जूजू तुर्कों के पास बहुत दिन से था। सबको डराया करते थे कि जहां उन्होंने जिहाद का झंडा खड़ा किया कि मुसलमान जहां होंगे वहीं खलीफ़ा के लिए बिगड़ खड़े होंगे। वह जूजू भी निकला पर नतीजा कुछ न हुआ। तुर्कों के शत्रु देश के मुसलमानों ने ज़रा साथ न दिया। अब वे फिर मिस्र की स्वेज़ नहर की तरफ़ रेंगते अंगरेज़ी विमानों को देख पड़े हैं। विपत्तिकाले विपरीतबुद्धि– की कहनत सिद्ध हो रही है। एक टर्की क्या कई टर्की मिल कर मिस्र की नहर पर सर पटकते रह जायंगे। ऐसी लंबी ठान जिस की पूर्त्ति हो नहीं सकती, ठाननी सिवा बुरे दिन के फेर के और क्या समझी जा सकती है।[43]

12. स्विट्ज़रलैंड कि स्थिति

...स्विट्ज़रलैंड प्रजातंत्र, विराज-राज्य है। अर्थात वहां राजा का नहीं, पंचायती राज्य है। आल्पस पहाड़ जो हिमालय का भाई है... स्विट्ज़रलैंड को अपने अंग में लिए हुए

है।... इन कैंटानों की अलग अलग राज्य-संस्थाएं हैं। सब विराज-राज्य हैं। ...पहले स्विट्ज़रलैंड एक तरह का एका करके थे जिसे हिन्दू-राज्यशास्त्र में 'अनुगुण' कहते हैं। पर नेपोलियन के बाद से ठीक एक सौ वर्ष हुए तबसे, वे संहति-राज्य बनाकर रहते हैं। इनकी संहति दांतों के बीच जीभ सी बिचारी है। ...स्विट्ज़रलैंड के विषय में भी योरोप के बड़े राज्यों में आपस में शर्त है कि वह उदासीन समझा जाएगा। उस पर कोई चढ़ाई न करेगा। वह 1815 ई. में उदासीनी कृत हुआ। पर आजकल षाड्गुण्य के धर्म पर शत्रु नहीं चल रहा है। जैसा कि बर्न हार्डी ने अपनी पुस्तक 'जर्मनी और भविष्य युद्ध' में कहा है, जर्मनी उदासीनी कृतता को कागज़ी पोश्तबंदी (Paper bulwark) समझती है।[44]

13. इंग्लैंड और युद्ध

रूस में कुछ लोग शिकायत करने लगे हैं कि इंग्लैंड युद्ध में अपना भाग पूरा नहीं कर रहा, वह दूसरों से कम साथ दे रहा। ...पर उनका अंग्रेज़ों को दोष देना बिलकुल बेजड़ है। इंग्लैंड एक सामुद्रिक बल का राज्य है। वह अपना मुख्य काम समुद्र पर कर रहा है। जर्मनी में माल रसद गोली बारूद की सामग्री बाहर से न पहुंच पाए इस का प्रयत्न भरपूर कर रहा है। अर्थात युद्ध की अवधि शत्रु के पर काट घटा रहा है। ...इसके आलावा इंग्लैंड एक दीर्घ सेना भी तैयार कर रही है जो मित्रदल का बल स्थगित हो जाने पर नवीन बनी रहेगी और शत्रु का सामना करने को ठीक मौके पर पहुंच सकेगी। ...यदि अंगरेज़ फ्रांस का साथ न देते तो आज जर्मनी का रंग कहीं तीखा होता। उसके लिए सारा संसार रोज़गार और धन के लिए खुला रहता। अंगरेज़ी सेना लाख सवा लाख सही, पर इंग्लैंड का युद्ध में मित्रों का साथ देना बहुत बड़ी बात है। मित्रों का पल्ला इंग्लैंड के साथ देने से बहुत मज़बूत पड़ गया। इंग्लैंड की छोटी सेना दाल में नमक की तरह अलबत्ता है, पर नमक बड़ी ज़रूरी चीज़ है। उसके बिना सब फीका रहता है।[45]

14. डारडनेल्स

...डारडनेल्स सर होने से भारत में गेहूं बहुत सस्ता हो जायगा। रूस में इतना गेहूं रुका हुआ है कि उसका कुछ भाग यहां भी आएगा। ...एक बार उन्नीसवीं सदी में (1808) अंगरेज़ी सेनापति डकवर्थ के द्वारा डारडनेल्स का मुहाना भेदा जा चुका है। इस बार भी वह भेदा जायगा और इस्तम्बुल फिर कांस्टेंटिनोपल हो जायगा। ...सोफिआ का गिरजा कांस्टेंटाइन सम्राट ने बनबाया था। वह सब गिरजा घरों का सम्राट है। अब इस के फिर गिरजा घर होने के दिन बाहर आए देख पड़ते हैं।[46]

These editorials written over a period of more than seven months (8 August 1914 to 13 March 1915) highlight the following concerns of KPJ:

(1) It is the first and the foremost duty of the Hindus and

Indians to fight on the side of the British, notwithstanding some reservation that "we might be having internally."

(2) Fighting on the side of the British is fighting a 'righteous war' (*dharma-yuddha*)—Germany was seen as being on the side of *adharma*—where there is *dharma*, the victory resides there.

(3) The Muslims of this land (India) must also be on the same side as the Hindus—there was no greater Holy Land than the battlefield.

(4) The Indian soldiers would bring laurels and preserve the glory of the British flag as well as of the famed Indian bravery.

(5) The 'Bengali brethren' were taking an unacceptable position when they sought a written undertaking from the government that they would not be expected to carry the injured on their backs. KPJ strongly taunted Bengalis by saying that nobody goes to the battlefield to do *babugiri*.

(6) Notwithstanding the extra-territoriality of the war, it was 'Our War' and an 'Indian War'. Helping the government in the War is indeed 'self-help'—None in the whole of Europe and Asia was as liberal as the British.

(7) Need for preparing for a long war, at least for three or four years. Though KPJ felt Russia could wage even a ten-year war because it was primarily an agricultural country, he did not expect the War to last that long.

(8) The Sikhs, Hindus, Muslims, the Baluchis, and soldiers of other native states considered France as their *swadesh* and a political pilgrimage centre (*tirtha*). European democracy rests on the fame of France. The merit (*punya*) earned by Indian soldiers in France would bear fruit in future.

(9) Unhappiness over Turkey joining hands with Germany despite divided opinion within the ruling establishment in Turkey itself and also amongst Muslims of other areas like Africa and India. Indeed, many Turks in Burma and Calcutta appealed to the British that they should be recognised as British subjects. Considering Turkey's decision to be a big mistake, KPJ expected that acquisition of Dardanelles by the Allies would make wheat cheaper for India.

(10) No justification for Russia's complaint about England not

fulfilling its role in the War. It was, as KPJ argued, the British navy that blocked the Germans and without British help to France, Germany could not have been countered. Though England's army was very small—almost like salt in the lentils—nonetheless, salt was indispensable. Things are tasteless without it.

(11) The War scenario was also used as an opportunity to express opinions about the bases of international diplomatic relations. For this, parallels from *Hindu Polity* were duly invoked, e.g. the 24-canton confederation of Switzerland was seen as *anuguna*. Further, in the context of the attempts of the Allies to create 'Neutralised States' such as Switzerland, a German view was recalled. KPJ cited Burn Hardy's work 'Germany and the Future War' which considered such states as 'paper bulwark' (*'kagazi poshtabandi'*).

The question of loyalty to the British Crown (*rajabhakti*) was so important for KPJ that he even suspended the conflict over the Bihari-Bengali question on which he had written a number of comments. He made an appeal:

> इस विषय पर युद्ध के अंत तक लिखा पढ़ी बंद रखी जायगी। ये पत्र सिर्फ राय बहादुर पूर्णेंदु नारायण सिन्हा और दूसरे बंगाली नेताओं को यह दिखाने को छापे जाते हैं कि उन्होंने अपने बिहारी भाइयों के भाव का यथेष्ट ख्याल न कर और समय बे-विचारे अपने नए निवासजात-स्वत्व पाने की देहि देहि मचाई। इस समय बिहार से हमारी यही प्रार्थना है की बंगाली भाइयों के उठाए झगड़े को मुलतवी रखे और राजभक्ति के पुनीत व्रत में दत्तचित रहे।[47]

Another editorial comment of KPJ is eye-catching:

> प्रत्युपकार की आशा से हम उपकार नहीं करते। हमारा धर्म ही है कि जिसके साथ हों संकट पड़ने पर उसके काम आएं। भारत ने इंग्लैंड से बहुत कुछ लाभ उठाया है। भारत को बहुत कुछ शिकायत और उलाहना भी इंग्लैंड को देना था, पर वह शिकायत और उलाहना इस समय एकदम भुला दिया। वह तन मन धन से इस समय राजा की सेवा में लगा हुआ है, साथ दे रहा है और अपना धर्म पालन कर रहा है। इसका बदला वह नहीं चाहता, क्योंकि ऐसा करना उसे अपनी पुरानी वीर प्रथा और अपना स्वभाव भूल जाना है। ईश्वर इंग्लैंड के राजा और भारत के महाराज को विजयी करे और हमारी पत रक्खे। और कुछ हम इस समय नहीं चाहते, दिन सबके फिरते हैं। भले साथ का भला फल होता है। पुष्प के साथ रेणु भी कहां कहां पहुंचती है। इंग्लैंड के साथ के कारण भारत भूमि के दिन फिर फिरेंगे। इस समय देश को वह संतोष हुआ है कि

जिसकी आशा स्वप्न में भी न थी। कुम्हलाई लता में अमृत सिंचन हो गया। भारतीयों को याद होगा कि वे अर्जुन, कृष्ण, और राम के वंशधर हैं। यह इंग्लैंड की सुसंगत का फल है, भारतीय योद्धा जो धर्म से सत्य और शौर्य की वेदी पर, जगत को स्वंत्रता दान देने वाले फ्रांस के लिए अपना रक्त गिरा रहा है, वह उस रक्त से इस देश को मुक्ति दे रहा है। वीरता का आदर करने वाले अँगरेज़ क्या कभी भारत को भूलेंगे? अपने रण प्रयास से ही भारत ने फ्रांस को मानो मोल ले लिया। प्रसिद्ध स्वतंत्रता प्रेमी सिलवन लेवी ने 'हिन्दू सेना' को अपनी सेना कह कर अपनाया। मीराबो और नेपोलियन का देश आज भारत को गले लगाता है। कोई कहता कि यह दिन आने वाला है तो वह ज्योतिषी हम से भी दुत्कारा जाता।[48]

Since it was the time of war, parallels were drawn between the 'Hindu' war ethics and the ongoing war. In an editorial piece 'Vijayadashami', KPJ wrote:

पुराने समय में आज के दिन हिंदुओं की शत्रुओं पर चढाई की तैयारी होती थी, उनकी युद्ध-दुंदुभि बजती थी। आज ऐसा संयोग है कि हिंदू धर्म के पक्ष में लोहा बजा रहे हैं और अपना लहू गिरा धर्म का विकराल करवाल लोहित कर रहे हैं। पर स्त्री-हरण करने वाले, दूसरों का घर जलाने वाले, दूसरों का घर लूटने वाले अधर्मनिष्ठ सबल शत्रु से छोटी हिन्दू सेना भिड़ रही है। परिणाम वही होगा जो सनातन से होता आया है। धर्म की ही पत करतार रखता है। हिंदुओं की पत वह इस वार भी रक्खेगा।[49]

For KPJ, "Vijayadashami is a day of 'national victory' and Rama became an ideal of Hindu *Maryādā* and *Puruṣottama* because he took pain and trouble for others and was brave and patient".[50] Caste does not matter, if anyone has a sense of sacrifice. "If an *Ahir* is brave, then the *vedi* could be built for him, but not for the famous intellectual or generous person, even if he dies."[51] In addition, "Even the *'jangali'* Hanuman of the South has been given the status of divinity for his bravery."[52] Parallels were drawn between Rama and Ravana representing *dharma* and *adharma* on the one hand and the two warring groups of Europe on the other, in which "Hindus are fighting and bleeding in favor of virtue." As far as the nation and community are concerned, they overlap in KPJ's view and when he talks about Hindu society, he includes every community without differentiation, "The Hindu society has unanimously decided to extend their support to the Government in the War. This is a matter of great satisfaction."[53] Further, describing the sacrifices of Ganga Singh of Kangra and Darwan Singh of Punjab in the European battle KPJ wrote, "To fly the victory flag in Europe, could this be an effort of one community? In this country, the unity of the community *(jati)* lies even in the words 'Hindu *Jati*' only.[54] It is important to note here that KPJ saw no antagonism, contradiction between the British colonialism and Indian subjugation. When he talked of the revival of old days, which means the revival of old/ 'Hindu' days, implicitly the medieval period was a 'dark age' for him.

'Hindu' war ethics was also drawn from the *Mahābhārata*, *Dharmaśāstras* and the *Arthaśāstra*. According to KPJ,

> The Hindu did not kill these people in the war: the sleeping warrior, the thirsty warrior, who is not willing to fight, those whose weapons have fallen, the enemy who becomes a beggar/*fakir*, those who are fleeing, those who are moving carelessly, those who are engaged in eating, or are mad or eccentric, the wounded, those who have become weak in the battle, those who have not waged war and trust you, those who have just started preparation and have not completed mobilisation, the enemy who is melting with grief, the artisans, the coolie, who are living outside the district (*kataka*), the labourers of the district, the messengers, the medical help, the *vargi* (soldiers-special?), standing at the door, who feel threatened, women and children, the beggar, and who is in a crisis.[55]

The continuous use of Hindu symbols and scriptures–*Rāmacaritamānas*, *Mahābhārata*, *maryādā-puruṣottama* Rāma, celebration of *Vijayadaśamī*, as the 'national' victory, Kṛṣṇa, Hindu *jati*, Āryan community, Āryan religion, Āryāvarta, etc., (Hindu/ Āryan were interchangeably used)–might have created different impact or distinct impact especially among the Muslim community. It is possible that Rāma of KPJ was not the belligerent Rāma of the Sangh Parivar, but the *maryādā puruṣottama* or the most perfect among the men. It is true that everybody had his own Rāma, as KPJ himself admits, "The Hindus have been writing the *Rāmāyaṇa* in their language again and again. From Vālmīki to Romesh Chandra Dutt, they became famous because they wrote the *Rāmacarita*. Any language of the Hindus does not fall in the category of literature, until they do not describe the *Rāmacarita*."[56] At the same time it is also possible that it is not fall easy—not at all natural—for some sections, especially the Muslims to identify with Rāma. Under such circumstances the image of Rāma was more alienating than attractive especially for the Muslims. KPJ, perhaps, was not unaware of this alienating potential of Rāma in a multi-faith society like ours. However, words have their social context and specific implication. 'Rāma' is not a simple word, shorn of history or legacy. Rāma became the symbol of projection of 'Hindu' masculinity, virility, and power and of the Hinduism. These words that have been mired in controversy and conflict do not become innocent simply because KPJ chooses to use them, as a renowned scholar. In this context, the selection of these symbols might have had a negative impact on the 'nationalist' mobilisation. At a personal level, KPJ might not have had communal feelings, as he himself expressed happiness over the way Hardinge handled the Kanpur Riots, "The people of the entire country are overwhelmed by your love for the people. By releasing the accused of Kanpur Riots and by repairing the damaged portion of the mosque and making them happy, you have respected not only the feelings of the Indian Muslims but of the Muslims of the entire world."[57] However, the use of Hindu symbols and metaphors could be read differently by different people, especially the Muslims.

The *Rāmacarita* is about a small-sized army fighting a force far greater in number. But large as it was, it was a force that did not have virtue on its side and had gone to the extent of kidnapping another person's wife, burning down houses and plundering others' properties. And at the end of the war, there was the victory of *dharma*, "The prestige of righteousness is protected by God and the prestige of the Hindus will be protected this time also as it has been happening since the *sanatan* times."[58] And finally, "India will get its due share for the brave feats performed by the Indian soldiers."[59] Its due 'share' was, perhaps, getting *Swarāj*, as he also wrote in the introductory editorial and at other places as well as in the case of Ireland. Since Rāma is his ideal hero, *Swarāj* is equal to *Rāmrājya* (the Rule of Rāma, traditionally regarded as the ideal political and social order). KPJ picked up such words from the lexicon of Hindu society and gave them a new and unique dimension, projecting an ideal social and political order, "The performance of Ramlila is not the annual repetition of the defeat of the enemy, but the celeberation of the glory and pride of the victory."[60]

KPJ took the religiosity of a thing to be its unquestioned proof. His otherwise sharp vision is unable to explode the walls of the caste system and the violent religious traditions. Religion is all-encompassing/accommodating for him, if one performs the religious duty of sacrifice. Religious identity is even more important to him than the national identity, "Now, the Turkish have no love for the religion, they have more love for politics—like the Germans, they love the Fatherland, not the Quran or Islam. In such a situation, like Khan Bahadur Ajijuddin, it is natural that the Muslims of India will pray for the coming of an Arab Government under the English flag."[61]

The above editorials and editorial comments clearly show the pro-British position of the *Pataliputra* and its editor. However, it has to be understood in the context of time. The outbreak of the First World War in 1914 gave a new lease of life to the nationalist movement which had been dormant since its heady days. Britain's difficulty was India's 'opportunity.' This opportunity was seized, in different ways and with varying success, firstly by the Ghadar revolutionaries abroad, and secondly by Lokamanya Tilak, Annie Besant, and the Home Rule League in India. The Ghadarites attempted a violent overthrow of British rule, while the Home Rule Leaguers launched a nation-wide agitation for securing Home Rule or *Swaraj*. There was another response, from the civil society (largely the elite) in the form of sycophancy to the British rule, and they offered all kinds of assistance to them in the War. In Bihar, a series of such meetings were organised by the upper caste elites to show their loyalty to the British empire, such as by the Bhumihar-Brahman Sabha, Maithil Sabha, etc.[62] Such meetings of loyalty to the British Crown were held in different parts of the country and even in England:

> इस समय लन्दन में जितने भी मुख्य मुख्य हिंदुस्तानी हैं उन्होंने राजभक्ति सूचक पत्र स्टेट सेक्रेटरी की मार्फत सम्राट की सेवा में भेजा। उसमें लिखा है की इस युद्ध के समय हम सब हिंदुस्तानी सदा की भांति अपने ब्रिटिश साम्राज्य की जय मानते हैं। भीतरी प्रबंध के विषय में सरकार से हमारा मतभेद शांति के समय हो सकता है किन्तु इस समय, जबकि एक बाहरी शत्रु से सामना है, हिंदुस्तानी मात्र ब्रिटिश विजय के लिए हृदय से उद्योग करने में तत्पर है। स्टेट सेक्रेटरी ने चिट्ठी सम्राट की सेवा में भेजते हुए हमारी राजभक्ति की सराहना की है।[63]

The above details show that the First World War provided an occasion for the Indian elite including non-residents to demonstrate their loyalty to the British Crown. This was the political-cultural milieu in which KPJ was the editor of the *Pataliputra*. It is important to note here that the Indian nationalist leaders, including Lokamanya Tilak, decided to support the war effort of the government. Sentiments of loyalty to the British empire and of the desire to defend it were loudly and widely expressed.[64] But, as

Jawaharlal Nehru has pointed out in his *Autobiography*, 'There was little sympathy with the British in spite of loud profession of loyalty. Moderates and Extremists alike learnt with satisfaction of the German victories. There was no love for Germany, of course, only the desire to see our own rulers humbled'.[65] The hope was that a graceful Britain would acknowledge India's loyalty with economic and political concessions enabling India to take a long step towards self-government, and that Britain would apply to India the principles of democracy for which she and the Allies were claiming to be fighting the War.

(B) Language and Script

The question of language and was another important concern of KPJ's journalistic writings. Language and script was one of the essential concerns of Indian reformers in the nineteenth century, a basic constituent of their discourse of progress and reform. Establishing Hindi as a public language and creating a group identity around it were themselves products of this concern. The Hindi movement started as an organised effort in the 1860s in Banaras, but it soon got widespread support from Agra to Calcutta.[66] The intelligentsia of Bihar had a significant role to play on this issue. Backed by support of government officials, the movement was able to establish Hindi written in the Nagari script, as the official language of Bihar in 1880, whereas in the United Provinces this happened only in 1890.

KPJ's love for Hindi could be seen from his writings from his young days. However, as the editor of the *Pataliputra*, KPJ's love for Hindi is clear from his introductory editorial, "पाटलिपुत्र के संचालकों की अभिलाषा है कि यह पत्र देश की सेवा में सदा अग्रसर रहे, देश के सामयिक पत्रों का बल बढ़ावे और हिंदी भाषा के साहित्य तथा सर्वोपरि हिन्दू धर्म का प्रधान पोषक हो।"[67] (It is the desire of the Directors of the *Pataliputra* that this weekly should be a frontrunner in the service of the nation, it must enhance the strength of the contemporary weeklies of the country, and it should be the main nourisher of the literature of the Hindi language and above all the Hindu *dharma*). The purpose of the weekly could appear thus as a duty and service to the nation and the 'Hindu community'. The influence of Bharatendu Harishchandra and Mahavir Prasad Dwivedi is clearly visible here. Echoing Harishchandra, Dwivedi wrote, "The progress of dharma of the country rests on propagating the mother tongue and on the growth and enrichment of national literature. To strive and work for the progress of Hindi, therefore, is presently the first and foremost duty of every patriot and right-thinking man."[68]

Bihar had a different dimension to the language and script politics. It was between Hindi vs Maithili, Hindi vs Bengali and Kaithi vs Nagari. KPJ felt proud about the progress of Hindi in Bihar but, with some regret, "Bihar is a Hindi-speaking province. The province has such pride in and love for Hindi, which are not seen in any other province. Bihar has monopolised the present Hindi literature. The colloquial Hindi of the poetry system, started by Late Babu Ayodhya Prasad Bihari will continue till the existence of Hindi. There are very few English educated people who do not read or write Hindi. In that matter, Bihar is more progressive than the centres of Hindi like the Antarveda and Awadha. Despite the huge progress of Hindi, there was no respect for the Hindi language in the Courts."[69] In his eyes, this was happening because of the use of Kaithi script. KPJ wrote two editorials— 'Maithil Bhasha' and 'Kaithi ya Nagari'—and made several editorial comments over these controversies.

मैथिल भाषा :

> मैथिल लोग कई बरसों से अपनी भाषा अलग प्रतिष्ठित किया चाहते हैं। इस पर हिंदी के पक्षपाती मिथिला में और बाहर, रुष्ट होते हैं। उनका कहना है कि जब सारे देश की यह कोशिश है कि जहाँ तक हो सके एक भाषा हिंदी का प्रचार हिंदुओं में हो, मैथिल भाषा चलाने वालों की चेष्टा छप्पर-नीचे खीचने वालों के कर्म समान कुत्सित और गर्हित है। मैथिल लोग इससे चिढ़ कर अब यह कहने लगे हैं कि हिंदी तो कोई भाषा ही नहीं है। **मिथिला के ब्राह्मणेतर जाति वाले अपनी साधु भाषा हिंदी ही मानते हैं। यही विचार गोप महासभा का है।** पर मिथिला के ब्राह्मण-लोग मैथिल बोली को भाषा का दर्जा देना चाहते हैं, वे अपनी भाषा अलग चाहते हैं। ऐसी दशा में समझाना या रोना वृथा है। जो लोग अपनी भाषा अलग करना चाहते हैं, वे भले ही विलग हो जाएं। हिंदी वालों को कोई रोक टोक नहीं करना चाहिए। क्योंकि कल्याण से कल्याण क्यों न हो, पर जो लोग उसे न चाहें तो दूसरों को अधिकार नहीं कि उनपर ज़ोर करे। यदि मिथिला के लोग अपने को अलग किया चाहते हैं तो उन्हें ज़बरदस्ती रोकने का अधिकार हम को नहीं है। **भाषा मनुष्य के लिए है, कुछ मनुष्य भाषा के लिए नहीं पैदा किया गया है। भारत की देशीयता यही है कि टुकड़े टुकड़े हों, सदा अपने से विलग होते रहना।** ऐसी दशा में सनातन रीति के अनुसार मिथिला के ब्राह्मण यदि आर्यावर्त के हिंदुओं से भाषा में अलग होना चाहें तो कोई नई बात नहीं है। हों, भले ही अलग हो जायं। चाहे यह बात कितनी भी हम लोगों को एकता-प्रिय दृष्टि से ना-गवार गुज़रे, **पर मूल बात यह नहीं भूलना**

चाहिए कि बलात्कार से प्रेम नहीं होता। मनुष्य को सदा अधिकार है कि अपनी भाषा वह चुन सकता है। वह अपनी भाषा का विधाता है। रही यह कि सरकार उनकी भाषा को तसलीम करे। इसका फैसला तभी हो सकता है जब मिथिला के अधिक निवासी वहां के ब्राह्मणों की भाषा सम्बन्धी बात मान लें। जिस भाषा को वहां वाले अधिक लोग चाहेंगे वही वहां स्कूलों में और अदालत में वर्ती जायगी। यदि अधिक लोग मैथिली चाहेंगे तो सरकार को मैथिली की प्रतिष्ठा करनी होगी। नहीं तो जब तक हिंदी के पक्षपाती अधिक हैं तब तक हिंदी ही वहां माननीय होगी। **मैथिली का झगड़ा इस बात की प्रमाण सुमिरनी का एक चमकता दाना है कि हिन्दू एक नहीं हो सकते।** जितने बड़े चक में यह हिंदी मैथिली का झगड़ा उठा है उस प्रदेश में कभी मुसलमानों ने मैथिली उर्दू या बिहारी उर्दू या सैयदी उर्दू चलाने या अलग करने की कामना न की। पर **'सच कहे तो मारा जाय' कटु-सत्य सुनते लोगों को खलेगा कि हिंदुओं से मुसलमान इस विषय में श्रेष्ठ जाति हैं।** इसलिए यदि सरकार उनका मान अधिक करे तो कोई अचरज की बात नहीं है। पर तौभी लोग सरकार को ही दोष देने की प्रवृत्ति रक्खेंगे। अपना मुंह अपने करतब के आईने में न देखेंगे।[70] (emphasis is mine).

The editorial is an early piece of evidence on how layered the language politics was in a place like Bihar, and it tells us how caste as a factor cannot be discounted (between Brahmins and non-Brahmins) in this debate which has by and large been characterised to have been a Hindu-Muslim question. On the testimony of new histories of Bihar, we can say that Bihar has had a tense relationship with the mainstream Hindi nationalist movement. KPJ, too, comes across as a Hindu-Hindi nationalist, if we go by his tone and the cultural material he mobilises to build his arguments. However, if we take a second look, we would also find a sense of irony in his diagnosis before he delivers a solution which is nothing less than the advocacy for self-determination of languages and linguistic nationalisms.

KPJ talked about two kinds of splits in the Hindu society on the question of language, especially, with regard to Hindi projected as the sole, unifying language of the Hindus. The editorial, cited above, constituted a comment on the differences between the advocates of Maithili and Hindi on the one hand, and those between the upper-castes (Brahmin) and other non-Brahmin castes (Gopas/ Yadavas, here) over the status of Maithili vis-a-vis Hindi. We would do well to remember that the weekly reported a proposal passed by the Gopa Sabha of Bhagalpur,[71] in which the Gopas objected to Brahmins and Kayasthas—the two most literate and educated castes of Mithila—of misappropriating the role of sole representatives of Mithila region, people, language and culture, and said that Hindi was the *Sadhu Bhasha* for them, and not Maithili. KPJ noted with a sense of despondency that there was no point explaining the situation or crying over it, and cited it as one more piece of evidence of how the Hindus were doomed to remain disunited. He wrote with sane anguish: "Fragmentation is the temperament of India. In such a situation, as per the *sanātan* system, if the Brahmins of Mithila want to separate themselves from the Hindus of the *Āryāvarta*, then it is not a new thing. If they want, they can get separated. Even if it is unpalatable from the standpoint of the unity of the land, it must not be forgotten that love does arise out of *rape*. If the people of Mithila want to separate themselves, then we do not have the right to forcibly stop them."[72]

Towards the end of the editorial he exhorted the Hindus to learn a lesson or two from the Muslims who had wisely desisted from advocating a 'Bihari Urdu', 'Maithili Urdu', or 'Syedi Urdu'![73] So, while the sense of despondency is unmistakable, he also ultimately reasoned that the Hindiwallas should not use force to make Hindi acceptable to the warring groups of Mithila. Although KPJ was a supporter of Hindi and Nagari, here he appears in favour of persuasion and self-determination: a far cry from the standard refrain of Hindiwallas then or now!

On the question of Hindi-Bengali dispute, KPJ offered another solution. In Dhanbad, the Bengalis had made Bangla as the official language of the court. The magistrates were generally Bengali. When the Bihar government ordered the use of Hindi in the court, the Bengalis sent a memorandum to the Lieutenant Governor saying that the Marwaris understand Bengali and not Hindi and the language of Dhanbad was Bangla! They had also started refusing applications written in Hindi and had consciously ignored the Biharis. KPJ suggested the boycott of the Bengali lawyers, "It would not be enough if the all Biharis take oath on this acute discrimination/suppression that they will not take assistance from the Bengali advocates".[74] It needs to be underlined that on the question of Hindi-Maithili controversy, KPJ advocated self-determination (although with pain), but on the question of Bengali-Hindi controversy he talked about the boycott of the Bengali advocates!

When efforts were being made by the Muslims of Madras and Bombay for the promotion of Urdu, the Gujaratis and the Marathas had criticised them. KPJ felt surprised, when some of the Hindi newspapers mocked their effort. He wrote,

> कितने ही मुसलमानों की यह इच्छा है कि हिन्दुस्तान में सब प्रान्तों के मुसलमान उर्दू पढ़ें, उनके बच्चों की प्रारम्भिक शिक्षा उर्दू में हो और उर्दू ही उनकी मातृभाषा कहलावे। इस इच्छा के वशीभूत होकर जस्टिस अब्दुर्रहीम ने मदरास की यूनिवर्सिटी में उर्दू के लिए स्थान ढूंढा और बम्बई प्रान्त के मुसलमान पूना बम्बई आदि शहरों में अपने बालकों के लिए मदरसे खोलाते खुलवाते हैं। बम्बई की तरफ तो शायद इसी के लिए मुसलमानों की एक शिक्षा समिति हर साल बैठती है। इस साल भी बैठी थी। गुजराती मराठे आदि मुसलमानों के इस उद्योग की निंदा करते हैं। उनका ऐसा करना स्वाभाविक है किन्तु यह देखकर आश्चर्य होता है कि कुछ हिन्दी पत्र भी मुसलमानों के इस प्रयत्न की दिल्लगी उड़ाते हैं। समझ में नहीं आता कि जो हिन्दी पत्र हिन्दी को राष्ट्रभाषा के आसन पर विराजमान देखना चाहते हैं वे मुसलमानों को उसी का दुर्गम मार्ग सुगम बनाते देख क्यों हंसते हैं और लेखा-जोखा लगा कर दिखाते हैं कि मुसलमान उन प्रान्तों में उर्दू चलाना चाहते हैं जहां इस समय उस को कोई नहीं पूछता! हिन्दी वाले जहां केवल 'हिन्दी राष्ट्रभाषा भवतु' का प्रस्ताव पास करके बैठे रहते हैं वहीं मुसलमान भाई स्कूल खुलवाकर उर्दू प्रचार का उद्योग कर रहे हैं। इस से हिन्दी वाले लज्जित होकर उनसे सबक क्या सीखेंगे उल्टे उनकी हंसी उड़ा रहे हैं। लेकिन हम तो मुसलमानों के इस काम की सराहना ही करेंगे क्योंकि इस से भी हिन्दी प्रचार का रास्ता खुलता दिखाई देता है। उर्दू हिन्दी में बहुत कुछ समानता है, दोनों की क्रिया, विभक्ति और सर्वनाम एक हैं केवल अक्षर और शब्द प्रयोग में भेद है। इसके कारण हिन्दी उर्दू में भारी भेद पड़ते जाने पर भी उर्दू प्रचार से हिन्दी प्रचार से बड़ी सहायता मिलेगी। इस समय जहां उर्दू को कोई नहीं पूछता और हिन्दी को भी कोई नहीं पूछता वहां के मुसलमान जब उर्दू बोलने चालने और लिखने पढ़ने लगेंगे तो उसका प्रभाव वहां के हिन्दुओं पर भी पड़ेगा और उनका भी उर्दू की ओर झुकना सम्भव है। फिर उर्दू से उनका ध्यान हिन्दी की ओर अवश्य जायगा जैसा कि पंजाब में हो रहा है। इसलिए हम तो समझते हैं कि मुसलमानों का यह उद्योग हिन्दी की भी भलाई करने वाला है।[75]

On the question of language, KPJ appears expressing his cosmopolitan desire and the necessity of multilingualism. On the one hand, he advocated vociferously the use of the local/regional language (*Deshbhasha*) and praised both the Japanese and Bengalis for that and regretted that not enough was being done in that direction in the Āryāvarta and Bihar. Simultaneously, KPJ was convinced that learning to use English was no less important, for, that provided international exposure and larger spread of ideas.[76] English for KPJ was the language of the world and Hindi, the language of the region to address the local masses. It seems that KPJ's notion of the Āryāvarta was restricted to the Hindi-speaking areas only.

It appears that KPJ's arguments were an extension of the line propagated by the earlier magazines of Bihar– *Sudarshan* and *Bihar Bandhu*. Madhav Mishra, the editor of *Sudarshan* wrote an article, '*Hindi Bhasha*' in February 1900, arguing that the progress and prosperity of a nation and its religion depend on the development of the mother tongue and national literature. Similar views were expressed by Pandit Keshavaram Bhatt, one of the early writer-journalists of modern Bihar and the editor of *Bihar Bandhu*.[77]

KPJ's understanding of the necessity of multilingualism were reflected in the commercial advertisements and he had no hesitation in giving space for advertisements focusing on speedy and magical learning of English language in the several issues of the weekly:

असली इंगलिश टीचर।

यह इतनी सहल है की बिना गुरु के तीन मास में अंग्रेजी लिखना पढ़ना और बातचीत करना बखुबी सीख लो। इसमें ग्रामर के ट्रांसलेशन और इडीएम, हजारों मुहावरे के शब्द और फिकरे मिलेंगे घर बैठे मिडिल पास की लीयाकत कर लो, मूल्य 1, 200 पृष्ठ वाली।

In another advertisements:

अंग्रेजी की सीढ़ी।

बाबू बनने की सहज उपाय।

इसमें एक ऐसा इंजन लगा है जिससे वर्षों का इल्म घंटों में सीख लो। नागरी पढ़ा अंग्रेजी उर्दू सीख लेगा। उर्दू पढ़ा अंग्रेजी नागरी सीख लेगा। उस्ताद की कोई जरूरत नहीं। नाम गाँव लिख लेना तो मिनटों में आता है। अंग्रेजी में बातचीत तार चिट्ठी ग्रामर आदि को सिखाने में रेल के तुल्य है। मूल्य 1/– डाक मूल्य माफ।

पता– मैनेजर श्रीविल्वेश्वर यन्त्रालय, सदर मेरठ।

लेखक की आवश्यकता।

गया के लक्ष्मी प्रेस में एक ऐसे आदमी की आवश्यकता है जो हिंदी और उर्दू का अच्छा लेखक हो और अंग्रेजी भी इतना अवश्य जानता हो की वह अंग्रेजी का भाषान्तर कर सके। प्रार्थना पत्र के साथ साथ लेखों के नमूने भी आने चाहिए। मासिक वेतन 30/

पता– लक्ष्मी नारायण लाल वकील

मालिक 'लक्ष्मी प्रेस', औरंगाबाद, गया। (14.11.14)

These were indeed commercial advertisements, and yet they reflect the policy decision of the weekly. It appears that the editor—KPJ, an advocate of the Hindi language and Nagari script—was not only aware about the necessity of multilingualism but also of the pragmatic role of English language, in which he himself was trained in India and England. It was a reflection of the understanding of

KPJ 'the international' and KPJ 'the national' on the language issue. Of course, the material requirements for running the weekly were an important consideration, and that was why the policy of carrying these particular advertisement was followed; but there had to be a process of selection at work. That English was seen as the language of opportunity, access and communication is obvious from these advertisements and its editor saw nothing wrong in publishing them. Notwithstanding, the basic framework of Hindi, Hindu and Hindustan remained the overall thrust of the weekly. The consensus on Hindi among nationalist leaders before 1920 concealed different agendas. What Malviya, Tilak and Lajpat Rai shared was a cultural affiliation to Hindi as the essentially 'Indian' language because of its Hindu core; Gandhi's support instead was for Hindi as the language of *swadeshi*, the antithesis to English, and he considered Hindi to be the *spoken* language of village India that transcended divides of literature, script, and religion. For this reason, he later rejected Hindi as too identified with Hindu interests and supported Hindustani.[78]

The weekly reproduced several articles from the reputed Hindi magazines like the *Saraswati*, *Jayaji Pratap*, *Bharatmitra*, etc., and invited several reputed Hindi scholars like Ramavatar Sharma, Haraprasad Sastri, etc., to contribute to it. Therefore, as a promoter of Hindi, KPJ provided a separate column, 'साहित्य प्रसंग' (Sahitya Prasang). Besides this, poems, stories, novels (translated from other languages as well), and other news and articles related to the progress of Hindi language and literature were also carried. The poems published in the weekly largely concentrated on the national anthems of different countries, such as of England,[79] France,[80] Belgium,[81] etc. Hindu regeneration, pride, valour, masculinity, and *vira rasa* are also the recurring features of the weekly:

1. आत्मस्मरण

प्रवासियों, भारतवर्ष वासियों!
हेय आर्यवर्यो रणबांकुरे सभी।
हे धर्मधीरो अभिमान हिन्द के
कृतार्थ है आज देश, पा तुम्हें।।
थे विश्व में ज्यों हम श्रेष्ठ, त्यों कभी
कोई हुआ या फिर हो सकेगा।
आदेश था मान्य सदा हमारा
आचार्य मणि हम सदा विश्व के रहे

दे कष्ट कोई खग या मृगों को
हिंसा करै निर्बल जीव, कीट की।
तो हिन्दुओं के मृदु प्राण हों दुखी–
थी यों हमारी दृढ़ विश्व–बन्धुता।।
तिरस्क्रिया हो यदि न्याय धर्म की
तो हिन्दुओं को वह सह्य हो कहां?
है यौन हमारे बलवीर्य की कथा
ऐसे हमारे रण का गुरुत्व था।
अखण्ड है भारतखण्ड–वीरता
प्रचण्ड है आर्य–घमण्ड चण्डता।।
(एक भारतीय प्रजा, पाटलिपुत्र, 5.12.1914, p. 2)

2. ...वहां आज बहती है गंगा की धारा

भागे गिर गए पर गोली न चलाना।
दुखी दीन को भूल कर मत सताना।।
सदा बच्चे और औरत को बचाना।
कभी हाथ मत बे–बसों पर उठाना।।
बहक, नाम पुरुखों का मत तुम डुबोना।
सपूतों बड़ों की बड़ाई न खोना।।
सदा बंस मरजाद का ध्यान रखना।
चरित द्रोन भीखम का अभिमान रखना।।
प्रताप और गोविन्द का मान रखना।
अयोध्या सिंह उपाध्याय (हमारे सपूत, पाटलिपुत्र, 26.12.1914, p. 2)

3. ...गुरखा, सिक्ख, डोगरा, सेना सारी

राजपूत रणवीर करो युद्ध की तैयारी
ब्रिटिश सिंह की ध्वजा धार सज–धज से धाओ
युद्ध भूमि से शीघ्र शत्रु को मार हटाओ
पुरखों की विख्यात वीरता विशद बड़ाई
नहीं भूलना ब्रिटिश छत्र की सुख छाया को
रक्षित रकना आर्यवंश की यश–काया को
श्रीधर पाठक (युद्ध–पुकार, पाटलिपुत्र, 27.2.1915, p. 2)

These are few lines of the above mentioned poems. However, the weekly was loaded with such poems. Publishing poems was one of the striking features of the Hindi publications at that time and it became the medium of almost everything: apart from literary enjoyment (*rasasvadan*), verse was the vehicle of religious discourse and controversy, social reform, women's upliftment, and political awakening.[82]

Script: Nagari or Kaithi

One of the sustained controversial issues at the time was the use of script: Nagari or Kaithi, an issue which was also interlinked with the use of language. During the British colonial period, the use of Kaithi was discouraged, except in Bihar, where it was made the official script of government offices and courts. As a result, it is also known as the Bihar script. Elsewhere it was used mainly by the Kayasthas, and Brahmins made up mainly of scribes and clerks. The name Kaithi is derived from Kayastha, which means 'scribe' in Sanskrit. Until the early twentieth century, Kaithi was widely used, but since then it has been largely replaced by Devanagari or other scripts, although it is apparently used to some extent in personal correspondence in rural areas.

The Government of Bengal, acting on the advice of the British Indian Association and others, decided on 24 March 1893 to adopt Nagari in place of Kaithi as the script to be used for writing the vernacular in the courts and offices in Bihar. There is plenty of evidence of the efforts made by educated people to support Nagari for official use in Bihar. The movement began with democratic aspirations, and the intelligentsia was trying to make use of a favourable situation created by the government's policy of introducing the vernacular in the courts and schools of Bihar. The role of the Hindi intelligentsia was crucial for the ultimate success of the Hindi movement in Bihar. The Bihar Landholders' Association and the Bhagalpur Landholders' Association also came forward to help the cause of Hindi in Devanagari script. The Muslim members of these Associations favoured the introduction of Urdu in Persian script as the court language.[83]

In the Hindi-Urdu and Kaithi-Nagari debate, KPJ advocated Hindi with Nagari script. The demand for Hindi with Nagari script in Bihar was growing because of its expanding social base. KPJ as the editor of the *Pataliputra* provided a forum for the debate on Kaithi versuș Nagari and invited opinions over the issue and opined that when the Nagari script was taught in the school, the text books of the schools were printed in the Nagari, and the papers of the entire province were being printed and read in Nagari; in such a situation the government papers should not be printed in Kaithi.[84] KPJ wrote a long editorial comment in favour of the Nagari script:

बिहार हिंदी भाषी प्रान्त है। हिंदी की उन्नति और हिंदी से प्रेम जैसा इस प्रान्त में है

> उससे अधिक दूसरी जगह नहीं। वर्तमान हिंदी साहित्य पर बिहार ने अपना सिक्का जमा दिया है। स्वर्गवासी बाबू अयोध्या प्रसाद बिहारी की चलाई हुई बोलचाल की भाषा में काव्य प्रथा जब तक हिंदी है जारी रहेगी। अंगरेज़ी पढ़े लिखे लोगों में ऐसे यहाँ बहुत कम हैं जो हिंदी न लिखते पढ़ते हों। इस बात में बिहार हिंदी-केंद्र अन्तर्वेद और अवध से बढ़ा हुआ है। किन्तु एक बात की शिकायत है। हिंदी का इतना प्रचार होते हुए भी हिंदी के अक्षरों की यहां की अदालत में अवमानना है। एक भदेस, मैली और भ्रान्त लिखावट जिसे कैथी कहते हैं, प्रचलित है। इसके टाइप भी सरकारी छापाखाने में बन गए हैं! हिंदी अक्षरों को छोड़ कैथी का बर्तना हीरे को फेंक कंकड़ी अपनाना है। बिहार के लोगों का इस पर ध्यान तो ज़रूर गया पर उचित उपाय उन्होंने अबतक न किया कि मैली लिपि निकाल बहार किया जाय। यहां छोटे बड़े सभी नागरी लिपि जानते हैं। अपर प्राइमरी से ऊंची कक्षा तक नागरी पढ़ाई जाती है। फिर मुसलमानों के कैथी से दांत खट्टे रहते हैं। वे नागरी लिपि को आसानी से सीख सकते हैं। इसका सबूत मध्य प्रदेश में मिल रहा है जहां नागरी अदालतों में जारी है। सय्यद बिलग्रामी भी नागरी की उत्तमता और सरलता स्वीकार कर चुके हैं। ऐसी दशा में यदि बिहार में थोड़ा भी आंदोलन किया जाय तो पुनीत नागरी लिपि का प्रचार हो जाय। मिथिला संस्कृत की भूमि है, पर वहां अदालतों में कैथी लिखी जाय! बिहार हिंदी की भूमि है, वहां हिंदी के अक्षरों को स्थान मिलाना चाहिए। यदि इस विषय पर स्थान स्थान पर कुछ लोग उठ खड़े हों और रईस, क़ानून पेश और सर्वसाधारण से सम्मति पत्र ले हमारे पास भेजें तो हम गवर्नमेन्ट से इस विषय में निवेदन कर कम से कम सरकारी कागज़ों पर नागरी छपवाने की कोशिश करें। इस विषय के जो पत्र आवें उनके ऊपर 'नागरी' एक कोने पर लिखा रहे और वे मुरादपुर पोस्ट ओफिस (बांकीपुर) के पते से भेजे जायं।[85]

(...Despite the huge progress of Hindi, there is the humiliation of Hindi script in the courts. Kaithi is being used, which is a clumsy, dirty, and confusing script. Its typefaces have also been made in the government press! The adoption of Kaithi, after leaving out Hindi, is like throwing away the diamond and retaining the pebble. The Muslims are also reluctant to use Kaithi. They can learn the Nagari script easily. The proof of that is coming from Madhya Pradesh, where Nagari has been used in the courts. The superiority and simplicity of the Nagari has also been accepted by Syed Hussain Bilgrami. In such a situation, even a small movement in Bihar will help the cause of the holy Nagari script. Mithila is the land of Sanskrit, but the use of the Kaithi in their courts! What a travesty of justice! Bihar is a land of Hindi; and the letters of Hindi script must get their due status here).

In another editorial 'कैथी या नागरी' (Kaithi or Nagri), KPJ wrote,

> ... जब स्कूल में नागरी अक्षर सिखलाए जाते हैं, स्कूली किताबें सब नागरी अक्षर में

> छपती हैं और सब प्रान्त के सब पत्र नागरी अक्षर में छपते और पढ़े जाते हैं ऐसी दशा में कैथी में सरकारी कागज़ न छपने चाहिए।...एक बार लोगों को स्कूल में नागरी सीखनी होती है फिर अदालत के काम के लिए 'कैथी' सीखने की आवश्यकता पड़ती है। नागरी के प्रचार से मुसलमानों तथा छोटा-नाग-पुर वालों को भी सुभीता होगा। मिथिला संस्कृत की भूमि है और वहां नागराक्षरों का राज्य है। छोटा-नागपुर में पादरियों द्वारा नागरी की ही शिक्षा दी जाती है। मुसलमान हाकिम नागरी किसी तरह पढ़ भी सकते हैं पर कैथी से वे हमेशा अपरिचित ही रहते हैं। ज़िलों में जज लोग शायद वकील लोगों से राय लेंगे। पटने में 100 में 95 कानून पेशा के लोगों ने नागरी के लिए राय दी है। दूसरे स्थानों में नागरी-प्रेमियों को सिद्धिलाभ की यत्न करनी चाहिए। इस समय अधिकतर लोग स्वयं नागरी का गुण जानने लगे हैं, तथापि वे बहकाए न जा सकें इसका नागरी-प्रेमी ध्यान रक्खें। इस समय हम लोगों का यत्न केवल इस बात का है कि सरकारी तौर पर नागरी का उच्च-पद इस प्रान्त में मान लिया जाय। अदालती लोग अभी कैथी में ही लिखें क्योंकि उसी की आदत उन्हें अधिक है। पर आगे चलकर इसका प्रयत्न हो कि यदि नागरी में लिखकर कोई कागज़ पेश किया जाय तो उस लेने में उज्र न किया जाय। नागरी के लिए इस प्रकार द्वार खुल जानेपर अभ्यासवश नागरी की उन्नति होती जायगी और 'हिंदी भाषी बिहार प्रान्त' में हिंदी अक्षरों की वस्तुतः प्रतिष्ठा हो जायगी।[86]

As a clever advocate, KPJ appealed to the judges in the district that they should take the opinion of the Bar Associations and told them that 95 out of 100 legal professionals in Patna had suggested the use of Nagari.[87] It is not surprising that all of the signatories were upper-caste Hindus. However, KPJ was not in favour of the sudden exclusion of Kaithi, "At this time our only effort is that at the official level the Nagari should be accepted as the first script in the province. The people working in the courts should continue with Kaithi because they are used to it. Later on, the effort should be made to see that if a paper written in the Nagari was presented, it was accepted without any hesitation."[88]

As far as the advocacy of Hindi and Nagari was concerned, KPJ tried to give all relevant information about the growth and development of both Hindi and Nagari. All news items, information reports, and all proceedings of the Lucknow session of All India Hindi Sahitya Sammelan were published very prominently. Expressing his pleasure about the success of the Conference, KPJ wrote, "One of the happiest outcomes of the conference is that a number of advocates of Awadh have taken an oath that they will do their signature etc, in Nagari from now."[89]

KPJ's overall position on the issues of languages and scripts as manifested in his writings in the *Pataliputra* is somewhat different from his contributions on these subjects in relatively more academic journals such as the *Saraswati*, *Hindi Pradeep*, etc. In the *Pataliputra* pieces, he certainly appears less jingoistic and far from being a participant in the Hindi-Hindu-Hindustan call. Do we take it as an example of the evolution of his ideas over a period of time? Or could it be the result of the need for addressing a different readership? The readers of the *Pataliputra* were, perhaps, the *hoi polloi* whereas the aforesaid Hindi literary journals had a niche readership. We think, it could be a blend of both the factors.

Women

As far as the women's question is concerned, only a few articles were produced during the entire period of KPJ's tenure as the editor: one is a reproduction, with the editor's comment, from a Bengali monthly '*Vijaya*', written by a Bengali lady Smt. Sarojvasini Gupta. The Hindi translation of her article was published as 'हिन्दू जाति में नारी का सम्मान और स्वाधीनता'[90] ('Hindu Jati mein Nari ka Samman aur Swadhinata'). The second is 'Parde ki Pratha' written by Pandit Lakshmishwar Sharma[91], and the third one is 'Dampati Kalah' by Gopal Ram.[92] These articles had been carefully selected, which show the personal interest of the selector as well. Except one editorial on Lady Hardinge,[93] which is an obituary editorial on the well-known white woman, the women's question does not appear in the editorials. This fact is intriguing because in his early days KPJ was associated with the Kalwar Sabha and tried to eradicate the social evils rampant in his community, such as dowry, child marriage, the objections to widow remarriage, etc. Interestingly, beautiful commercial advertisements with the pictures of young women with attractive titles were given more space to lure the consumers—for women in general and for the male to lure his beloved one in particular!

KPJ's personal understanding of the issue is well reflected in the editor's note on the article, 'हिन्दू जाति में नारी का सम्मान और स्वाधीनता' (18 July 1914). It reads thus:

> हिन्दुस्तान में गत पच्चीस तीस वर्षों से एक प्रकार का नया युग सा आ गया है। हर तरह की उन्नति की चर्चा चारों ओर से सुनाई देती है। कहीं राजनीतिक आंदोलन है तो कहीं समाज सुधार है, कहीं धार्मिक समारोह है तो कहीं साहित्य-सेवियों का सुखद सम्मलेन है। इन सभी प्रकार के आन्दोलनों के अतिरिक्त स्त्री-जाति की वर्त्तमान दुरावस्था को दूर कर समाज में उनकी मान मर्यादा बढ़ाने के लिए भी

आंदोलन जारी है। इस आंदोलन में हमारी अनेक सुशिक्षिता भगिनियों का हाथ है और हमारे कुछ उत्साही स्त्री शिक्षा प्रेमी और नारी-जाति के उन्नति-कामी भाई भी शामिल हैं। इस लक्षण को हम देश के कल्याण का कारण समझते हैं, किन्तु कुछ हमारे भाई नारी जाति को पूर्वीय आदर्श के अनुसार शिक्षित न कर उन्हें पाश्चात्य आदर्श पर ले जाना चाहते हैं जिससे हमें भय होता है कि हिन्दू स्त्रियां भी कहीं कालान्तर में वैसी ही उच्छृंखल न हो जायं जैसी इंगलैंड की मतभिलषिणी स्त्रियां हो गयी हैं।

अस्तु, दोष गुण या अपनी अभाव-आवश्यकताएं जितना हम समझ सकते हैं उतना और कोई नहीं। हिंदुस्तान के पुरुषों की वर्त्तमान अवस्था और उनके भविष्य के कल्याण के लिए जो कुछ कर्त्तव्य है उसपर जितनी अच्छी तरह से हम विचार कर सकते हैं उतना और कोई नहीं। इसी प्रकार हमारी महिलाएं स्त्री-जाति के हिताहित की बातों को जिस तरह ठीक ठिकाने के साथ कह सकती हैं उस तरह हमलोग कभी नहीं कह सकते। इसीलिए हम उपर्युक्त विषय पर स्वयं कुछ अधिक न कहकर एक पढ़ी लिखी बंग महिला के विचारों का सारांश नीचे देते हैं और आशा करते हैं कि पाठक इसे ध्यानपूर्वक देखेंगे और प्राच्य तथा पाश्चात्य भावों का मिलान करेंगे। वास्तव में जिस शिक्षा से हिन्दू नारी आदर्श हिन्दू नारी न बनकर सुशिक्षिता होते ही आधी पूरब की और आधी पश्चिम की हो जाय हम उस शिक्षा को दूर से नमस्कार करते हैं।''[94]

Very clearly, the editor has expressed his opinion and the rest of the details have been reproduced as they were in the original article of Sarojvasini Gupta. The editor's opinion and the content of the article are on the same lines. He was in favour of the movement for women's rights and considered it as a symbol of the welfare of the nation. He also talked about gendered sensibilities and argued for self-advocacy for women: "The way we can better understand the present condition of the men and our responsibility for their future welfare, similarly a woman can better understand the interests of women; we cannot do that." However, he was not in favour of imparting them western education and supported the eastern ideal for education. Although KPJ was educated in England, the patriarchal Hindu *saṃskāras* (sacraments) was still a dominant part of his understanding on the issue, as it was for the Hindi/Hindu intellectuals at that time. He was in favour of limited freedom within the *maryādā* (moral limits).[95]

The second article, on the *purdah* system, went into the history of the *purdah* practice and considered its desirability for modern women. It did not find any exact or conclusive evidence of whether *purdah* was pre-medieval, or whether it was introduced in India by the *Yavanas*, meaning Muslims. It certainly did not exist in the Vedic times, and even the *Mahābhārata* mentions women's participation in assemblies, etc. Whatever the case, it then presented the *pūrvapakṣa* opinion of the anti-*purdah* thinkers: *purdah* was bad for women's health, which was evident in their deteriorating health as soon as they came to their husbands' homes. Lack of exercise or movement meant low digestion. Their social behaviour too was shaped by the *purdah*, so even in cases of emergency they would not venture out or show their faces. These people also rhetorically asked if their character was all right in their fathers' homes, what was the need to change their status in father-in-laws' homes? Moving along with others kept the couples healthy and happy. Some people even argue, the article reported, that women being human beings deserve as much liberty as men, especially since their behaviour and disposition are purer than those of men. So *purdah* was really unwarranred, they say. Then the author offered a very weak reasoning in defence of the *purdah*—it was necessary for preserving women's modesty and honour. It zeroed in on Bihari women especially those from the genteel backgrounds, for whom *purdah* functioned as the primary training ground, and advocated its continuance till such time that they were educated enough and became fit for self-defence. It also offered a sectarian reading of the situation: "विशेषत: बिहार की स्त्री के लिए परदे की प्रथा पाठशाला का काम देती है जिसमें वे अपना आचरण शुद्ध रखना सीखती हैं।... जब तक बिहार में स्त्रीशिक्षा सामान्य रूप से भी न होगी और हमारी अबलाएं विद्या की निहाई पर कूट कर ठोस न बनाई जायंगी तब तक परदा पद्धति का यहां रहना बहुत ज़रूरी है। पहले उनमें विद्या प्रचार होना चाहिए जिस से वे आत्मरक्षा में समर्थ हों। इसलिए मैं परदे की प्रथा उठा देने के विरुद्ध हूं।"

To take one example from the occasional works of fiction published in the paper, let's turn to 'Dampati Kalah' ('The Couple in Quarrel'), a story penned by Babu Gopal Ram (aka Gahmari), who edited *Jasoos*, a thriller magazine in Hindi. The story is about a clerk, Seetaram, and his educated and moderately-travelled wife, Yashoda. The structure of the story is somewhat similar to the *pūrvapakṣa-uttarapakṣa* organisation of the example discussed above. So the story opens with a fiery speech by Yashoda, who had gone to meet her editor friend of a women's magazine, *Abala*. Her speech was occasioned by her husband's long speech after she was found missing from the house on his return from the office. In the dispute that ensued she argued for her right to equality with her husband

and freedom to move about, while he emphasised that she was supposed to take care of him. She read newspapers and had seen women working as booking clerks in Calcutta and wanted no unnecessary questioning by her husband. The peeved husband went out of the house announcing his late return but in fact kept wandering about in the city. In the meanwhile, Yashoda found sleep hard to come by and started conjuring up all kinds of fearful scenarios she had read in *Jasoos*. So when her husband came she thought it was a thief and would not let him come in. He thought she was angry, and that was why she did not let him in. When he finally broke through and got inside, she was senseless with fear. She came literally and figuratively to her senses at the climax, apologising for her bad behaviour in the past and promising to behave in the future: "अच्छा अब मैं बराबरी नहीं चाहती! सदा तुम्हारी दासी हो कर रहूंगी। नाथ! अब तुम्हारी आज्ञा से मैं कभी बाहर नहीं रहूंगी। जो बीत गया उसको बिसार कर मुझे क्षमा कर दो... स्वामी की अधीनता से स्त्री की स्वाधीनता नहीं जाती। प्यारी यशोदा! यह तो हिन्दू स्त्री का आभूषण है। ...इसके बिना स्त्री कौड़ी काम की नहीं है। ...जो तुम चाहते हो वही पाओगे नाथ!"

All these situations published in the *Pataliputra* could be seen as attempts at straining the shackles of orthodoxy. Even though the denoument was always in favour of *purdah*, or restrained movement and *sevābhāva* model for a *pativratā strī*, there were always radical arguments put forward in the *pūrvapakṣa*. So the readers could weigh the comparative strengths and weaknesses of arguments and decide for themselves, as the essay on *purdah* custom clearly argued. In both cases it was the fear of the rogue world outside, whether real or imaginary, that seemed to swing the argument in favour of conservative positions. The authors could not take outright radical positions, but they definitely wanted to generate a sense of doubt in their readers' minds—even this kind of ambivalence was a movement forward for them.

The question of women's education was one of the chief concerns of the Hindi intelligentsia and social reformers of the nineteenth and early decades of the twentieth century. It was as personal for them as their religion. Nobody could interfere in that matter. Before the coming of the British they could not even get education in their vernaculars. The staunch Vaishnava reformer and one of the propounders of the movement of Hindi language and the Nagari script, Madan Mohan Malviya was against widow remarriage and voting rights for the women and in the Banaras

Hindu University, founded by him, women did not have access to Vedic studies till after several decades of the twentieth century.[96] Interestingly, in Banaras 500 girls coming from the lower strata of the society were getting education in the school sponsored by the Maharaja of Vijayanagaram, and they were given some stipends to support themselves. However, there was reluctance among the elite and the upper-caste people to send their daughters to school. Vir Bharat Talwar has shown how a bigger chunk of Western-educated reformers considered women as the carriers of their religion and as an index of their culture and civilisation they had to keep a safe distance from the influence of Western education. This was the reason that is they did not want to impart western education to them, and when they did, they would limit it to imparting religious and moral education. They considered scientific education necessary for Indian men but not for girls. Commenting on this attitude of the social reformers, Uma Nehru wrote in 1920s, "The Indian male imitates the West completely and wants to create a model for development on that basis, but wants that the girls should look eastern only."[97]

Presenting the idealised picture of women's glory and idealising what are typically women's qualities, like sacrifice, tolerance, and purity, *maryādā*, etc., KPJ does not recognise the existence of power in gender-relations. It is also surprising that KPJ himself was educated in the English system in India and London, and yet, why was he opposing Western education for women? The projection of womanhood is something that today's feminist might find irrational and unacceptable. Once again, on the women's question, Hinduism and *Śāstric* references occupy the central position in KPJ's journalistic writings.

History

As a budding historian turned journalist, KPJ gave appropriate space to history in the *Pataliputra* and even the first issue starts with an article titled 'Pataliputra' written by Haraprasad Sastri. Apart from articles of pure historical interest such as '*Dhamma-lipi* of Aśoka', 'Hindu Polity', 'Origin of Lucknow', '*Raso* of Chand Bardai', 'An Old Copy of Gītā' etc., there was a separate informative column about matters of general interest titled, इतिहास-प्रसंग (*Itihas-Prasang*). Most of the articles are anonymous. Historic autobiography titled 'इतिहास का रोड़ा' (*Itihas ka Roda*) written by R.D.

Banerji was serialised over several issues. However, the most interesting in the section are the articles 'Hindu Polity' and '*Dhamma-lipi* of Aśoka', perhaps written by the editor himself because in the subsequent years, he wrote on such issues in English. These were serialised in seven and ten issues respectively. Efforts were also being made to popularise 'Hindu Rājyaśāstra' among the general readers by giving advertisements generally on the front page of the weekly from 14 November 1914 to 3 April 1915. Not only that, the following six editorials were also written during his tenure as an editor: 1. 'Gatha Sattasai',[98] 2. 'Aśoka ki Dharma-lipi',[99] 3. 'Bharat Mein Veerpooja',[100] 4. 'Aśoka aur Bharatavarsha',[101] 5. 'Hamara Samvat',[102] 6.'Mahakavi Bhāsa ke Natak'.[103]

KPJ's contributions to history-writing will be discussed separately in the next chapter. However, we have selected a few articles here for understanding KPJ's perspective as a Hindi journalist and historian. It is important to note here that these were, perhaps, the first journalistic writings in Hindi and through which KPJ tried to make the Hindi readers aware about ancient Indian literary treasures and history. He tried to tell his readers that the literary classics should be made available to the Hindi readers. Writing about Bhāsa's plays, KPJ wrote, "It is a matter of great shame, if the Hindi translations of those plays are not available in Hindi from which Kālidāsa had learnt to write his plays." [104] He also stated that one of the plays of Bhāsa had been performed in a theatre of the city of Paris and regretted that the Indian people were not familiar even with his name. He argued that it was necessary to have several Hindi translations of these plays, out of which the best ones would become treasures of the language and literature.

In one of his historical editorials, KPJ chose to comment on a Prakrit text called *Gaha Sattasaī* i.e., *Gāthā Saptaṣatī* in Sanskrit. The Sattasai in its original format followed a particular arrangement of *dohās* with certain *mātrās*. He tells us that the *gāthās* were actually focused on *śrṅgārā*, even in the Prakrit age. Apart from discovering Hāla the poet for posterity, KPJ pointed out, quite presciently, that it was also a popular register for women poets. On the basis of their philological differences with the language of the inscriptions of the times, the language of this poetry was described by KPJ as non-artificial and homely. As already noticed in the second chapter, KPJ considered Prakrit as the mother of Hindi, much against the mainstream Hindi establishment view that set up a direct blood lineage with Sanskrit, the *devavānī*. KPJ could not read most of the names of these women poets since most were pulped as a result of degeneration of paper, but the ones he could recover are the following: Reva, Prahata, Rodda, Anulachhi, Asuladdhi, and Madhavi. KPJ also cited some of their remarkable couplets from the collection. To give one example—simply because it has a contemporary relevance, —for its resemblance with Raj Kapoor's first reported sighting of his beloved Nargis, which, incidentally, was recreated in his film Bobby. Anyway, here goes the gatha poem, cited by KPJ: 'यथा, प्रियतमा के रसोई बनाने से कालिख लगे हुए हाथ से उसके मुख पर कालिख लग जाने पर पति ने हंसी की, क्यों आज तो खासी चान्द की छटा है।'

This was a remarkable philological feat of KPJ finding women poets 1900 years before his own time. He definitely updated our knowledge on Vedic women *riṣis* and poets.

Hero worship and glorification of ancient India is a recurring phenomenon in KPJ's journalistic writings. The editor tells his readers that the system of hero worship was in practice in this country since the beginning and the heroes were worshipped cutting across the caste system[105] (KPJ, here overlooked the fact that the duty of the warrior was only assigned to the Kṣatriya). He argued that these heroes had become venerable because of their contribution to the welfare of the people and the country. The profession of the soldier was kept even above that of the Brahmin and produces evidence from the *Arthaśāstra*, "The Brahmin desires to reach heaven through the activities such as sacrifices and asceticism, and the brave reach that stage even earlier through sacrificing his life in the battle."[106] Implicitly, this was an appeal for such sacrifices, and they became the perfect nationalist icons for those times, in that they synthesised selfless activism, heroism, wisdom, etc.

For making it glamorous, the duty of sacrifice was contextualised in the global context,

> The hero worship has always been held in high esteem by the Hindus, the Parsis, the Greeks, and the Romans. The Chinese, however, did not do so. Amongst all, the hero worship by the Hindus is quite exceptional. Even the brave monkey character (*bahadur bandar*, perhaps Hanuman) was considered as equal to God. He had a large number of worshippers because of his bravery, which is not found anywhere else. Further, the beacome of the Hindu dharma, such as

> Tathāgata Buddha, and the Jains were also so overwhelmed by bravery that notwithstanding their thrust on not killing even insects, they were been calling themselves as 'jina' (victorious), Mahāvira, etc. Guru Gobind Singh started the religion of bravery— 'lion-ness' (*Sihpan*) became his religion.[107]

While talking about history, KPJ's otherwise sharp vision is unable to pierce the walls of caste system and religious traditions (of Budhists, Jains, Sikhs), and he does not see here the possibility of power play. On the contrary, every caste and community, except Muslims, harmoniously fits into his Hindu understanding of India's past. For KPJ, Guru Gobind Singh was the role model for the Hindus, whose name will be remembered as long as Hinduism lasted. In an editorial commemorating his birth anniversary he wrote, "Guru Gobind Singh was one of the great personalities of India, whose name will be remembered as long as the Hindu *jati* exists. Earlier such great personalities were considered as the incarnations of God, i.e. they were operated through God and whatever the Hindu society desired of them required, they fulfilled them. They were the very images of masculinity and the sources of pride for the community. Neither the incarnations were considered separate from the community, nor was the community considered different from them."[108] Further, Guru Gobind Singh was equated with Viśvāmitra,

> He took the responsibility of hunting the hawk of the injustice with a small bird and he proved it. He was like a second Vishvamitra. This Vishvamitra did not have Rama and Lakshmana, but he created another universe out of mere dust. He made the 'other' (itar) and the shudras into a lion, and killed the hawk with a bird."[109] Guru Saheb started the Singh-cult, and trained his disciples, so that the country would get emancipated from injustice (rule of *Adharma*). In this endeavour, he took a vow to keep hair uncut and keep his weapon on his persons for life.[110]

According to KPJ, Shivaji and Guru Gobind Singh were the two towering personalities of India in the seventeenth century. KPJ goes on to say, "Because of these two incarnations, the reign of Aurangzeb got demolished and amongst the supporters of these two great souls were the right-thinking Muslims as well."[111] The editor carefully chose his words and he did not want to brand himself as sectarian or communal, therefore, in his opinion the conflict between Aurangzeb and Guru Gobind Singh was a conflict between the just and the unjust, and not between two different religions. The Muslims who were fighting against Aurangzeb were seen as fighting for a just cause. Such an interpretation the medieval period of Indian history was indeed an oversimplification! And finally,

> "पौष सुदी 7 को श्री गोविन्द सिंह जी के जन्मस्थान 'हरि-मन्दिर' पर जा सर नवाना हिन्दू जाति का कर्त्तव्य है। यह जन्म दिन, कृष्णाष्टमी, रामनवमी, दीपावली आदि जाति के पुण्य दिनों की भांति जब तक हिन्दू जाति जीती है मनाएगी।"[112]
>
> ("It is the duty of every Hindu to visit the birthplace of Shri Govind Singhji at Sri Harimander Sahib to pay homage to him. Hindus should celebrate his birthday hike they celebrate Kṛṣṇāṣṭamī, Rāmanavamī Dīpāvalī, etc., till the Hindu religion is alive.)

KPJ wrote two editorials on Aśoka and his *dhamma* policy.[113] The Hindi translation of *dhamma-lipi* was serialised and published in ten parts between 14 November 1914 and 13 February 1915. The editor informs the reader that the Aśokan pillar inscriptions were considered extraordinary all over the world and many works thereon were published in English, German and French, but it is yet to published in any regional language of India. He claimed that he was publishing it for the people of the country of Aśoka.[114] And his 'people' of the country were Hindi readers!

Aśoka does not appear in favourable light in KPJ's assessment because he did not fit into his Hindu framework. He argued that Aśoka had made the entire country Buddhist. He also changed such policies of Candragupta (his grandfather) which had been responsible for stopping beggary amongst his subjects and for curbing the power of 'anti-national' (*rāṣṭraghātī*) monasteries. Such transformation had never took place even later on in any country. There were a number of upheavals in the world because of this king.[115] It was the policy of *dharma,* which was responsible for the decline of the Mauryas.[116] These arguments had by then been advanced by Haraprasad Sastri.[117] However, such arguments are now considered untenable.[118]

Another important marker of the 'Āryan'/'Hindu' culture, for KPJ, was the use of eras based on chronological events. There was definite nationalist *Swaraj*-based anti-colonial politics in the ways people used their calendars. And his solution is disarmingly simple: just keep using the Vikrama Saṁvat (Era) to keep it alive. As a historian, he considered the 'Hindu' calendar superior to those of the Muslims and Christians. He says that the former originated as a symbol of victory while the latter, were reminders of tragic incidents.[119] So KPJ, the historian-turned-journalist, was practising what he preaches, himself inscribing it on the pages of his newspaper, but, how? The main, front page masthead uses both systems, Christian and Vikrama Saṁvats. The mast of the editorial and all the other pages, however, carries dates only in the Vikrama Saṁvat. But a closer look at the *Pataliputra,* at the reports, for example, reveals that the Christian dates were being used for everyday reporting, which was a practical choice he had to make. But what is interesting about this editorial page is that KPJ, while taking stock of political events in the year gone by, gives the pride of place to the Vikrama Saṁvat, and Caitra Śukla 4 of the Hindu calender. He also associates it with the rumours floated by several Pandits on different occasions about the certain demise of the British government at the national level, or some prediction about the plunder and siege of local Patna Treasury. Needless to say, as a loyalist, he praises the liberalism of the empire that it did not take any action against the culprit-Pandit-practitioners of useless *phalit jyotish,* and let the rumours die their natural death.

Articles on 'Hindu Rājyaśāstra' which were serialised and published in seven parts between 15 August 1914 to 17 October 1914 constituted another area of KPJ's interest. KPJ had already delivered a long lecture at the Hindi Sahitya Sammelan session in Calcutta in 1912 and its English translation in several parts had already been published in the *Modern Review* in 1913. Finally, it was published as a monograph—*Hindu Polity*—in 1924. By publishing it for the common reader of Hindi was, perhaps, a part of his larger political agenda because for the first time, colonial hegemony in the writing of political history was being categorically challenged and he wanted to make his reader aware about the rich political system in ancient India. The publication of such articles in the Hindi weekly was, perhaps, first journalistic writing and KPJ brought such issues to the notice of the Hindi intelligentsia and common readers from out of the confines of libraries, seminars, and intellectual discussions.

The detailed discussion on the topic will be done later on in the chapter on history. However, it will be important to note here that for the first time, KPJ showcased the importance of republics in ancient Indian history and tried to prove that the 'Hindu political system', partly of republics of the Athenian type, and partly of constitutional monarchies such as that of Great Britain thrived in ancient India. There were popular assemblies such as *samiti* and *sabhā*, which were called twin sisters in *Atharvaveda*. According to KPJ, *samiti* was the mother of a number of institutions. All political and public matters were discussed in these assemblies and there were no hierarchies in the republics, and everybody was equal. While discussing 'Hindu monarchy', he wrote on a number of things—the origin, rights, and the duties of the king, the types of checks on the rights of the king, taxation, land ownership, etc.

KPJ's interpretation and conclusions have been questioned by the later generations of historians. However, understanding the context in which he was writing would be profitable. In KPJ's days, there was an intense nationalist zeal and associated movements were sweeping across the country. The nationalist movement stimulated the search for ancient manuscripts, resulting in the discovery of the *Arthaśāstra* of Kauṭilya in 1905 and its publication by R. Shamasastry in 1909. The discovery was an epoch-making event in the history of the study of ancient Indian polity, for it provided valuable raw material which could be utilised in yielding 'political precedents for modern controversies'. This was an important factor which contributed to many critical and descriptive studies of the ancient Indian polity.

Caste

It is surprising to note that the caste issue is conspicuously absent in KPJ's writings in general and appears in journalistic writings only marginally, despite the fact that he himself belonged to a backward community (Kalwar) and wrote a piece on Brahmin caste (already discussed). The news items related to the upper castes sabhas find place in the *Pataliputra*, but the news items related to the lower caste sabhas are absent, although such sabhas were very much in existence.[120] He did see injustice in the caste system and emphasised that the country was yet to find the recipe which would unite all castes:

> भारत में द्रविड़ देश–दक्षिण में ब्राह्मण और ब्राह्मणेतर जातियों में महाद्रोह चल रहा है। ब्राह्मण दूसरी जातियों को दबाए रक्खा चाहते हैं और दूसरी जातियां अब इसे पसंद नहीं करतीं। इस भाव के कारण वहां क्लब, फुटबॉल मैच आदि सामुदायिक कार्य प्राय: बिगड़ जाते हैं। अभी सर शंकर नायर ने एक सभा में कहा है कि इस देश में सार्वजनिक कामों में ब्राह्मणता से हानि पड़ती है, यदि पुराने ब्राह्मण विचारों की

> श्रेष्ठता अब भी मानी जायगी तो उन्नति कदापि न होगी, अब समय क्षत्रिय-विचार की श्रेष्ठता का है। सर शंकर नायर ने हिन्दू यूनिवर्सिटी का भी विरोध इस मतलब से किया था कि उस में ब्राह्मणों और 'ब्राह्मणता' का जोर रहेगा जिस से ब्राह्मणेतर जातियां खटाई में पड़ेंगी।
>
> खेद है कि घर में ऐसा दुर्भाव रहे। यदि दिल की सफाई हो तो कोई संदेह और अविश्वास की जगह न रहे। सब बातों को देखते हुए स्पष्ट है कि अंगरेज़ी राज्य न रहने से आपस में जातियां लड़ बैठेंगी और एक दूसरे को दबा कर रखने का अन्याय करेंगी। इस देश में एका का मसाला अब तक नहीं मिला जिस के द्वारा सब जमकर एक हो जायं। समाज संगठन ऐसा है कि हिंदुओं का एक होना असंभव प्रतीत होता है।[121]

What Dalit ideologue Chandrabhan Prasad is arguing today 'अंग्रेज लेट आए और जल्दी चले गए' (The British came late and went early) was visualised by KPJ quite early 'अंगरेज़ी राज्य न रहने से आपस में जातियां लड़ बैठेंगी' (without the British state, all castes will fight among themselves). However, the remedy KPJ offers is quite interesting - purity of heart. The four-fold division and hierarchy of the caste system is not a problem, only a 'change of heart' is enough to make him happy. Strangely, like gender relations, KPJ does not see here —in these social relationships—the possibility of power play.

The theory of 'Sanskritisation' does not fit in KPJ's case, as he contested the claims of the Kalwars for their Kṣatriya-status, which created tension amongst the people of his caste. KPJ did attend his caste sabhas meetings and extended help to his caste brethren. However, he did not make his caste brethren very happy and he did not come up to their expectations. Once a Kalwar delegation went to KPJ's place for some help but they did not find him more helpful, and therefore, the editor of the *Kalwar Kesari* wrote a sarcastic article.[122] The theory of class might work in his case. Economically, he was well-off since his childhood and he might not have faced any social problems in day-to-day life. Second, his immediate surroundings comprised people from upper castes and the sponsors—Hathuwa and Darbhanga Maharajas of the weekly also came from that background. It appears, therefore, that he might have delibertly avoided such issues.

KPJ was the editor of the *Pataliputra* for a period of nearly a year. However, the reasons for his resignation are not explicit. There were perhaps multiple reasons. One reason might have been political interference or conflict with the government. The first controversy occurred just after the publication of the second editorial titled 'Rath Yatra', on the 4 July 1914. It was a sarcastic article on Lord Jagannath. Anticipating some kind of tension, the government had warned the editor and the publisher. It was also noted that the owners of the paper were a syndicate of respectable gentlemen; that is why the paper was exempted from depositing security money under the Press Act, but in the eyes of colonial masters, the paper was a political one and the editor, KPJ was still a suspected revolutionary.[123]

Significantly, the first editorial 'Hamara Parichay' is very clever. The British empire was not directly challenged, and India was shown to be on the path of progress because of the imperial connection. On the other hand, it was categorically stated that the empire would become powerful in every sense once India attained autonomy in administration. Therefore, to achieve the autonomous institution of self-governance was the fundamental goal of the *Pataliputra*.[124] This clever tactic did not really work, "It soon earned the ire of the Governor, and Kashi Prasad Jayaswal had to say good-bye to the Weekly."[125]

The government was not the only source of trouble for KPJ, the editor. He had differences with his colleagues as well, and Pandit Ishwari Prasad Sharma had to leave precisely because he did not get along well with KPJ.[126] Moreover, the dominant caste configurations in the world of journalism were also actively involved in seeing the back of KPJ. For example, the all powerful editor of the *Saraswati*, Mahavir Prasad Dwivedi, in his letter to Maithilisharan Gupt dated 25 July 1914 wrote: "What is the caste of Jayaswalji, was not hidden from the owner of the *Patliputra*. If they wanted to have a Brahmin then why did they appoint Jayaswalji in the first instance? What is the real issue we cannot know."[127] Caste issues of the Hindi intelligentsia might also have been at work. As a legal practitioner he might have tried to keep himself aloof from such controversies, because his clients were also coming from the upper caste background. Another reason was, perhaps, the beginning of BORS in 1915. KPJ was associated with the Society and its Journal - *JBORS* - in various capacities. Therefore, because of excessive work, it might not have been possible for him to continue with the weekly.

The *Pataliputra* did pretty well during KPJ's brief tenure as its editor. He was, perhaps, a non-paid editor. He might have had in mind that demanding money for *sahitya-seva* (service to literature), would be improper. According to the historians of Hindi journalism, the weekly could not maintain its stature after he left.[128] The popularity and the expanding base of readers could be seen from commercial advertisement pages, which went from quarter page of the first issue to two and half pages during his editorship and the sponsors were coming from distant regions like Aligarh, Mathura, Calcutta, Poona, Bombay, Almora, etc. The editor himself wrote, "A correspondent has been appointed in Shimla. He has good connections over there. Till the time Government of India stays there, he too will be staying there, thereafter he will come back to Delhi. The readers, therefore, will be getting the news of the Government regularly. It will lead to considerable expenditure, but because of the huge demand of the weekly, we have got the necessary confidence to bear the cost."[129] There was a separate column entitled 'Shimla ki Chitthi'. The weekly had a London correspondent as well because a separate column 'Hamari Vilayat ki Chitthi' was regularly published.

The growing demand of the weekly could be seen from another instance: a report of the theft of the copies of the weekly. One gentleman, Kanhai Lal, complained to the manager that he was a subscriber of the weekly but he was not getting it regularly. On his own enquiry, it was found that the issues were being sold off by the postal peon. Kanhai Lal, therefore, made a complaint to the postal inspector as well as the officials of the *Pataliputra*. In response to the complaint, the manager of the *Pataliputra* wrote that he was sending those issues again to the person concerned, but made an appeal to the other customers to be as watchful as Kanhai Lal.[130]

Looking at the entire content of the *Pataliputra*, it appears that it was a combination of both news and transference of knowledge and KPJ was successful in fulfilling his promise made in the inaugural editorial. Broadly, it can be reiterated that the political posturing of the weekly was pro-British—specially in its handling of the First World War; it showed a fairly progressive outlook on issues of languages and scripts; notwithstanding its awareness about caste discriminations, it failed to take a confrontationist position; and on the question of women, too, it blew hot and cold simultaneously. Overall, the weekly was 'useful' for the Hindi readers.

NOTES

1. Chunder, Bholanath, *Travels of a Hindoo to Various Parts of Bengal and Upper India,* cited in Hitendra Patel, *Communalism and Intelligentsia in Bihar*, 1870-1930, Orient Blackswan, New, Delhi, 2011, p. 92.
2. In 1911, only 18 newspapers and periodicals were being published from Patna whereas the number was 243 from Calcutta. There were 165 Bengali newspaper and periodicals at that time whereas there were only 25 in Hindi, see, Hitendra Patel, op. cit., p. 97.
3. Shridhar, Vijaydatt (ed.), *Bharatiya Patrakarita Kosha,* Vol. 2, New Delhi, 2010, p. 592 & 663-64.
4. Political Special, File No. 178/1914, Bihar State Archives (BSA).
5. *The Express,* 16.6.1914.
6. *Pataliputra,* 27.6.1914, p. 3.
7. Ibid.
8. Political Special, File No. 178/1914, BSA.
9. *The Biharee,* 30.6.1914.
10. History Sheet of KPJ, File No. 118c.
11. For a detailed discussion of the political-culture of the Hindi writers/ intellectuals of 19th century, see, Talwar, Veer Bharat, *Rassakashi: Unnisavi Sadi ka Navjagaran aur Paschimottar Prant*, (2nd edn.), Saransh Prakashan, New Delhi, 2006.
12. KPJ and Har Dayal were together in England, KPJ came to India, and Har Dayal went to America from England. Har Dayal launched the Urdu weekly *Ghadar* on 1 November 1913 and its Gurumukhi edition on 9 December 1913. The weekly was responsible for organizing revolutionary activities among the non-resident Indians in America and in other parts of the world, and later on the Ghadar movement in India. The purpose was to overthrow the British rule through armed revolt. On the other hand, the weekly *Pataliputra* was quite opposed to the position of Ghadar and it was absolutely pro-British. No news related to the Ghadar movement or any anti-government activities were published during the editorship of KPJ.
13. For details of the incident, see, Chandra, Bipan, *India's Struggle for Independence 1857-1947*, Viking, New Delhi, 1987, pp. 149-52.
14. 'British Upanivesh (Kalony) aur Bharatvasi', *Pataliputra*, 27.6.14, p. 3.
15. 'Komagata Maru' *Pataliputra,* 25.7.1914, p. 5.
16. 'Sikhon ka Danga' *Pataliputra,* 10.10.1914, p. 5, 'Budge Budge mein Danga', *Pataliputra,* 10.10.1914, p. 5.
17. 'Sikhon ka Danga', *Pataliputra,* 24.10.1914, p. 3.
18. *Pataliputra,* 08.08.1914, p. 3.
19. *Pataliputra,* 15.8.1914, p. 3.
20. *Pataliputra,* 22.8.1914, p. 3.

21. *Pataliputra*, 29.8.1914, p. 3.
22. *Pataliputra*, 05.9.1914, p. 3.
23. *Pataliputra*, 12.9.1914, p. 3.
24. *Pataliputra*, 19.9.1914, p. 3.
25. *Pataliputra*, 10.10.1914, p. 3.
26. *Pataliputra*, 24.10.1914, p. 3.
27. *Pataliputra*, 31.10.1914, p. 3.
28. *Pataliputra*, 14.11.1914, p. 3.
29. *Pataliputra*, 28.11.1914, p. 3.
30. *Pataliputra*, 09.01.1915, p. 3.
31. *Pataliputra*, 13.02.1915, p. 3. (Date is misprinted, it is 13.3.15).
32. *Pataliputra*, 8.8.14, p. 3.
33. 'Hamara Utsah' *Pataliputra*, 15.8.1914, p. 3.
34. 'Yudh mein Bharat', *Pataliputra*, 22.8.14, p. 3.
35. 'Yudh mein Hamara Yog', *Pataliputra*, 29.8.14, p. 3.
36. 'Yudh ko Bharatiya Yudh Samajhana Chahiye', *Pataliputra*, 5.9.1914, p. 3.
37. 'Lambi Ladai ki Taiyari', *Pataliputra*, 12.9.1914, p. 3.
38. 'Shatruon ki Haar', *Pataliputra*, 19.9.1914, p. 3.
39. 'France mein Hindustani Sena', *Pataliputra*, 10.10.1914, p. 3.
40. 'German Jal-Sena', *Pataliputra*, 24.10.1914, p. 3.
41. 'Neutralised State athwa Udasin Banaye Hue Rajya', *Pataliputra*, 31.10.1914, p. 3.
42. 'Room ki Bhool', *Pataliputra*, 14.11.1914, p. 3.
43. 'Turkon par Chipkali', *Pataliputra*, 23. 1. 1915, p. 3.
44. *Pataliputra*, 28.11.1914, p. 3.
45. 'England aur Yudh, *Pataliputa*, 9. 1. 1915, p. 3.
46. 'Dardanelles' *Pataliputra*, 13.02.1915, p. 3. (Date is misprinted, it should be 13.3.15).
47. *Pataliputra*, 22.8.14, p. 4.
48. *Pataliputra*, 5.12.14, p. 3.
49. 'Vijaya Dashami' *Pataliputra*, 26.9.1914, p. 3.
50. Ibid.
51. Ibid.
52. Ibid.
53. *Pataliputra*, 5.9.14, p. 3.
54. *Pataliputra*, 26.12.14, p. 4.
55. 'Hinduon ka Yudhdharm', *Pataliputra*, 24.10.1914, p. 3.
56. 'Vijaya Dashami' *Pataliputra*, 26.9.1914, p. 3.
57. 'Lord Harding', *Pataliputra*, 11.7.1914, p. 3
58. 'Vijaya Dashami' *Pataliputra*, 26.9.1914, p. 3.
59. 'France mein Hindustani Sena' *Pataliputra*, 10.10.1914, p. 5.
60. 'Vijaya Dashami' *Pataliputra*, 26.9.1914, p. 3.
61. 'Arab ke Islamic Tirth' *Pataliputra*, 5.12.1914, p. 3.

62. *Pataliputra*, 15. 8. 1914, 22.8.1914, p. 5.
63. *Pataliputra*, 12.9.14, p. 6.
64. Bipan Chandra, op. cit.
65. Nehru, Jawaharlal, *An Autobiography*, The Bodley Head, 1936, p. 31
66. The origin and development of Hindi movement and its impact on KPJ's writings has already been discussed in the chapter number 2 on Hindi.
67. 'Hamara Parichay', *Pataliputra*, 27.6.1914, p. 3.
68. Mahaveer Prasad, Dwivedi, 'Deshvyapakbhasha', *Saraswati*, November 1903, quoted in Orsini, p. 128
69. 'Bihar mein Nagari', *Pataliputra*, 29.8.1914, p. 3.
70. 'Maithil Bhasha', *Pataliputa*, 16.1.1915, p. 3.
71. 'Mithila Bhasha mein Shiksha' *Pataliputra*, 19.12.1914, p. 7.
72. 'Maithil Bhasha', *Pataliputra*, 16.1.1915, p. 3.
73. Ibid.
74. 'Dhanbad mein Bangali Vakilon ka Atyachar', *Pataliputra*, 13.3.15, p. 3.
75. 'Bombay-Madras mein Urdu', *Pataliputra*, 24.10.1914, p. 3.
76. 'Desh Bhasha ka Barappan', *Pataliputra*, 23.01.1915, p. 3.
77. Patel, op. cit., pp. 67-68.
78. Orsini, op. cit., p. 138.
79. *Pataliputra*, 5.9.1914, 26.9.1914,
80. *Pataliputra*, 10.10.1914.
81. *Pataliputra*, 24.10,1914.
82. Orsini, op. cit., p. 74.
83. Patel, op. cit., p. 78.
84. 'Kaithi ya Nagari'?, *Pataliputra*, 20.2.1915, p. 3.
85. 'Bihar mein Nagari', *Pataliputra*, 29.8.1914, p. 3.
86. 'Kaithi ya Nagari'?, *Pataliputra*, 20.2.1915, p. 3.
87. 'Kaithi ya Nagari?', *Pataliputra*, 20.2.1915, p. 3.
88. Ibid.
89. 'Sahitya Sammelan', *Pataliputra*, 12.12.1914, p. 3.
90. 'Hindu Jaati mein Nari ka Samman aur Swadhinata', *Pataliputra*, 18.7.1914, p. 1.
91. *Pataliputra*, 5.9.14, p. 6.
92. Ibid.
93. *Pataliputra*, 18.7.1914, p. 3.
94. 'Hindu Jaati mein Nari ka Samman aur Swadhinata', *Pataliputra*, 18.7.1914, p. 1.
95. A study on this question has been done by Orisini, see Women and the Hindi Public Sphere, in *Hindi Public Sphere*, pp. 241-308.
96. Talwar, Veer Bharat, op. cit., also see, Chatterjee, Partha, *The Nation and its Fragments: Colonial and Postcolonial Histories*, Princeton University Press, 1993, especially chapter, The Nation and its

women.

97. Quted in Orisini, op. cit., p. 38.
98. *Pataliputra*, 17.10.1914, p. 3.
99. *Pataliputra*, 7.11.1914, p. 3.
100. *Pataliputra*, 21.11.1914, p. 3.
101. *Pataliputra*, 12.12.1914, p. 3.
102. *Pataliputra*, 20.03.1915, p. 3.
103. *Pataliputra*, 03.04.1915, p. 3.
104. Ibid.
105. 'Bharat mein Veerpooja' *Pataliputra*, 21.11.1914, p. 3
106. Ibid.
107. Ibid.
108. 'Guru Govinda Singh ki Varshganth', *Pataliputra*, 19.12.1914, p. 3.
109. Ibid.
110. Ibid.
111. Ibid.
112. Ibid.
113. 'Aśoka ki Dharma-lipi', *Pataliputra*, 7.11.1914, p. 3, 'Aṣoka aur Bharatvarsh', *Pataliputra*, 12.12.14, p. 3.
114. 'Aśoka ki Dharma-lipi', *Pataliputra*, 7.11.1914, p. 3.
115. Ibid.
116. 'Aśoka aur Bharatvarsh', *Pataliputra*, 12.12.14, p. 3.
117. See, *JASB*, 1910, pp. 259-62.
118. See, Thapar, Romila, *Aśoka and the Decline of the Mauryas*, Oxford University Press, New Delhi, 2008, pp. 197-212.
119. 'Hamara Samvat' *Pataliputra*, 20.3.1915, p. 3.
120. 'The Dusadh Vanshiya Mahasabha' (1891), 'Ist Kurmi Conference' (Lucknow 1894), 'Gopa Mahasabha' (Madhepura, 1911), 'Koeri Hitkari Sabha' (Mirzapur 1912) etc. For a detailed discussion of the activities of these Sabhas see, Jata Shankar Jha, *Early Revolutionary Movements in Bihar*, KPJRI, Patna, 1977, Mishra, Girish and Pandey, Braj Kumar, *Sociology and Economics of Casteism in India: A Study of Bihar*, New Delhi, 1996.
121. 'Bharat mein Ghar ka Jhagada', *Pataliputra*, 20.2.1915, p. 3.
122. *Kalwar Kesari*, Sampadakiya Tippaniyan, Vol. 2, No. 2, Āśvina-Śukla, Saṁvat 1981, pp. 122-23.
123. See, political Special File Nos. 178/1914, 106/18, BSA.
124. *Pataliputra*, 27.6.1914, p. 3.
125. Shridhar, Vijaydatt, (ed.), *Bharatiya Patrakarita Kosha*, Vol. 2, New Delhi, 2010, pp. 663-64.
126. Mangalmooratti (ed.), *Shivpujan Sahay Sahitya-Samagra*, Anamika-Publishers', New Delhi, Vol. 2, p. 325.
127. *Mahavir Prasad Dwivedi Rachanawali*, Vol. 14, p. 214.
128. Vajpeyi, Ambika Prasad, 'Hindi Patrakarita ka Sinhawalokan' in

Shri Venkateshwar Samachar (weekly) Hirak Jayanti, Vol. 1896-1956, 1956, p. 175.

129. *Pataliputra*, 25.7.1914, p. 1.
130. *Pataliputra*, 26.9.1914, p. 5.

4

Conformist and Confrontationist: The Multifaceted Historian

KPJ is known to the world primarily as a historian. In this chapter, we will analyse his contributions to history-writing. We have divided his contributions into three segments: (A) Monographs: *Hindu Polity; Manu and Yājñavalkya: A Comparison and Contrast; History of India AD 150-350; An Imperial History of India (700 BC to c AD 770)*, and *Chronology and History of Nepal*, (B) Edited and translated works such as: *Rājanīti-Ratnākara by Chaṇḍeśvara; Bhaṭṭa-Svāmin's Commentary on Kauṭilya's Arthaśāstra; Descriptive Catalogue of Manuscripts in Mithila*, Vol. I, *Smṛiti* Manuscripts (with A.P. Sastri); *Descriptive Catalogue of Manuscripts in Mithila*, Vol. II: Literature, Prosody; *Adhyarddhaśatka* by Mātṛcetā, and *Vigrahavyāvarttanī* by Ācārya Nāgārjuna (with Rahul Sankrityayan), *Lassen's History of Indian Commerce*, (translated jointly with A.P. Banerji-Sastri) and (C) Research articles, further divided into several segments: (a) Epigraphic studies, (b) Numismatics, (c) Writings on Indian Arts, (d) Paintings, (e) Monumental structures and Consenvation of Monument, (f) Writings an Political Developments, (g) Miscellaneous Articles.

As is fairly well-known, modern research in history of ancient India began only in the second half of the eighteenth century to serve the needs of the British colonial administration and to legitimise the colonial rule. This effort culminated in the setting up of societies such as: the Asiatic Society of Bengal in 1784, Bombay Asiatic Society in 1804, and the Asiatic Society of Great Britain, London in 1823. Another, and perhaps the greatest impetus, to the Indian historical studies was first given by scholars described as the Orientalists or the Indologists, the best known amongst whom was F. Max Muller (1823-1902). His *Sacred Book of the East* series ran into 50 volumes. Max Muller and some other Western scholars made certain crude generalisations about the nature of ancient Indian history and society. They stated that the ancient Indians lacked a sense of history. So obsessed the natives were with the spiritual concerns about of the next world that they were unconcerned about the problems of this world. They promoted the theory that Indians had experienced neither a sense of nationhood nor any form of self-government and they were absolutely in love with despotism.

However, the first important history of India did not come from the house of the Orientalists, but from a totally different source. In 1817, James Mill published his *History of British India*, a lengthy work divided into three major sections—the 'Hindu civilization', the 'Muslim civilization', and the 'British period'. There is plenty of literature on Mill and colonial historiography—from the 'nationalists' to Marxists and non-historians like Edward Said and Bernard Cohn, and the advocates of the Subaltern studies. On the basis of their writings we can safely say that there are interesting parallels in Mill's take on India and that of the early Orientalists. Their writings describe India, rather anachronistically, as a changeless, static society, and the impact of this dominant description can be seen even in the writings of Karl Marx, the lover of a scientific and global perspective for history, who had to invent a new mode of production (Asiatic Mode of Production) to accommodate India and Asia!

Many of these generalisations were repeated in the *Early History of India* by V.A. Smith (1843-1929), published in 1904, the first 'systematic' history of ancient India. His book, which was based on an in-depth study of the available sources, gave primacy to political history. Smith emphasised the role of foreigners in ancient India. Alexander's invasion accounted for almost one third of his book. India was presented as a land of despotism which had not experienced political unity until the establishment of the British rule. He observes: "Autocracy is substantially the only form of government with which the historian of India is concerned".

In sum, British interpretation of Indian history served to denigrate the Indian character and achievements, and justify colonial rule. We know by now that the generalisations made by colonialist historians were by and large either false or grossly exaggerated, but served as good propaganda material for the perpetuation of their own despotic rule and to demonstrate that Indians were incapable of governing themselves.[1]

All this naturally came as a great challenge to Indian scholars, particularly those who had received Western education. A band of scholars took upon themselves the mission not only to reform Indian society, but also to reconstruct ancient Indian history in such a way as to make a case for social reforms and, more importantly, for self-government. During the War and the Post-War periods, the nationalist and revolutionary movements sweeping over Europe and Asia gave a huge impetus to such writings. No other period of the twentieth century has produced so much research work on ancient Indian polity as the period of nine years between 1916 and 1925.[2] Most prominent among such scholars were R.G. Bhandarkar, V.K. Rajwade, P.V. Kane, D.R. Bhandarkar, H.C. Raychaudhuri, R.C. Majumdar, K.A. Nilakanta Sastri, etc. KPJ belonged to the same age and creed. He was one of the first historians who challenged the ideological foundations of British empire; through his new researches and innovative interpretations of ancient Indian history. The overall range of KPJ's writing is quite large and covers issues such as polity, law, epigraphy, numismatics, arts, the 'regional', 'national' and 'international' histories, etc.

(A) Monographs

(a) *Hindu Polity*: KPJ started writing articles of historical importance in Hindi at the age of nineteen.[3] However, KPJ's chief claim to eminence lies in his monograph, *Hindu Polity*, whose genesis was first spelt out at the third Hindi Sahitya Sammelan in Calcutta in 1912, when KPJ read a paper entitled 'Hindu Rajyashastra', which was later translated into English, serialised and published in the *Modern Review* as 'An Introduction to Hindu Polity', and finally as a monograph in English in 1924. Before the 'Introduction' appeared in the *Modern Review*, there had been no work in any modern language on the subject. Therefore, KPJ argued that his 'Introduction' fulfilled its purpose. Soon, it found its place in the university curriculum. And the author had the satisfaction of seeing his work quoted and reiterated, with and without acknowledgement, almost every year; the subject had indeed become popular: "the truth ha[d] become recognised, accepted, and adopted".[4] Soon after publication, *Hindu Polity* was put on the syllabus of almost every university in India. The first edition of the book sold off very quickly. Keeping in view the demand for the book, the author published its second cheap and revised edition in 1936, both for students and the general public. The third edition was published from the Bangalore Press in 1943.[5]

Hindu Polity consists of two parts: the first part deals with the so-called republics, and the second deals with monarchy. There are thirty nine chapters and four appendices. The story takes off from the Vedic period to the middle of the fourth century A.D. to the Gupta imperial system and further till the seventeeth century. He began with a brief discussion on the variety of sources for the reconstruction of Indian history: indigenous, religious and non-religious, foreign (Greek), inscriptions, as well as numismatic pieces of evidence. On the basis of these sources, KPJ demonstrated the existence of eighty-two republics in different parts of the sub-continent from the post-Vedic to the Gupta period.[6]

KPJ starts with the conviction that the "Hindu race has experimented with great and various systems of state and political machinery. We are not yet in a position to reconstruct a complete history of the constitutional development of the race."[7] The main discussion began with the Vedic assemblies, the *Samiti* and the *Sabhā*, in which *Samiti* was described as the sovereign assembly of Vedic times.[8] According to him, the *Samiti* discussed and decided upon all matters concerning the state. Likewise, he viewed the *Sabhā* "as the standing and stationary body of selected men working under the authority of the *Samiti*", and to him "the *Sabhā* was the National Judicature and passed judgments on criminals."[9] Clearly, KPJ was using modern lenses and terminology to describe these historical institutions.

With Chapter IV begins the actual discussion on 'Hindu republics' which rose in the post-Vedic period. There is no doubt that Thomas William Rhys Davids was the first scholar to point out the existence of republics in Buddha's time. However, it was KPJ who thoroughly examined the problem and tracked down the references to republics in ancient Hindu literature. He pointed out that *gaṇa* in the then literature meant republic and *saṁgha* had similar connotations. KPJ collected evidence from Buddhist sources, Pāṇini, *Mahābhārata*, and other texts to prove that the meaning of *gaṇa* was indeed republic.[10] KPJ showed that with the end of the fifth century, republics disappeared from 'Hindu India'.[11] He made a critical analysis of the strengths and weaknesses of the republics:

a high sense of justice, adherence to discipline, belief in the equality of all citizens, economic prosperity, and existence of people's militias accounted for their success and longevity, while the smallness of the units and their vulnerability to intrigues, bitter hostility, and dissensions contributed to their fall.[12]

To show the great constitutional progress or rather the experiments made by the ancient Hindus, KPJ looked upon *bhaujya* (temporary rulership), *svārājya* (self-ruling system), *vairājya* (kingless system), *dvairājya* (the rule of two), and *arājaka* (non-ruler state) as different forms of the state flourishing in ancient India.[13] Relying upon democratic procedures in the Buddhist *saṁgha*, KPJ believed that ancient 'Hindu republics' introduced resolutions, debated on them and finally decided by vote of the majority. An overenthusiastic KPJ also proclaimed, "We might have seen a vast republic, vaster than the country had yet seen."[14]

In Book II, Chapter XXII begins with a detailed discussion on 'Hindu monarchy'. To KPJ the Ṛgvedic king once elected, "He becomes the sole taker of the taxes from the people; he becomes the king of the people... It shows that the idea of the state as an organism is realized as early as the Vedic kingship."[15] According to him, "The actual election at times did take place even in post-Vedic times; ...the theory of elective kingship was a widely current national theory."[16] The theory of limited monarchy could not be better expressed than in these words of KPJ, "The fact, if not the theory, was clear that the office of the king was a creation of the people and was held conditionally. Above him there was always the National Assembly, the *Samiti*, which was the real sovereign."[17]

KPJ was the first scholar who drew attention to the constitutional significance of the coronation ceremony of the 'Brahman period.'[18] In his view, "No room for a theory like divine origin existed... The Theory of Mānava (Mānava-Dharma-Śastra) was never approved or adopted by a single subsequent law-book. He further cited references from *Manusmṛti*, where the king is again brought under law and observed, "The Hindu theory of kingship was not permitted to degenerate into a divine imposture and profane autocracy."[19] His theory that the Hindu kingship was contractual in nature and could not be constitutionally autocratic, naturally led him to search for institutional checks on royal authority. This led him to propound the theory of sovereign popular assemblies—*paura* and *janapada*—in ancient 'Hindu' kingdoms.

According to him the *paura-janapada* deliberated on the nomination of *yuvarāja* or king-assistant[20] and could interfere with succession and prevent an undesirable prince from coming to the throne. Citing *Mahāvaṃśa*, a Ceylonese Buddhist chronicle, he asserted that the *paura* in India could depose and banish the king for illegal acts, and they, mindful of the good of all, could choose another in his place outside the dynasty, by deciding upon it in their meeting.[21]

KPJ concludes:

> We had an organism or a twin organism, the *Paura-Janapada*, which could depose the king, who nominated the successor to the throne, whose kindly feelings towards a member of the royal family indicated his chance of succession, whose president was apprized by the king of the policy of the state decided upon in the council of ministers, who were approached and begged by the king in all humility for a new tax, whose confidence in a minister was regarded an essential qualification for his appointment as chancellor, who were consulted and referred to with profound respect by a king aspiring to introduce a new religion, who demanded and got industrial, commercial and financial privileges for the country, whose wrath meant ruin to provincial governors, who were coaxed and flattered in public proclamations, who could enact statuettes even hostile to the king, in fine, who could make possible or impossible the administration of the king- an organism with these constitutional attributes was an institution which we will be justified in calling the Hindu Diet (Japanese Parliament). The *Paura-Janapada* combine was a powerful check on royal authority.[22]

The Council of Ministers was another constitutional institution, which according to KPJ, was a great check on royal absolutism and they never lost their Vedic prestige even in the most powerful days of the Hindu monarch. Thus "the king was constitutionally a servant of the people."[23]

While talking about taxation, KPJ was of the opinion that "The Hindu theory of taxation is of immense importance from the constitutional point of view." Taxes had been fixed by Law and the scales had been embodied in the Sacred Common Law. As against the royal ownership of land, KPJ produced numerous instances of gifts and sales of land by private individuals. Above all, it is expressly and emphatically declared that the king has no property in the soil and this is declared in no less an authority than the very logic of 'Hindu' law.[24]

As far as the position of king is concerned, KPJ sums up the position thus: "With this defined position, shackled with the checks and limitations we have noticed, subjugated under the great constitutional power of the *Paura-Janapada*, with a conscience trained to be prone to listen to the public voice, his position really was that of the servant of the State, i.e he was the constitutional slave. And finally, the king is the servant of the people getting his wages.[25]

In KPJ's view,

> The period after 700 A.C. (A.D. 700) is a period of darkness and disruption. Popular institutions decayed and Hindu traditions dwindled. But then there was a Hindu revival in the time of Śivāji and the Sikhs. The Sikhs as a polity failed. They failed because they could not connect themselves with the past... But the movement in Maratha country had a different history. There they looked into past history and drew up a constitution and founded a polity on materials that were easily available to them but the materials which connected them with the past... Yet the system tried was only one portion of Hindu polity, one half of the whole body. They had the *Parishad* but they had not the *Paura Janapada*. To their great credit it must however be said that in modern times they were the first to realise that one man's rule was not allowed by the wisdom and experience of their forefathers... Their limitations were the limitations of darkness and ignorance about the constitutional history of the country, a darkness which we have not yet fully removed three centuries after.[26]

KPJ concludes, "The constitutional progress made by the Hindus has probably not been equalled, much less surpassed by any polity of antiquity... The 'Golden Age' of his polity lies not in the Past but in the future." KPJ made huge temporal jumps and excluded the entire medieval period in his reconstruction of political structures. Interestingly, His modern history begins, rather early, with the seventeenth century when Vaiṣṇavism preached the equality of all men, when the Śūdra, the helot of the ancient 'Hindu' India, preached shoulder to shoulder with the Brahmin (who welcomed and encouraged it), when the God of the Hindu was for the first time worshipped with hymns composed by a Muhammadan, when Rāmadāsa declared that man is free and he cannot be subjected by force, and when the Brahmins accepted the leadership of the Śūdra in attempting to found a State... Constitutional and social advancement is not a monopoly of any particular race.[27]

KPJ's *Hindu Polity* made a deep impact on the contemporary scholars and activists, and also on a later generation of historians. F.W. Thomas, Boden Professor of Oxford University, leading authority in England on Indian history and culture, prefaced his review in the *JRAS* (1925) with these remarks: "Mr. Jayaswal is to be congratulated upon the publication of a long meditated work. We may also congratulate the student of ancient Indian institutions: for in addition to an unusual vigour of mind Mr. Jayaswal as a trained legal practitioner and theorist brings to bear upon the history of Indian state a more concrete realization of the value-in-use of terms that is natural to scholar as such. It was this that enabled him in his first publication to direct upon the political Samghas (aristocratic or republican governments) of ancient India the light obtainable from the procedure of the Buddhist ecclesiastical organizations."[28]

Later on, A.L. Basham remarked:

> As the nationalist movements progressed, and as slow steps were taken in the direction of more representative government for India, her ancient history was called upon to show that she was fitted by her traditions for democracy and self-government. The most important examples of this practice are to be found in the works of K.P. Jayaswal, a lawyer who was also a brilliant Sanskritist. If we use Bhandarkar's analogy, Jayaswal appears more often in the role of counsel for the defence than in that of impartial judge. In his most famous work, *Hindu Polity,* he sought to show that representative institutions had existed in ancient India, that the ancient Indian king was not an 'oriental despot' but a constitutional monarch, and that the states generally known as republics were in fact little different in constitution from the republics of the contemporary West. In order to prove this thesis Jayaswal employed a large range of sources, but used them in a manner of a barrister trying to win a favourable judgment, emphasizing every passage which tended to support his case, and interpreting it in the most favourable light, while virtually ignoring the evidence which went against him. *Hindu Polity* was an enormous success, and is still widely read. I believe it has played a very real part in the movement for India's independence.[29]

Commenting on the political implications of *Hindu Polity,* R.S. Sharma wrote, "Jayaswal's readings of ancient Indian political institutions presented the first solid ideological contrast to the colonial interpretations of India's ancient past and must have provided ideological support for those who were fighting for the complete independence. It is because of this that no thesis on ancient Indian history has been so frequently quoted as his monograph *Hindu Polity*. It became the Bible of the Indian nationalists. Meet any educated old man, he knows about *Hindu Polity*. Jayaswal was followed by a host of scholars, who flooded *Modern Review*, *Hindustan Review*, and *Indian Antiquary* with a spate of articles and wrote a number of theses."[30] Similarly, A.R. Kidwai, the Governor of Bihar, remarked, "Dr. K.P. Jayaswal's writings not only served the cause of Indian history and oriental learning but they also raised high the morale of the freedom-fighters for whom his *Hindu Polity* had become the second *Gītā*."[31]

Whatever political purpose *Hindu Polity* might have served during the nationalist movement, most of its conclusions and interpretations have become obsolete by now. KPJ's understanding of *Sabhā-Samiti* and its functions, coronation ceremony, the theory of limited monarchy, the role of the council of ministers, the role of *paura* and *janapada*, land ownership, taxation, etc., have been challenged and refuted by the later generation of historians.[32] However, KPJ's main weakness, as B.P. Sinha remarks, "appears to be his over-enthusiasm to build-up his pet theories about the glorious heritage of the ancient Hindus in the political and constitutional fields, and to see the full maturity of modern constitutional ideas and political system in ancient India. For this he often appears to run away with the slenderest evidence and build up his vast edifice on foundations not carefully checked."[33]

(b) *Manu and Yājñavalkya*: *A Comparison and a Contrast*: This monograph was published in 1929 from Patna. It is a collection of KPJ's lectures delivered as Tagore Law Lectures in 1917, organized by the University of Calcutta. Before the lectures, KPJ published a few articles in the legal journal, viz., the *Calcutta Weekly Notes* between 1911 and 1913.[34] The method deployed by KPJ had found approval from Joseph Kohler, Professor of Jurisprudence at the University of Berlin, who till his death retained his position as the foremost comparativist. He made an observation on those articles..."They marked a new stage in the history of Indian Law."[35] KPJ developed the same line of inquiry on the same historical method which he had already set for his studies during 1911-13.

The whole body of 'Hindu' law, the bulk of which had been neglected, had been brought under survey in those lectures. As there were numerous references in these lectures to the results stated in his constitutional history (*Hindu Polity*), KPJ deferred the printing of the lectures until the publication of the latter.

The monograph compares and contrasts the two treatises on the basic 'Hindu' law by Manu and Yājñavalkya. KPJ applied the historical method and used a variety of other sources, both literary and epigraphic, to establish the continuity and change in the 'Hindu' legal system over centuries. The monograph is divided lecture-wise in thirteen chapters. It tries to evaluate the elements of continuity and change between Manu and Yājñavalkya on several issues apart from origin and evolution of these texts and consequently 'Hindu' law. The chosen themes are:

> The role of reason and good conscience, theory of punishment, caste and administration of law, the theory of state, kingship, divine theory, fatalism in politics, Brahmin ownership of land, laws of war, republics etc., the court house, king's penal authority, caste courts in districts, king's cases, pleadings, counter cases, law of evidence, the burden of proof, contrary pleadings, possession, witnesses, and their examination, witness-box, and cross-examination, oath, ordeals, perjury, witness-jury, costs of witness, documentary evidence, criminal law—defamation, blasphemy, slander of assembly, assault, assault on trees and animals, constructive assault, theft, plea of self-defence, strīsaṁgrahaṇa, five high-offences, Brahmin and tonsure, corporate bodies, quacks, Brahmin vs Śūdra, treason, regulations, capital punishment and prison, contract, void and voidable contracts, public policy, definiteness, acts of God and state, debts, interest, rule of 'dandupat', rules about interest, limitation in debts, rule of priority, bonds, novation, attestation and registration, liability of heirs for predecessor's debts, 'pious' duty of son and grandson, Śrīdhara vs Mahidhara, *lexi loci* in contracts, execution against the person of the debtor, contract and transfer of property: surety, joint and several liability, heir's liability, agency, torts by agents, contract of carriage, contract of service, slavery, partnership, corporations, transfers, mortgage, pledge, mortgage and doctrine of trust, redemption, limitation, conditional sale, registrar of ādhi, trust deposits, title and possession, purchase in market overt, law of finder, recession of contracts, warranty, contract of marriage, divorce, specific performance, family law,

> history of marriage, women's inheritance, forms of marriage, marital relations between *dvija* and Śūdra, sons and adopted sons, their inheritance, primogeniture, partition, early doctrine of *Dāyabhāga* and *Mitākṣarā* doctrine, succession to *strīdhana*, daughter, her rights, mother, partition by father, self-acquisitions, exclusions, order of succession, succession to son, and escheat.

The last chapter deals with miscellaneous topics such as the law of gift, gifts in perpetuity, examples of appeals and original cases, security of costs in appeal, court-fees, professional lawyers, pardon by crown, eugenic rules, *sapiṇḍa* doctrine, prohibition in selection, age to be parents, telegony, sex in embryo, commentators, later *Smṛti* codes, Megasthenes and 'Hindu' law.

KPJ divides the legal literature of the 'Hindus' into three classes: the *Dharma-sūtras* or *Aphorisms of Law* of different schools, the *Dharmaśāstras* or the *Codes of Law* attributed generally to the sages well-known in sacerdotal history, and the commentaries and treatises ('digests') by 'Hindu' *jurisprudentes* which cover a period as expansive as ten centuries—from about the eighth to the nineteenth century of the Christian Era. The third class, according to KPJ, might be regarded as being still in progress and was the most important from the practical point of view, for the British law courts have made the opinion of the 'Hindu' *jurisprudentes* as the ruling and binding law of 'Hindu' society. For KPJ, the ancient scriptures remained valuable as the ultimate guides. They were the bases of the present 'Hindu' law and they must be referred to where the *jurisprudentes* ran amok.[36]

KPJ argued,

> Amongst such Codes the position of the Codes of Manu and Yājñavalkya is pre-eminent. The former is supposed to be the foundation of the whole orthodox system of Hindu Law. Its authority is regarded as supreme by the unanimous verdict of both the lay and legal literature of Hindu India, and as such it occupies a unique position in the legal history of the land. The latter is the present-day binding law of the majority of the Hindus... It has, in effect, superseded the Code of Manu. It seems clear that it was with the object of superseding the orthodox but unworkable provisions of the earlier Code that Yājñavalkya's Code was promulgated. It became the accepted code of law of the Hindus not only on account of its repealing virtue but also for its advanced and liberal juridical norms.[37]

That is why, KPJ felt it necessary to make a comparative study of the two Codes. He made a thorough enquiry into the dates of the two law Codes and argued that the Code of Manu was a product of the early days of the 'Brahmin Empire', (Śuṅga period) *circa* 150 B.C., and the final revision and the present form would have been fixed by A.D. 100-150, not later[38] and the Code of Yājñavalkya followed it about three centuries later. The period of the Code would be about 150-200 A.C. (A.D. 150-200) It cannot be earlier, and it cannot be much later."[39] On the basis of the analysis of varieties of sources, KPJ argued, "We can only say that the Code (Yājñavalkya) is based on (1) the Mānava Code as pointed out by Stenzler, (2) the Vishṇu- Smṛiti, as pointed out by Jolly, and lastly, and for law proper mainly, on the Arthaśāstra of Kauṭilya."[40] KPJ fixed the date of the Code of Kauṭilya about 300 B.C. His studies, therefore, cover a period of about five centuries of legal development.[41] In fixing these chronologies, KPJ invoked the material progress of the society reflected in these texts.

KPJ further argued,

> In our study, however, we cannot do without taking into account the Imperial Code of Law of the Mauryas in the Artha-Śāstra of Kauṭilya. ...While Yājnvalkya borrows bodily from the Artha-Śāstra. The *Dharmasthiyam* in the Artha-Śāstra is a unique code in legal history. It is one of the earliest codes of law in the world, and in quality it is far superior to the most of the early codes. Its authority embraced an area greater than that covered by any ancient Code. It is absolutely secular. In Hindu legal literature it is the only secular Code before the Nārada-Smṛiti, and the Nārada- Smṛiti closely follows the *Dharmasthiyam*. You cannot have a comparative view of Manu and Yājñavalkya without reference to Artha-Śāstra. They both are connected with it. Points which in the domain of Hindu Law appeared as so many riddles to earlier writers, can be now solved with the help of the Artha-Śāstra. The Artha-Śāstra was the missing link.[42]

In KPJ's opinion, "A correct appreciation of the different codes and their different provisions without reference to the social, political, and economic history of the country is not possible. The law codes are not so many idiocyncratic productions of Brahmins; they are the children of their times."[43]

By quoting examples from *sūtras*, KPJ argued that they *"conclusively establish the fact that the secular laws or king's laws in the sūtra period were different from the Dharma law*. The provinces of the

Dharma and the Artha laws were separate. But in the *Māṇava-Dharma-śāstra*, for the first time, we find the Dharma-śāstra invading upon and appropriating the province of the Artha law and making the latter only an appendage to its own system." The reason, KPJ argued, "That the sacerdotal power became also the political power in the country. The law of politician, therefore, got merged into the law of sacerdotalist. The invasion of law proper by the Dharma-Śāstra explains the sudden appearance of a fully developed system of law in the Dharma literature in the shape of Mānava Code."[44] According to KPJ, "The Mānava Code thus suffers from its political, social, and sacerdotal prejudices. It is a code as well as a controversy. But if we transfer ourselves to its times, we can imagine how ready approval it would have received from the race to which it was preached. Buddhism and Buddhist State stood discredited."[45] While describing the Yājñavalkya, KPJ argued, "...Work being a purely scientific book, the scientific attitude and freedom from prejudice made the work acceptable throughout India."[46]

According to KPJ, the development in law has its full counterpart in developments of commerce, of political institutions and of social welding of orthodox and Buddhistic thought. KPJ argued,

> The psychology of the Hindu nation of the Brahmin Empire is pictured in the Mānava-Dharma-Śāstras, and the voice of prosperous and the liberal empire of the Sātavāhanas is recorded in the Code of Yājñavalkya. The Brahmin in the Mānava Dharma-Śāstra claims to be 'lord of all', he claims exemption from capital punishment, he argues for a special criminal law for his caste, and he pleads for local sovereignties as against imperialism.... The Brahmin, when the Code of Manu was composed, was the Emperor of India, he was the lord of all, his empire recognised sub-kings, he had smarted under the Mauryan law seeking to establish uniformity and equality before the Criminal Court in contravention of the common law which was based on caste. The Code of Manu practically ignores women, because that was the view of the old common law.[47]

KPJ further argued,

> The last chapter of Manu bears a striking resemblance to the doctrines of *Gītā* in several places. The Bhaviṣya Purāṇa which describes Pushyamitra as the saviour of Hindu society and Dharma and as subjugating Kali, makes him also a special student of *Gītā*. The *Gītā* is

> a gospel of war composed to combat the Buddhist doctrine of 'no war.' It is very likely that the *Gītā* was not only a favourite of Pushyamitra but a work of his period. The doctrinal affinity between Manu and the *Gītā* is easily explicable. The Śuṅga period, in the light of recent studies has to be counted as the epoch of the first Sanskrit revival, and of great literary activity... So does the Brahmanisation of *Mahābhārata*. Sanskrit histrionics, the beginning of Kāvya style, Sanskrit inscriptions, and fuller Sanskritic forms on coins and seals which appear for the first time in that period, all indicate a great Sanskrit literary upheaval in the period, which even Buddhism, the great advocate of Prakrit, does not escape. During and after the Śuṅga epoch even the Buddhists had to adopt Sanskrit as the medium to spread their cult. The Mānava Code studied as part of the literature of the Śuṅga revival becomes explicable in its character.[48]

There is marked difference between the two Codes. KPJ argued,

> We can understand it if we remember that the Sātavāhana rule combined orthodoxy with Buddhism and that Buddhism had made woman an equal of man. The corporation of nuns had held property as much as that of monks; likewise, the woman of Sātavāhana regime could inherit property from her husband and father. Similarly, the privilege of Brahmin is cut down to a minimum in Yājñavalkya. The largest space in Civil Law is given in Contract in the latter Code. Partnership of sea-traders and artisans and the law of Corporations find place in Yājñavalkya. All this is a reflection of the economic life of the country in the Sātavāhana epoch. Commerce with the West was at its zenith. The corporate life of the artisans is a known feature of the economic prosperity of the time.[49]

As far as the position of Śūdra is concerned, KPJ argued,

> ...With the Brahmin revolution, and with the hostility of the Śūdra dynasty (i.e. Mauryas) and Śūdra religion (i.e., Buddhism), the Śūdra greatly suffers in the Mānava Code. With the fall of the Śuṅgas, his position is so much improved as he had never attained before. Yājñavalkya has no repressive law against a Śūdra disputing with the Brahmins, or against a Śūdra teaching, a Śūdra owning property and so forth. Manu's hostility to the Śūdra is primarily towards the learned Śūdra, towards the controvertilist Śūdra, claiming equality and freedom. That claim is almost tacitly allowed in Yājñavalkya. And herein lies the greatness of Yājñavalkya as a lawyer. He accepted facts and bowed to the change that had taken place.[50]

After analysis of the contents of Yājñavalkya, KPJ came to the conclusion,

> It raises the position of the Śūdra, allow him Chāndrāyaṇa penance which had been open only to the twice-born, enjoins respect to be shown to him when gifted with knowledge, and allows trade to him. The extravagant punishments for his suppression are omitted. Likewise, the extravagant claims of the Brahmin for total immunity are set aside, and he is brought under king's law. The profession of arms is once more forbidden to the Brahmin. His claim to sovereignty is ignored.... Yānjñavalkya bears the stamp of the kindly conscience bequeathed by Buddhism during its past revolution. Punishments are, like penances, much less severe, and here the Code is an advancement not only on Manu but also upon Kauṭilya. Laws about women are brought in conformity with their social position, already immensely raised by Buddhism... The Code may be taken to have replaced and repealed Manu's Code throughout the land of Aryan civilisation.[51]

Further,

> Yājñavalkya with his progressive tendency still retains orthodox conservatism. It is due to this feature that it outlived the true codes of law like that of Nārada. The orthodox school favoured Yājñavalkya. Yājñavalkya may be credited to have given a permanent life to the Dharma-Vyavahāra mixed system of law in the country. Without him probably today we would have been more used to Nārada, or Bṛihaspati and Kātyāyana, and we would not have lost the latter two.[52]

KPJ made a significant comparison between the Manu and Yājñavalkya regarding the criminal law. He argued,

> The Mānava Code, with a ferocious puritanism and a blood-thirsty religious zeal, remained a controversy, rather than the law, on the subject of crimes. Yājñavalkya sat down to remedy this defect, and succeeded in giving a workable code of criminal law. He defines crime with reference to the older law which had been in force before the Code of Mānava, classified offences and laid down the old punishments in milder form. He gave a code without any controversy, unlike the object and reasons of the so-called Manu on the law about the Śūdra, without citing any opinion, without any fear of the name of Manu and even contradicting him. He does not deserve credit for originality as he had the Code of Kauṭilya before him. Yet he deserves greater credit than that of originality. He boldly cured the injury done

> to the society by the Code of Manu. He prescribed uniform laws, removed the weight of social depression off the limbs of the nation. What Aśvaghosha did as a preacher, Yājñavalkya silently did as a legislator, and even so an orthodox legislator...Legal genius of the race kept pace with other activities and reached the pinnacle of glory in the latter period, but in criminal law it found nothing to add; it accepted Yājñavalkya as final.[53]

KPJ gave special attention to the law of judicial procedure. For him, "The Law of Procedure is a branch of Hindu Law well worth a critical study which will richly repay the student of comparative jurisprudence. It marks a high development in the legal history of the world. Then, it has also some, though rare, application, and utility to our present-day Hindu Law... Anquaintance with the Procedure Law also helps us in appreciating provisions of Substantive Law."[54] KPJ also expressed surprise to know that the procedure as to pleadings, which was prevalent in the courts of the East India Company towards the end of eighteenth and the beginning of the nineteenth century and which had been the subject of judicial dicta of the courts, really came down and developed from the procedure of the Yājñavalkya Code. KPJ also provides evidence of the existence of a professional lawyer. However, he argued that the working system of the court—the judge and the *Sabhā*—is not to be fully gathered from the codes, and the provisions in that respect have to be illustrated from general literature, in the light of which the *Sabhā* were the real judges to whom the judge only explained the law. There was also the King-in-Council sitting in appeal. The codes also place the laws of prescription and limitation among the Laws of Procedure. The laws of eugenics also draw KPJ's special attention.

KPJ also discussed the theories of politics given in the two codes and the underlying idea being the interrelation between politics and law. According to him,

> Yājñavalkya adopts a higher standard. Manu's Code, for instance, advocates royal absolutism. This was clearly against the old tradition of the country and against the old common law. ...But, the Mānava-Dharma-śāstra had to uphold a political revolution which was also a social revolution—a political rule by the Brahmin. Yājñavalkya gives up the position of Manu. Manu's Code, however, does not allow the king to make the law as he did in the Mauryan regime. Yājñavalkya's attitude on the subject is characteristic. He does not count the king

among the sources of law, yet he recognizes laws made by kings. The attitude is one of liberal conservatism throughout.[55]

The family law is another topic to which KPJ gives more attention because the two codes bear more accentuated points of difference which are sometimes bewildering. For example, the forms of marriage prohibited by Manu are allowed by Yājñavalkya. The kinds of sons disinherited by Manu have been enfranchised by Yājñavalkya. Woman is brought in the list of heirs by the latter. Different provisions as to maintenance, succession to *strīdhana*, and a number of other differences, along with the views of commentators thereon, are important studies for the lawyer today. KPJ saw the rise of the different schools of 'Hindu' law in these differences.[56]

Some other marked difference between Manu and Yājñavalkya highlighted by KPJ are:

(1) Manu defined Āryāvarta from sea to sea in the east and west, and from mountain to mountain (the Himalayas and the Vindhyas). The country of *mleccha*s is beyond that.[57] Yājñavalkya does not give any definition of Āryāvarta.[58]

(2) Manu is hostile towards *mleccha*s, Yājñavalkya is not.[59]

(3) For Manu, *Śruti* (Vedas) and *Dharmaśāstra* are the only sources of Dharma-law, and for Yājñavalkya, along with these *Aṅgas*, *Purāṇa*s were also sources of the Dharma-law.[60]

(4) Manu introduced a new theory—divine theory of kingship with the right of perfect arbitrariness. This was opposed to all traditions, Vedic rituals of kingship and coronation, and the very spirit of 'Hindu' law which refuses to place even gods above the law and which distinctly places the king under it. Yājñavalkya ignored this theory and only translated the undertaking of the coronation oath.[61]

(5) Manu is hostile to the republics, Yājñavalkya is not hostile.[62]

(6) Manu expects the state to be puritanical and of correct morals, while Yājñavalkya expects the king to be more practical, to reduce the incident of vice by administrative methods rather than by moral crusade.[63]

(7) Manu was not only a lawyer and law-giver, but also as an advocate and preacher of anti-Buddhist Brahmin revolution; Yājñavalkya is not anti-Buddhist.[64]

(8) Both enjoin that the royal judge should be only one and

that should be a Brahmin. But when Manu requires the jurymen also to be brahmins, Yājñavalkya did not accept it.[65]

(9) The slave had been regarded as a chattel in *Dharma*. However, Yājñavalkya applied principles of contract to slavery... a slave saved the life of his master and held to have completed his service was free; if he paid his price or the cost of maintenance he was entitled to obtain liberty.[66]

(10) Yājñavalkya's name must always be remembered for endowing women with the right of inheritance. He lays down the list of the heirs of a sonless deceased, with the wife and the daughter. Without his law, daughters and widows could not have been heirs to-day in this country, The Mānava code does not admit either of them in its list.[67]

This monograph may be classed in the category of *Hindu Polity*, as KPJ tried to see all the modern political institutions developed in ancient/'Hindu' India; similarly he tried to find out all the developed modern legal institutions, such as Constitutional Law, 'Hindu' court, 'Hindu' legal system, 'Hindu' lawyer, doctrine of legitimacy, cross-examination, oath, plaintiff, defendant, etc. *Sabhya* for KPJ, "The people who decided the case were the Sabhyas... The Sabhyas were the real judges... They very much resemble the present jury: in spirit both are the same. Yet both had different origin and history. The English jury first came in as witness of the neighbourhood. But the *Sabhā* was a remnant of the national assembly of the Vedic times... The *Sabhā* and the English jury are essentially different in genesis, though they both arrive at the same judicial goal and perform there the same function."[68] Describing the inaugural speech by the judge in the court room, KPJ believes, "...In full conformity with the high traditions of Hindu judiciary, and worthy of being followed in any age and civilisation."[69] Similarly, while describing the law of judicial procedure KPJ argued, "Yājñavalkya's law of procedure is far in advance of Kauṭilya and Sumati. Yet he does not reach the level attained by Nārada and Bṛhaspati, whom the most technical rules of pleadings of Modern Europe have not yet surpassed."[70] While tracing the principles of contract, "Almost all the principles of contract which we know to-day are to be found in the laws of Artha-Śāstra."[71]

As a historian, KPJ was fully aware of his sources, time, and place and argued that whatever changes are visible in Manu and

Yājñavalkya, they were due to the social, economic, and political changes. Some of the conclusions and interpretations drawn by KPJ might appear irrelevant today. However, this monograph created a deep impact on the historians and jurists soon after its publication.

Fitz Gerald, I.C.S., Lecturer to the Inns of Courts on 'Hindu' law, described this work in the *English Law Quarterly Review* in these terms:

> 'Hindu Law', said J.D. Mayne 'has the oldest pedigree of any known system of Jurisprudence'. Yet its ascertained history has hitherto been a miscellaneous collection of dry bones without flesh or blood and with even the position of the bones in the skeleton disputed by the anatomist. Generalization of the widest type—for instance, that the age of Dharmasūtras preceded that of Dharmashāstras; dates which were seldom within half a millennium of certainty; these were all that the scholar had to offer a lawyer anxious to understand the growth of the system which he has been called upon to administer. Max Muller and Būhler destroyed the Anglo-Brahmanical legend (enshrined in Mayne's Ancient Law and in the Holman Hunt fresco at Lincoln's Inn) of the Manudharmāshāstra as a code of laws claiming obedience in the same manner as e.g., the XIIth Tables or the 'Corpus Juris': but they put nothing in its place. Little or no attempt was made to connect the history of thought with the political history of India; though it must be obvious that, however detached from the world's affairs the Ṛishis might be, great kingdoms could not rise and fall nor great religious system strive for acceptance without some effect on the jurisprudence and ethics of the schools. It is to the credit of Mr. Jayaswal that he makes a real constructive attempt to bridge the gap. Sanskritist and lawyer, he adds to these qualifications a rare independence of judgment.[72]

The Vice Chancellor also spoke in glowing terms: "The book is studied not only in Indian Universities but also in Continental Universities and is recognised as a standard work of Ancient Law."[73] The monograph finds numerous references in the recent publications on Manu and Yājñavalkya[74] and one can find numerous references to KPJ in the fourteenth revised edition of *Mayne's Hindu Law and Usages.*[75]

(c) *History of India c. A.D. 150 to 350 A.D.*: The constitution and law were not to remain KPJ's sole fields of study. He was conducting researches into all branches of the comprehensive subject—Indian history and culture. His interest in the problems of reconstructing political history and chronology of ancient India was shown as early as 1915 and he had written a number of articles in *JBORS*. But his most widely read and discussed book on political history is the *History of India c. A.D. 150 to 350 A.D.* He christened the period as Nāga-Vākāṭaka imperial period. This appeared in volume IX of *JBORS* and was published as a monograph in 1933. The period A.D. 150-350, from the fall of the Kuṣānas to the rise of the 'Imperial' Guptas, was dubbed as the Dark Age in Indian history. KPJ, by piecing together bits of information scattered here and there in the Purāṇic literature, in the inscriptions and coins, tried to disprove this theory of Dark Age and to reconstruct the political history of the period to show that it was an era of great national resistance and a bright epoch in the political and cultural history of India. Viewed through his eyes, the Gupta empire and its cultural excellence emerge as natural successors of the Nāga-Vākāṭaka age.

The monograph is divided into five parts: (i) India under the Nāga Dynasty (c. 150 A.D.-284 A.D.), (ii) The Vākāṭaka Kingdom, (248 A.D. - 284 A.D.): the Vākāṭaka Empire (284 A.D.-384 A.D.), with an Appendix on the later Vākāṭaka period (348 A.D. 550 A.D.), (iii) Magadha (31 B.C.-340 A.D.) and the Gupta India at 350 A.D., (iv) Southern India (150 A.D.-350 A.D.) and the Unification of the North and the South; and (v) Conclusion (Effects of Gupta Imperialism). Looking at the contents of the monograph, it appears that this monograph is an anti-thesis to V.A. Smith's *Early History of India* (1924 edition). Smith had dubbed the period as 'Dark Age'. Therefore, before the beginning of the discussion, KPJ prays; 'Lead me from darkness to light'.

KPJ begins with the chief arguments of Smith:

(A) 'So much, however is clear, that Vāsudeva was the last Kushān king who continued to hold extensive territories in India. After his death there is no indication of the existence of a paramount power in Northern India'.

(B) 'Probably numerous Rājās asserted their independence and formed a number of short-lived states... but historical materials for the third century is so completely lacking that it is impossible to say what and how many those states were'.

(C) 'The period between the extinction of the Kushān and the Āndhra dynasties, about A.D. 220 or 230, and the rise of the imperial Gupta dynasty, nearly a century later, is one of the darkest in the whole range of Indian history'.

After working on the materials available, KPJ found that none of the three statements can be accepted and need to be repeated in future. KPJ argued that the statement that there was no paramount power before the 'Imperial' Guptas is thoroughly incorrect and cannot be maintained even for a moment. According to him, "The history of Imperial Hindu revival is not to be dated in the fourth century with Samudra Gupta, not even with the Vākāṭakas nearly a century earlier, but with the Bhāra-Śivas half a century earlier still. There is not a line about the Vākāṭakas in the history of Dr. Vincent Smith, nor a line about the Bhāra-Śivas in any text-book."[76]

The rise of the Bhāra-Śivas is dated roughly about A.D. 150 and their seat was between Kauśāmbī and Banares. KPJ believed that the real contribution of the Bhāra-Śivas is the foundation of a new tradition—"The tradition of Hindu freedom and sovereignty... The tradition initiated by the Bhāra-Śiva was kept up by the Vākāṭakas and was taken over by the Guptas and fully maintained by the subsequent emperors from Chandra Gupta Vikramāditya to Bālāditya. If there had been no Bhāra-Śiva there would not have come into existence a Gupta Empire and the Gupta Vikramādityas."[77]

The period of the Gupta rule was characterised as 'Golden Age' in the writings of some contemporaries of KPJ. However, KPJ's own remarks on Samudragupta, the first important king of that dynasty, read as follows:

> ...Samudra Gupta, like Alexander, killed the free spirit of his country. He destroyed the Mālavas and the Yaudheyas, who were the nursery of freedom; and many others of their class. Once those free communities were wiped out, the recruiting ground for future heroes and patriots and statesmen disappeared. The Gupta themselves, both from their mother's side and their father's side, had descended from those republican communities. They themselves were crops of those seed communities but they totally destroyed them.[78]
>
> The social system of the republican communities was based on equality. They knew no caste. They consisted of one caste only. The o rthodox system, on the other hand, was based on inequality and caste where mass patriotism could not be mobilised as it could easily be done amongst the Mālavas, the Yaudheyas, the Mādrakas, the Pushyamitras, the Ābhīras and the Lichchhavis. They were the exercise-ground for state-making, for patriotism, for individual ambitions, capabilities and leadership. But under Samudra Gupta and

> his descendants they all merged into an organised, officialised, orthodox caste-system and an orthodox political system which recognised and fostered monarchy and imperialism. The seed-pot for the rise of a Kṛishṇa, the prophet of rightful war and the prophet of the cult of duty, the seed-pot to produce a Buddha, the prophet of a universal religion and universal equality, was consumed forever; the seed-pot of the production of a future Bhāraśiva or a future Gupta was made extinct. And the Hindu sank. The Republics of Rajaputana dissolved into Rajputs who forgot all the traditions of their republican ancestors. And the Republics of the Punjab dissolved into the Jaṭs with all their past lost. The life-giving element was gone. The Hindus did not remember the name of Samudra Gupta with any gratitude, and when Alberuni came to India he was told that the Guptas were a wicked people. This is another view of that picture. They were the tyrants of the Hindu constitutional freedom, though excellent rulers to the individual subject.[79]

In contrast, one century of Bhāra-Śiva rule was a period of the germination of 'Hindu imperialism', of the foundation of a 'new tradition—the tradition of Hindu freedom and sovereignty', and the period which took the Āryāvarta and India out of the 'Dark Age' and enlightened them. Taking recourse to prognostication and a few verses of the *Vana-parvan* of the *Mahābhārata*, KPJ designated the period of the Kuṣāṇas as 'Buddhist India' and drew inferences about the terrible state of 'Hindu nation'. The *Mahābhārata* verses read as follows:

> ...The whole world will be Mlechchhanized; all rights and sacrifices will cease. The Brāhmaṇas, Kṣatriyas and Vaiśyas will disappear; at this time all men will become one caste... men will no more gratify the Celestials with *śrāddha* or manes with libations. Prohibiting the worship of Celestials, they will worship bones. In the settlement of the Brāhmaṇas, in the Āśramas of the Great Ṛishis, in place sacred to gods, in sacred spots and in temples which had been dedicated to the Nāgas—the land will be marked with tombs ('Eḍūkas' = Buddhist stūpas) containing bones. They will have no temples dedicated to the Celestials.[80]

KPJ comments, "The description seems to be a description of an eye-witness." With such an assumption and ascribing these descriptions of the *Mahābhārata, Vana-parvan* to c. A.D. 150-200, KPJ compared them with the description of the Śaka rule in *Garga-Saṁhitā* and several *Purāṇas*. His own assessment of the Śaka rule is:

> The Śakan rule aimed at denationalising the Hindus and at the basic destruction of the national system. The social revolution which the Śakas strove for with a calculated policy, was a scheme to depress the high and the aristocrati, the custodian of national culture and the trustee of national liberty—the Brahmin and the Kshatriya... They aimed at sapping character from the common people by systematic terrorisation and proselytisation. The *Garga Saṁhitā* says that they carried away one-fourth of the total population from Śiprā to their own capital, i. e. Bactria. Their massacres are noted both by the *Garga Saṁhitā* and in their summing up by the *Purāṇas*. They must have carried away as well great wealth from the country to Bactria. Their infamous greed was notorious. They systematically imposed a non-Brahmanical religious system on the Hindus. Hindu life, in short, was suspended. No book written between 78 A.D. to 180 A.D. is to be traced in the orthodox literature of Northern India. It became, therefore, imperatively necessary for the Hindus to undertake to deliver their country from such a political and social scourge.[81]

The Bhāra-Śivas are supposed to have taken upon themselves the responsibility of freeing the nation from this national calamity, and they also raised the yogic/ascetic and destructive *tāṇdava* form of Mahādeva Śiva as the symbol of 'National Cult and Faith'. KPJ emphatically wrote:

> The presiding God to whom political service was this time dedicated, was the God of Destruction. The Bhāraśivas called in Śiva who stood up in Yoga for a partial Tāṇdava through his people of the Gangetic valley. We find Śiva everywhere in this period. The air is surcharged with the belief that the Destroyer Himself has founded the Bhāraśiva State, that He is guarantor of the king and the people of the Bhāraśiva kingdom. He has stood up to see His people free—free to follow their *dharma,* free to be their own masters, free to be in Āryāvarta, the land of the Āryas, their God-given home...He must do it by His own method, by His own process, the dance of destruction. The Nāga kings became *Bhāraśiva*. They undertook to execute and they successfully executed that national dance of destruction in the valley of Ganges. The names assumed by the Bhāraśiva Nāgas—'Vīrasena', 'Skanda Nāga', 'Bhīma Nāga', 'Deva Nāga', 'Bhava Nāga'—all prove that the sense of Śaiva responsibility and necessity which the time required. Their repeated *aśvamedhas,* like the revival of names of divine heroes, are records in themselves. A series of acts of valour continued, and repeated exertions resulted in progressive destruction of the Kushan power in Āryāvarta... The Kushans were so pressed by the Bhāraśivas

> that they ultimately sought the protection of the Sassanian Emperor Shapur (between 238 and 269 A.D.) whose effigy they had to stamp on their coins... The hills up to Kangrā once more were under Hindu rulers when Samudra Gupta appeared on the scene. Most of the achievement is to be credited to the Bhāraśiva Nāgas, performers of ten *aśvamedhas*; and the maintenance of that free inheritance for 50 years, with further progress, to the Vākāṭakas, who carried on the Bhāraśiva policy.[82]
>
> The Bhāraśiva rule was marked with Śiva's asceticism. They have no grandeur except the grandeur of their severe and austere undertaking. They ignore the imperial coinage of Kushans and revert to the old Hindu coinage. They assume no grandeur, unlike the Guptas. Like Śiva, they have a self imposed non-richness. Like Śiva, they bestow and not partake. They give freedom to the Hindu Republics; they give them freedom to mint their own money and to live their own full life. Like Śivas's domestic polity, they have a member of *gaṇa*, of Hindu States around them. They are the true Śiva-made Nandi, the lord of the *gaṇas*. They merely preside over a confederacy of states and foster freedom everywhere. They perform *aśvamedhas*, but do not function as *eka-rāṭ* Emperors. They remain political Śaivas and international ascetics amongst their countrymen.[83]

Since the Kuṣāṇa emperors were the killers of cows and bulls, the Bhāra-Śivas decided to make the bull their sacred symbol, depicting it on their coins, and it was only thereafter that the sacredness of the bull came to be recognised universally throughout the length and breadth of their empire, 'punctuating the difference of their age from the last political period when the bull was freely slaughtered for the kitchen of the Kuṣāṇas... In total contrast to the rule of the Guptas, that of the Bhāra-Śiva kings of the Nāga dynasty was responsible for raising a confederacy of states where considerable freedom and autonomy was reposed in the confederating units. The Bhāra-Śivas were truly political Śaivas. KPJ concluded, "The foundations of modern Hinduism were laid by the Nāga Emperors and that edifice was reared by the Vākāṭakas and elaborated by the Guptas."[84]

KPJ also discussed with pride, the 'Hindu notion' of imperialism:

> Further India was recognized as part of India in the Bhāraśiva-Vākāṭaka Period... Between the Himavat and the sea, Bhāratavarsha stands, but it covers a larger area on account of Indians *Bhāratī-prajā*

living in eight more islands (dvīpas),...All these dvīpas were to the east, that is, they constituted or sea-grit lands what we call to-day Further India. *Indradvīpa,* the first dvīpa in the list, has been satisfactorily identified with Burma. The Malay Peninsula was well known to Indians at that time... *Kaseru* or *Kaserumat* dvīpa which is mentioned next to *Indradvīpa* meant the present Straits Settlements. The next class begins with Tāmraparṇi (the older name of Ceylon): Tāmraparṇa, Gabhastimān, Nāgadvīpa, Saumya, Gāndharva, and Varuṇa dvīpas. Nāgadvīpa is Nicobar. ...It is certain that the Purāṇas in the third and the fourth centuries are conscious of the Hindu colonies in Further India, and treat them as parts of Bhāratavarsha. Their Bhāratavarsha, which was primarily India, was at this point of time interpreted as India-cum-Greater India, which latter taking Ceylon, consisted of eight units of divisions, called *dvīpas.*[85]

....*the King of Siṁhala and all other islanders* (or, Ocean rulers), who made their submission and acknowledged Samudra Gupta as their Emperor. They paid no taxes but brought presents and expressly accepted his headship. Samudra Gupta describes this as *uniting the whole land Pṛithivi within his two arms.* His India or Pṛithivi, therefore, embraced within its bounds Further India. *'All the dvīpas'* here meant all India colonies of Bhāratavarsha, of the *Bhārati prajā*... We have in the third century a Sanskrit inscription in Chaṁpā (Cambodia) of a king belonging to the dynasty of Śri Māra Kauṇdinya, anticipating the favourite *Vasantatilakā* metre and the language and style of the Vākāṭaka and Gupta inscriptions. This inscription establishes that the connection of the colonies with the Bhāraśiva and Vākāṭaka India and with the revivalism of Sanskrit in the home-land had been fully maintained... The connection of the Hindu king of Funan with India since 245 A.D. is also a recorded fact... About the same time in the Hindu colony of Western Java we find inscriptions being written in Sanskrit in the script of 'the fourth and fifth centuries A.D.' And Sumatra gets so much of orthodox Hindu culture just before the arrival of Fa Hien that he found: *'various forms of error and Brahmanism flourishing while Buddhism in it is not worth speaking of.'*[86]...Evidence of art further establishes a Guptan connection with Indian colonies.[87]

Samudra Gupta in every respect carried out the Hindu ideal of imperialism... According to that ideal the whole of India including Afghanistan must be comprised in that empire. But the empire must not go further west and be at the cost of the liberties of the countries beyond Afghanistan. The traditional international morality of Hindu India was noted by the Greek writers and the Arab Sulaiman. The Law of Manu, which fixes the western boundary of India, was

> scrupulously observed by Samudra Gupta...But Samudra Gupta had a law laid down to him by his Dharmaśāstra—the code, 'the *rule (Śastra) of civilisation*' (dharma). And that dharma was followed: that dharma limited a Hindu monarch's action, both international and imperial. The history of Samudra Gupta's conquests shows that his actions were well-regulated by that law, and that he did not become a militarist.[88]

And look at another instance of the hegemonic role of the North India over South:

> The history of South for the period is really a history of Northerns in the South, both new and old, and of their efforts to introduce and establish a common civilization, *viz.* that Hinduism which proved so successful at the time in reforming and reviving the society in the North. The South becomes so united with the North through these efforts that truly the old definition of Bhāratavarsha had to be revised and extended to include the whole of the South. The northern Hindus introduce the language, the script, the worship and the culture in general, of the North into the South. They infuse new life in Further India from there, and make history. They make One India by common culture, the legacy of which has come down to us.[89]

The above representation of the Bhāra-Śivas-Vākāṭakas and Gupta imperialism appears to be an over-glorification. The appearance of Śiva and his role in emancipation and then sudden disappearance is like a kind of dramatisation. However, it is to be admitted that KPJ's writing, in the context of the time, did serve Indian nationalism? The national consciousness and pride in the progress in the constitutional field in the past, seldom emphasised by scholars before, certainly served a useful purpose. An ardent 'nationalist' with a history of political activity and association, KPJ was proud of the national heritage and the versatile genius of the Indian people in bygone days. He hated the contemporary foreign rule and consistently condemned the foreign rulers of ancient days. The 'nationalist' in him would never allow him to give the devil his due; he could never accept that a foreign ruler could ever be the best beneficial ruler in any sense or aspect. The total anti-Indianness of all foreign rulers was what he believed in and what he tried to show to his readers. Impartial Indian scholars have given some credit to and shown their appreciation of Kuṣāṇa contribution to the development of Indian religions and culture, art and literature, not only in this country but outside. To KPJ, Kuṣāṇa policy was "a policy of social tyranny and religious fanaticism, both actuated by political motives."

KPJ goes further, after indulging in specious arguments, concludes that "Kuṣāṇa rule destroyed them (the pre-Gupta Hindu temples)." His strong 'nationalist' bias leads him to strongly defend the Varṇāśrama system and the ritual-ridden brahmanic religion, which he regards as essential elements of ancient 'Hindu nationalism'. He observes: "The Śaka rule aimed at denationalising the Hindus and at the basic destruction of their national system. The social revolutions which the Śakas strove for with a calculated policy, was a scheme to depress the high and aristocratic, the custodians of national culture and the trustees of national liberty - the Brahmins and the Kshatriyas." Impartial critics of the Kuṣāṇa rule will not find enough evidence to credit or discredit the Kuṣāṇas with the alleged successful scheme to destroy the Varṇāśrama Dharma and Hinduism. Kadphises II and Vāsudeva could not be accused of anti-Hinduism. But KPJ's main concern was to show the totally unacceptable character of all foreign rule and its calculated policy to denationalise the enslaved nation. Probably he was transferring the attributes of British rule in his days, as he saw them, to the Kuṣāṇas. And, as any movement against the British rule and for reassertion of Hindu ideas and cultural norms would be a nationalist movement, he saw in the rise of the Bhāra-Śiva-Nāgas and the growth of the Vākāṭaka power the fulfilment of national aspirations of the period (A.D. 150-350) against the degraded and tyrannical rule of the alien Śaka-Kuṣāṇas. He, therefore, wove a story from scattered slender threads, often of doubtful authenticity, of a national regeneration movement against the foreign rule, and tried to demonstrate the resounding success of the movement.

According to KPJ, "The undertaking to deliver the country from such a national calamity was shouldered by Bhāra-Śivas in the valley of Ganges... They undertook to execute and they successfully executed that national dance of destruction in the valley of Ganges". In order to enhance the so-called achievements of the Bhāra-Śivas, the enemy's—the Kuṣāṇas'—power is at first magnified, and then the success of the Bhāra-Śivas from humble beginnings against such a great power is admirably dramatised. He argued, "That power now to be challenged by a leader raised from obscurity was a bigger fact than the challenge by the subject Greeks against the mammoth

Persian empire... It was not the question of merely throwing off a suzerainty, it was not the case of merely tearing off the veil of prestige hanging from a distance, but attacking directly a mighty power bodily installed in the country. The Bhāra-Śivas did it and did it successfully." Should we not read here the mighty British empire and the Indian nationalist movement under Gandhi for the Kuṣāṇa empire and the humble Bhāra-Śivas respectively? Could not his conclusions inspire the confidence of the nationalist leaders about their ultimate success just to prove that history repeats itself? According to KPJ "The greedy imperialism of the Kuṣāṇa was destroyed: the Hindu people were purged of deteriorated morals. And when the task was done, the Bhāra-Śivas retired... They restored the Hindu imperial throne and the national civilisation and gave a new life to their country... they left their deeds and obliterated themselves". In doing so, KPJ was making sweeping generalisations, which were ruthlessly criticised by later scholars.

KPJ's above monograph is again a kind of glorification. However, the immediate impact of the publication of *History of India* was so effective that E. Edwards, who revised the standard book of V.A. Smith on the *History of India* stated in his preface that new knowledge gained from KPJ's researches, necessitated a revision of the book. V.A. Smith's two titles on *Indian History* bear numerous references to KPJ's fresh discoveries on the topic.[90]

Several hypotheses of KPJ have been questioned by the later generations of historians.[91] His entire laboriously built-up theory of the Bhāra-Śiva-Vākāṭaka all-India empire, resting on questionable readings of legends and attribution of coins and on very infrequent and scattered references in the Puranic literature, have been very plausibly shown by A.S. Altekar to be almost a castle in the air. But, KPJ's main weakness appears to be his overenthusiasm to build up his pet theories about the glorious heritage of the ancient 'Hindus'... For this he often appears to run away with the slenderest evidence and build up his vast edifice on foundations not carefully checked.[92] KPJ again tries to see the history from A.D. 150 to 350 as a binary opposition of Smith's writing. There had been several developments in realm of religion, art, polity, society during the period following the Mauryan period, and some of the credit for these developments must certainly be attributed to the 'foreign rulers', which have been purposely denigrated by KPJ. Again, by no means the political control of the

Kuṣāṇas was less than the Guptas; however, KPJ was so obsessed with the Guptas that he termed them as 'Imperial Guptas' but never mentioned the Kuṣāṇas as 'Imperial', when he discussed in this context the Nāgas or the Guptas. As far as the notion of imperialism in ancient India is concerned, KPJ was trying to do for Southeast Asia what the Western Indologists did in the context of India, "His approach to the history to this region did not really differ much from Vincent Smith's approach to the history of ancient India. This certainly is an unacceptable face of Indian nationalist historiography."[93]

KPJ's *History of India*, however, made a deep impact on the scholars and intellectuals coming from different disciplines. It is important to read Amritlal Nagar in this context:

> सन '45 में दो फिल्मों के संवाद लिखने के वास्ते मद्रास गया था। इसी के आस-पास किसी समय मद्रास के एक मंदिर में दर्शन करने गया था। मंडप में एक पुराणवाचक तमिल भाषा में कथा सुना रहे थे। कथा कहने के ढंग में मुझे अपने यहाँ के कथावाचकों जैसे ही झटके दिखलाई दिए। मौज में आकर थोड़ी देर के लिए वहीं खड़ा हो गया। पुराणवाचक महोदय ने एकदा नैमिषारण्यत्तिल कहा, तो मेरे मन में अपनेपन की फुरफुरी-सी दौड़ गई। लगा हमारी गोमती नदी के तट पर राष्ट्रीय महत्त्व का कम-से-कम एक पावन क्षेत्र तो है ही, जहाँ सारे पुराण, भगवत, महाभारत आदि ग्रन्थ सुनाए गए थे। नैमिष के सम्बन्ध में केवल यह प्रश्न ही अरसे तक मन में उठता रहा कि अयोध्या, काशी, प्रयाग, हरिद्वार, और मथुरा जैसे सरनाम तीर्थों को छोड़ कर सूत-शौनकादि ने सारे पुराण वहां क्यों बांचे? यह चौरासी हजार संतों का मेला किसने आयोजित किया था?
>
> इसके कई बरस बाद डॉ. काशी प्रसाद जायसवाल लिखित 'अन्धकारयुगीन भारत' में भारशिवों और वाकाटकों के शासन काल में एक महान सांस्कृतिक सामाजिक आन्दोलन चलाए जाने की बात पढ़कर फिर नैमिषारण्य के 84000 संतों वाले मेले की याद आई। सोचा, हो न हो यह मेला उसी समय से जुड़ा होगा। बात को ऐतिहासिकता का कुछ सहारा मिला, तो वह क्रमश: जोड़ पकड़ती गई। सबेरे नहाते समय पढ़े जाने वाले 'गंगा बड़ी गोदावरी कि तीरथ बड़े प्रयाग' या 'गंगा सिन्धु सरस्वती च यमुना गोदावरी गण्डकी' अथवा 'अयोध्या मथुरा माया काशी कांची ह्यवंतिका' जैसे सप्त नदियों और सप्त पुरियों के श्लोक, जो अब तक अनगिनत बार अनेक धार्मिक लोगों से सुने थे, सहसा एक नया राष्ट्रीय अर्थबोध लेकर सामने आए। विष्णुपुराण का भारत गीत 'गायन्ति देवा: किल गीतकानि धन्यास्तुये भारत भूमि भागे' पढ़कर तो मेरी यह धारणा पक्की हो गई कि चौरासी हजार संतों का यह पौराणिक सेमिनार कोरा धार्मिक तमाशा या गप नहीं है, इसके पीछे राष्ट्रीय महत्व का कुछ इतिहास भी है।[94]

He further wrote,

> मुझे हुमायूँ की जान बचाने वाले भिस्ती की तरह अगर चार घड़ी की हुकूमत मिल जाये, तो मैं नगर-नगर, गाँव-गाँव डॉ. जायसवाल की मूर्तियाँ लगवाने का हुक्म दे दूँ। इस महापुरुष ने दुनिया और भारतीयों को भी, भारतीय इतिहास देखने समझने की सही दृष्टि प्रदान की। उनका यह उपकार भुलाया नहीं जा सकता। इनके द्वारा लिखे गए ग्रन्थ 'अन्धकारयुगीन भारत' ने बिच्छू के से डंक मारने वाली इस पहेली का अता-पता दे दिया की गंगा, यमुना, बद्री, केदार, हरिद्वार, काशी, मथुरा, अयोध्या, प्रयाग, आदि के रहते हुए हमारी गोमती नदी पर बसे नैमिशारण्य को क्यूँ चुना गया।[95]

While speaking on the occasion of KPJ's Birth Centenary Ceremony in 1981 in Patna the then Vice-President of India M. Hidayatullah, made the following remarks about KPJ's *History of India:*

> My first acquaintance with Dr. Jayaswal was made in 1946 through his writings. That was in the first case I decided as a Judge of the High Court at Nagpur. Although I had offered History as a one of the papers for my B.A. Examinations, we were required to begin Indian History from 1526 which was the beginning of, what is called, the Mughal Period. In that case it was necessary to go into the Hindu period. The question was the limits of the expansion of Telangana and the spread of the people of Telangana in India. In Hindu Law there are many schools of law, as all lawyers know. The question was which school of Hindu Law governed Komtis who were living in Chanda (now Chandrapur) district of Maharashtra. As you know river Godavari is the boundary between Andhra Pradesh and Chanda. Unfortunately each Province in India had *lex loci* and the *lex loci* of Chanda were Mitāksharā School of Hindu Law. Therefore, the *lex loci* applied to them without anything more. But if they had migrated across the river then they would be presumed to have brought their law with them and that would be rules recognized by *Smṛiti Chandrika* and *Saraswati Vilasa* and not the *Mitāksharā*. Now there is a *non-possumus adamant* rule that migration must be proved and the evidence of migration is found in the histories rather than in oral evidence. There was no evidence of migration by the family in recent times.
>
> We were faced with this difficult problem and I solved it by looking into Dr. Jayaswal's *History of India* for 200 years beginning from 150 A.D. According to Dr. Jayaswal, Telangana extended beyond Godavari and right further north and thus the Komtis were not migrant but autochthonous. No other historian had anything to offer. With the Komtis living in the Chanda district always, the *lex loci* was applied. It was then that I learnt about Dr. Jayaswal and began to

have great admiration and great respect for his erudition and research.[96]

(d) *An Imperial History of India (c. 700 B. C. - c. 770 A.D.):* This is another important monograph by KPJ, published in 1934. This monograph is based on the Tibetan version of *Mañjūśrī Mūlakalpa,* which was edited in collaboration with Rahul Sankrityayan. This monograph is enriched with KPJ's comments, contains new information about the political and cultural history of the country, particularly with regard to the Gupta and later Gupta history.

If KPJ's *History of India* was a rebuttal of V.A. Smith's contribution to the post-Mauryan centuries, the *Imperial History of India* was similarly a rejoinder to that colonial administrator's understanding of the post-Gupta centuries in North India. Smith in his *Early History of India* had argued: (i) "Very little is known about the history of India during the second half of the sixth century. It is certain that no paramount power existed" (p. 341), (ii) "Interior India was exempt from serious foreign aggression for nearly 500 years, from the defeat of Mihirakula in A.D. 528 until the raids of Mahmud of Gazni at the beginning of the eleventh century, and was left free to work out her destiny in her own fashion. In political institutions no evolution took place, no sovereign arose endowed with commanding abilities" (371), (iii) "Harsha's death loosened the bonds which restrained the disruptive forces always ready to operate in India, and allowed them to produce their natural result, a medley of petty states" (371). KPJ contended that the above conclusions were based on fragmentary views presented by inscriptions and for want of a written history. Inscriptions by themselves are powerless to delineate a full picture of the past. And a partial picture is a dangerous thing. KPJ argued, "From 78 A.D. we have in our new text a connected history down to the close of eighth century. And what is still more gratifying is the imperial feature of that history."[97]

KPJ argued, "In a Buddhist work called *Mañjūśrī Mūlakalpa,* which is in Sanskrit, there is a 'Book of Royal History'. This book gives the history of India (a) from the time of the Buddha up to the Mauryas, (b) the prosecutors of Buddhist religion, then, (c) the revival of Buddhism under the Kuṣāṇas, (d) the provincial histories, it takes up, (e) the imperial history of inner-India. This imperial history begins with the Śaka dynasty and has the following continuous successions of empires down to the rise of the Pāla empire: (1) Śaka Dynasty, (2) Nāgas and Senas, (3) Imperial Guptas up to the end of Budhagupta's reign, (4) Vardhanas, (5) Maukharis, (6) Dynasty of Thāneśvara, (7) Dynasty of Valabhī, (8) Later Guptas (9) The Pālas, beginning with Gopāla. On the basis of these descriptions KPJ argued that numbers 4, 5, 7, and 8 have been sadly missed by V.A. Smith and his followers.[98] KPJ attacked the imperialist historians, "The *Mañjūśrī Mūlakalpa* decides once for all that the treatment of Indian history from the Gupta times up to the Pāla period has to be radically revised and that the bible of the Early History printed at Oxford will henceforward be obsolete."[99]

KPJ also cautioned the Indians against the imperialist history-writing, "Let us hope that Indians will now execute the imperative duty of writing a history of their country and of completing the tradition which their forefathers carried on for several centuries through their Purāṇas and chronicles as preserved in the *Mañjūśrī Mūlakalpa*. It is a humiliation unworthy of any civilised nation and more so for the countrymen of Kālidāsa and Kalhaṇa, to read their histories written by the outsiders who are least fitted to understand and interpret it."[100]

KPJ also re-affirms his ideas of Farther and Insular India given in his monograph *History of India*, on the basis of his reading of *Mañjūśrī Mūlakalpa*. KPJ argued,

> I am gratified to find that the *Manjuśri* author has treated the history of Indian Archipelago and Farther India as part and parcel of the history of India... *Mañjūśrī Mūlakalpa* notes that the Gauḍa dynasty of Bengal ruled up to Burma in the reign of Prakataditya. It also has given names of certain Hindu artists who went from Southern India to the islands and beautiful Buddhist monuments and monasteries there... The book gives at the end a short history of religious and political leaders, artists, and philosophers of art (iconography) both Brahmanical and Buddhist. Some of them were Śūdras. The survey covers the whole land from the north up to Ceylon and embraces Greater India.[101]

Coming to the book, KPJ argued the book was published by M.M. Ganapati Sastri in 1925 (Trivandrum Sanskrit Series No. 84), but is a poor production as an edition, because he was unfamiliar with the Buddhist technical terms. However, KPJ had the privilege of having both the editions—Buddhist and Tibetan.[102] Comparing both these texts, KPJ argued, "Geographically it is to Gauḍa and Magadha that the author pays his greatest attention... To him Gauḍa means the whole of Bengal and includes generally Magadha... I would, therefore, regard the work as one of circa770 A.D. (the death of Gopāla), or roughly 800 A.D. It was translated into Tibetan in about 1060 A.D. by the Hindu Pandita Kumārakalaśa in co-operation with the Tibetan interpreter Śakya-blo-gros."[103]

Analysing the style of the content of the text, KPJ argued, "The history is put in the prophetic style in the mouth of the Buddha, who undertakes to narrate the future vicissitudes of his Doctrine and the Church, and in that connexion royal history is dealt with. It is not strictly speaking, history proper as in the *Purāṇas*, but a secondary reference, the primary note being the history of Buddhism... The language and style has a striking resemblance with the *Yugapurāṇa* in the *Garga-Saṃhitā*."[104]

According to KPJ, "The historical narration is a lengthy one, the chapter covering 1005 verses in the printed Sanskrit *Mañjūśrī Mūlakalpa* and about 25 less in Tibetan *Mañjūśrī Mūlakalpa*."[105] KPJ further argued, "Half of this will not interest the present day materialist reader, for the writer does not forgive like the modern historian, the wickedness and arbitrariness in kings. He would have thrown into the waste-paper basket all modern histories as so many veiled and covert panegyrics on force and fraud and virtueless greatness. His outlook is different. He emphasises the relentless law of morality, the avenging principle of *Karma* and he follows the rascally kings to their torture in hell."[106]

It appears that there is a paradox in KPJ's understanding as far as his handling of Buddhism and Buddhists is concerned, which is visible several times throughout his writings. Aśoka is not portrayed in favourable light by KPJ possibly because of his pro-Buddhist leanings. KPJ glamorises Puṣyamitra, his 'Brahmanic Revolution', and anti-Buddhist prosecution and criticised the Kuṣāṇas for their pro-Buddhist leanings. It is also mentioned above that while dealing with the Nāgas or the Guptas, KPJ never used the term 'Imperial' for the Kuṣāṇas. However, if it was the question of a reply to Smith's interpretation, KPJ had no hesitation in accepting them as 'Imperial'.[107] It seems that on the inside issue, the Kuṣāṇas were foreigners and on the outside issue they were the locals. The author of the Buddhist-Sanskrit text, *Mañjūśrī Mūlakalpa*, is also respectfully called by KPJ as 'Our Buddhist Historian' and KPJ felt no hesitation in constructing his theory of Greater India on the basis of this text. It is also interesting to note that one of his closest friends and associates was Rahul Sankrityayan, who adopted Buddhism and at one point of time KPJ also confessed that he was willing to accept Buddhism.[108]

(e) *Chronology and History of Nepal (600 B.C.-A.D. 880):* This monograph was published in 1937 from Patna and reprinted in 1976 from Banaras. This monograph is divided into three sections, including fourteen sub-sections: (A) Licchavis and Ṭhākurīs [A.D. 350 to 880 A.D.] (B) Early Dynasties of Nepal, (C) Retrospect. Why did KPJ choose to discuss the later history of Nepal in the first chapter and the early history later is not clear. However, the overall contents show that the monograph begins with 600 BC, i. e., the beginning of the early dynasties of Nepal. The major part of the monograph is given to the later part of the history of Nepal - Licchavis and the Ṭhākurīs. The history of early dynasties is dealt with in only a few pages. The major portion deals with relationship of Nepal with the Licchavis, the Guptas and India in general. In reconstructing the history of Nepal, KPJ used a variety of sources: Chinese, Buddhist, Tibetan, inscriptions, coins, etc.

While discussing the history of Licchavis and Ṭhākurīs, KPJ argued that the date of Aṁśuvarman is a pivot of Nepalese chronology. For fixing the date of Aṁśuvarman, KPJ a used variety of sources both primary (inscriptions, Chinese and Tibetan literary sources) and the secondary (readings of Bhagawanlal Indraji, J.F. Fleet, Waddell, Sarat Chandra Das, etc.), and argued that Aṁśuvarman was the founder of the Ṭhākurī era, the era of Aṁśuvarman, which is counted from his coronation as *mahāsāmanta* in 595 A.D. Analysing different sources, KPJ argued that Aṁśuvarman worked as *mahāsāmanta* till 635 A.D., with full royal paraphernalia and was probably re-anointed in the very last year of his reign with the full title of sovereignty—*mahārājādhirāja* — which appears on one series of his coins.[109]

As far as the constitutional position of Aṁśuvarman is concerned, KPJ drew the following conclusions: (i) that the title *mahāsāmanta* was given up after the 34th year by Aṁśuvarman [although the Lichchhavi king still applies it to him up to 639 A.D.]; (ii) that Śrī was used as title of full sovereignty, which according to book on constitutional forms and preceedents may alone denote 'His Majesty'. The same Śrī alone is found on the coins of Māna and Guṇa; (iii) that the higher imperial title of *mahārājādhirāja* must have been assumed by Aṁśuvarman after or in the year 44/45 and before the year 48, and that he had died before the inscription of Jishṇu Gupta of the year 48; (iv) that Aṁśuvarman was never a subordinate of the Tibetan king even up to his death. If Aṁśuvarman had given his daughter to the Tibetan king, so had done the emperor of China. The alliances prove the importance of Tibet but not suzerainty in either case; (v) that Aṁśuvarman adopted full kingship between the years 34 and 39, and the imperial title after 639 A.D. in or after and 44th year (vi) that the era of the 44th year would therefore began in 595 A.D., not later.[110]

KPJ further discussed the names the kings of the three dynasties in detail—the Licchavis, the Guptas, and the Ṭhākurīs—and gives the chronological order of each dynasty[111] and discussed the Gupta dominance over Nepal in the light of the Allahabad inscription of the time of Samudragupta. Further, the Gupta influence is also seen in Nepal making Vaiṣṇavism the royal cult."[112] However, KPJ further underlined the continuous change in the religious history of Nepal,

> Buddhism reigned supreme after the Imperial Gupta influence disappeared in the reign of Mānadeva I (576 A.D.). Coming after the Śaiva Aṁśuvarman who patronised Buddhism merely as a ruler, Vṛishadeva about 660 A.D. made Buddhism again popular. But his son Śaṅkaradeva, about 680 A.D., is regarded as a second Śaṅkarāchārya for having revived Śaivism at the cost of Buddhism. He has left his monuments at Paśupati and is universally credited by the Buddhists to have abolished monasticism in Nepal Buddhism (Mahāyāna), forcing every *Bhikshus* to lead a married life. There have been no wifeless *Bhiksus* in Nepal ever since; the vihāras are occupied by married Buddhist priests. After Śankaradeva the Lichchhavis remain markedly Śaiva and Vaishṇavite.[113]

On the basis of the account of the Chinese travellor Wang-Hieun-t'se, KPJ discussed the people, currency, arts, sciences and worship, the King, architecture and temples.[114] While discussing writing and sculpture, KPJ argued, "As Gupta writing persisted in Nepal, so did Guptan and post-Guptan style in sculpture in Nepal."[115]

KPJ extended the history of Nepal up to the 'Moghul period' and argued,

> We have thus positive proof of the fact that at least in the time of Rāma Pāla Nepal was under Pāla suzerainty. It is very likely that under Dharma Pāla and Deva Pāla a similar state obtained. We do not find Nepal striking her own coins from about 800 A.D. onwards.

> This is probably explained by the fact of the Pāla domination, which was immediately followed by the Kārnāṭaka domination beginning with Nanyādeva. At the close of the Kārnāṭaka period we find Nepal imitating the coin of Alauddin Khilji. Then follows a troubled period until stability is restored under Jayasithimalla (1380-1394). Nepal acknowledged nominal suzerainty of Delhi as noted by Travernier. And naturally we do not find a Nepal coinage until permission for establishing a mint was obtained from the early Moghuls."[116]

Explaining the Indian connection with Nepal, KPJ argued, "Nepal thus from 800 A.D. or at any rate from 1080 A.D. remained as part of the Indian Empire up to the Moghul days in international theory, which found a tangible expression in the history of her coinage - the absence of coinage. The same is to be predicated of her in the Imperial Gupta times as well."[117] KPJ also explored the dual sovereignty of Nepal, "The Lichchhavi monarchy in Nepal probably retained its original character of divided sovereignty, otherwise the position of Aṁśuvarman's dictatorship and Śivadeva's sovereignty is not explicable. Probably even before Aṁśuvarman some similar arrangements obtained."[118]

KPJ concluded his studies on Nepal:

> The history of Nepal is a part of the history of India and of Hindu race. The valley was colonized by the Hindus both consciously and by mutual process of expansion. Yet it is history of a colony, with distinctive features. Those features may be summarised in this way...The ruling dynasties though mostly Hindus from the plains of India—the Mauryas, the Lichchhavis, the Kārnāṭakas, the Gorkhas—have a tendency to establish a system of divided sovereignty which works happily in that valley of Paśupati. There is much less cause for jealousy in that system on the soil of Nepal than anywhere else. Joint rules and regencies are a familiar problem in the Lichchhavi times, in the Ṭhākurī times, in the Malla times and in the Gurkha times—two kings occupying the same town or contiguous towns afford a picture of Mitāksharā family agreeing upon..., A 'division for the convenience of enjoyment' rather than upon an actual division by metes and bounds. This divided sovereignty would baffle the theories of political science but has been a familiar, good working system in Nepal.
>
> There is always a sort of internal weakness, but to the outside world Nepal has always shown strength. Throughout her history there has been no case of traitorous betrayal. Internally weak, but externally strong is again a political problem which is explainable by its

> republican origin. Nepal's whole history bears out the rule that the little kingdom can defend itself most effectively—it defeated Tibet in her palmiest days when Tibet was the first power in Asia, it defeated Kashmir when Kashmir was the first power in India, it defeated King Shamsuddin, the most brilliant Muslim soldier of the 14th century. Small, and 'internally weak', Nepal is a successful state against the invader. Its republican Lichchhavi origin explains the mystery. Its strong political sense is a Lichchhavi heritage.
>
> Nepal has been in Hindu times mostly a member of Indian Empire. But for centuries, being situated between two large empires —China and India—Nepal has evolved a wise international policy, wherein she has hardly ever taken a false step. Owing to this wise policy, her international position today is such as it had probably never been before. She enjoys and rightly the complete confidence of her powerful neighbour.[119]

Looking at the conclusions KPJ drew from his studies, it appears that it was a part of his concept of Further India.

(B) Edited and Translated Works

KPJ edited with learned commentaries many hitherto unpublished texts: (a) *The Rājanīti-Ratnākara by Chaṇḍeśvara,*[120] (b) Bhaṭṭa-Svāmin's commentary on Kauṭilya's *Arthaśāstra,*[121] (with A. Banerji-Sastri) (c) *Descriptive Catalogue of Manuscripts in Mithila,* Vol. I., Smṛiti Manuscripts, (With A. P. Sastri),[122] (d) *Descriptive Catalogue of Manuscripts in Mithila,* Vol. II Literature, Prosody,[123] (e) *Adhyārddhaśataka* by Mātṛcetā,[124] (f) *Vigrahavyāvarttanī* by Ācārya Nāgārjuna,[125] (g) *Lassen's History of Indian Commerce* (Vikramāditya to the later Guptas),[126] translated in association with A.P. Banerji-Sastri.

Numbers a (c) and (d), were part of KPJ's expedition for the search of Mithila and Puri manuscripts, which was initiated by the government in 1918 and entrusted to the BORS and KPJ himself directed and supervised the work.

(a) *Rājanīti-Ratnākara*: While examining the list of manuscripts catalogued during the first few months, KPJ noticed the title of *Rājanīti-Ratnākara* and felt surprised to see a book on 'Hindu politics' composed in the medieval period, and that by a well-known lawyer of the status of Caṇḍeśvara.[127] The present edition was prepared from three manuscripts found in the region of Darbhanga. They are all written on paper and belong almost to the same period, speaking roughly, the eighteenth century. None of them is dated. They are all in Maithili script. In editing the text, KPJ preserved faithfully the language of the manuscripts except correcting the very obvious grammatical inaccuracies resulting from copyist's carelessness and ignorance. KPJ has given variants even of the slightest importance.[128]

Caṇḍeśvara, the famous lawyer of Mithila and minister of the state, was the author of *Rajanīti-Ratnākara*. The family of Caṇḍeśvara was given to orthodox learning. Caṇḍeśvara's style is pointed and not pedantic; he does not ramble about like other digest-writers, and in his remarks, both on law and *Rājanīti,* he has his eyes on the changing times. But it seems that much of his work is based on the labour of earlier authors whom he expressly designates in the beginning or the end of his work as his sources.

After analysing the text, KPJ highlighted the importance of the text and argued that Caṇḍeśvara was quick to change and he differed from the theory of the *dharmaśāstra* writers. Sacrament of coronation was not essential for kingship. This was quite in conformity with the hard facts and the new facts. The Delhi emperors had been on the throne, even over 'Hindu' kings, without any Vedic consecration. They had got established and there was no hope for a 'Hindu restoration'. Theories must change with facts, and Caṇḍeśvara, an old statesman, realised that the *Aitareya* and *Śatapatha Brāhmaṇas* had ceased to rule. He laid down the definition —one who protects is the king... His views on general subjects are, of course, traditional, and they are very valuable as such. For instance, on succession to a kingdom he writes that the ordinary rule of division and succession cannot apply to a kingdom, for the royal property is owned by the whole people—they all have shares in it (the poor, orphans etc.), that leadership, if divided, would destroy the state.[129]

KPJ analysed the value of the text,

> The *Rajanīti-Ratnākara* has got sixteen chapters related to statecraft and administration... The chief value of *Rājanīti-Ratnākara* lies in the fact that it introduces us to a new branch of literature and it is the oldest work of that branch yet published. Politics, as a separate study, is traced back in India to the seventh century BC... The subject was a popular one and had a succession of masters. In the period from the early Christian centuries, down to the fifth or sixth, it seems, some important books, e.g., *Kāmandakīya* and *Nāradīya,* were composed.

> After that there appears to be a cessation in the composition of new books for about five centuries. On the analogy of what happened in the literature in Hindu Law, to which Hindu politics is closely allied, this was probably a period of commentaries."[130]

As to why this change happened, KPJ did not give any answer. Since the 'Muslim' rule was not a factor between the sixth and the tenth centuries it can't be a plausible explanation—even if one were to feel tempted to invoke it. D.D. Kosambi's hypothesis about the broader decline in quality of Sanskrit texts (situated within the feudal context) also does not explain the phenomenon completely. The question is: How did polity-centred texts emerge in a period which saw considerable proliferation of state 'polities' in different regions?

KPJ also traced the genesis of commentary writing,

> About the eleventh century a new class of literature on political science came into existence, viz., digests of 'Hindu politics', mainly based, not on the former *Artha-Śāstra* and *Daṇda-nītis*, but, on *Dharma-Śāstra*... They ignored, also the old titles, *'Artha-Śāstra'* and *'Daṇda-nīti'*, and adopted a new term *'Rājanīti'*, or 'Royal Principle (or Policy)'. The writers of this class of works were lawyers of the *Dharma-Śāstra* school and composers of Dharma law-digests. To this class belongs our *Rājanīti-Ratnākara*. One of the earliest, if not the earliest, Digests of Hindu Politics was *Rājanīti-Kalpataru* by Lakshmidhara Bhaṭṭa, the senior foreign minister under King Govindachandra of Kāśī, the grandfather of Jayachandra... No complete copy is yet available in India. It is largely quoted in *Rājanīti-Ratnākara*. Another work of this class was *Rājanīti-Kāmadhenu* of which we only know of from references in our Ratnākara. Like Chaṇḍeśvara and his successors the later digest-makers, Vāchaśpati, Mitra Miśrā and Nīlakaṇṭha, who also composed sections on Rājanīti.[131]

KPJ further argued,

> The *Rājanīti-Ratnākara*, in addition to the information as to the existence of earlier digests of Hindu Politics, discloses to us the fact that there was a work attributed to Nārada dealing with politics. This becomes evident by looking at the passages quoted under the name of Nārada or the Nāradiya. Some of them are traceable to the law-book of Nārada while others are not to be found there and they cannot be referred to as a law-book. It is not very clear but it seems probable that some *Artha-Śāstra* work was attributed to the name of Hārita. Chaṇḍeśvara quotes largely from a work called 'Rāja-nīti'. The book

cannot be identified without discovering the earlier digests. The Śukra-nīti referred to in the *Ratnākara* differs completely from the *Śukra-nīti* that we have got today. The Ratnākara is thus valuable for the history of political literature and deserves attention on that ground as well. Still more important are the norms which obtained at the close of the Hindu and the beginning of the Muhammadan periods. Originality and force are on the decline, yet there is no lack of interest and no total surrender of reason.[132]

(b) *Bhaṭṭa-Svāmin's Commentary on Kauṭilya's Arthaśhāstra*: This commentary is part of the text of Bhaṭṭa-Svāmin called *Pratipadapaīcikāyama*. This manuscript was handed over by a Pandit of the Tanjore District to the Mysore Oriental Library. Kangle mentions that R. Shamasastry thinks that it is not more than a century or two old. Bhaṭṭa-Svāmin was from Kerala.[133] The text was serialised and published in six parts. The commentary consists of various chapters of the second *adhikaraṇa* of the *Arthaśāstra* dealing with various aspects of administration and polity. The language of the *sūtras* of the *Arthaśāstra* is simplified in the commentary, meant for the common reader of Sanskrit. KPJ was the first scholar who published the commentary, although he did not give any editorial comment on it.

(c) *Descriptive Catalogue of Manuscripts in Mithila*, Vol. I and II: Another contribution of KPJ was the editing of the Mithila manuscripts. Cataloguing of the manuscripts was one of the important agenda items of the Indologists since the middle of the nineteenth century. In 1868, the Government of India instituted a programme of manuscript cataloguing and collection. In the Bombay and Madras Presidencies, there were series of regional searches by Sanskrit scholars including such renowned figures as Franz Kielhorn (1840-1908), Georg Bühler (1837-1898) and R.G. Bhandarkar (1837-1925), who published reports on their findings, catalogued local collections, acquired manuscripts where available, and commissioned copies of others. In Bengal Presidency, this responsibility was taken up by Rajendra Lal Mitra (1823-1891) and Haraprasad Sastri (1853-1931). During the nineteenth century, Indian manuscripts began to be identified, studied and catalogued in all parts of India, often by European scholars who lived and worked in India most of their lives. The first major Indian manuscript catalogues in Europe were those of Theodore Aufrecht (1822-1907) at the Bodleian Library (Oxford) and Albrecht Weber

(1825-1901) in Berlin.[134]

The Government of Bihar had also initiated the expedition for the search of Mithila and Puri manuscripts in 1918; the work was entrusted to the BORS and KPJ himself supervised and monitored the expedition. On the basis of the findings of this expedition, KPJ prepared and published the *Descriptive Catalogue of Manuscripts in Mithila* in two parts. As embodying the results of the first decades of the search, the Mithila manuscripts have been arranged for publication under the eleven heads: Smṛiti, Veda, Vyākaraṇa, Kāvya, Philosophy, Tantra, Jyotiṣa, Purāṇa, History and Geography, Buddhist and Jaina, and Miscellaneous Manuscripts.

The first volume, i.e., *Smṛiti* Manuscripts deals with ancient 'Hindu' sacerdotal law on the basis of remembered authority as recorded by old sages. On the material available in the Manuscripts, KPJ divided the entire catalogue into eighteen segments: 1. *Smṛiti* Manuscripts, (2) Complete Codes (11th to 20th century), (3) Works on Sacred Law (13th-17th century) 4. *Ahṇika*, 5. Marriage, 6. *Aśaucha*, 7. *Śrāddha*, 8. *Vyavahāra*, 9. *Dāna* 10. Consecration and Dedication, 11. *Prāyaśchitta*, 12. *Śānti*, 13. *Smṛiti-Jyotiṣa*, 14. *Pūjā-Pātha*, 15. *Vrata*, 16. *Castes*, 17. *Tīrthas*, 18. Miscellaneous. The second catalogue is on literature manuscript. It has been divided into five segments: *Chandas*, *Alaṅkāra*, *Kāvyas*, *Nāṭakas*, Works on Letter-writers and *Praśastis*.

A distinguishing feature of these catalogues is the reference to previous notices in any published catalogue so far, which will enable readers to verify different versions and see at a glance manuscripts which were noticed before but are described here for the first time. By cataloguing these thick volumes, KPJ tried to present the literary and intellectual traditions of Mithila. He quotes Haraprasad Sastri, "Forty years of search for Sanskrit Mss. have not enabled me to get even a Ms. copied in Muslim Bengal during the 13th and 14th centuries, not to say of the composition of any work either in vernacular or in Sanskrit." KPJ argued, "Mithila, on the other hand (beyond a strip along the Ganges occupied by the Muhammadans) under the Kārnāṭakas and the *Śrotriya* Brāhmaṇas, produced important works in Sanskrit in the 13th and the 14th centuries... But the *Smṛiti* Mss. of the 13th and 14th centuries are extremely rare."[135]

After analysing contents of the manuscripts KPJ argued, "It may be claimed that Mithila though creditably represented in every branch of the *Smṛiti* literature, is especially remarkable for her *Nibandhas* or Digests. Another striking feature is the uninterrupted continuity of the growth and development of *Smṛiti* in Mithila." However, KPJ also highlighted its evil effect,

> While during the 15th, 16th, and 17th centuries, the whole of Northern India was convulsed by the religious and social upheavals, *e.g.*, with Nanak in the Punjab, and Chaitanya in Bengal, Mithila remained unaffected, deeply engrossed in the details of the Karmakāṇḍa. In the 19th and the 20th centuries, it has, to a certain extent, hampered the growth of that critical and liberal education which obtains elsewhere in India as a result of knowledge of the West. But it has been compensated for by conferring on Mithila her unique position as the only surviving centre in the whole of Northern India where the whole of *Smṛiti* may be studied in all its successive stages from the earliest time to the present day.[136]

The systematic cataloguing of these manuscripts reflects the sharp editorial skills of KPJ. He took care of every substance and detail of the texts, such as; character, paper, size, date (if available), place and person from where the text was found, subject of the text etc. Details provided by KPJ in these two volumes of the catalogue provide a useful model that seems to have been invoked later in the 1950s in the Government of India's Sanskrit Commission's recommendations for cataloguing of manuscripts.

(d) *Adhyārddhaśataka* by Mātṛcetā: Another work of KPJ is the editing of the book *Adhyārddhaśataka*, a famous work by the poet, Mātṛcetā, in association with his friend Rahul Sankrityayan.[137] Mātṛcetā was an elder contemporary of Kaniṣka (78 A.D.). The title of the text means that it comprises 150 verses. The text was very popular and it was due not only to its simplicity, good choice of words and easy and graceful style but it also served the purpose of a manual of Buddhism for the novices.

After analysing the text, KPJ argued,

> The work is based on an ancient Buddhist canon. ...It is a mistake to imagine traces of Mahāyāna in any work which eulogises the sublime ideal of Bodhisattva. Such praise of a life of self-denial and suffering for the benefit of others is common to both Hīnayāna and Mahāyāna Schools. The Jātaka stories of the Hīnayāna school are nothing but attempts to popularise the high ideal of Boddhisattva. We find such passages in this work but on account of that it will be wrong to assume that Matṛcetā has some leanings towards the Mahāyāna School. The

> invention of *Trikāyā* (three bodies) i.e. *Dharmakāyā*, *Sambhogakāyā*, and *Niramāṇakāyā*, is no doubt the speciality of the Mahāyāna School, but from verse 146, we know that our poet has no notion of the theory of three bodies. There, instead of three bodies, he mentioned only two *Dharmakāyā* (the body of law) and *Rūpakāyā* (the material body)—which are the notions found in the Hīnayāna canons. In the *Mahāparinibbānasutta* of the *Dīghanikāya* we find the Buddha exhorting his disciple at the time of his death to take refuge in the Dharma after the demise of his physical body."[138]

Both KPJ and Rahul reason out that Mātṛcetā is different from Aśvaghosa as was often believed in view of the Tibetaṇ translation and second, the text is not a completely Mahāyāna text.

(e) *Vigrahavyāvarttanī* by Ācārya Nāgārjuna: The last contribution in this category was the editing of *Vigrahavyāvarttanī* by Ācārya Nāgārjuna, which was edited in association with Rahul Sankrityayaṇ.[139] Nāgārjuna, the revolutionary philosopher and founder of the Mādhyamika school of Buddhism was born in a Brahmin family in the country of Vidarbha according to the Tibetan authors. He was the contemporary of a Sātavāhana king. From his work we know him as a great philosopher; but Nāgārjuna was known in India and in Buddhist countries outside India, as a magician and alchemist too; and perhaps it was due to his association that in later times Śrīparvata became a most sacred seat of the Tāntrika cults of both Hinduism and Buddhism.

In going through the pages of *Mādhyamika-Kārikā* and this work, the editors found that Nāgārjuna's idea was not to have an innovation in Buddhistic thought. His *Śūnyatā* or voidness was nothing but a logical corollary of *Pratītya-samutpāda*, i.e., dependent origination, or discontinuous continuation. The Buddha saw

> Impermanence in everything. According to him, all changes were without any permanent substratum. In the light of this he has to change the law of cause and effect into that of *Pratītya-samutpāda* (origination of the successor after the extinction of the predecessor). In fact all the mental and physical phenomena are devoid of any permanent substance like matter or ego. This was Buddha's own conception and Nāgārjuna's *Śūnyatā* or voidness is only a more appropriate word for that conception. We can thus understand well, why Nāgārjuna's heart overflowed with gratitude to the Master.[140]

The editors further explain,

> Invalidity of *Pramāṇa* (source of knowledge) for the establishment of the theory of voidness is the chief theme of the *Vigrahavyāvarttanī*. In the first 20 verses he gives all the objections against his theory of voidness, which proposes to refute the reality of existence and the source of real knowledge, since the outer phenomenon is unreal and no standard remains for two moments which can be utilized for comparison to establish the existence of a thing. In the remaining 52 verses, he refutes all the arguments of his opponents.[141]

After analysing the texts, the editors come to the conclusion,

> ...The advent of Nāgārjuna opens a new epoch of activity in philosophical thought, which led to the formulations of six systems of Brahmanical philosophy. At the present stage of our information we cannot assert anything definitely but the meagre materials which we have at our disposal indicate that the personality of Nāgārjuna is not less important than the personality of Dignāga who is rightly called the father of Medieval Indian Logic; and of Gaṅgeśopādhyāya the founder of Modern Brahmanical Logic (*Navyanyāya*). The importance of *Vigrahavyāvarttanī* is great since among the works known up to the present, it is the oldest work which deals with a logical subject.[142]

Vigrahavyāvarttanī text was translated into Tibetan by (i) Paṇḍita Jīnagarbha (A.D. 874) and the translator (ka-va) Dpal brts-egs; and again (ii) revised by Paṇḍita Jayānanda (A.D. 1060) of Kashmir and the Tibetan interpreter (khu) Mdo-sde-dpal. The commentary was translated by the same Paṇḍita Jīnagarbha with the help of Ban-de-rakṣita. The present manuscript of *Vigrahavyāvarttanī* was discovered in the monastery of Sha-lu in July 1936.

(f) *Lassen's History of Indian Commerce*: KPJ, in association with A.P. Banerji-Sastri also translated *Lassen's History of Indian Commerce.*[143] It was a translation from German to English. In 1858, the third volume of Lassen's *Indische Alterthumskunde* was published. The first chapter, *Geschichte des Ilandels die Zeit Von Vikramāditya bis auf die spatern Gupta*, deals with the history of Indian commerce from the time of Vikramāditya to that of the later Guptas. The published translation was of that chapter.

The subject of Indian commercial history had become a subject of popular study. The translators, having noticed that the researches of Christian Lassen, the first writer on the subject, were not, as a rule, availed of by Indian writers and students, felt the necessity making available an English translation of Lassen's chapter on the subject. In translation, they endeavored to adhere to the original more than to the elegance of language which had to be sacrificed more or less in almost every rendering of a scientific nature. In the introduction they observed, "Since Lassen's time, Indology has progressed much, but Lassen can never be superseded. Lassen is the classical in the field of Indian history. Without Lassen, for generations after, no one could have easily conceived of producing an Indian History of Hindu times dealing with political, social and intellectual development. The wonder is that no other author, except Duncker on a much smaller scale, has since attempted a comprehensive work like Lassen's *Indische Alterthumskunde.*" While thus indicating the importance of translating Lassen's chapter into English they added, "It might be useful to prepare a bibliography bringing the subject up-to-date and the translators hope that it would be done later." However, the bibliography was added only in 1973, when its third reprint was published from the Society. Citing this translation, A.L. Basham wrote, "This is the only translation of Lassen known to me, though others may exist."[144]

Within a short period of time, KPJ in association with his colleagues, edited, catalogued, translated, and published seven texts, which may be classed in the category of classics. Through the publication of these works KPJ, perhaps, tries to indicate that the intellectual, literary, and political tradition was alive in India throughout the ages. The more you discover, and publish, the more you will be able to tell the western world that we were not living in the 'Dark Age'. This understanding of KPJ was against the colonial interpretation of India's ancient past.

(C) Research Articles

(a) Epigraphic Studies: KPJ made a valuable contribution to the Indian epigraphic studies. He wrote 34 articles on epigraphy, which were published in several journals.[145] For the purpose of convenience, we have classified the articles broadly into three categories: (i) Hathigumpha inscription, (ii) Aśokan inscriptions and (iii) incriptions of the miscellaneous variety.

(i) The Hathigumpha inscription: KPJ spent almost one third of his nearly 30-year career of literary and academic activities in deciphering and editing king Khāravela's Hathigumpha inscription in Udayagiri-Khandagiri hills of present-day Orissa. Though the existence of this inscription had been known for more than 90 years.

It was noticed for the first time by A. Stirling in 1825 and was published by James Prinsep from an eye-copy prepared by Lieutenant M. Kittoe in 1837. In 1871 Cunningham published a tracing in the first volume of the *Corpus Inscriptionum Indicarum*. In 1880, R.L. Mitra published another version of this inscription. The first reliable version of the record was published by Bhagwanlal Indraji in 1885. In 1895 and 1898 Bühler proposed certain corrections. The first inked impression was taken by T. Bloch in 1906 and sent to Kielhorn from whom it passed on to Fleet, who published two short notes proposing certain corrections in the reading of 16th line. In the same year H. Lüders of Berlin published a summary of this inscription. In 1913 R.D. Banerji examined portions of this record at the request of KPJ, and in 1917 he prepared two inked impressions at the request of V.A. Smith and KPJ. KPJ spent more than ten years—visiting the site several times during these years and studying the inscription on the spot facing numerous odds. His findings appeared in print in several articles in English and Hindi published between 1917 and 1930. Most of his readings of crucial terms, expressions, identification of personages, events, and his overall assessment of the historical significance of this inscription, have remained invaluable till this day—even after over a century.

On the basis of his reading of the Hathigumpha inscription, KPJ tried to reconstruct the political, economic, religious, and cultural history of Kaliṅga during the reign of Khāravela. The major highlights of his readings are concerned with: (a) Khāravela's exploits on the battlefield against several contemporaries of the Deccan, the Magadhan empire and the Yavanarāja Dimita... (identified with Demetrius), (b) invaluable contribution to the history of the Jainas in the region—specially underlining some popular practices of their faith, viz, raising and worshipping relic memorials, and Khāravela's instrumentality in the compilation of the *Aṅgas* (sacred canon of the Jainas), (c) the role of Khāravela in developing the economic potential of the region—building a structure of taxation and identifying centres of mobilisation of financial resources, (d) building activities of the hero of the inscription - places, temples, canals, reservoirs etc., and (e) relatively greater importance of Khāravela in comparison with the Mauryan emperor Aśoka. For KPJ, the Ceṭi king deserved a higher rank because he defended Brahmanical system.

Some of the readings of KPJ might have been challenged, as in the case of the existence of *paura-janapada*.[146] The real significance, however, of the reading of this inscription lies in the fact that for the first time it was successfully read and it was a triumph of the modern scholarship. Before the recovery of this inscription, not a line about Khāravela had been found in the literature of the country. What we know about Khāravela is what the mystic voice of the rock was made eternally audible by KPJ.

(ii) Aśokan Inscriptions: KPJ made valuable contributions to reading and interpreting Aśokan edicts, which appeared in different leading journals of the period.[147] While reading several inscriptions of Aśoka, KPJ interpreted and defined the context and the meaning of numerous terms and names found in the Aśokan inscriptions, some of these include: *nijhati, pariṣad, mukhato,*[148] *priyadarśī, devānām-priya, supathya, dharma, samāja, chola, Pāṇḍya, Satiyaputra, Kerala, Antiyoka, rājuka, prādeśikas, parisa, samvarta, arambha, vimāna, dharmācāraṇa, jana, mahā-mātras,*[149] *anubandha and kṛtabhikāra,*[150] *ashashu,*[151] *Pāladas* and the so-called *rāja-viṣaya,* Definite Location of the Northern *Āndhras* and *Pāladas* in the *Purāṇas, Aparānta.*[152]

As far as KPJ's understanding of Aśoka is concerned, it presents a kind of paradox. While KPJ felt proud about the publication of the proclamation for the first time being made accessible to the modern representative of Aśoka's '*jana*' or nation and said:

> ...These Proclamations inscribed on stone to be mightier than Time, they have living interest. For the modern country-man of Aśoka still bears marks of the Social Revolution brought about through these very Proclamations. And indeed those marks are so prominent that they constitute the main features of Modern Hindu. The present day Hindu is still a subject of Pious Despot, 'the original author', as Aśoka proudly calls himself, of both the spirit and the letter of these fateful Proclamations. Opinion no doubt will be divided, as it was divided twenty centuries ago, whether Aśoka was inscribing the epitaph of the Hindu race or was leaving to them a legacy 'to last and benefit the community, up to what he called the end of the Kalpa. In any case the importance of the documents must be admitted on all hands in this country. The chiselled history of Aśoka is not a mere pastime of the antiquary: it is a living law still governing the national life -I hope, not the national destiny - of the 'nation' of Aśoka.[153]

Yet, at another place he wrote:

> The Dharma is of course the particular Dharma of Aśoka which in the beginning he refrains from preaching in all its details. As a preparatory step in his propaganda of Buddhism, he preaches a set of morals which were common both to the Jains and Buddhists and in fact all dissenting sects and which generally by themselves were not antagonistic to the orthodox national ethics. *But in the last analysis they were destructive of the national religion.*[154] (emphasis is mine).

KPJ also defined the geographical location of the spread of Aśokan inscription as well as the influence of the Aśokan empire:

> The actual area covered by the Proclamations comprises all that lies between Mysore and the Persian frontier, and copies of the Proclamations in situ have already been discovered both beyond the frontier of India where the Yusufzai roams and rules and over the plains of "Jambudvīpa" as far south as the apostolic seat of the undying Śaṅkarāchārya. The subject-matter of the Proclamation embraces a wider world, a world of three continents—Asia, Europe and Africa, for the Messages of Aśoka deal with the kingdoms of his 'neighbours' Antiochus, King of Syria, and of the Kings of Macedonia, Egypt and Cyrene, where the Emperor had established his hospitals for men and for beasts and introduces his missionary propaganda.[155]

One of the important concerns of KPJ was the question of language Aśoka used in his inscriptions. KPJ argued that Aśoka used a language which was understood from Ceylon to Afghanistan and a script which was current in the same area excepting beyond our North-Western borders.[156] However, KPJ was aware of the occurrence of linguistic variations and argues, "That except two Kharoshṭhī scripts (foreign), all other editions are in Brāhmī script, the parent of Devanagari, Bengali, Tamil, and other *Hindu scripts of modern India...* the variation was due to local phonetics and local idioms of the time."[157] While publishing the translation of the proclamations of Aśoka, KPJ highlights the use of the vernacular and the existence of a common national script, "It is needless to remark that the proclamations presuppose literacy in the populace for whose use they were composed in the vernacular. The percentage of that literacy is considered by an English expert to have been "higher than it is now in many provinces of British India." The proclamations also furnish an instance of the existence of a common national script and a common *national language* from Indian History."[158] (emphasis mine).

KPJ considered Aśoka as one of the greatest sons of India.

However, because of his pro-Buddhist policy and KPJ's affection for the old system, Aśoka was not held in very high esteem by him.

(iii) Miscellaneous Articles: KPJ wrote several articles on inscriptions and seals underlining the issues such as polity, religion, script, and regions such as Jạva, Nepal, Mithila, and Gaya.[159] It covers a period from the Harappan time to the medieval period. Analysing the contents and script of some of the inscriptions, KPJ argued that some of the inscriptions are pre-Aśokan, such as Vikramkhol inscription,[160] Jogimara cave inscription[161] and Barli stone inscription.[162]

Some of the inscriptions have been identified by KPJ as belonging to different dynasties and kings. *Śreṇika* of Rajgir stone image has been identified by KPJ as Bimbisāra, a contemporary of the Buddha, and king of Magadha with its capital Rājagṛha or present day, Rajgir.[163] The 'Brahmanical revolution' of the Śuṅgas had been one of the favourite subjects of KPJ which were discussed extensively in his monographs—*Hindu Polity* and *Manu and Yājñavalkya*. However, KPJ also highlighted a Sanskrit inscription from Ayodhya to support his theory of 'Brahmanical revolution' under the Śuṅgas.[164] Reading the Girdharpur pillar inscription of the Kuṣāṇa ruler Huvishka, KPJ argued that this inscription records a perpetual gift (*akṣaya-nīvi dinna*) for the benefit of the Devaputra Śāhi (king) Huviṣka and those dear to him and the whole land. It was evidently inscribed at the *puṇyaśāla* (charitable pavilion) which it mentions. 550 and 550 (1,100) *purāṇas* were deposited with two guilds, and from the monthly interest of the funds, daily alms (like modern sadabrat) were to be given. KPJ especially underlined that this gift was in favour of Brahmins and the general public, and it is not a Buddhist endowment.[165]

KPJ also supported his theory of *paura-janapada* on the basis of the reading of Nalanda seal.[166] When he offered a constitutional interpretation of the term *paura* and *janapada*, several critics asserted that the term denoted merely a man of *paura* (city), and a man of a *janapada* (country), without any constitutional significance. According to KPJ,

> This controversy is set at rest by a Nalanda seal. It is a seal of the *Janapada* of Purika: with the legend—*Purika-grāma-Janapadasya* in Gupta characters of the fifth century or sixth century... Purika figures in the inscription of Bharhut. The *Janapada* office was located at the

> capital. Purika represented a small principality in its best days. Probably it remained a small unit under the Guptas. *Janapada* would represent the grāmas or townships, according to *Vivāda-Ratnākara*. *Purika-grāma-janapada* would mean the *Janapada* of the *grāmas* of Purika. It is also possible that the main *Janapada* represented local *Janapadas* in the Gupta times. In any case, this much is certain that *Janapada* was a body and that in the Gupta times it was still a living institution."

KPJ also ventured to reconstruct the regional history of Bodh-Gaya[167] and Mithila.[168] Describing the Janibigha inscription, KPJ argued, "...Is of very great importance to the history of the Sena epoch. It is dated in the era of Lakshmaṇa-Sena, the year being 83, i.e., the third year (1202 AD), after the expedition of Muhammad, son of Bakhtyar. This inscription now proves that the neighbouring district of Gaya remained under a scion of the Sena family in the time of Muhammad ibn Bakhtyar."[169] However, they were subjugated by Muhammad Khiliji through a stratagem. All the great families of Hindustan had been already reduced by the new victors. The surprise of the great Sena monarch at Nadiah meant merely the last blow to the already weakened morale of the eastern Hindus.[170] While reconstructing the history of Mithila, KPJ argued that Khandāhā inscription was the first inscription of the Oinwār or Kāmeśvara dynasty of Mithila. On the basis of his reading, KPJ established the genealogy of the dynasty beginning with Bhavasiṃhadeva, then [Ha]rasiṃhadeva and Narasiṃhadeva and established its date as 1375.

Some of KPJ's epigraphic contributions threw useful light on religious developments. While deciphering the Ghosundi Inscription,[171] KPJ argued that this was the earliest inscription in Sanskrit yet discovered in the country and was of great importance from the point of view of religious history. It was the earliest monumental proof of the fact that temples were erected to Vāsudeva, and to his brother. It was dedicated to gods Saṁkarṣaṇa and Vāsudeva. KPJ analysed a variety of sources and came to the conclusion that Kṛṣṇa's worship began before 200 B.C., and that the antiquity of the cult probably did not go too far back in time. The two inscriptions (Naṇaghat and Ghosundi) and Baudhāyana's *Dharmasūtra*, therefore, are the earliest records establishing the deification of Kṛṣṇa. While the Nanaghat record still refers to the family of the two brothers, the Ghosundi inscription detaches them completely from their human associations and treats them as *devas* pure and simple. The *garuḍa-dhvaja* dedication of Heliodorus similarly treats Vāsudeva as god, and it is noteworthy that is does not mention the elder brother Saṁkarṣaṇa at all. This history of the worship of Vāsudeva would place the Nanaghat evidence as the first piece chronologically, the Ghosundi as the next and the Besnagar as the last.[172] This sequence was also supported by palaeographic arguments.

KPJ's reading of the Janibigha inscription was also invoked for the history of the Bodh-Gaya shrine in the medieval period. He argued that the Buddhist monk was the guardian of the whole shrine at Bodh-Gaya. It is interesting to note that Hīnayāna school still held the shrine and abbots for their knowledge of the *Tripiṭaka* were imported from Ceylon as late as at the beginning of the thirteenth century. The Buddhist guardianship of the shrine seems to have come to an end in the fourteenth century. This shrine as a Buddhist institution survived 'Hindu revolutions.' Even the Brahmanical Sena rulers respected and supported it. It fell only when the Hindu power fell before the Islamic zeal. The possession of the orthodox *sannyāsins*, probably originated during the period of the rehabilitation of Gaya by 'Hindu crusaders' under Rajputana warriors.[173]

Another feature of KPJ's reading of inscriptions and the seals was the tracing of the evolution of scripts such as Śaṅkha and Brāhmī.[174] KPJ was, perhaps, one of the earliest scholars who tried to read the Harappan seals. In 1912, Fleet published three Harappan seals in the July issue of the *JRAS*. KPJ proposed a tentative reading of the seal and argued that the characters, on the whole, are the nearer system of the old Brāhmī than their pictorial predecessors. Two other pieces are also very important.[175] He compared the script of the Vikramkhol inscription with the Harappan script and concluded, "A theory that Brāhmī is an indigenous Indian writing, receives confirmation from these finds, for its letters are nearer Brāhmi than any other script." The Vikramkhol inscription supplied a link between the passages of letter-forms from the Harappan script to Brāhmī. The Vikramkhol record, however, need not necessarily be an 'Aryan piece of writing', "The writing is certainly earlier than the earliest specimen of Brāhmī known so far; and Brāhmī was completed before 1500 B.C. We should be within the range of a fair approximation in dating it about 1500 B.C."[176]

KPJ also tried establish a link between India and Java by interpreting Shell Character rock inscription from Ci-Aruton.[177] He studied the "box-headed" writing of the Javanese inscriptions and argued that the writing was bi-scriptory and very likely the Pauṣkarasādiya, one of the three main *lipis* (scripts) of Northern India mentioned in the Buddhist texts. The shell writing was always found in Northern India, and its present instances were found on certainly Gupta monuments; the Rajgir writings on the road may be much earlier. Its cursive form shows that it was non-monumental, i.e., book writing. The system was purely Hindu; the forms, though different, have basic unity with Brāhmī forms. It seems that Puṣkarādi with whose personal name the system is associated, invented the system from Brāhmī. A modern example of a similar type of invention is Gurumukhi. The head of each letter of the inscription was headed with a line as in Nagari, Bengali and other modern Indo-Aryan scripts of the North.

One of the important contributions in the epigraphic studies of KPJ was that he broke the Nepalese myth that Nepal was never invaded by any Muhammadan conqueror.[178] In April 1936, he visited Nepal. At the Paśupati temple, he found some stone images having broken noses. The local explanation by the common people and scholars of this fact offered was that the damage was accidental. KPJ found that the damage was not accidental. He examined the well preserved inscriptions at Svayambhu Nath. The script was Newāri and except for few passages, the whole was readable. The inscription when read gave the history of an invasion by *Suratrāna Samasdina 'along with a large Bengal army'*. The inscription was in incorrect Sanskrit. The inscription is dated in the 492nd Year of the Nepal era (A.D. 1371-72). Among other things, it says that Sultan Shamsuddin along with a large army of Bengal, having come into Nepal, broke and burnt completely the Dharma-dhātu Stūpa (the pious relic shrine), the banner of the *muni* (Buddha), which had been founded by the predecessors of the king (or, by earlier people). The Sultan Shamsuddin of the inscription is undoubtedly Shamsuddin Iliyas who ruled in Bengal as an independent king from A.D. 1342 to 1357. Taking into account the other contemporary source of the inscription, KPJ established the chronology of the invasion. KPJ concluded, "It has now become clear that it was this Muhammadan invasion which indirectly led to the supersession of the Malla dynasty of Nepal. With Jayasthiti Malla begins the

Kārṇāta dynasty of Nepal which lasted up to A.D. 1768 when the Gurkha dynasty dispossessed them."

The Nepal visit of KPJ was arranged by Pandit Rājaguru of Nepal. However, the publication of the above article created a furore in Nepal and ultimately led to permanent rupture of relations between the Rājaguru on the one hand and KPJ and Rahul on the other because the Rājaguru and the King of Nepal were not willing to accept the theory of 'Muslim invasion' of the Himalayan kingdom.[179]

(b) Numismatics: KPJ was quite aware of the importance of the numismatic studies for the reconstruction of the Indian history. Speaking as the President of the Reception Committee of the sixth All India Oriental Conference, he highlighted the importance of numismatic studies, "We should not forget that some chapters of Indian History are exclusively contributed by coins. It is our duty not to let this branch of study become feeble."[180] Further, he said,

> In the absence of written history, coins and inscriptions necessarily play a very important part in this country in the recovery of our history. Time is a relentless destroyer. But man fights against that destroyer. Dynasties enter the mouth of all-consuming time obliterating chronology; man endeavours to rescue it for his knowledge and derive benefit from that knowledge. In that process the little piece of metal called coin is a powerful and an indestructible means. The little piece, otherwise not worth much, makes important disclosures. It tells unsuspected tales of truth. May we hope that our countrymen would attach due importance to the not negligible piece?[181]

In June 1935, he was invited to deliver a lecture at the Royal Asiatic Society in London, where he dwelt on some coins of the Mauryas and the Śuṅgas. The lecture was illustrated by lantern slides.[182] He was the first Indian scholar to receive such an honour from that illustrious Society. He was elected President of the Numismatic Society of India twice and presented distinctive addresses focusing on the development of the numismatic studies in India.[183] He was awarded a special medal for conspicuous original work on the science of Indian coins.[184] However, before these learned speeches, KPJ wrote several articles on numismatics, which were published in the leading journals of the time.[185] It is, however, interesting to note here that the first article on numismatics was written by KPJ,[186] when he was merely 23 and it was after a gap of 27 years, that he started writing on the subject more regularly.

The range of KPJ's readings of Indian coinage covers from the pre-Mauryan times to the medieval period. He not only read the coins but also discovered new coins. On the basis of his studies of coinage, he tried to reconstruct the history of ancient India. He also critically examines the information and authenticity of coins, whenever required. In his Presidential Speech at the 26th session of the Numismatic Society in Udaipur, KPJ said,

> Numismatists have to devote increasing attention to the early Hindu period, as that is the only period where coins can render unique contributions to Indian History. For later centuries we have already worked upon materials to a point where very little is left to be done. For instance, on the Moghul period we are reduced to counting the lines of the milled edge. The later periods in Indian Numismatics have been exhausted. The real task of the Indian Numismatists is the early Hindu period.[187]

During his lifetime, KPJ gave three important lectures on numismatics. Speaking at the Royal Asiatic Society on 'Some Coins of the Mauryas and Śuṅgas', he highlighted the importance of the 'moon-(or crescent)-on-hill' mark on the government pottery and the coins.[188] The mark, according to him, was found on silver punch-marked coins from Peshawar to Patna and throughout the Deccan. Among other things, KPJ highlighted the question of signed coins in ancient India. He argued, "We cannot yet fix the limit of antiquity of the signed coins of Ancient India: but on the present data they certainly go back as far as c. 500 B.C., having regard to the pre-Maurya coin of the Dharma-Pāla of Avanti, and that of Āryaka (hitherto misread as Eraka)."[189] He contended that public coinage is not such a cultural characteristic which could have sprung up in a day. The successors of the Mauryas in the South were the Āndhras or the Sātavāhana dynasty, just as the Śuṅgas were in Āryāvrata. The Sātavāhana certainly had signed coins bearing royal names. It is natural, therefore, to accept that their contemporaries and rivals, the Śuṅgas also minted their own coins. From these and various other indications it is certain that the Śuṅgas, from the very beginning of their rule, minted both silver and copper coins inscribed with their names.[190] Oldham, present at the lecture, appreciated KPJ and drew comparisons between KPJ's work and that of another pioneer, Cunningham, whose views, not always accepted at the time, had since been mostly justified.[191] KPJ further elaborated the above thesis with additional evidence and fresh data in his first Presidential Speech at the annual meeting of the Numismatic Society of India in Mysore in December 1935.[192]

In his second Presidential Speech at the Udaipur session of the Numismatic Society of India, KPJ highlighted, among other things, the large evidence of cast copper coins of the Yaudheya mint recovered from Rohtak.[193] These coins belong to 100 B.C. and KPJ read the legend as *Yaudhéyāna Bahudhānake,*

> The last part of the legend had not been read before. *Bahudhānake,* according to *Mahābhārata,* was one of two main provinces over which the community ruled from Rohitaka, i.e. Rohtak. The other province was Maru, i.e. Rajputana. Bahudhānyaka was the rich fertile territory which was to the west of Rajputana extending to the Jumna and including the district of Saharanpur. These coins of the Yaudheyas bear the Śuṅgan emblems—elephant and bull—as opposed to the Yaudheya symbols of their later coinage. We should call the series the Bahudhānyaka series.[194]

KPJ argued that the *Mahābhārata* did not give the names of the rulers of Maru and Bahudhānyaka - a lacuna that is filled by coins. On the basis of his studies of coins and inscriptions, KPJ concluded:

> Now the coins and inscriptions establish that the whole of Northern Rajputana, Eastern Punjab and the land up to the borders of Kurukshetra, that is, the large tract between the Sutlej and the Jumna was under the united states of the Yaudheya republic in the early centuries before the Christian era. Their coins are largely found between the Sutlej and Jumna, and their name survives in Johiyabar in the Sutlej Valley and in monuments in Bahawalpur. Rajputana was still under the republican Yaudheyas in the time of Samudragupta. The Yaudheyas, according to the Puranic history, were from an ancient aristocratic Kshatriya stock. Coins, along with inscriptions, prove that we had, before the foundation of the United States of America, the largest federal republican state in the Yaudheya federation. We know from the coins that the Yaudheya organisation was a federation of at least three more republics. In the Yaudheya history, we have the most authentic history of the race which inhabited Rajputana up to and in the fourth century of the Christian era. That race must have survived as the prominent element in the population of Rajputana later. The medieval aristocratic constitution of some of the Rajput States, where a council of noble families ruled along with the Rāṇā, is explainable in the light of the ancient Constitution of the Yaudheyas. *Rājanya*

> which is the original word for Rāṇā denoted the president of a particular type of aristocratic republics. In any case, it is sure that the Rajputs of Rajputana are mostly survivals of the Kshatriyas who composed the Yaudheyas."[195]

KPJ identified some of the coins of the Nāga-Vākāṭaka period. The coin in question was known by popular name the 'lanky bull type' and its chief feature is the 'humped bull of very lank shape'. The coin was collected by Srinath Shah of Benares from Kosam. KPJ found that the letters are undoubtedly pre-Guptan and post-Kuṣāṇa and the symbols (nāga) and system of dating (30th year on the back) is quite in line with the Nāga coinage.[196] Reconstructing the historical value of these coins, KPJ concluded,

> The dynasty of Nava is known to the Purāṇas. And if coins struck with the name *Nava* are found with the letters of the period, it is unfair to ignore the identification and its historical consequences. Coming as the coin does, in fairly large numbers, from the territory which had been directly under the Kushans, and bearing Kushan letters, and years, not of the Kushan era but of the king's (Navas) own regnal years, it cannot but prove a political revolution denoting replacement of the Kushans by Nava in Central Hindustan—the area of the coin.[197]

KPJ also explained the term 'Garutmadaka' of the Allahabad pillar inscription as the coin bearing Garuḍa.[198]

KPJ made a study of the Radhia hoard of Champaran and found that they were copper coins of Kuṣāṇas, "The hoard proves the extension of Kuṣāṇa rule up to Champaran, and lends support to a recent conclusion which I have hesitatingly expressed in the *History of Nepal* that a century which is a gap in Nepalese history was probably covered by Kuṣāṇa rule whose coins were dug out in Nepal; but, as they were little, the evidence was inconclusive. Now Kuṣāṇa rule having been established in Champaran by this large hoard, it becomes a probable conclusion that their rule covered Nepal."[199]

The overall writings of KPJ on numismatics are unlike his writings on epigraphy and far less intensive. He may have been put at par with Cunningham, but the overall impact of his numismatic forays would not deserve very serious attention today. Neither the quantity nor the quality of his numismatic essays would make his achievements enviable.

(c) Writings on Indian arts: KPJ's contribution towards ancient

Indian arts is also remarkable. He wrote extensively on varied subjects relating to monuments, sculpture, paintings, etc., which range from the pre-Mauryan times to the medieval period.[200] The major highlights of these writings are: KPJ's efforts to establish the antiquity of the representation of human form and its indigenous origin; every form of art for KPJ is 'Hindu' and indigenous; cultural imperialism of the Hindus; KPJ's concern as a conservationist, etc. And, finally all of them are answers to the colonial interpretation of India's ancient past.

(a) Statues and Sculptures

(i) Pre-Mauryan: KPJ's contributions in this category can be divided in two phases: in the first phase (1898-1919), he published only three articles in Hindi and in the second phase from 1919 onwards, he published articles only in English. His first publication 'Bharatavarsha Ki Purani Imaraten' was the Hindi translation of Lord Curzon's speech on India's old monumental structures given at the Annual Conference of the Asiatic Society of Bengal in February 1900. KPJ's second publication 'Kausambi' was also a translation of V.A. Smith's article. Both of these articles were published, without any comment by KPJ. KPJ's third article 'Buner ke Prachin Sansthano ka Anusandhana' was based on the report published by the Principal of the Lahore College, M.A. Stein. Buner is a part of North-West frontier region. KPJ argued that the antiquity of Buner was not found in any of the inscriptions and in Indian history, it is only through the accounts of Chinese travellers, we are able to get information about Buner. We, therefore, should be thankful to those Chinese travellers. On the basis of the report, he argued that before 1897, no archaeologist had any idea about the Buner region. He tried to reconstruct the history of the region since the time of the Buddha and claimed that the sculptures lying there were 'Hindu' sculptures. He also discussed several Buddhist stūpas and structures of the site.

One of the important and controversial discoveries of KPJ was his identification of the two statues as early Śaiśunāka emperors Udāyin and Varta-Nandi.[201] The importance of KPJ's reading was such that it led to the joint meeting of Asiatic Societies held in England on 5 September, 1919. In the meeting, L.D. Barnett questioned KPJ's reading of the inscription and KPJ also gave a detailed explanation of his criticism.[202] The existence of these statues had been known for more than 100 years. These statues were discovered near Patna in 1812 by Buchanan and in 1879 Cunningham offered a tentative reading of the inscription. The distinguished archaeologist identified the figures as of Yaksha and ascribed on the basis of the form of scripts a date later than Aśoka. However, KPJ argued that these statues had really been discovered only, in 1919, i.e., after KPJ's readings.

KPJ challenged Cunningham's readings and identification and underlined the following: (i) the inscriptions on the statues are contemporary to the statues, (ii) the script, polish etc., are pre-Aśokan, (iii) the inscriptions reads: *chhonidhise* (His Gracious Majesty Aja, King [lit. Over-ruler of the land or Earth]) and *Sapakhate Vaṭa Nandi* (of the complete empire (dominion), Varta Nandi), (iv) the initial date of Udāyin-Aja is 483 B.C. and of Nandi 449 B.C. and the date of the statues be fixed *circa* 467-449 B.C. in the case of statue A (Udāyin) and *circa* 409 B.C. in the case of statue B (Varta-Nandi), (v) Magadha and Vaiśālī were the capitals of Udāyin and Nandi respectively, (vi) the language was the vernacular which was found in canonical Pali. That, not Sanskrit seems to have been the official language under the Śaiśunākas, and (vii) as historic monuments they are not only the most important remains in India but have to be classed amongst the important pieces of the world.

The reading by KPJ led to an intense debate. Chairing the meeting of the Royal Asiatic Society, V.A. Smith, congratulated KPJ with some reservation,

> The inscriptions have been studied carefully first time by Mr. K.P. Jayaswal... That result, if established, revolutionises the history of Indian art. Hitherto the assumption that stone sculpture began with Aśoka had been generally accepted. If the Patna statues and their inscriptions are as old as supposed, it must be admitted that the art of sculpture in stone was well matured two centuries before Aśoka. The execution of the image is such that it presupposes a long prior development of plastic art.[203]

Barnett, however, raised serious questions on linguistic grounds and concluded,

> To sum up the result of this epigraphic study: the name of Aja does not appear in inscription A; the inscription B has indeed four syllables which may without violence be read as Vaṭa Nandi, a name which might be Sanskritized as Varta-Nandi but as the Purāṇas say nothing at all about a king called Varta-Nandi, Mr. Jayaswal's effort to identify his Vaṭa-Nandi with the Puranic Nandivardhana must be pronounced

> a failure; and the type of writing points to a Mauryan date at earliest and probably is considerably later.[204]

KPJ re-examined the whole question and the letters on the statue with reference to the criticism of Barnett. KPJ not only answered the questions raised by Barnett, but also mentioned new facts having a bearing on the question. In his reply, KPJ took help from Haraprasad Sastri, the Sanskritist, and F. Green, the stone expert and argued that here the testimony of Sastri's position is invaluable as scholars abroad could not physically see the monument.[205]

Before KPJ, it was generally argued that the beginning of art came from Persia. However, before the discovery of these statues, KPJ had already come across a piece of evidence which had greatly shaken his belief in the current archaeological theory which ascribed art (undoubtedly in the absence of pre-Mauryan monuments) to Persia. KPJ saw a neolithic piece which is generally known as '*Vajra*' (thunderbolt) with the polish! That, according to him, unmistakably pointed to an Indian origin of the polish coming down and was developed from the art of pre-historic times, when primitive man devoted much attention to his stone. The latest evidence now comes in the shape of these statues which carry the art two centuries back from the date assigned for its import from Persia. The origin of the art, in his opinion, was to be sought in the art of Dravidian India which shaped the polished *vajra* and not in Persia.[206] KPJ's reading of the inscription met with favourable reception from some other experts, "He deserves the gratitude of all students for opening up a new vista in the most distant horizon of ancient Indian history."[207]

Some other pre-Mauryan monuments were also discussed by KPJ. Some of the cave houses at Rājagṛha were described by KPJ as belonging pre-Buddhist and Buddhist phases and corroborated with the accounts of Chinese travellers. At Rājagṛha the Śākyamuni Buddha lived in a hill hermitage called Gridharkūṭa. The hill was identified by Cunningham, but he could not find any of the cave-houses described by the two Chinese travellers (Huen-Tsang and Fa Hien). During his survey, KPJ found that one of these caves was one that was occupied by the Buddha and the description of Huen-Tsang fully corresponded to some details still in situ. KPJ seemed quite convinced that some of these remains went beyond the time of the Buddha. Some of the brick buildings were certainly contemporary with the Buddha, and the Chinese authors have recorded true archaeological information that they were built by Bimbisāra as confirmed by the inscribed bricks.[208]

KPJ examined the statue of Ajātaśatru-Kuṇika.[209] In 1885, a statue from village of Parkham (Mathura) was brought to light by Cunningham and since then its identification had been a big issue in early Indian art. Before KPJ, three scholars had attempted to read the inscription; Alexander Cunningham, J.Ph. Vogel, and Sten Konow.[210] But those readings gave no meaning and had been so unsatisfactory that H. Lüders in his list declared the line as undeciphered.[211] The statue was examined by KPJ and he made a comparison between the letters of the Bhita seal, the sigloi coins, and the Piprahwa vase and those of the Parkham statue and placed the Parkham record before the dates of the former.[212] He found that the art of statue-building was carried to a period much earlier than the sixth century B.C. and in execution the statue was nearer to the Besanagar piece.[213] KPJ further argued,

> The absence of the Buddha statue at Bharhut and Sanchi is not conclusive for the argument that no statue of the Master was made in early days. In view of the Śaiśunāka statues the arguments in favour of that view disappear on the artistic side. The statue of Jina in Kalinga in the fifth century B.C. and the ancient wooden statue of a Kalinga prince, referred to in Khāravela's inscription, further weaken M. Foucher's theory that Hindus could not make statues before Menander.[214]

KPJ read from the inscription that the Jaina name *Kuṇika*, spelt also as *Koṇika*, etc., was the real name of the king, and the Purāṇic 'Ajātaśatru' (the Enemy-less) and 'Aja-satru' a *viruda* name. 'Kuṇika' had been a well established name in the Vedic literature... The form in the inscription probably indicated the name of the founder of the family to have been *Śevas-Nāga* or *Śevas-nāka*, "the auspicious" (*śevas*, Vedic Sanskrit) *Nāga* or *Nāka* (*Nāḳa*, 'Heaven').[215]

Another inscription of Kuṇika was found by KPJ on the female figure, worshipped as 'Manasa Devi' at village Sinaut, Mathura and he argued, "The details of statue are pure Hindu style of Besanagar statue."[216] According to him, the statue was important for the history of art and was a further proof to contest M. Foucher's theory that Hindus learnt the art of making statues from the Greek residents of India. The statue was not noticed in any of the official reports.

(ii) Mauryan: During the Patna excavations of the 1930s, KPJ collected several antiquities that were ultimately given to the

Museum that he was creating in Patna.[217] Amongst important antiquities were: (i) a carved ivory plaque, (ii) a plaque of pure gold images—identified by KPJ as those of Śiva and his consort, (iii) a highly polished torso from Lohanipur (compared with Mohenjo Daro torso), (iv) an unpolished statue of a 'Jaina thirthankar,' (v) a brick structure identified as a temple. KPJ's accent in making sense of these finds was to assign them to either the Mauryan period (largely on the ground of 'polish') or even to the pre-Mauryan period. Further, KPJ enthusiastically believed that the images of Jain tirthankaras were in existence long before those of the Buddha, Śiva or any other Hindu deity.

(iii) Kuṣāṇa: KPJ's attention was also drawn towards some sculptures from Mathura (and housed in the Museum there), which enabled him to reflect on developments in the region in the early centuries of Christian Era.[218] Some of these sculptures were identified as those of the Śaka chief Caṣṭana, Wema Kadphises and Kaniṣka. Curiously, KPJ treated 'Kuṣāṇa not as a race' name but only a personal name. Regarding Kaniṣka as the founder of the Śaka era, KPJ also underlined that Kuṣāṇas were called Śakas by their contemporaries in India! Bihar was under the suzerainty of the Kuṣāṇas from the days of Kaniṣka to those of Vāsudeva, argued KPJ.

(iv) Nāga-Vākāṭaka: KPJ discussed some of the Nāga-Vākāṭaka sculpture, the Caturmukha (four-faced) Śiva bust at Nachana.[219] The issue finds numerous details in his monograph, *History of India*, as well. KPJ found: (i) the chief feature of this bust of Śiva is the ascetic *mudrā* of *dhyāna*, (ii) the motive originated in the time of Bhāraśiva Nāga emperors, and was followed up in the next epoch of the Vākāṭaka emperors, and then taken up by the Guptas, (iii) the Trikamala image of the Buddha from Bodh-Gaya belongs to this class and that is dated in the Cedī era, (iv) Nachna bust is more pronounced in its spiritual aspects than the Bodh-Gaya Buddha, (v) for a Brahmanical sculpture it is earlier than the entire true Gupta image.

(v) Gupta: A sandstone head in a three quarter profile and housed in the Indian Museum (Kolkata) was noticed by KPJ for its pleasant expression—*priyadarśana*, "which is enjoined for the Hindu kings." Struck by its prominent nose, masculinity, and royal dignity, KPJ tangentially suggested that it was perhaps of Samudragupta. Characteristically, it was also described as 'a secular face' —

apparently because KPJ did not see any sign/mark of any divinity. The Museum label marked its find-spot as Magadha.[220]

Another piece, considered to be of the Gupta period, was a terracotta panel/plaque from Chausa depicting what KPJ called a 'Rāmāyaṇa scene' (specificity of the scene remained unidentified). Invoking the example of the brick temple at Bhitargaon that also had such decorative terracotta plaques, KPJ speculated that the panel under reference might have adorned the walls of a temple at Chausa.[221]

(vi) Post-Gupta: Among the post-Gupta findings the most notable are 240 metal images (of which 105 were inscribed) at Kurkihar monastery in Gaya.[222] For KPJ, the highlights of these finds are: (i) the collection as a whole is Pāla, but there are a few pieces which are pre-Pāla (ii) images buried in the monastery prove that the religious foundation had existed for several centuries, (iii) Bihar was effectively invaded by the Muhammadans for the first time and religious establishments were looted and destroyed, (iv) the images once buried could not be restored to the position of worship, owing to the political and consequent religious upheavals in the country following the "fateful year of 1197", (v) the Buddha images, represent the connecting link between the Gupta and Pāla plastic traditions, (vi) with the decline of Buddhism, a class of monk-artists arose who became philosophers in the science and art of image-making and who sought to revive Buddhism through the art-appeal of newly fashioned images—'Crowned Buddha images' suggesting 'Hindu theory of the Buddha as an *avatāra* of Viṣṇu.' Though KPJ had realised that 'this compromise in art was wholly unsupported by Buddhist canons, yet he contended, "The artist invented it to draw the Hindu to his church."

To the family of the art of Kurkihara and Nalanda belonged the Gaya black stone image (favourite material of the Pāla artist) of the Buddha's "Great Resolution" [Either I will discover *the truth* (the cause of human suffering) *or my body shall perish*]. The image was owned by Lady Holmwood of London and KPJ showed his gratitude to the lady for providing him with a photograph of the sculpture. 'The piece is unique, marking the zenith of the Pāla art", remarked KPJ.[223]

KPJ also kept his eyes and ears open and whenever he came to know about any unknown statues, he reported them. When Rahul Sankrityayan visited Tibet and found statues of three Indian scholars: Śāntarakṣita, Paṇḍita Gayadhara, and Śākya Śrībhadra, KPJ wrote an article, gave descriptions of these statues, and also their scholarly contribution towards the spread of Buddhism in Tibet.[224]

(b) Paintings: KPJ also wrote a few pieces on paintings. While still in England, KPJ had developed an interest in appreciating paintings. Writing his travelogue, KPJ described the religious significance of the painting—Mary and Christ—and also tried to establish an emotional relationship in India and Europe. He wrote, "There was a feeling of devotion among the old Christians. That is why; they were idol worshippers like us." Again, citing the opinion of the German and other historians, he wrote,

> They have proved with great endeavour that near the place which is shown as the birthplace of Christ, there was a Buddhist colony, for which there is historical proof. They say that on the basis of the stories of the Buddhist texts, the birth of the imaginative Christ is believed and it was on the basis of the sermons of the Buddha, Christ's sermons were written. They have also shown that the rituals of the Christian religion are absolutely taken from the Buddhist religion. No scholar has challenged these opinions yet. Acceptance or non-acceptance of these arguments is left to an individual's judgment. It is my personal belief that the research of these scholars is right."

However, KPJ was conscious of the nature of information he was giving to the readers of the *Saraswati*, "I have to show the example of the craftsmanship of the fine art. I do not have to give the religious sermon.[225]

KPJ contested V.A. Smith's view that no text on the art and science of painting in India was available, except a stray quotation from *Citralakṣaṇa* cited in the commentary on the *Kāma-śāstra*.[226] Contrarily, KPJ argued that there was a vast literature in Sanskrit on the subject and produced evidence from the *Jātakas, Arthaśāstra, Kāmasūtra*, as well as visual examples from Pāṭaliputra excavations, Ajanta, Ḅagh, Sigiri and other places. On the basis of his reading of the text of 16th century, called *Śilparatna* by Śrīkumāra of the Travancore State, KPJ argued that though it dealt mainly with the subject of civil engineering, yet it also had an interesting chapter on painting '*Citralakṣaṇa*'. The treatment of the subject in the book shows a strong adherence to the ancient *Śilpasāstras*. Similarly, his discussion on painting had all the traditions of the orthodox school.

KPJ further argued that this text discussed every minute thing of a painting like: definition, categories, and forms, colour combination, preparation of colour, technical directions, place (what kind of painting should be placed at what place), etc. Since the art of painting was a complex phenomenon, therefore, KPJ argued that the 'Hindu painter' was supposed to be a man not merely literate but thoroughly educated, as he had to distinguish between versions of a particular story according to particular Vedic schools. It was not an art for the unlearned. This is supported by the *Kāmasūtra* of Vātsāyāyana, which directs that the *nāgarika* or Hindu educated in polite literature should practise painting and should have his board, brush, and paints in his drawing room. KPJ further argued that the fresco painting is the most prominent method before the 'Hindu writers'. Examples of it are well known —Ajanta, Bagh, Sigiri, and walls of palaces mentioned in the Sanskrit literature, "Examples of painting on boards have not survived, but they too are a familiar topic of Hindu dramatists and polite writers in general."

(c) Monumental Structures and Conservation of Monuments: Monuments and their conservation also drew KPJ attention. On the basis of *Śilpaśāstras*, the origin of the Nāgara and Vesara styles of the temple architecture went back a long way and were well-development: (i) Unlike the Dravida and Kaliṅga, Nāgara and Vesara were not territorial appellations, (ii) Nāgara meant a building on a square plan, and Vesara meant an "ornamental" voluptuous style having a round plan, both of them may be *śikhara* or non-*śikhara* edifices, (iii) Nāgara is derived from Nāga, the dynastic name of the Nava Nāga kings, who drove the Kuṣāṇas out of Āryāvarta, (iv) Dravida and Kaliṅga are ethnic or territorial, but that does not necessarily mean that the other two terms must be similarly ethnic. Nāgara might be an ethnic expression but Vesara cannot be so regarded. Throughout this short article, the accent is on crediting the Nāga with the origin of the two styles—Nāgara and Vesara. Obliquely, it was also argued the Guptas were recipients of this legacy.[227]

While discussing the origin of *śikhara* style, KPJ criticised Codrington, when he argued, "There is no reason to believe that *śikhara*... existed before the medieval period."[228] KPJ gave examples from Bodh-Gaya, Suraj Man, Bhilsa, Khajuraho etc. Citing *Matsya Purāṇa*,[229] he argued that in the century before the Gupta period the *śikhara* style must have been a favourite and must have been practised in 'Hindu' architecture. The inscription of Khāravela (2nd c. BC) also mentions the construction of "excellent *śikharas*."[230]

While discussing the Udaipur temple of Malwa, KPJ observed: (i) the sculptures are probably superior even to the sculptures at Khajuraho, and is the most beautiful religious building of Āryāvarta, (ii) the builder of the temple was king Udayāditya, son of king Bhoja of Paramāra dynasty, (iii) Udayāditya raised this monument to the family deity Śiva.[231]

As a practising historian and conservationist, KPJ was only too well aware about the importance of preservation of monuments. During his field surveys, he visited a number of places of historical importance: Rupanath edict of Aśoka, Gupta temples at Deo Barnark, the Nachna temples, the Bhumara temple, the Datiya palace, the Orchha palace, Digh and Chhatarpur palaces, Nalanda, Rajgir, etc., and gave details of their monumental structures. However, KPJ's main focus was on the dilapidated and deteriorating conditions of these structures. The neglect of monuments, in his eyes, was a crime perpetrated on the future generations. Describing the pathetic conditions of the Rupanath inscription, he wrote, "It lies neglected, exposed to the attack of rains and ill-treated by man. A record which lasted fairly well for some 2,175 years has been subjected to a rapid process of obliteration when the public revenues provide for a highly-paid staff and organisation to look after ancient monuments." Without any fear KPJ voiced his protest publicly, "Probably local officers would have done much more and taken effective measures, had the care of monuments been in the hands of the Local Governments and not the Government of India."[232]

At another place, on the Mauryan rock-cut hermitage at Barabar, "No civilised administration should neglect these ancient monuments in this manner. In no other country under a civilised government, their neglect in this manner would be tolerated. There is no placard, no notice for the guidance of the public to trace and see the caves and the inscriptions. If the caves are not protected from wanton destruction their value will go on decreasing."[233]

KPJ also smelled discrimination in the conservation of the monuments, "Non-Hindu remains are treated differently by the Archaeological Department, e.g., lakhs have been spent on Taxila, because there they discovered Persian, Greek and Kushan remains. But a few thousands will not be spared for these Gupta temples

(Deo Banmark, Nachana and Bhumara temples). Gupta temples in brick are very few in the whole country. To Buddhist and other sites the purse readily opens, but to Hindu remains the Archaeological Department is more often as cold as a step-mother."[234] However, he was also critical of the Hindus for the negligence of the Nachna temples, "It had escaped destruction at the hands of the Musalman rulers owing to its secluded position. But Hindus themselves have completed its ruin which it had escaped in the past ages. No action seems to have taken by the State, and a private individual was, on the other hand, permitted to destroy the Parvati temple—an impious deed which time itself had refused to perform for over 1600 years."[235] KPJ did praise those, who had taken care of the monuments, "The small and the poor State of Chhatarpur has maintained every Bundela palace of the late dynasties in perfect order. In this respect no State, British or Indian, can come to the standard attained and kept up by the State of Gwalior. It has looked after every monument with laudable care."[236]

KPJ's conservation concerns were not confined to monumental structures. Apparently, he was championing the cause of broader heritage as we understand it today. Highlighting "the civilising mission of the Indians", he reported zealously the recovery of lost manuscripts of texts, irrespective of their religious affliations. While describing the high philosophical learning and civilising mission of the Buddhists, KPJ wrote;

> तीसरी-चौथी शताब्दी में एक तरफ हमारे दर्शन-शास्त्र ग्रीस और रोम में आदरपात्र हो रहे थे, दूसरी तरफ सांख्य सम्भूत बौद्ध मत मंगोल जाति को सभ्य और शान्ति बना रहा था। धन्य थे कुमारजीव आदि, जिन्होंने घोर कष्ट सहकर एक बहुत बड़े भूभाग पर भारतीय धार्मिक और दार्शनिक भावों के बीज वपन किये। आजकल के पादरियों की तरह धर्मोपदेश के बहाने औरों की राजनैतिक स्वाधीनता पर दाँत लगाना कुमारजीव जैसे सात्विक साधुओं को स्वप्न में भी नहीं ख्याल हुआ था। काश्यप, धर्मरक्ष, धर्मपाल, बोधिरुचि, बोधिधर्म, कुमारजीव, परमार्थ, प्रज्ञतर, आदि इसी भारत के सुपुत्र थे। उन्होंने हिमालय का उल्लंघन करके विदेशियों की भाषाओं में इतनी पारदर्शिता प्राप्त की जितनी आज तक एक भी योरप-निवासी नहीं प्राप्त कर सका, क्योंकि आज तक किसी योरपवासी ने चीनी भाषा में कोई दार्शनिक ग्रन्थ नहीं लिखा। भारतीय परिव्राजक अपना धर्म अन्यान्य देशों में फैलाते थे। पर आजकल खुद भारत-वासियों को अन्य धर्म में ले जाने की चेष्टा हो रही है। अहो कष्टम।[237]
>
> (On the one hand, during the 3rd-4th centuries our philosophical pursuits were being treated with respect in Greece and Rome, and on

the other hand the Buddhists were trying to civilize the Mongols and spreading the message of peace among them. People like Kumārajīva were great because despite the having to suffer great torture they spread the religious and philosophical ideas of India over large parts of the world. They would have never thought of even in their dreams, like the modern priests who are encroaching upon the others' political space through religious preaching. Kaśyapa, Dharmarakṣa, Dharmapāla, Bodhiruci, Bodhidharma, Kumārajīva, Paramārtha, Prajñatara, etc., were the great sons of this very India, who have crossed Himalaya to learn foreign languages and achieved proficiency to that extent which has not been achieved by any Europeans because till date they have not written any philosophical text in Chinese. The Indian priests were spreading their religion in other countries, but nowadays there are efforts to convert the Indians to other religions. What a pity!)

KPJ also appears worried about the deteriorating condition of Sanskrit and proposed a kind of an exchange programme between China, Japan and India,

> Would it not be better that the Indians sponsor some of the Chinese and Japanese students and invite them here to learn Sanskrit? They have forgotten Sanskrit completely. After learning Sanskrit, they will certainly respect our ancient civilisation from the core of their heart. Nowadays, after hearing from the foreigners they have also started considering us as savages. Although, Sanskrit is like dead, however, those who go deep into it, cannot stop themselves from turning towards us.[238]

When Rahul Sankrityayan recovered rare manuscripts from Tibet, KPJ made an appeal,

> It is necessary that both the educated public and specialists should be apprised of the importance of the discovery of manuscripts made by the Tripitakacharya Mahapandita Rahul Sankrityayan. The discovery is epoch-making. For centuries the name of this successful explorer will be cited with gratitude by writers of Indian philosophy and Buddhism.[239]

(D) Writings on Political Developments

KPJ wrote several articles on the political developments, dynasties, individual kings, etc.; most of these articles have already been discussed in the monographs and articles discussed above.

However, reconstructing political chronology, KPJ took literature (*Purāṇas, Mahābhārata* etc.) at its face value and accepted it in totality.[240] Comparing the Purāṇic data with Buddhist and the Jaina sources, KPJ fixed the chronology of the three important dynasties: the Śaiśunākas, the Nandas and the Mauryas and the date of Buddha's *nirvāṇa* at 544 B.C.[241]

KPJ was, perhaps, the first scholar who used folk songs as a source of history and identified 'Vir Varshal' of the Punjabi ballad song as Candragupta Maurya. He argued,

> There is a ballad sung in the Punjab by *Dandhis* who are mendicant-musicians ...and they sing a ballad of a king *'Vir Varshal'* by name, *Vir* [= *Vīra*] in Punjabi means 'hero'. *Vir Varshal* was the king of the territory on the side of the Ravi and the other side was held by another king who was the enemy but whose daughter, he (Vir Varshal) ultimately married. The ballad is mainly a love-story of Vir Varshal and Vir Varshla's war with the king (whose name I have not yet learnt). Vir Varshal's friend was *Chāṇak*. Vir Varshal was a Hindu, while his enemy was a foreigner.[242]

KPJ further argued, "Now here for the first time we get the popular and pre-imperial personal name of Candragupta Maurya as *'Varshal'* which is rendered in the *Mudrārākṣasa* as Vṛishala (lit., 'powerful').[243]

Reconstructing Mauryan history, KPJ utilised Tārānātha's *History of Buddhism*, with some new data and concluded: (i) that Bindusāra continued the process of the unification of India after his great father Candragupta Maurya; (ii) that in this undertaking he, like his father, had the help of the counsel of the Chancellor Kauṭilya (Cāṇakya); (iii) that this Mauryan Bismark, before his death, saw the imperial system much extended: all the land between the 'Western and the Eastern oceans', comprising about 16 capitals, was brought under the imperial control; (iv) that the administration of Bindusāra and Cāṇakya was vigorous, marked with a stern policy in new annexations; (v) that the success was mainly attributed to the policy of the Chancellor whose capacity greatly impressed the popular mind; (vi) that the Chancellor died of some painful disease in the reign of Bindusāra.[244]

The history of the Śuṅgas, perhaps, inspired KPJ the most. Therefore, he wrote several pieces on the Śuṅgas.[245] KPJ surmises: (i) the Śuṅgas were Brahmins, (ii) Puṣyamitra was equal to Cromwell of the English history, and like him Puṣyamitra was a hero and patriot, (iii) Puṣyamitra was not an usurper, and that the last Maurya ruler Bṛhadratha was killed in the sight of the whole army, and therefore, evidently with their approval. The deed has thus popular approval, (iv) The weakness of the sovereign, the critical moment, and the long suffering of the persecuted religion, along with other facts conspired together to bring about the "un-Hindu" deed.[246]

KPJ further highlights and defends several changes under the Śuṅgan regime, such as: the religious persecution of Buddhists, revival of Brahmanism and *aśvamedha* sacrifice, disappearance of centralised administration and revival of the Sanskrit literature, and observes that although the Śuṅga revolution resembles the Maurya revolution—both being products of national crises, the former (the Mauryas) lacked the cement of the system of the latter (the Śuṅgas). One was mainly destructive (the Mauryas), while the other had been pre-eminently constructive (the Śuṅgas).[247]

In a very long article inspired by and in response to Konow edited volume on Kharoṣṭhī inscriptions (excepting those of Aśoka and published as *Corpus Inscription Indicarum* Vol. II, Pt. I), KPJ discussed several problems of Śaka-Sātavāhana history and reflected upon the political developments, linguistic issues and chronological markers in the immediate post-Mauryan scene of northern India and the Deccan. Some of the issues highlighted by him in these remarkably forthright contributions are:[248]

(i) There is no room for two Kuṣāṇa eras—one started by Wema Kadphises and the other soon after him by Kaniṣka,

(ii) There were two Śaka eras —the earlier one (called 'Old Śaka era' by Konow) starting in B.C. and the later one of A.D. 78.

(iii) It was not just the case of continuous eras following deaths of the Buddha and Mahāvīra but that such practice (in addition to regnal reckonings) was not unknown to the *Purāṇas*, even before 58 B.C.

(iv) Immediately after the exit of the Mauryas, there was some kind of a battle for supremacy amongst the four prominent players, viz, Puṣyamitra Śuṅga, Demetrius, Śātakarṇi I and Khāravela. The last named challenged all, and even had his way for some time. However, Puṣyamitra and Śātakarṇi I outlived him. They seem to have asserted their preeminence in their respctive spheres—former in the

> northern India and the latter in the Dakṣiṇāpatha (the Deccan). KPJ particularly emphasises, "both were Brahmins and both ultra-Brahmanical".

KPJ wrote quite a few articles on the Guptas.[249] The name Sifar or Siqar of Arab writer Abū Sālih was identified by him with Śikhara, as the Prime Minister of the Candragupta II. Abū Sālih renders the name of Śikhara's book as *Adabu-l Muluk* or *Instructions to Kings* which is a rendering of *Rājanīti*. Taking a clue from *Kāmandakīya Nītisāra*, KPJ assigns it to the reign of Candragupta II.[250] As far as the origin of the Guptas are concerned, *Mañjuśri-Imperial History of India* regards them Jats from Mathura. On the basis of a Nepalese chronicle, KPJ also opined, "The alleged caste of the Guptas as Aheer, Sanskrit Ābhīra or Goala (cowherd), which in popular estimation are interchangeable terms, brings them near the Jats who are always classed popularly as a variety of Goalas or Aheers. That the Guptas were regarded in Nepal as Goalas or Aheer is a fairly good piece of evidence on their original caste."[251]

KPJ in an article entitled 'Historical Data in the Drama Kaumudī-Mahotsava' (which KPJ ascibes to the Gupta period), builds a case of the low origin of the Guptas. The female author of the drama describes its hero Caṇḍasena (identified by KPJ with Chandragupta) as a Kārāskara, who according to *Baudhāyana Dharmasūtra*, were beyond the pale of Hindu orthodoxy. Additionally, matrimonial links of the Guptas with the Licchavis did not improve their status, for, the latter too were looked down upon by the orthodox people of Magadha as *mlecchas*.[252] While describing the origin of the Guptas, KPJ appears to be a defender of the Varṇa system, "Samudragupta becomes a Hindu of Hindus... Candragupta the Kārāskara was the earliest Shivāji of India, or the second early Shivāji, the first being Candragupta Maurya. The powerful Śūdra protectors of Hindu culture rivalled the race of Rāma and Parikshit in upholding orthodox rites, the cause of Brahmanism, the preservation of the cow, and the support of the sacred Sanskrit."[253]

On the basis of another Gupta period drama, *Devīcandraguptam*, KPJ tried to establish the historicity of Candragupta II's attack on the Śakas and Rāmagupta's immediate successor. *Devīcandraguptam* is cited by king Bhoja in his anthology *Śṛṅgāraprakāśa*. It was noted by Bhoja there that 'Candra-Gupta, concealed in a female disguise, went to the enemy's camp (Alipuram) to kill the Śaka king'. But

Levi declared the statement implied in the *Devīcandraguptam* of Viśākhadatta 'to be far from historical reality' in respect of Rāmagupta being the elder brother of Candragupta and Dhruvadevī being Rāmagupta's wife. The ground for his doing so, evidently, was that the lady is referred to in the official inscriptions of the Gupta dynasty as the wife of Candragupta II and that is also stated there that Candragupta had been selected by his father Samudragupta as his successor; there was, therefore, no room for a Rāmagupta to come in between Samudragupta and Candragupta. KPJ, however, argued that the fact seemed to be otherwise. KPJ analysed a variety of sources - Bāṇa (620 A.D., *Harṣacarita*), Amoghavarṣa (A.D. 873 Sanjan plate), Rājaśekhara (900 A.D., *Kāvyamīmaṁsā*), Bhoja (A.D. 1018-60, *Śṛṅgāraprakāśa*), Arab historian Abū Sālīh (A.D. 1026), *History of Rawwal and Barkamaris*), and Śaṅkara (A.D. 1713), Gupta inscriptions and coins, which he believed constituted a rare combination in the field of historical material. After analysing these independent sources, KPJ concluded that the evidence of the *Devīcandraguptam* must be accepted.[254]

(E) Miscellaneous Articles

KPJ wrote numerous articles defining several terms in inscriptions and Sanskrit literature, identifying places, persons, events, and geographical and topographical boundaries, the use of era, etc. Such identifications are: as *kumārāmātya* of Hindol plate as 'title prince'[255], 'the Yaunus' of the *Purāṇas* as the last Kuṣāṇa emperor in India,[256] King Udayāditya of Malwa as the direct descendant of Bhoja,[257] the 'dharma-mita-tama-viddhaṛ' of *Garga Saṁhitā* as Demetrios,[258] '*Gaṇa*' of the *Mahābhārata* as non-monarchical communities,[259] 'Malayaketu' of *Mudrārākṣasa* as Seleucus,[260] '*Dvirashtas*' of *Vāyu Purāṇa* as Arattās (band of robbers"), who helped Chandragupta Maurya against the Nandas,[261] Bandhu-bhṛitya of *Mudrārākṣasa*as Bandhuvarman, son of Viśvavarman of Mālawā, as a governor of the Gupta emperor in Mandasor,[262] 'Satrapa Vanaspara', as a lieutenant of Kaniṣka,[263] Śaka-Pārthiva of Kātyāyana as the "Scythian Parthian" King,[264] 'Kākas' of Samudragupta's inscription on the Allahabad Pillar as an autonomous community of Kakapur near Bhilsa,[265] *Barha-Takin* as the Takin (Ruler) of *Varha* (Bactria), and Khasa is Khasadhipati, as ruler of Kashgarh (Central Asia)—a description of the Kuṣāṇas,[266] 'Danta', as a Weapon—a short stab-instrument, with a round point, straight or curved,[267] 'Tāmralipti', as a Dravidian town, founded by the Dravidians before the Gangetic delta and Orissa were colonised by the Āryans,[268] Arikina of the Gupta inscriptions, as the name of a district wherein Samudragupta made his *(sva) bhọga-pura*, an imperial resort in Eran and Sanchi as Kakanada,[269] 'Alipura' of Gupta History, as Ali-Madras, a subdivision of Madras and the Vatadhanas of Hindu geography as Vrātyas, like the Licchavis, that is non-orthodox Hindus.[270] KPJ identified the Puranic Kalki as a historic person Yaśodharman of Śākambhari, in the late fifth and the early sixth century A.D. as the Napoleon of India,[271] *Mlechchhita* as the name for political cipher-writing of 'Hindu' state.[272] KPJ also made a comparative analysis of the some of the terms occurring in the inscriptions on the basis of his reading of the *Arthaśāstra*.[273] He tries to find out the origin of *Nārada-Smṛiti* and argued that the procedure law of the *Nārada-Smṛiti* was greatly based on the Dharmasthīya of *Arthaśāstra* of Kauṭilya.[274]

One of the major contesting terrains of ancient Indian history was the use of the era and again KPJ wrote several articles on the issue.[275] For him, Saṁvat is the chief symbol of the civilisation, pride of the country and community. KPJ considered the 'Hindu' calendar to be superior to those of the Muslims and Christians. He says that the former originated as a symbol of victory while the latter was a reminder of tragic incidents. There is definite nationalist *swarajist* anti-colonial politics in the ways people used their calendar and KPJ's solution is quite simple: just keep using the Vikrama Saṁvat to keep it alive and suggested various ways to do so.[276] On the basis of the comparative analysis of Jaina sources, Nasik inscription, Khāravela's inscription and the *Purāṇas*, KPJ fixed the beginning of the Vikrama Era as 58/57 B.C.[277] Taking the Puraṇic chronicle as true, KPJ fixed the beginning of 'Hindu history' at 6788 B.C. and two phases of Kali Age at 1388-388 B.C. and 388-188 B.C. According to him, with the Śuṅga revolution Kali Age expired.[278]

Describing the boundary of Āryāvarta, KPJ compares the description given in the *Dharmaśāstras* and some of the modern scientific research and gave the curious description, "Of all the animals the Kṛiṣṇa-Sarạ (black antelope) has been selected for the description of the 'holy land', the Āryāvarta; and beyond that land the world was declared to be 'foreign'. It is thus evident that the Āryāvarta was believed by the Hindus to be the only home of the black antelope. The Āryāvarta includes the area stretching from the Arabian Sea to the Bay of Bengal and from Himalayas to the Vindhyas."[279]

KPJ tried to locate the source of the Nile River in India. Basing his studies on the Purāṇas and two relatively modern writers—Francis Wilford, an Army officer (1791), and Speke (1862)—KPJ echoes their conclusion that the source was the lake called Victoria Nyanza, the Amara Lake. He also argues that the Nil is a Hindu word.[280] KPJ also discusses 'Hindu' scientists on earthquakes such as Varāhamihira, Vasiṣṭha, Parāśara etc., and discuss the circumstances, symptoms, regions, and effects of the various types of earthquakes.[281]

KPJ took region into consideration while reconstructing history. Recalling the role of Pāṭaliputra in history, KPJ said with considerable sense of pride:

> When once more—we thought—the heirs of Pāṇini and Patañjali, Aśvaghoṣa and Āryabhaṭa would meet here in this Capital and discuss here once more the problems of language and linguistics, literature and science, the traditions of our old city might revive. If not in our own right, certainly in the right of our eternal town—the Rome of Hindu India—to which all roads of arts, philosophy, law, and sciences led for no less than ten centuries—in the right of that Pāṭaliputra,... Pāṇini, the first and still the foremost philologist of the world; your Kauṭilya, the Hindu Aristotle; your Aśoka who chiseled on the page of history the greatest royal truth: '*Real conquest is Duty*'; your Patañjali, the grammarian, who has ruled over the Sanskrit language for the last two thousand years; your Umasvati (62 A.D.) who still leads in Jaina philosophy; and your Āryabhaṭa, the astronomer and mathematician, who at the age of 23 in 498 A.D. formulated the theory of the earth's gravitation and whose science, as he himself recorded, was honoured by the citizens of this town. Most of the best Sanskrit dramas were composed and staged at Pataliputra. In the fourth century, women wrote plays here in Sanskrit with ease and elegance, and the Emperor Samudragupta, the greatest general of his time, struck his coins here with his picture in the pose of a musician, and took care to note, on stone, his literary powers along with his Alexander-like career. Full fifty percent, if you make an appraisement of your national achievement, centres in and round this city. Nalanda, the Oxford of Hindu India, Oriental Library, the Bodleian of India.[282]

During the search for manuscripts in Mithila, KPJ was also able to trace the intellectual and political history of Mithila since early medieval times and he wrote several pieces, which were published in the *JBORS*.[283]

There are a large number of cross references to religious conditions in the overall writings of KPJ. However, he wrote very little on the religious history of ancient India. Discussing the Viṣṇu-pada hill at Gaya and the Vedic legend of Viṣṇu's stepping over the earth, KPJ tried to analyse the history of Viṣṇuism and early Buddhism.[284] He drew attention to a piece of evidence which carries one aspect of the Vaiṣṇava cult to a period not later than 700-600 B.C. This was the worship of Trivikrama Viṣṇu, curiously enough the form of worship was the worship of footprints. The custom of worshipping footprints, it shows, had already been an old institution before the time of the Buddha. It probably originated in this Vedic legend of Viṣṇu's stepping over the earth. His supposed footprints were worshipped by the Aitihāsikas and those who believed like them. KPJ argued that the identification of the Trivikrama was complete before the *Baudhāyana-dharmasūtra*. Further, child Kṛṣṇa (Dāmodara) and the cowherd-Kriṣṇa (Govinda) were also known deities before that text. This disposes of the view held by Indian and European scholars that the Kriṣṇa worship in the child-form is post-Christ. KPJ had accepted date of *Baudhāyana-dharmasūtra* as 'before 400 B.C.'

Tracing the evolution of Sanskrit literature and language (the language of Rāma and Kriṣṇa for KPJ), KPJ identified certain phases. According to him, there were several phases/stages of the revival of the Sanskrit: Śuṅga period, Gupta period and the continued in the sixth and seventh centuries. It revived once more in the eleventh century when every soldier-king of 'Hindu India' could wield the pen of poetry and sword of heroism with equal grace—a chapter of brilliant personalities, not known before, not known after, a chapter unparalled in the history of the world. Yet another revival happened in the fourteenth century and in the Mughal period. In KPJ's times, three states—Travancore, Baroda, and Benares were engaged in this pious act and individuals were vying with government in this pious game. KPJ also enumerates the name of the individual who contributed to the publication of the Sanskrit classics such as Ramakrishna Ravi of Rajahmahendry. The publication of *Śṛṅgāraprakāśa* of the time Bhojadeva (1018-1060)—prepared by Yatirāja Svāmin of Mysore—draws KPJ's special attention.[285]

As far as the history of the medieval period is concerned, KPJ's writings are almost negligible. However, Bundela Rajput chief Chhatrasal, contemporary of Shivaji, attracted KPJ's special attention.[286] He emphasised the following: (i) Both Shivaji and Chhatrasal were ideals of 'Hindu independence' against the mighty Muhammadan power, emperor Aurangzeb. (ii) both ruled independent 'Hindu' states; both were impelled by patriotism and devotion to Hinduism and both succeeded, (iii) it is strange that the name of the one (Shivaji) is on the lips of every school throughout India, while that of the other (Chhatrasal) is hardly known beyond Bundelkhand and that silent society of historians. Shivaji has been rightly raised to the plane of supermen by Ranade, while for the lack of a Hindu Carlyle, Chhatrasal has remained relatively unknowns, (iv) Hinduism stood liberated by the joint spiritual personality of Shivaji and Chhatrasal, though physically they were separated by about 1000 miles. Interpreting Aurangzeb on the one hand and Shivaji and Chhatrasal on the other, KPJ saw a binary opposition between the two representing Hinduism and Islam.

Overall KPJ's historical writings are quite heterogenous, covering fairly large spatial and chronological boundaries. Some of the conclusions and findings of KPJ were questioned by the later generations of historians. Some of them are even not relevant today. However, in the world of historiography, it is a golden rule that histories are written only to be re-written in the course of time. KPJ's writings are no exception to this rule.

NOTES

1. Thapar, Romila, *Past and Prejudice*, National Book Trust, New Delhi, 2012.
2. Sharma, R.S., *Rethinking India's Past*, Oxford University Press, New Delhi, 2009, pp. 4-5.
3. 'Lanka aur Sinhala' published in *Hindi Pradeep*, April-June 1900, Vol. 23, No. 4-6, pp. 26-30, 'Kausambi' in *Nāgari Pracharini Patrika*, Saṁvat 1900, pp. 1-6.
4. *Hindu Polity*, Preface, p. viii.
5. Ibid., p. vii. B.K. Sarkar noted that a lot of historians simply appropriated the footnotes provided by *Hindu Polity*.
6. *Hindu Polity*, Appendix B, pp. 375-78
7. Ibid., p. 3.
8. Ibid., p. 12.

9. Ibid., pp. 19-20.
10. Ibid., pp. 23-29.
11. Ibid., p. 164.
12. Ibid., pp. 169-176.
13. Ibid., pp. 79-89.
14. Ibid., p. 163.
15. Ibid., p. 195.
16. Ibid., pp. 191-92.
17. Ibid., p. 198.
18. B.P. Sinha, 'Kashi Prasad Jayaswal', *KPJCV*, p. 39, for details also see, *Hindu Polity*, pp. 210-22.
19. *Hindu Polity*, pp. 236-37.
20. Ibid., p. 255.
21. Ibid., p. 258.
22. Ibid., p. 279.
23. Ibid., pp. 306-22.
24. Ibid., p. 343.
25. Ibid. p. 355.
26. Ibid., p. 365.
27. Ibid., pp. 366-67.
28. Quoted in Vice-Chancellor Speech at the occasion of the conferment of Ph.D to KPJ, see, file no. XIII E-41/96, Bihar State Archives, also *Hindu Polity*, pp. xxxvii-xxxviii.
29. Basham, A.L., 'Modern Historians of Ancient India' in C. H. Philips ed., *Historians of India, Pakistan and Ceylon*, OUP & SOAS, 1961, p. 283.
30. Sharma, R.S., *Rethinking India's Past*, p. 66
31. A.R. Kidwai Speech on Centenary Celebrations of KPJ in 1981, *Prajñā-Bhārati*, Vol. 3, Part 1, 1983, pp. 12-14.
32. For details see, Altekar, A.S., *State and Government in Ancient India*, Motilal Banarasidas, New Delhi, 1949, Thapar, Romila, *Aśoka and the Decline of the Mauryas*, reprinted, Oxford University Press, New Delhi, 2007, Basham, A.L., *The Wonder that was India*, 3rd edn. Picador, 2004, Sharma, R.S., *Political Ideas and Institutions in Ancient India*, Motilal Banarasidas, Delhi, reprint, 2012, C. H. Philips ed., op. cit.
33. B.P. Sinha, op. cit., pp. 41-42.
34. Jayaswal, K.P., *Manu and Yājñavalkya*, reprinted, Cosmo Publications, New Delhi, 2004, Preface, p. v.
35. Ibid., p. v.
36. Ibid., *p.* xviii.
37. Ibid., p. xix.
38. Ibid., pp. 49-50.
39. Ibid., pp. 60-61.
40. Ibid., 59.

41. Ibid., p. xx.
42. Ibid., pp. xix-xx.
43. Ibid., p. xx.
44. Ibid., pp. 17-18.
45. Ibid., p. 42.
46. Ibid., p. 61.
47. Ibid., p. xx- xxi, For the details of privileges given to the Brahmin by Manu, see, pp. 102-5.
48. Ibid., pp. 52-53.
49. Ibid., p. xxi.
50. Ibid., pp. 91-92.
51. Ibid., pp. 61-62.
52. Ibid., p. 62.
53. Ibid., pp. 144-45.
54. Ibid., pp. xxii-xxiii.
55. Ibid., p. xxiii.
56. Ibid., p. xxiv.
57. Ibid., p. 30.
58. Ibid., p. 60.
59. Ibid., p. 60.
60. Ibid., pp. 66-67.
61. Ibid., pp. 96-98.
62. Ibid., p. 107.
63. Ibid., p. 108.
64. Ibid., p. 109.
65. Ibid., pp. 114-15.
66. Ibid., p. 210.
67. Ibid., p. 233.
68. Ibid., pp. 113-14.
69. Ibid., p. 121.
70. Ibid., p. 128.
71. Ibid., p. 175.
72. Quoted in Vice-Chancellor's Speech on the occasion of the conferment of Ph.D to KPJ, see, file no. XIII E-41/96, Bihar State Archives, also *Hindu Polity*, p. xxxix.
73. Ibid.
74. See, Gharpure, J. R, *Yājñavalkya-Smīiti*, Bombay, 1937, p. 199, Virdi, P.K., *The Grounds for Divorce in Hindu and English Law: A Study in Comparative Law*, Motilal Banarasidas, New Delhi, 1972, p. 28, Jha, Sureshwar, *Yājñavalkya*, Sahitya Academy, New Delhi, 1998, p. 41, Richard, W. Lariviere, *The Nāradasmṛiti*, Motilal Banarasidas, New Delhi, 2003, p. 2.
75. Mayne's *Hindu Law & Usages*, Revised by Justice Alladi Kuppuswami, Bharat Law House, New Delhi, 1991.

76. K.P. Jayaswal, *History of India*, Motilal Banarasidas, Lahore, 1933, p. 4.
77. Ibid., pp. 6-7.
78. Ibid., p. 210.
79. Ibid., pp. 210-11.
80. Ibid., p. 47.
81. Ibid., p. 48.
82. Ibid., pp. 49-50.
83. Ibid., pp. 51-52.
84. Ibid., p. 61.
85. Ibid., pp. 154-55.
86. Ibid., pp. 156-57.
87. Ibid., p. 158.
88. Ibid., pp. 158-59.
89. Ibid., pp. 202-3.
90. Quoted in Vice-Chancellor's Speech, *op. cit*.
91. See, K.M. Shrimali, 'Religion in Complex Societies' in Irfan Habib (ed.), *Religion in Indian History*, Tulika Books, New delhi, 2007, pp. 36-70.
92. Sinha, B.P., op. cit, pp. 41-42.
93. For detailed discussion about the Nationalist Historiography, see Chakrabarti, D.K., *Colonial Indology: Socio politics of the Ancient Indian Past*, Munshiram Manoharlal, New Delhi, 1997, pp. 207-42.
94. Nagar, Sharad, *Amritlal Nagar Rachanawali*, Vol. 1, Rajpal & Sons, New Delhi, 1992, pp. 49-50. (Andha Karungi in Bharat is a Hindi translation of KPJ's *History of India)*
95. Nagar, Sharad, *Amritlal Nagar Rachanawali*, Vol. 10, Rajpal & Sons, New Delhi, 1992, p. 209.
96. *Prajñā-Bhārati*, Vol. 3, Part I, 1983, pp. 14-15.
97. K.P. Jayaswal, *An Imperial History of India (700 B.C. - C. 770 A.D.)*, Lahore, 1934, reprinted, Eastern Book Houre, Patna, 1988, p. 1 (The main arguments of the book were published in the *Modern Review* with same title, Vol. LIV, August 1933, pp. 136-41).
98. K.P. Jayaswal, 'An Imperial History of India (600 B.C. - C. 770 A.D.)', *MR*, Vol. LIV, p. 137.
99. Ibid., p. 137.
100. Ibid., pp. 137-38.
101. Ibid., pp. 140-41.
102. *An Imperial History of India (700 B.C. - C. 770 A.D.)*, pp. 2-3.
103. Ibid., p. 3.
104. Ibid., p. 4.
105. Ibid., p. 4.
106. 'An Imperial History of India (600 B.C. - C. 770 A.D.)', *MR*, Vol. LIV, p. 141.

107. *An Imperial History of India (600 B.C. - C. 770 A.D.)*, p. 26.
108. *Rahula Vangmaya*, Vol. II, Part I.
109. Jayaswal, K.P., *Chronology and History of Nepal (600 B.C. - 880 A.D.)*, Patna, 1937, reprinted, Bharati Prakashan, Varanasi, 1976, pp. 16-17.
110. Ibid., pp. 24-25.
111. Ibid., pp. 29-55.
112. Ibid., pp. 56-58.
113. Ibid., p. 58.
114. Ibid., pp. 86-88.
115. Ibid., p. 92.
116. Ibid., 104-05.
117. Ibid., 105.
118. Ibid., 107-08.
119. Ibid., pp. 110-12.
120. *JBORS*, Vol. X (IV), December 1924, Appendix, reprint, XXII (IV), December 1936, pp. 1-77.
121. *JBORS*, (XI (I) March 1925, Appendix, pp. 1-24, XI (II), June 1925, Appendix, pp. 25-54, XI (III-IV), September-December 1925, Appendix, pp. 55-92, XII (I), March 1926, Appendix, pp. 93-130, XII (II), June 1926, Appendix, pp. 131-68, XII (III), September 1926, Appendix, pp. 169-214.
122. *BORS*, Patna, 1927.
123. *BORS*, Patna, 1933.
124. *JBORS*, Vol. XXIII (IV), December 1937, Appendix, pp. 1-14.
125. *JBORS*, Vol. XXIII (IV), December 1937, Appendix, pp. 1-29.
126. *JBORS*, Vol. X, part III, September 1924, pp. 227-316.
127. *Rājanīti Ratnākara*, p. 9.
128. Ibid., p. 10.
129. Ibid., pp. 24-25.
130. Ibid., pp. 26-28.
131. Ibid., p. 28.
132. Ibid, p. 29.
133. Quoted in Gautam, P.K., *One Hundred Years of Kauṭilya's Arthaśāstra*, Indian Institute of Defence Studies and Analyses, New Delhi, 2013, pp. 44-46.
134. For detailed discussion on cataloguing, see Dominik Wujastyk, *Indian Manuscripts*, University of Vienna, 2011.
135. *Descriptive Catalogue of Manuscripts in Mithila, Preface*, Vol. I, p. v.
136. Ibid., p. xiv.
137. Appendix, *JBORS*, Vol. XXIII, published after KPJ's death.
138. Ibid., pp. iv-v.
139. Appendix, *JBORS*, Vol. XXIII, also published after KPJ's death.
140. Ibid., pp. ii-iii.

141. Ibid., p. v.
142. Ibid., pp. vii-viii.
143. *Lassen's History of Indian Commerce, JBORS*, Vol. X, part III, September 1924, p. 1, reprinted by BROS, Patna, 1976.
144. Basham, A.L., op. cit., p. 262.
145. ***JBORS***: 1. 'Hathi-Gumpha Inscription of the Emperor Khāravela' (173 B.C.-160 B.C.), III (IV), December, 1917, pp. 425-72, 2. 'Further Note on Hathi-Gumpha Inscription', III (IV), December, 1917, pp. 473- 507, 3. 'The Terms 'Anusamyana', 'Rājuka' and Former Kings in Aśoka's Inscription', IV (I), March, 1918, pp. 36- 43, 4. 'A Note on Hathi-Gumpha Inscription (Elephant Ships)', IV (I), March, 1918, pp. 96-98, 5. 'Aśoka's Inscription' II, IV (II), June, 1918, pp.144-47, 6. 'Importance of the Janibigha Inscription of the year 83 of the Lakshmaṇa-Sena Era', IV (III), September, 1918, pp. 266-72, 7. 'Hathigumpha Inscription Revised from the Rock (with plates)', IV (IV), December 1918, pp. 364-404, 8. 'Copper-Plates in Bhubneshwar Temple', V (II), June 1919, pp. 298-99, 9. 'An Inscription of the Śunga Dyansty (with plate)', X (III), September 1924, pp. 202-208, 10. 'Hathigumpha Inscription of the Emperor Kharavela (Correction)', XIII (III-IV), Sptember-December 1927, pp. 221-46, 11. 'The Sunga Inscription of Ayodhya', XIII (III-IV), September-December 1927, pp. 247-49, 12. 'Hathigumpha Notes', XIV (I), March 1928, pp. 150-51, 13. 'An Important Brāhmi Inscription, Barli Stone (with plate)', XVI (I), March 1930, pp. 67-68, 14. 'Girdharpur Pillar Inscription', XVIII (I), March 1932, pp. 4-7, 16. 'Khandāhā Inscription of King Narasiṃhadeva of Mithila (Oinwar Dynasty dated S. 1357)', XX (I), March 1934, pp. 15-19, 17. 'Rājgir (Maniar Math) Stone Image Inscription (with plate)', XXII (II), June 1936, pp. 79-80, 18. 'An unrecorded Muhammadan Invasion of Nepal (with Appendix)', XXII (II), June 1936, pp. 81-95.

    IA: 19. 'The Rock Edicts VI of Aśoka', XLII, November 1913, pp. 282-84, 20. 'Notes on Aúoka Inscriptions: The term Ashasu in Rock Edict XIII', XLVII, December 1918, p. 297, 21. 'The Jogimara Cave Inscription' XLVIII, July 1919, p. 131, 22. 'Evidence of an Aśokan Pillar at Bhuvanesvar in Orissa', LVIII, November 1929, pp. 218-19, 23. 'The Vikramkhol Inscription', LXII, March 1933, pp. 58-60, 24. 'Places and Peoples in Aśoka's Inscriptions', LXII, July 1933, pp. 121-33, 25. 'Proclamation of Aśoka as a Buddhist and His Jambudvipa', LXII, September 1933, p. 167.

    MR: 26. 'Proclamation of Aśoka: With a Revised Translation', Vol. XVII, January 1915, pp. 75-85, 27. 'An Inscription of Śunga Dynasty', Vol. XXXVI, October 1924, pp. 430-432, 28. 'Mahasthan (Bogra) Mauryan Inscription', Vol. LIII, May 1933, pp. 508-09. ***EI***: 29. 'The Ghosundi Stone Inscription', Vol. XVI, 1921-1922, pp. 25-27, 30. 'The

Hathigumpha Inscription of Khāravela', Vol. XX, 1929-1930, pp. 71-89, 31. 'The text of the Sohagaura Plate', Vol. XXII, 1933-1934, pp. 1-3, 32. 'Shell Character Rock Inscription at Ci-Aruton (Java)', Vol. XXII, 1933-1934, pp. 4-5.
Nagari Pracharini Patrika: 33. 'Kalinga Chakravarti Maharaj Kharvela ke Shilalekh ka Vivaran, Vol. 8, pp. 301-22, 34. 'Shri Kharavela Prashasti aur Jain Dharma ki Prachinata, Vol. 10, Saṁvat 1986, pp. 499-502.

146. In support of his theory of the *Paura-Janapada*, KPJ provided a seal from Nalanda, see, 'A Seal of a Janapada', *IA*, LVIII, July 1929, pp. 139-40. However, his theory of the *paura-janapada* was vehemently criticised by A.S. Altekar, see, *State and Government in Ancient India*, pp. 101-09.
147. 1. 'The Rock Edicts VI of Aśoka', *IA*, XLII, November, 1913, pp. 282-84, 2. 'Proclamation of Aśoka: With a Revised Translation', *MR*, Vol. XVII, January, 1915, pp. 75-85, 3. 'The Terms 'Anusamyana', 'Rājuka' and Former Kings in Aśoka's Inscription', *JBORS*, IV (I), March 1918, pp. 36-43, 4. 'Notes on Aśoka's Inscription II', *JBORS*, IV (II), June 1918, pp. 144-47, 5.'Notes on Aśoka Inscriptions: The term Ashasu in Rock Edict XIII', *IA*, XLVII, December, 1918, p. 297, 6. 'Evidence of an Aśokan Pillar at Bhuvanesvar in Orissa', *IA*, LVIII, November, 1929, pp. 218-19, 7. 'Mahasthan (Bogra) Mauryan Inscription', *MR*, Vol. LIII, May 1933, pp. 508-09, 8.'Places and Peoples in Aśoka's Inscriptions', *IA*, LXII, July 1933, pp. 121-33, 9. 'Proclamation of Aśoka as a Buddhist and his Jambudvipa', *IA*, LXII, September 1933, p. 167, 10. 'The Text of the Sohagaura Plate', *EI*, Vol. XXII, 1933-1934, pp. 1-3.
148. 'The Rock Edicts VI of Aśoka', *IA*, XLII, November 1913, pp. 282-84.
149. 'Proclamation of Aśoka: With a Revised Translation', *MR*, Vol. XVII, January 1915, pp. 75-85.
150. 'Notes on Aśoka's Inscription II', *JBORS*, IV (II) June 1918, pp. 144-47.
151. 'Notes on Aśoka Inscriptions: The term Ashasu in Rock Edict XIII', *IA*, XLVII, December 1918, p. 297.
152. 'Places and Peoples in Aśoka's Inscriptions', *IA*, LXII, July 1933, pp. 121-33.
153. 'Proclamation of Aśoka: With a Revised Translation' MR, Vol. XVII, January 1915, p. 76.
154. Ibid., p. 81.
155. Ibid., p. 76.
156. Ibid., p.76
157. Ibid., pp. 76-77.
158. Ibid., p. 77.
159. 1. 'An Inscription of the Śuṅga Dynasty (with plate)', *JBORS*, X (III),

September 1924, pp. 202-08, 2. 'An Inscription of Śuṅga Dynasty', *MR*, Vol. XXXVI, October 1924, pp. 430-32, 3. 'The Śuṅga Inscription of Ayodhya', *JBORS*, XIII (III-IV), September-December 1927, pp. 247-49, 4. 'The Ghosundi Stone Inscription', *EI*, Vol. XVI, 1921-1922, pp. 25-27, 5. 'The Vikramkhol Inscription', *IA*, LXII, March 1933 pp. 58-60, 6. 'The Jogimara Cave Inscription', *IA*, XLVIII, July 1919, p. 131, 7. 'An Important Brāhmi Inscription', Barli Stone (with plate)', *JBORS*, XVI (I) March 1930, 67-68, 8. 'Rājgir (Maniar Math) Stone Image Inscription (with plate)', *JBORS*, XXII (II), June 1936, pp. 79-80, 9. 'Girdharpur Pillar Inscription', *JBORS*, XVIII (I), March 1932, pp. 4-7, 10. 'Importance of the Janibigha Inscription of the Year 83 of the Lakshmaṇa-Sena Era', *JBORS*, IV (III), September 1918, pp. 266- 272, 11. 'Kandahā Inscription of King Narasiṃhadeva of Mithila' (Oinwar Dynasty dated S. 1357)', *JBORS*, XX (I) March 1934, pp. 15-19, 12. 'Shell Character Rock Inscription at Ci-Aruton (Java)', Vol. XXII, 1933-1934, pp. 4-5, 13. 'An Unrecorded Muhammadan Invasion of Nepal (with Appendix)', *JBORS*, XXII (II), June 1936, pp. 81-95, 14.'The Harappa Seals', *IA*, XLII, July 1913, p. 203, 15. 'Brāhmi Seals Newly Discovered at Patna', *JBORS*, X (III), September 1924, pp. 189-93, 16. 'A Seal of a Janapada', *IA*, LVIII, July 1929, pp. 139-40, 17. 'Some unpublished Seals', *JBORS*, XX (I), March 1934, pp. 1-6, 18. 'Branding Seals of the Second Century A.D. (with plates)', *JBORS*, XXIII (I), March 1937, pp. 128-29.

160. 'The Vikramkhol Inscription', *IA*, LXII, March 1933, pp. 58-60.
161. 'The Jogimara Cave Inscription', *IA*, XLVIII, July 1919, p. 131.
162. 'An Important Brāhmi Inscription', Barli Stone (with plate)', *JBORS*, XVI (I), March 1930, pp. 67-68.
163. 'Rājgir (Maniar Math) Stone Image Inscription' (with plate), *JBORS*, XXII (II), June 1936, pp. 79-80.
164. 'An Inscription of the Sunga Dynasty' (with plate), *JBORS*, X (III) 202-208, September 1924, 'An Inscription of Śuṅga Dynasty', *MR*, Vol. XXXVI, pp. 430-432, October 1924, 'The Sunga Inscription of Ayodhya', *JBORS*, XIII (III-IV) 247-249, September-December 1927.
165. 'Girdharpur Pillar Inscription', *JBORS*, XVIII (I), March 1932, p. 5.
166. 'A Seal of a Janapada', *IA*, LVIII, July 1929, pp. 139-140.
167. 'Importance of the Janibigha Inscription of the year 83 of the Lakshmaṇa-Sena Era', *JBORS*, IV (III), September 1918, pp. 266-272.
168. 'Kandahā Inscription of King Narasiṃhadeva of Mithilā (Oinwār Dynasty) dated S. 1357 (1435 A.D.)', *JBORS*, XX (I), March, 1934, pp. 15-19.
169. 'Importance of the Janibigha Inscription of the year 83 of the Lakshmaṇa-Sena Era', *JBORS*, IV (III), September, 1918, pp. 266-72.
170. Ibid., p. 271.
171. 'The Ghosundi Stone Inscription', *EI*, Vol. XVI, 1921-1922, pp. 25-

27.

172. Ibid., pp. 26-27.

173. 'Importance of the Janibigha Inscription of the year 83 of the Lakshmaṇa-Sena Era', *JBORS*, IV (III), pp. 271-72.

174. 1.'The Vikramkhol Inscription', *IA*, LXII, March 1933, pp. 58-60, 2. 'Shell Character Rock Inscription at Ci-Aruton (Java)', *EI*, Vol. XXII, 1933-34, pp. 4-6, 3. 'The Harappa Seals', *IA*, XLII, July 1913, p. 203, 4.'Brāhmi Seals Newly Discovered at Patna', *JBORS*, X (III), September 1924, pp. 189-93.

175. 1. 'The Vikramkhol Inscription', *IA*, LXII, March 1933, pp. 58-60, 2. 'Shell Character Rock Inscription at Ci-Aruton (Java)', Vol. XXII, 1933-1934, pp. 4-5.

176. Ibid.

177. 'Shell Character Rock Inscription at Ci-Aruton (Java)', Vol. XXII, 1933-1934, pp. 4-6.

178. 'An Unrecorded Muhammadan Invasion of Nepal (with Appendix)', *JBORS*, XXII (II), June 1936, pp. 81-95.

179. D.R. Regmi, 'K.P. Jayaswal: Reminiscences', *Prajñā-Bhārati*, Vol. 3, Part 1, 1983, pp. 49-53, Rahul Sankrityayan, 'Dr. Kashi Prasad Jayaswal', *KPJCV*, 1983, p. 55.

180. *Proceedings and Transactions of the Sixth All India Oriental Conference*, Patna, December, 1930, pp. xxiii-xxxiii.

181. Presidential Speech, 26th Session, Udaipur, 13 Nov. 1936, see, Gupta, P.L., *Sixty Years of the Numismatic Society of India*, p. 148.

182. *JRAS*, pp. 788-796, No. 4, Oct. 1935.

183. Presidential Speech, 25th Session, 30th Dec. 1935, Mysore, and 26th Session, Udaipur, 13 Nov. 1936. For the text of these addresses, see, *Sixty Years of the Numismatic Society of India*, pp. 128-148.

184. Vice-Chancellor's Speech, op. cit.

185. 1. 'Pathani Sikkon par Nāgari', *Saraswati*, No. 11, Part 5, November 1904, pp. 380-85, 2. 'Purana Coin and the Date of the Mānava-Dharma-Śastra', *JBORS*, XVII (IV), December 1931, p. 398, 3. 'A Passage in Samundra Gupta's Inscription at Allahabad and Gupta Coinage', *JBORS*, XVIII (II) June 1932, pp. 207-11, 4. 'Six Unique Silver coins of the Śuṅgas, *JBORS*, XX (I), March 1934, pp. 7-9, 5. 'A Coin of Dasarath Maurya', *MR*, Vol. LV, May 1934, p. 516, 6. 'Coins of Samprati Maurya', *MR*, Vol. LV, May 1934, p. 647, 7. 'Early Signed Coins of India', *JBORS*, XX (III-IV), September-December 1934, pp. 279-308, 8. 'The Punch-Marked Coins: A Survival of the Indus Civilization', *JRAS*, (14th June 1935), 9. 'Early Signed Coins of India (Additions and Corrections)', *JBORS*, XXI (III), September 1935, pp. 191-93, 10. 'On Some Hindu Coins of Pre-Christian Centuries (With plates)', *JBORS*, XXII (II) June 1936, pp. 59-69, 11. 'New Coins of Nāga-Vākāṭaka Period', *JBORS*, XXII (II), June 1936, pp. 70-78, 12.

'Mauryan Symbol', *JRAS*, 1936, 13. 'Numismatic Notes on Some Hindu Coins of Pre-Christian Centuries', *JBORS*, XXIII (I), March 1937, pp. 148-49.

186. 'Pathaṇi Sikkon Par Nāgari' written in association with Mahavir Prasad Dwivedi. The article has already been discussed in the chapter No. 2 on Hindi.
187. Presidential Speech, 26th Session of Numismatic Society of India, Udaipur, 13 Nov. 1936, see, Gupta, P.L. op. cit., p. 146.
188. *JRAS*, No. 4, Oct. 1935, p. 788.
189. Ibid., p. 791.
190. Ibid.
191. Ibid.
192. For Presidential Addresses see, Gupta, P.L., *Sixty Years of the Numismatic Society of India* (1910-71), Banaras, 1973, pp. 128-142.
193. Ibid., pp. 143-148.
194. Ibid., pp. 143-44.
195. Ibid., pp. 144-45.
196. 'New Coins of Nāga-Vākāṭaka Period', *JBORS*, XXII (II), June, 1936, p. 72.
197. Ibid., p. 75.
198. 'A Passage in Samundra Gupta's Inscription at Allahabad and Gupta Coinage', *JBORS*, XVIII (II), June, 1932, pp. 207-08.
199. Gupta, P. L., op. cit., p. 148.
200. ***JBORS***: 1. 'Statues of Two Śaiśunāka Emperors' (483-409 B.C.), V (I), March 1919, pp. 88-106, 2. 'Chastana's Statue and the Date of Kanishka', V (IV), December 1919, p. 511, 3. "Śaiśunāka Statue", V (IV), December 1919, pp. 512-49, 4. 'Another Śaiśunāka Statue', (515 B.C.), V (IV), December 1919, pp. 550-51, 5. 'The Statue of Wema Kadphises and Kushan Chronology', VI (I), March 1920, pp. 12-22, 6. 'The Statue of Ajātaśatru-Kuṇika and a Discussion on the Origin of Brāhmi', VI (II), June 1920, pp. 173-204, 7. 'A Hindu Text on Painting', IX (I), March 1923, pp. 30- 39, 8. 'Jaina Image of Maurya Period', XXIII (I), March 1937, pp. 130-32.

   MR: 9. 'An Ancient Statue at Muttra', Vol. XXX, November 1921, pp. 611-14, 10. 'Hindu Culture in Mesopotamia', Vol. XXX, December 1921, pp. 682-84, 11. 'A Hindu Text on Painting', Vol. XXXIII, June 1923 pp. 732-35, 12. 'A Sand stone Head of the Gupta Period', Vol. XLVII, January 1930, pp. 26-27, 13. 'The Udaypur Temple of Malwa and its Builder', Vol. LI, June 1932, pp. 603-06, 14. 'A note on a Terracotta Ramayana Panel of Gupta Period and on Śikhara Temples', Vol. LII, August 1932, pp. 148-50, 15. 'Buddha's Hermitage', Vol. LIII, February 1933, pp. 179-81, 16. 'Neglect of Monuments', Vol. LIII, April 1933, pp. 385-91, 17. 'Mauryan Rocks cut Hermitage at Barabar', Vol. LIII, May 1933, p. 705, 18. 'Śiva Busts at Nachana' (Ajaigarh State, C. I) Circa 320-50 AD, Vol. LIV, July 1933, p. 68, 19. 'Great Resolution', Vol. LXI, January 1937, p. 16, 20. 'Statues of Indian Scholars in Tibet', Vol. LXI, April 1937, pp. 401-02.

JISOA: 21. 'Nāgara and Vesara', Vol. I, No. 1, June 1933, pp. 57-58, 22. 'Pataliputra Śiva-Pārvatī Gold Plaque', Vol. II, 1934 p. 1, 23. 'Metal Images of Kurkihar Monastery', Vol. II, 1934, pp. 70-82, 24. 'Terracotta Dug Out at Patna', Vol. III, No. 2, December 1935, pp. 125-26, 25. 'An Early Ivory', Vol. IV, No. 2, June 1936, pp. 75-82.

JA: 26. 'Oldest Jaina Images Discovered', Vol. III, 1937, pp. 17-18, (This article was originally published in The Searchlight on 20 February 1937).

Saraswati: 27. 'Bharatvarsh ki Purani Imaraten', No. 3, Pt. 3, April 1900, pp. 96-105.

NPP: 28. 'Kausambi', Pt. 4, 1900, pp. 75-95, 29. 'Buner ke Prachin Sansthano ka Anusandha', Vol. 15, No. 1, Saṁvat, 1991, 150-68.

201. 'Statues of Two Śaiśunaka Emperors', *JBORS*, (483-409 B.C.), V (I), March 1919, pp. 88-106.
202. For the entire proceedings see, "Śaiśunāka Statue", *JBORS*, V (IV), December 1919, pp. 512-49.
203. 'Śaiśunāka Statue', *JBORS*, V (IV), December 1919, pp. 512-13.
204. Ibid., p. 516.
205. Ibid., pp. 516-19.
206. 'Statues of Two Śaiśunāka Emperors', *JBORS*, (483-409 B.C.), V (I), March 1919, pp. 104-05.
207. Gangoly, O.C., 'A Note on Mr. Jayaswal's Discovery of Two Śaiśunāka Statues'(?), *MR*, July-Dec., 1919, pp. 419-24.
208. 'Buddha's Hermitage', *MR*, Vol. LIII, February 1933, pp. 179-81.
209. 'The Statue of Ajātaśatru-Kuṇika and a Discussion on the Origin of Brāhmi', *JBORS*, VI (II), June 1920, pp. 173-204.
210. Ibid., p. 175.
211. Ibid., p. 184.
212. Ibid., p. 185.
213. Ibid., pp. 176-77.
214. Ibid., p. 177.
215. Ibid., pp. 178-179.
216. 'An Ancient Statue at Muttra', *MR*, Vol. XXX, November 1921, pp. 611-14.
217. 'Pataliputra Śiva-Pārvati Gold Plaque', *JISOA*, Vol. II, 1934, p. 1, 'Terracotta Dug Out at Patna', *JISOA*, Vol. III, No. 2, December 1935, pp. 125-26, 'An Early Ivory', *JISOA*, Vol. IV, No. 2, June 1936, p. 75, 'Oldest Jaina Images discovered', *JA*, Vol. III, pp. 17-18, 'Jaina Image of Maurya Period', *JBORS*, XXIII (I), March 1937, pp. 130-32.
218. 'Chastana's Statue and the Date of Kanishka', *JBORS*, V (IV),

December 1919, p. 511, 'The Statue of Wema Kadphises and Kushan Chronology', *JBORS*, VI (I), March 1920, pp. 12-22.

219. Śiva Busts at Nachana (Ajaigarh State, C. I) Circa 320-350 A.D.', *MR*, Vol. LIV, July 1933, p. 68.
220. 'A Sand Stone Head of the Gupta Period', *MR*, Vol. XLVII, January 1930, pp. 26-27.
221. 'A Note on a Terracotta Ramayana Panel of Gupta Period, and on Śikhara Temples', *MR*, Vol. LII, August 1932, pp. 148-50.
222. 'Metal Images of Kurkihar Monastery', *JISOA*, Vol. II, 1934, pp. 70-82.
223. 'Great Resolution', *MR*, Vol. LXI, January 1937, p. 16.
224. 'Statues of Indian Scholars in Tibet', *MR*, Vol. LXI, April 1937, pp. 401-02.
225. 'England ki Jatiya Chitrashala', *Saraswati*, No.12, Part 8, December 1907, pp. 496-99.
226. 'A Hindu Text on Painting', *MR*, Vol. XXXIII, pp. 732-35, June 1923 & 'A Hindu Text on Painting', *JBORS*, IX (I), pp. 30-39, March 1923.
227. 'Nāgar and Vesara', *JISOA*, Vol. I, No. 1, June 1933, pp. 57-58.
228. 'A Note on a Terracotta Ramayana Panel of Gupta Period, and on Śikhara Temples', *MR*, Vol. LII, August 1932, pp. 148-50.
229. Ibid., (KPJ dates this text differently. While in this article it is placed in the fourth century, in another the article on 'Nāgara-Vesara Style' (1933), it is ascribed to 250 AD).
230. 'A Note on a Terracotta Ramayana Panel of Gupta Period, and on Śikhara Temples', *MR*, Vol. LII, August 1932 pp. 148-50.
231. 'The Udaypur Temple of Malwa and its Builder', *MR*, Vol. LI, June 1932, pp. 603-06.
232. 'Neglect of Monuments', *MR*, Vol. LIII, April 1933, p. 385.
233. 'Mauryan Rocks-Cut Hermitage at Barabar', *MR*, Vol. LIII, May 1933, p. 705.
234. 'Neglect of Monuments', *MR*, Vol. LIII, April 1933, p. 386.
235. Ibid., p. 387.
236. Ibid., p. 391.
237. 'Chin Japan Mein Sanskrit Granth', *Saraswati*, October, 1907, reprinted in *Saraswati*, October 1963, pp. 372-76, (This article was written when KPJ was studying in Oxford and provides a long list of Sanskrit Buddhist texts including copies of some manuscripts on wood and birch-bark that were obtained from China and Japan and kept in the Bodleian Library), also see, 'Lost Sanskrit Works Recovered from Tibet', *MR*, Vol. LXI, February 1937, pp. 159-64.
238. 'Chin Japan Mein Sanskrit Granth', *Saraswati*, October 1963, pp. 372-76.
239. 'Lost Sanskrit Works Recovered from Tibet', *MR*, Vol. LXI, February

1937, pp. 159-64.

240. 'The Brihadrath Chronology', *JBORS*, IV (I), March 1918, 26-35.
241. 'Śaiśunāka and Maurya Chronology and the Date of Buddha's Nirvana', *JBORS*, Vol. I (I), September 1915, pp. 67- 116, (The date of the Buddha *Mahaparinirvāṇa* continues to be a hotly debated issue till date).
242. 'Chandra Gupta Maurya as 'Vir Varshal', *JBORS*, Vol. XVIII (I) March 1932, p. 79.
243. Ibid.
244. 'The Empire of Bindusara', *JBORS*, Vol. II (I), , March 1916, pp. 79-83.
245. 'Revised Notes on the Brahmin Empire', *JBORS*, Vol. IV (III), September, 1918, pp. 257-65, 2. 'Revised Notes on the Brahmin Empire', *JBORS*, Vol. XIV (I), March 1928, pp. 24-27, 3. 'Historical Data in the *Garga-Saṁhitā* and the Brahmin Empire', *JBORS*, Vol. XIV (III), September 1928, pp. 397-421, 4. 'On the Rule of Puṣyamitra Śuṅga', *JBORS*, Vol. XV (III-IV), September-December 1929, pp. 583-84.
246. 'Revised Notes on the Brahmin Empire', *JBORS*, Vol. IV (III), September, 1918, pp. 260-61.
247. Ibid., pp. 263-65.
248. 'Problem of Śaka-Satavahana History', *JBORS*, Vol. XVI (III-IV), September-December 1930, pp. 227-316, & Śaka-Satavahana Problem, *JBORS*, Vol. XVIII (I), March 1932, pp. 7-16.
249. 1. 'The Book on Political Science by 'Śikhara', Prime Minister of Chandra Gupta II', *JBORS*, Vol. XVIII (I), March 1932, pp. 37-39, 2. 'Historical Data in the Drama Kaumudī Mahotsava', *Annals of Bhandarkar*, Vol. XII, 1930-1931, pp. 50-56, 3.'Origin of the Imperial Guptas', *MR*, Vol. XLVI, November 1929, pp. 499-501, 4. 'Chandra Gupta II (Vikramāditya) and his Predecessor', *JBORS*, Vol. XVIII (I), March 1932, pp. 17-36, 5. 'Nepal Chronicles on the Caste of the Guptas', *JBORS*, Vol. XXII (II), June 1936, pp. 108-10.
250. 'The Book on Political Science by 'Śikhara', Prime Minister of Chandra Gupta II', *JBORS*, Vol. XVIII (I), March 1932, pp. 37-39.
251. 'Nepal Chronicles on the Caste of the Guptas', *JBORS*, Vol. XXII (II), June 1936, p. 109.
252. 'Historical Data in the Drama Kaumudī Mahotsava', *Annals of Bhandarkar Oriental Research Institute*, Vol. XII, 1930-1931. pp. 50-56.
253. Ibid., p. 56.
254. 'Chandra Gupta II (Vikramāditya) and His Predecessor', *JBORS*, Vol. XVIII (I), March 1932, pp. 17-36 (On the basis of the letter written by Kavi that he had recovered a manuscript of the drama *Devīcandraguptam* (fragmented piece) KPJ gave date of Śaṅkara as 1713 AD, and argued that there is no doubt that the fragmentary

manuscript is of the same book which is cited by different authors and that its author was Viśākhadatta. However, Vasudeva Upadhyaya in his book, *Gupta-Samrajya ka Itihas* (1957), identified the commentator as Śaṅkarācārya of ninth century A.D. (p. 69).

255. 'Kumarāmātya', *JBORS*, Vol. XVII (IV), December 1931, p. 399.
256. 'The Yaunus of Purāṇas and the last Kuṇāṇa Emperor in India', *JBORS*, Vol. XVIII (II), June 1932, pp. 201-06.
257. 'King Udayāditya', *MR*, Vol. LII, August 1932, pp. 171-72.
258. 'Demetrios, Khāravela and the *Garga-Saṁhitā*', *JBORS*, Vol. XIV (I), March 1928, pp. 127-28.
259. 'Republics in the Mahabharata', *JBORS*, Vol. I (II), December 1915, pp. 173- 78.
260. 'The Date of the Mudrā-Rākhasa and the identification of Malayaketu', *IA*, XLII, October 1913, pp. 265-67.
261. 'Kauṭilya and the Arattas', *IA*, Vol. XLIII, June 1914, p. 124.
262. 'Bandhu-bhritya of the Mudrā Rākshasa', *IA*, Vol. XLVI, November 1917, p. 275.
263. 'Identification of some of the Post Andhrabhritya Rulers of the Purāṇic List', *IA*, Vol. XLVII, December 1918, pp. 298-99.
264. 'Kātyāyāna and Parthia', *IA*, Vol. XLVIII, January 1919, p. 12.
265. 'The Kakas – their Location', *JBORS*, Vol. XVIII (II), June 1932, pp. 212-13.
266. 'A Note on 'Tikina' and 'Khasa', *JBORS*, Vol. XVIII (II) June 1932, p. 225.
267. 'Danta', a Weapon', *JBORS*, Vol. XVIII (III-IV), September-December 1932, p. 391.
268. 'Ethnic Origin of Tāmralipti', *IA*, Vol. XLIII, April 1914, p. 64.
269. 'Airkina and Sanchi', *IA*, Vol. LXI, August 1932, pp. 159-60.
270. 'Some Notes on Names in Hindu Geography', *IA*, Vol. LXII, June 1933, p. 119.
271. The Historical Position of Kalki and his Identification with Yaśodharman, *IA*, Vol. XLVI, July 1917, pp. 145-53.
272. 'Political Cipher-Writing in Hindu India', *MR*, Vol. XXII, , December 1917, pp. 662-63.
273. 'The Arthaśāstra Explains', *IA*, Vol. XLVII, February 1918, pp. 50-56.
274. 'On the Origin of the Narada-Smṛitī', *IA*, Vol. XLII, December 1913, p. 306.
275. 1. 'Hamara Samvat aur Uski Raksha,' *Saraswati*, No. 3, Part 9, March 1908, pp. 135-37, 2. 'Chronological Summary in the Purāṇic Chronicles and the Kali-Yuga Era', *JBORS*, Vol. III (II), June 1917, pp. 246-62, 3. 'The Week-days and Vikrama', *IA*, Vol. XLVII, April 1918, p. 112, 4.'The Vikrama Era', *MR*, Vol. XV, January 1914, pp. 98-99.

276. 'Hamara Samvat aur Uski Raksha,' *Saraswati*, No. 3, Part 9, 1908, pp. 135-37, (see also a discussion of relevant issue in chapter No. 3).
277. 'The Vikrama Era', *MR*, Vol. XV, January 1914, pp. 98-99.
278. 'Chronological Summary in the Purāṇic Chronicles and the Kali-Yuga Era', *JBORS*, Vol. III (II), June 1917, pp. 246-62.
279. 'A Note on the Black Antelope and the Āryāvarta', *MR*, Vol. XIII, March 1913, pp. 329-30, (also see discussion on this issue in chapter 3 on the *Pataliputra*. Interestingly, while discussing the spread of Hindi language, KPJ restrict the Āryāvarta concept to the Hindi speaking area only).
280. 'The Discovery of the Source of the Nile by Ancient Hindus', *MR*, Vol. XVII, April 1915, pp. 517-19.
281. 'Hindu Scientist of Earthquake', *MR*, Vol. LV, March 1934, pp. 310-11.
282. *Proceedings and Transactions of the Sixth All India Oriental Conference*, Patna, December, 1930, pp. xxiii-xxxiii.
283. *JBORS*: 1. 'A Judgment of a Hindu Court in Sanskrit', VI (II), June 1920, pp. 246-58, 2. 'The Unexplained Passage', VII (II-III), June-September 1921, pp. 123-24, 3. 'Contributions to the History of Mithila (King Nanya Deva of Mithila and an Inscription of His time)', IX (III-IV), September-December 1923, pp. 300-10, 4. 'Contributions to the History of Mithila', X (I-II), March-June 1924, pp. 37-46, 5. 'Hridaya Narayana of Mithila', X (I-II), March-June 1924, pp. 47-48, 6. Date of Vardhamāna, XIV (II), June 1928, p. 311, 7. 'A Deed of Acquittance in Sanskrit', XIV (I), March 1928, pp. 63-64, 8. 'Dating in Lakshmaṇa-Sena Era', XX (I), March 1934, pp. 23-24.
284. 'Vaishnava Worship and Buddhism', *IA*, Vol. XLVII, March 1918, p. 84.
285. 'Sanskrit Revival and King Bhoja's Art Criticism of Lyrical Poetry', *IA*, Vol. XLIII, June 1928, pp. 722-25.
286. 'King Chhatrasal Champion of Hindu Independence, and Queen Kamalavati, the Devoted Wife', *MR*, Vol. LI, May 1932, pp. 545-48.

5

Pedestalling Bihar's Intellectual Identity: KPJ as an Institution Builder

To protect their interests, to legitimise colonial rule and to establish their supremacy, the British created a number of modern institutions in India such as research societies, museums, universities, law courts, printing presses, etc. They also set up such pioneering branches of study as Indology or Orientology. This study arose principally because the East India Company required that its officers, in order to administer properly the territory, which it had acquired, become familiar with the laws, habits, languages, and history of the people they were governing. That was the context in which the colonial administrators had created a number of modern institutions dedicated to the study of India's past.[1]

In 1912, a new province—the province of Bihar and Orissa—was created from out of the Bengal province. As a consequence, a number of important institutions were created in this newly created province, namely, the Patna High Court, the BORS, the Patna Museum, and the Patna University, etc. KPJ, once described as the 'cleverest Indian' of his time and the most 'dangerous revolutionist' by the colonial administrators, was closely associated with these institutions from their very founding stages. His association with all these institutions was both diverse and intense.

KPJ's organisational skills were evident at a very early stage in his life, when, soon after his early education at the Queen's College, his public spirit found three different outlets. In the first place, he organised a Chapra Sabha (Shellac Association) for the protection of economic interests of shellac traders of different strata. Secondly, he organised a Kalwar Sabha or an association of his caste people for the purpose of social reform. Besides, he began writing articles in Hindi journals such as Pt. Mahavir Prasad

Dwivedi's *Saraswati* and Bal Krishna Bhatt's *Hindi Pradeep*. This last activity at once brought him to the notice of the nationally inclined intelligentsia of Northern India, and between 1898 and 1912 his articles kept appearing in these journals even while he was away in England for higher studies.[2]

When KPJ came back to Patna, via Calcutta, in 1914, Sir Edward Gait was the administrative head of the newly formed province. He was himself a scholar interested in India's past. KPJ found a ready friend in him for his historical studies and with his help and with the support of the leaders in the Province, he was able to organise a number of activities. They equally shared the credit of founding in 1915, the BORS, its journal *JBORS*, and the Patna Museum. But KPJ in particular had a paternal affection for these institutions and he devoted a good deal of time in directing their various activities, which is evident from a letter dated, 14 April 1937 in which Sir Edward Gait wrote from London, "I may have a hand in forming the Bihar and Orissa Research Society, but it was you who had been the mainstay from beginning up to the present time." KPJ was the editor of the Society's journal from its inception in 1915 to the last days of his life and he made it one of the leading research journals of the world. As G.P. Ambastha also concurred, "With Mr. Jayaswal's arrival in Patna and with the foundation of the BORS started the second period of his research contributions."[3]

Bihar and Orissa Research Society

The inaugural meeting of BORS (hereafter called "the Society"), held on the 20 January 1915 and chaired by Charles S. Bayley, Lieutenant-Governor of Bihar and Orissa, was attended by thirty intellectuals, bureaucrats, lawyers and other distinguished individuals including KPJ. After a brief and sympathetic inaugural speech of the Lieutenant Governor, Sir Edward Gait explained why it was considered desirable to establish a research society in the new province:

> I need not dilate at length on the necessity for a society to promote research in the Province. We all know that the Aryans were already settled here in very ancient times, and even when the Vedas were compiled, parts of Bihar had already been occupied by the Indo-Aryans. Several centuries before the Christian era, Patna was the capital of an extensive empire. But in spite of its antiquity the Province boasts of few regular historical records, and our knowledge of the

past has to be laboriously pieced together from various source of information, such as references in religious books, inscriptions on rocks, stones, and coins, and the excavation of ancient sites. A great deal has already been done by individuals, but the field is too great to be covered by any individual, however, learned and energetic he may be. In order that the best results may be obtained, it is necessary to undertake organized research under the auspices of a Society, which will not only ensure steady and sustained effort but will also arouse the interest and stimulate the energies of anyone who may be able to contribute to our knowledge and which will, in its journal, provide a means of recording all the information that may be collected. In the absence of a Society it often happens that interesting facts come to light, but pass unrecorded and are again forgotten.

There is no danger of such a fate overtaking the great work now being done by Dr. Spooner, but it is constantly the case with discoveries on a smaller scale if they are not duly recorded. As a case in point I may mention that, last year, an accident brought into my hands an old copper axe-head that had been dug up by a cultivator in the Palamau district. I sent it to Dr. Coggin-Brown of the Indian Museum, who reported that it was a very perfect specimen of the copper age, which intervened between the ages of stone and iron, and the first discovered in this Province. In the absence of a printed record, this find would soon be forgotten; while it is only reasonable to suppose that if systematic search were made, other similar implements might be discovered. Again I learnt only the other day from my friend, Babu Sarat Chandra Ray from Ranchi that cinerary urns containing copper ornaments are from time to time dug up in the Munda country. Hitherto their friends have disposed of the article found in these urns to local copper-smiths, and much valuable information has thus been lost. In Assam much light has been thrown on a period, otherwise unknown, by discovery of the copperplate land grants, in which interesting details were given regarding the dynasty of the kings making grants and the areas under their rule. Most of these copperplates were found in the course of a special search which was instituted about twenty years ago. There is reason why similar copperplates should not be forthcoming in this Province. A search for Sanskrit manuscripts might have also valuable results. It is believed that the pandits of Tirhut and Orissa have many ancient manuscripts in their possession which might add greatly to our knowledge of the past history of the province.

There is also ample field for research in the domain of anthropology. A great deal of interesting information has already been placed on

> record in various books such as Risley's Tribes and Castes of Bengal, but in these books the surface only has, as it were, been scratched, and a great mass of information remains to be collected. This is especially the case in Chota Nagpur, where the aboriginal tribes have retained to some extent the primitive beliefs and practices that probably prevailed throughout India before the advent of the Aryan culture. Babu Sarat Chandra Roy, who has written a very valuable account of the Mundas, and has now in the Press an even more valuable account of the Oraons, has more than once urged the necessity of starting an anthropological journal for the province.
>
> It will, I think, be generally admitted that there is ample scope for a Research Society such as the one which we propose to inaugurate. Many such Societies have of late sprung up in other parts of India. Now the Bihar and Orissa has its own Government, and will shortly have its own High Court, and, as we hope, its own University, it should also have its own Research Society.
>
> It was unanimously agreed that the Society should be called "The Bihar and Orissa Research Society."[4]

Four disciplines were identified as the Society's research priority: history, archaeology and numismatics, anthropology and folklore, and philology. It was agreed that the government might properly be approached for assistance in official recognition and financial aid. The council of the new Society was to formulate definite proposals, which would then be submitted for the consideration of government through the proper channel.

The constitution of the Society was as follows: 1. Patron, 2. Five Vice-Patrons, 3. President, 4. A council of 12 members (excluding the President), 5. General Secretary and 6. Treasurer, who would be an *ex-officio* member). It was proposed that the first council should hold office for three years, a fresh council was to be elected annually thereafter at a general meeting of the members of the Society.[5] A suggestion was made that the journal might perhaps be called the *Magadha Review*, but it was decided that this title would not be so appropriate, inasmuch as the scope of the Society would extend beyond the limits of ancient Magadha. It was ultimately agreed that the most appropriate title would be *JBORS*.[6]

In the same meeting, Sachidanand Sinha moved another proposal that a provincial museum and library should be established for which he offered to place at the disposal of the Society his own well-known large collection of books. That is how the idea of the provincial museum and library was given concrete shape.[7] The rules of the Society were also framed, like its object, constitution, election of the members, subscriptions, registration and absence of members, officers, council, re-election, joinder of offices, vacant offices, meetings, general rules regarding meetings, visitors, proxy and the journal.[8]

Contribution of KPJ to the BORS

KPJ was not only the founder-member of the Society, but he also remained closely and intimately associated with the Society till his death on the 4 August 1937, for more than twenty-two years. As his friend and colleague, P.C. Manuk, observed, "For many years I had been a member—interested but ignorant—of the B&O Research Society, of which [KPJ] was a main pillar and stalwart."[9] He served the Society in various capacities. As a contributor, he wrote articles on his historical research, book reviews, obituaries, etc, which are more than a hundred in number, which is the largest number ever by any member of the Society. He was also the editor of the journal for the longest time; no other editor served the Journal for such a long period. Another colleague, Ambastha, wrote, "K.P. Jayaswal was the editor of this Journal from its start in 1915 to the last days of his life and he made it one of the leading research journals of the world."[10] However, the available records say something else. The first issue of the Journal was published in September 1915. Till 1920 it does not mention the name of any editor. In 1921, it mentions the name of the editor as Jadunath Sarkar and sub-editors as Azimuddin Ahmed and S.N. Mazumdar.[11] In 1922, a 'Journal Committee' appears with G.S. Bhate as convener and Jadunath Sarkar as a member.[12] In fact, it is only in 1923, that the name of KPJ appears in the journal committee as an editor and S.N. Mazumdar and A.P. Banerji-Sastri as the members.[13] Since then, he continued as the editor of the journal till his death. In August 1933 he wrote a letter, asking to be relieved of the editorship of the Society's Journal. But the Society rejected his request.[14]

After KPJ's death, the next editor of the journal A.P. Banerji-Sastri wrote the following obituary, "The members of the Bihar and Orissa Research Society will have heard with deep sorrow the news of the death of Dr. Kashi Prasad Jayaswal, one of the Foundation [sic] members of the Society and the Editor of its journal for the greater part of its existence."[15] The fourth part of the journal

(*JBORS, vol. XXIII, December 1937*) was published as a commemoration volume, in which Rajendra Prasad and P.C. Manuk wrote their memoirs about KPJ.

Presenting the annual report for 1937-38, the Honorary Treasurer, S. Bahadur wrote,

> The Society has this year sustained an irreparable loss in the death of Dr. Jayaswal, who has been so intimately connected with the Society since its inception, and has been for 19 years the editor of the Society's Journal. The Society and its Journal stand today high in the learned world's esteem largely, even chiefly, from what Dr. Jayaswal has given to it.[16]

If we accept the year 1923 for KPJ's formal appointment as the Editor of *JBORS*, then he edited 58 volumes of the journal during his life. However, it appears from certain other references that KPJ had been looking after the editorial work of the journal even before his formal appointment. Presenting the annual address in 1920, Sir Edward Gait had remarked, "I regret to say that Mr. Jayaswal has found it necessary to give up the work of editing the Journal, which he has done so well during the last two years."[17] Why was KPJ excusing himself from the editorial work at such an early stage would require further investigation.[18] The fact is that he remained committed to the responsibilities of the Journal for the rest of his life. On 17 March 1937, KPJ attended the last meeting—Annual General Meeting—of the Society, in which The President, His Excellency Sir Maurice Garnier Hallett was in the Chair, and at the end of the meeting KPJ proposed thanks to the Chair.[19]

Acknowledging the tremendous devotion and editorial commitment of KPJ, McPherson, the Vice-President of the Society had commented in 1924,

> The Society also owes a great debt of thanks to Mr. Jayaswal who, as the Editor of the Journal, with the assistance of the Editorial Committee has got through an enormous amount of work since the last meeting. It is no light task to edit nearly 1,000 pages of a learned Journal like ours and Mr. Jayaswal has applied himself to the work with a devotion that merits the highest praise. In this connection also the gratitude of the Society is due to Mr. Mackenzie, Superintendent of the Government Press, who has given the Editor all possible assistance in his work. Last March, when the new executive assumed office, the Journal was four issues in arrears and members were beginning to complain of its non-receipt. In the last twelve months,

> all the arrears of the years 1922 have been cleared off, while for 1923 all four issues have been brought out.[20]

The Editorial Committee led by KPJ prepared a table, outlining a system of transliteration to be followed in articles published in the Society's journal, and this table was published once every year in the pages of the journal since 1924.

Positions held by KPJ in BORS*

KPJ served the Society in various other ways. Till his death, nearly 150 meetings of the Society were held, out of which he attended 131 meetings,[21] several of which he also chaired. Having gone through the entire proceedings of the Society, we have found that attendance of KPJ was the maximum compared to that of any other member of the Society, which shows his dedication towards the organisation and its agenda of historical research.

KPJ was the General Secretary of the Society for two years (1918-1919) and presented the Annual Report of that period in 1920. He had been a member of the council from the inception of the Society till his death, except for two years, when he was the General Secretary. KPJ was the Departmental Secretary for history section from 1915 to 1920 and Secretary for Archaeology and Numismatics in 1921. KPJ also served as a member of the sub-committee of Archaeology from 1915 to 1922. In the capacity of the editor, KPJ remained a member of the Library Committee till his death. Apart from editing the journal of the Society, he was actively involved in the task of supervising the collection, cataloguing and editing and publication of Sanskrit manuscripts from Mithila/Tirhut and palm leaf MSS in Puri district and other parts of Orissa.[22] KPJ was also appointed as Honorary Treasurer for three months in 1928, during the absence from Patna of Mr. D.N. Sen.

K.P.J's Contribution as a Research Scholar

The greatest of his contributions to the Society was as a research scholar. Most of the KPJ's writings, approximately ninety in number, appeared in the *JBORS*, ranging from quarter pages to thick hundred-page long articles. KPJ also edited and reproduced some of the Classics in the journal: *Rājanitī-Ratnākara* of Chaṇḍeśvara, *Lassen's History of Indian Commerce*, co-edited with A.P. Banerji-Sastri, *Vigrahavyāvarttanī* of Ācārya-Nāgārjuna, *Adhyārddhaśataka* of Mātṛcetā, co-edited with Rahul Sankrityayan.

Except one year 1922, he contributed papers every year. No scholar produced such a big number or carried out original research in the Society's journal as KPJ did.[23] He threw new light on various issues and created a stir in the academic circles in India and abroad in the field of ancient Indian history and the journal provided a forum for informed debate. Sir Edward Gait remarked, as early as 1919,

> The Journal has continued to appear with fair regularity. It has maintained the reputation which it had already gained, and I have more than once received gratifying letters from England telling me of the interest which some of the papers published in it have aroused amongst European savants. This is specially the case in regard to several papers by our talented Honorary Secretary, K.P. Jayaswal, who is rapidly making a name for himself as an investigator and epigraphist.[24]

In the annual Presidential Address of the Society in March 1920, Sir Edward Gait again singled out KPJ for praise:

> Our Society has now been in existence for five years and has continued to show vigorous growth and development. When the Society was inaugurated there were many who doubted whether Bihar and Orissa contained sufficient persons interested in the subjects, which it deals to ensure its survival for any considerable time. Those doubts have now, I hope, been dispelled. Each year has been a steady improvement in the variety and value of the papers published in the journal, the reputation which continues to grow both in this country and Europe. This gratifying result is largely due to the researches of Mr. K.P. Jayaswal, who is rapidly acquiring European reputation and whose successful work in deciphering the Kharavela inscription in Hathi-gumpha cave at Udaigiri has aroused the widest interest. The same may be said of his discoveries in connection with what are known as the Patna statues. Controversy still continues regarding his reading of the inscriptions on these statues, but I hope it will not be long before his views on the subject gain general acceptance, in which case, as has been truly said, he will have succeeded in revolutionizing the history of Indian Art... The editing of the great inscription of Kharavela has been described by the late Dr. Vincent Smith as the most notable achievement of our Society. Last October Mr. Jayaswal again visited the Hathigumpha cave, accompanied with Mr. R.D. Banarji, to make a further study of the inscription. Apart from a few minor emendations in the results previously announced, only one fresh discovery was made, but that was a highly important one: it consisted of the reading

> of the name of the Greek king Demetrius, who is said to have retired from Mathura on hearing of Kharavela's deeds of valour in the siege of Gorathagiri and Rajagriha in the eighth of that monarch's reign.[25]

Delivering a lecture on 'Historical Research in Bihar and Orissa' at the annual meeting of the Society in March 1923, Sir Asutosh Mookerji commented on the comprehensive study made by KPJ till that time and he also highlighted his personal effort (personal study on the spot) in deciphering the Hathigumpha inscription in particular."[26]

Other Contributions of KPJ

The Society under the steady leadership of KPJ was not an instrument of research and publications alone. The latter was also instrumental in conferring honorary membership of the Society on eminent persons from diverse backgrounds. It appears that he wanted to create a pool of resource persons by roping them in for the activities of the Society. The Society and its journal could sustain themselves only if there was a healthy flow of funds and goodwill from the elite quarters of the society.

In 1918 twelve members were elected, out which six names were proposed by KPJ, which included a bureaucrat, an intellectual, an advocate, and a businessman.[27] The following scholars and dignitaries were inducted in the Society on KPJ's recommendation: Hermann Jacobi, Professor of Sanskrit at the University of Bonn,[28] J. Jolly, Professor of Sanskrit at the University of Wurzburg[29], the Sanskritist Mahamahodhyaya Haraprasad Sastri[30], Maharajadhiraja Kameshwar Singh of Darbhanga was elected Vice-Patron of the Society,[31] KPJ also seconded the proposal of the induction of one of the big *rayees* of Patna and artifact collector, Radha Krishna Jalan as one of the Vice-Patrons of the society.[32] These are a few examples of how KPJ had mobilised dignitaries for the better functioning of the Society. It should also be noted that the Maharaja of Darbhanga had contributed Rs.10,000 for the search of Mithila and other manuscripts.[33]

Quite clearly, KPJ was also an ambassador and the public face of the Society. He represented the Society at various academic fora as delegate or as a representative. He was the Society's first representative to the Senate of the Patna University. He was unanimously elected on the 8 August 1919, although there were eight other nominations; some were not approved and a few others had withdrawn their nominations.[34] He served the Senate as the Society's representative till September 1924. He was elected a member of the organising committee and the President of the Reception Committee of the sixth All India Oriental Conference be held in Patna in 1930, where he delivered a long speech.[35] He was also nominated as a delegate to the first Bombay Historical Congress held in December 1931.[36] In 1933, he was nominated as one of the representatives of the Society to the seventh All India Oriental Conference in Baroda.[37] As the General President of the Baroda session, he delivered another long speech on Indology.[38] He was invited to attend the anniversary celebration of the Asiatic Society of Bengal in March 1934.[39] He was also requested, along with Sham Bahadur, to represent the Society at the eighth All India Oriental Conference held in Mysore in 1935.[40]

Administrative Measures/Interventions/Initiatives

From time to time, KPJ also initiated efforts for the amendment of the Rules of the Society for better and transparent functioning.[41] Surely, his legal eye and acumen would have played an important part in such initiatives. Having donated his own volumes to the library, he requested the Lieutenant-Governor for a special donation and the latter was pleased to allow Rs. 2,000 towards the library.[42] Sometimes he even bore the cost of publishing the articles, obviously for distribution among his friends and the purpose was, perhaps, to make them aware about the recent and new discoveries in Indology.[43] From time to time, he was also entrusted with the task of selecting suitable speakers.[44]

There was no branch in the Society or its journal, where KPJ's influence could not be seen. The preparation of the library catalogue was started as early as 1919 under KPJ's supervision and after final revision by KPJ and Samadhar the catalogue was printed. KPJ was also conscious of the cost of the running of the society, and therefore, he tried to keep a skeleton staff.[45] He also provided his personal Remington typewriter at a low cost of Rs. 150. It should be noted here that the staff of the Society were not appointed on a permanent basis, and the same system continued till 2007, when Society was taken over the Government of Bihar. It ran on the contributions made by the government and the donations by some generous persons like Radha Krishna Jalan, the Maharaja of Darbhanga, etc. Knowing these facts, KPJ as an instinctive institution builder, did everything possible within his capacity. For meeting the requirements of funds he tried to keep several well-heeled people on the board.

Most importantly, as a resource mobiliser, KPJ invited scholars of diverse disciplines and regions to contribute to the Journal. The list of the contributors is quite long; some of the prominent contributors were: Haraprasad Sastri, Rev. Heras, Jayachandra Vidyalankar, Ramavatar Sharma, R.D. Banerji, L.V. Ramaswami Aiyar, A.S. Altekar, B.C. Majumdar, Jadunath Sarkar, Sten Konow, G.R. Hunter, V.H. Jackson, K.S. Coldwell, Shams-ul-Ulema Nawab Syed Imdad Imam, Saiyid Zamir-ud-din Ahmad, saiyid Wasi Ahmad Bilgrami, Sarat Chandra Roy, Rahul Sankrityayan, H. Panday and so many others.

From the inception of the Society till KPJ's death, KPJ contributed to all branches of the Society and its journal. As a token of its gratitude, the Society paid him a handsome tribute after his death, by publishing a commemoration volume in his name.[46] Reminiscing his prolific contributions, the Vice-President of the Society, Justice J.F.W. James said:

> From the time of the institution of this Society Dr. Kashi Prasad Jayaswal was its most active member and he more than any other has contributed to maintain and secure the high position which the Society enjoys in the learned world. In his early youth when as an under-graduate in Oxford he obtained the rare distinction of a University scholarship, he showed a flair for difficult and little-known oriental languages; and in later life, he combined painstaking and successful work at the Bar with work in epigraphy, numismatics, archaeology and history which won him an Asiatic and a European reputation. All of us here mourn the loss of a friend; the loss to the Society is irreparable; but his work will live after him to inspire future generation of scholars in Bihar.[47]

V.R. Ramchandra Dikshitar, the then Vice-Chancellor of Madras University, remembered him in the following words: "Above all, Dr. Jayaswal was the life and soul of the Bihar and Orissa Research Society. He was the distinguished Editor of the Journal of Bihar and Orissa Research Society for years together, maintaining a high standard of excellence."[48]

The Patna Museum

No State in the Twentieth Century can afford to be without a museum, when even a municipality realises the necessity and utility of such institutions.[49] **KPJ**

One of the founding members of another historic institution, the Patna Museum, KPJ was closely associated with it in various capacities: as its President for the longest period, as advisor, as a member of its managing committee, as a donor of antiquities and artifacts, and as a resource mobiliser. After the formation of the province of Bihar and Orissa in 1912, it was proposed that a museum at Patna be set up to house for displaying the antiquities of Bihar. The excavations of the multi-pillared hall at the close-by Kumrahrar in 1913 gave a further impetus to this idea. In July 1915, at the inaugural meeting of the Society, Sachchidanand Sinha moved the proposition that a provincial museum and a library be established. A committee with KPJ as a member was appointed to work out a scheme for the purpose. The committee's report was published in October 1915, and the scheme was well received. In view, however, of the fact that the expenditure on the building would be large to give effect to the committee's proposals, further consideration was deferred till financial conditions improved. In the meanwhile, the collection of the exhibits for the Museum was commenced with the Commissioner's Bungalow acting as a provisional shelter for the collectibles.[50]

Annual Report of the Patna Museum (*ARPM*) from the year ending 31 March 1918 to 31 March 1938 and the proceedings of BORS are the basic primary sources for these readings. The proceedings of the Society are not available in the Library of the Society. Therefore, we have accessed it from the different libraries: the Society Library, Patna Museum Office, and the Library of the Archaeological Survey of India.

The BORS and the Patna Museum were twin institutions, in the sense of a shared moment of birth, but their life histories also remained interconnected in several important ways. While the Society represented the theoretical work of research and criticism, as evidenced by the learned articles in its Journal on objects of historic and archaeological interest, the Museum sought to gather up whenever possible, and preserve the objects themselves. Thus, functioning together, each institution complemented the other. The Museum also presented a popular, living, material interface for things historical.

The Patna Museum is widely known in India and abroad for

its rich collections consisting of stone sculptures, architectural pieces, bronze images, terracotta figurines, pre-historic implements, copper-plates, stone-inscriptions, coins, seals, pottery, various kinds of jewelleries, weapons, tools, and many other antiquities. There are no less than eleven thousand objects of antiquarian interest ranging from the early Mauryan period, third century B.C., to the present times.[51]

In April 1917, the Patna Museum was formally established by Sir Edward Gait, who succeeded Sir Charles S. Bayley as Lieutenant Governor; and the distinguished ethnologist and anthropologist Rai Bahadur Sarat Chandra Roy was appointed as the Museum's first curator. A managing committee of five members, with Mr. Walsh, as President, was also constituted by the same government resolution. After the formal inauguration of the Museum in 1917, the antiquities were removed to the northern wing of the Patna High Court premises where the Museum was relocated, in view of the growing number of antiquities, to five rooms in the southern annexe of the Court allotted to the Museum by the government in 1924. It was in 1929, that the Museum was moved to its present building on the Buddha Marg (i. e., Patna-Gaya Road) constructed in Indo-Saracenic style, one of the most elegant buildings of Patna.

KPJ was appointed a member of the managing committee in 1927.[52] He was appointed against the vacancy created by the new appointment of P.C. Manuk, as President of the Museum. Before his appointment as the full-fledged President, KPJ acted as the Officiating President thrice, when President Manuk was on leave in London: From 18 May 1927 to the 25 October 1927,[53] 27 June 1928 to 31 October 1928[54], 6 May 1929 to the 28 October 1929.[55]

KPJ was appointed full-fledged President of the managing committee, Patna Museum, with effect from 12 June 1930.[56] For a short period, H. Lambert, Principal, Patna College, was appointed a member of the managing committee in place of KPJ. In 1933 KPJ resigned from the post of President[57] and was again re-appointed President in December 1934.[58] The tenure was for three years with effect from the 1 December 1934. However, before the expiry of his tenure, he left this world. KPJ was on leave for a few months during his entire tenure, from 23 April 1935 to 23 July 1935.[59] KPJ was the fifth full-fledged President of the Museum and he served the Museum as the President for the longest ever period.

What was the driving philosophy behind the creation of the

Museum? Let us listen to the answer that was given at the inaugural ceremony of the present building of the Museum by the Governor Hugh Lansdown Stephenson:

> [The occasion] surely forces us to realize that the present is not a self-created, self-sufficing age; we are the products of the past and should be proud of our heritage; we do not want to turn back the pages of history, to replace the motor car by the bullock cart, but still less can we afford to obliterate the past, to endeavour to create a new heaven and a new earth out of the resulting chaos. We may fervently believe in the future of united India, but we are fundamentally in the past of Bihar, of Orissa, of Chota Nagpur. The list of the workers shows that the past of the province is of interest not only to those whose lot it has been to work in the province, but to the outside world that has never been here at all; it is a common platform on which all races can meet, but it is of vital interest to the direct inheritors of that past. And this is why we cannot be content to be merely a section of the Calcutta Museum or any other Museum. We must have the tangible evidences of our past history here in our midst. We must have our own Museum, not merely to house objects of archaeological interest, but as an outward and visible sign that we have a past, and that it belongs to us. The educational value of such a Museum is enormous and I trust that full advantage will be taken of it, but I am more interested to-day in the Museum as the symbol of the fact that the province has a history of his own. And if we are proud of that history, it is right that the Museum should be a stately building worthy of our pride...

Speaking of the work to be done he continued:

> It is the function of the Museum, not only to recapture our past, but to link it with the present; it is our ambition that it shall be enriched, not only by original research and the purchase of individual antiquities, but also by gift or loan of private collections which will thus be made available to the province as whole. I will now open the building so that you may see that the inside is in no way unworthy of the outside.[60]

Quite clearly, the Museum was intended as a repository of a collective past with an inevitable link to the present and future. It was not seen as an actual return to the past but as an instrument that would engender a sense of identity, heritage and history to the people in the region, away from the shadows of a cosmopolitan Calcutta. Having thus allayed the fears of a possible allegation about an obsession with the past, the speaker also put to rest any message of sectarian autonomy that the very fact of a regional museum might send. The speech thus walked a fine line between the past and the present, regional and Indian, local and global by adequately emphasising its supreme pedagogical value and geographical immediacy. The somewhat defensive stance of the speech could be said to have been balanced by an unequivocal invocation of a collective 'we' which could be inclusive as well as assertive in identity terms. If one could generalise on the basis of this one speech, one would have to say that a "museum project was not always 'national' in its imagination", as Benedict Anderson has suggested.[61] The peculiar colonial context that we are dealing with was a complex phenomenon irreducible to terms such as 'nation', 'unity', 'progress'. The speaker's sense of pride in the architecture and what was housed within is unmistakable.

The fantastic building of the Patna Museum had availed the engineering skills of Sohan Lal, the Engineer-in-Charge of the construction. But KPJ had a say in its design, which is obvious from its similarity to the design of his own house in Mirzapur constructed before the museum building.[62] Speaking of KPJ's acute aesthetic sense, P.C. Manuk observed,

> The learned Jayaswal loved beauty—no matter in what form or shape or material it evinced itself. Often he held forth to me on the beautiful symmetry and proportions of the Taj at Agra, comparing its glorious arches with those of the West, and its general architectural effects with Rajput architecture. Particularly was he struck by the skill with which the decorators of the Taj had proportioned the sizes of the letters in Persian inscriptions over the entrance arch so that all the letters of the different lines, one above the other, appeared to be of the same length to the observer below? "After that", he used to say, critics say we Indians had no sense of perspective.[63]

The Patna Museum was built during Manuk's presidentship. Previously the Museum had been housed in a wing of the High court for want of an adequate building. After much insistence, the government of the day sanctioned an adequate sum for a home worthy of the many excellent exhibits already collected. Detailing the deliberations behind the architecture, Manuk wrote,

> That day Jayaswal, a member of the Committee, was a happy enthusiastic man. He was determined that the building should combine the grace and merits of both the Mogul and Rajput styles of architecture, within the limits of the grant. We all agreed. Backwards

> and forwards went the plans from the Committee to the capable engineers charged with the construction. With such an excellent "fidus Achates" at my elbow, my task was easy. Again mine was the pen-his the inspiration, helped by that other profound scholar and Jayaswal's colleague in Research work, Dr. Banerji Sastri. Thus emerged the beautiful Museum, in the Mogul-Rajput style of which Bailey Road in Patna boasts today.[64]

While taking an active interest in the Patna Museum, KPJ also acted as a statesman at large for such projects elsewhere. Read his words of praise and disappointment in the following speech, delivered as the President of the seventh All India Oriental Conference in Baroda, which deserves to be cited *in extenso*:

> I would take this occasion to thank publicly on your behalf the State and Government of Gwalior for the care which they take in the preservation of the ancient monuments in their State. Mr. Gadre, the Archaeological Superintendent, deserves special mention. Their administration in this behalf is an example to the rest of India. Every ancient building, both major and minor, is carefully conserved, roads made for its approach, and the approaches to the buildings notified and placarded on the spot. The Government of Hyderabad has won the admiration of scholars and artists by the scrupulous care they take of Ajanta frescoes and by their admirable volumes on the Ajanta paintings and sculptures. The publications of the Archaeological Department of His Exalted Highness the Nizam and of His Highness the Maharaja of Mysore are always awaited with interest.
>
> It is, however, a matter of regret that in some of the Indian States monuments are suffering from a terrible neglect. The State of Ajaigarh has allowed a most important temple at Nachna to be destroyed by its subjects. This was a pre-Guptan or early Guptan monument the like of which was nowhere to be found in the whole of India. Historical and artistic remains are so widely scattered all over India that unless the public take a dutiful interest in their preservation, they cannot be effectively protected from vandalism and natural decay. An Indian State is especially expected to protect its ancient temples and objects in art.
>
> The work of the Imperial Archaeological Department has been great in the past and the British Indian Government may look back upon it with rightful pride. In recent years, however, the work of the Department has suffered for want of adequate financial provisions at the hands of The Imperial Government. Owing to the financial difficulties, every State-undertaking has suffered, but the

Archaeological Department seems to have been outstandingly a victim. This has been due to want of interest at the hands of public men and politicians. The Department has found no advocate for its help. This is, indeed, a deplorable fact. The work of the Archaeological Department should be a matter of keen interest of the cultured members of the Imperial Assembly. They should note that not a single pre-Buddha site of importance has yet been excavated in India. The interest of the late Director-General of Archaeology created round post-Alexander sites, and it was by a mere chance that Mr. R. D. Banerji lighted upon Mohenjo Daro and by his genius realized its significance. History in India does begin with Alexander, and the sites which are well-known and are lying in numbers, crying for spade, remain untouched. Add to this a number of new sites along the fringe of the Khirthar range, in the Ravi valley, in the ancient Saraswati-Ghaggar basin, etc., which have been recently traced. It will be a great pity if the present apathy and neglect continues. If steps are not taken to direct our energies to this vast and virgin soil, the result will be that expeditions from foreign countries will possess the fields and crowd us out. We must remember that no inscription in Brahmi has yet been found of a period before the death of the Buddha. This is for the simple reason that no truly ancient Hindu site has so far been excavated, with the consequential result that what is medieval in the eyes of the Hindu historians is being treated as the beginning of Indian history. In the eyes of Hindu historian, ancient history ends with the Mahabharata War, at about 1400 B. C., while the spade knows nothing apart from Mohenjo Daro, anterior to 500 B. C. In this connection, I might appeal to private societies, like the Historical Society of Allahabad, to undertake the excavation work which the law now permits. If they dig at Kausambi, I am confident that pre-Buddhan remains and documents will be discovered. The dynasty of the Bharatas, after giving up Hastinapura, came and settled at Kausambi. Personally, I have not the least doubt, if proper operations are conducted and the right sites selected we shall get at the remains of the family of Shatanika and Sahasranika.

We cannot shut our eyes to what the academic institutions in Europe and America are doing to fit out costly expeditions of exploration in distant lands. The other day we read of a proposed Italian expedition to Nepal. Are our Universities and other institutions merely to sit and look on while others win undying glory in fields which legally belong to us?

What private effort can do in one field is well illustrated by the Museum of the Allahabad Municipality, equipped in less than three

> years. You have their sculptures and remains from the Asokan time down to the eleventh century A.D., almost every period being represented. You have two unique inscriptions there- one being on copper in inlaid gold letters. A single individual, Mr. Vyas, the Executive Officer of the Municipality—without spending any significant funds did it. If every Municipality did the same, what a treasure we should gather with but little effort. Such Museums should be objects of local civic pride, and collectively national wealth. The Allahabad Municipal authorities have similarly gathered a number of ancient coins through their peons and employees and a number of paintings as free gifts from the citizens. I mention this in detail for guidance in founding such priceless civic institutions—priceless both in sense of being costless, and priceless in sense of being immeasurable in value.
>
> The educative value of museums needs not to be told to the modern world. It is self-evident. And when we hear that the State of Kashmir has made a retrenchment by abolishing its Museum, we have to draw the attention of the Darbar that the institution should be resuscitated. No State in the twentieth century can afford to be without a museum, when even a municipality realizes the necessity and utility of such institutions.[65]

The speech is a comprehensive, passionate appeal, backed by KPJ's deep knowledge of the past and present developments in the fields of archaeology, numismatics, and museology and also his historical insight. He praised the governments that lived up to his expectations and decried the ones that did not pay enough attention to research, conservation, and excavation of new historical material. He was an *avante-garde* historian, incessantly pushing the boundaries of the discipline in time and space. And he took the pedagogic role of the museums as self-evident.

Inside the Museum, various improvements were introduced in the working of the Museum during KPJ's tenure. The exhibits were arranged on scientific lines especially in the Art Gallery and in the Geological room. The Coin Cabinet was rearranged by the Curator. Arrangements of exhibits on scientific lines in the Archaeological section were also completed. Old arms and war trophies were rearranged. There was also a plan to keep a handbook on the Museum to act as a guide to the reading visitors.

Apart from the general acquisitions and research work of the Museum, KPJ took great care in supervising every aspect of the Museum work. It was during his presidentship that we see a mention of the garden in the *Annual Report*. He took up the cause of its beautification with the help of the government. During 1931-35, a large number of permanent low growing trees and flowering plants were planted. He asked for the setting up of two hydrants, one at the front and another at the back of the Museum, for watering the garden. The tank on the west of the museum was completed and made over to the Museum. It was fenced. Reporting its progress, he also had a set of demands; he always had an agenda, a to-do list. Whether it was the issue of tanks drying up in the summers, or of plantation of shrubs around the tanks. A turnstile was built in 1935 to allow the police-constables and office peons to go out and enter the Museum without the main gates being kept open. This was to prevent cattle from entering the compound at night and causing damage to the garden. It facilitated access to the public when the main gates were closed. Clearly, KPJ was conscious of both the environment and the habitat around the museum, he knew that for it to grow, it needed to be both environment and people-friendly in a quotidian sense of the term.

Visitors

The Museum was opened for the public for the first time in 1921 and the place witnessed an average of forty visitors a day. However, there was a sharp rise in the number of visitors during KPJ's tenure. KPJ managed to spread his personal sense of enthusiasm for the museum in the public at large. The overwhelming increase in the number of visitors shows that he was successful in inculcating a sense of pride in Bihar's historical riches in art, architecture and craftsmanship.

Number of visitors:

1930-31	119,144
1931-32	117,110
1932-33	129,607
1933-34	109,223
1934-35	132,971
1935-36	143,983
1936-37	163,958
1937-38	147,994

The fall in visitors, during 1933-34, was due to the disastrous earthquake on the 15 January 1934. Owing to the damage to the

Museum galleries, domes etc., the building was declared unsafe by the Chief Engineer, and the Museum galleries were closed to the public from the 16 January 1934 to the 20 May 1934 with the permission of the government.[66]

Among some of the distinguished visitors to the Museum were:

(i) The members of the sixth All India Oriental Conference and the members of the Indian Historical Records Commission, both held in the month of December 1930.[67]

(ii) Sir Hugh Stephenson visited the Museum at a Tea party given by KPJ.[68]

(iii) Members of Indian Historical Records Commission on 23 December 1930.[69]

(iv) Prince Purachhatra of Siam with the President of the Managing Committee. Prof. C.C. Webb of Oriel College, Oxford, and was pleased with it.[70]

(v) Dr. Magnus Hirschfeld, Berlin, Germany, on 9 October 1931.[71]

(vi) Members of All India Philosophical Conference on 21 December 1931.[72]

(vii) Delegates of the Science Congress held at Patna, on 3 January, 1933.[73]

(viii) Dr. Pran Natn, of Banaras Hindu University, on 15 January 1933.[74]

(ix) Signor G. Scarpa, Counsel-General of Italy, on 21 February 1933.[75]

(x) Dr. Hiranända Sastri, Epigraphist to the Government of India, on 30 March 1933.[76]

(xi) The Hon'ble Mr. Justice J.R. Das of the Rangoon High Court on 25 November 1933.

(xii) Dr. Heinrich Meinhardt, Assistant Curator, State Museum of Ethnology, Berlin, Germany, visited 24 March 1934.[77]

(xiii) His Excellency the Governor of Bihar and Orissa and Lady Sifton on 24 March 1935.

(xiv) H.C. Prior, Esq., I.C.S., Secretary Finance Department, Government of Bihar and Orissa, on 9 January 1935, and

(xv) J.W. Houlton, Esq., I.C.S., Secretary, Revenue Department, Government of Bihar and Orissa on 19 January 1935.[78] These are a few names of who's who, of the visitors to the Museum.

If we look carefully at the events organised during KPJ's tenure as President, it becomes clear that organising high-profile events was part of his strategy to popularise the Museum. He took full advantage of the contacts he had developed to invite these high profile leaders of opinion to the Museum. It would naturally be covered by the newspapers, thus taking the news of happenings at the Museum to far-flung areas, ensuring a further publicity, attracting the big crowds that it did. But the biggest gain must have been its magnetic quality in attracting more historical pieces by travelling collectors such as Rahul Sankrityayan, who contributed several valuable manuscripts from Tibet, Nepal and other parts of the Himalayan valley.

Some Notable Acquisitions

An important finding of KPJ's tenure was that of Kurkihar images in the excavations carried out between 1931 and 1934.[79] The site was visited by him and the images brought to the Patna Museum at the direction of Government Revenue Department where it was duly cleaned. The images had inscriptions and dates in the regnal years of the Pala kings. KPJ followed up the excavation work by writing an illustrated article about the Kurkihar images.[80]

KPJ himself contributed a number of artefacts to the Museum.[81] He also utilised his personal relations in the overall growth and expansion of the Museum. It was because of his close association, that Rahul Sankrityayan came in to contact with the Patna Museum and made valuable contributions. KPJ persuaded Rahul to donate his Tibetan collection of MSS to the Museum. Rahul wrote,

> In 1930 I returned from Tibet from my first visit and went to Lanka with 20 khacchars loaded with material-books, painting, etc. In 1932-33, I took three dozen paintings out of 150 paintings to Europe. It was there that I was able to understand the value of these historical and artistic paintings. People were ready to pay several thousands for one painting. Then I thought, it must be kept in safe keeping. At that time I thought of the Museum of our Province. On 28th October, I wrote a letter to Jayaswal ji from London, 'I am ready to give my Tibetan paintings to the Museum, however, if a secure place can be found at Nalanda, then it should be shifted there'. I got the telegram of Jayaswal ji on 22 November in Paris, 'I accept your offer with thanks and writing Thomas Cook to ensure safety in transit.'[82]

It is important to note that Rahul Sankrityayan's Tibet expedition in search of manuscripts and paintings was sponsored by KPJ. So a friend was returning the favour when he thought of the Patna museum as the right place for it. However, it should be noted that he had offered them with the caveat that if he was unable to build within twenty years a private Museum at Nalanda, they would be kept there: 'If the Nalanda Museum is not built within twenty years, the objects will be regarded as absolute gifts to the Patna Museum.' The Committee accepted this offer.[83] The Nalanda Museum was not constructed and Rahul's donations are still kept safe in '*Rahul Sankrityayan Gallery*' of the Patna Museum, which was established in Rahul's memory. From 1933 to KPJ's death, Rahul donated hundreds of items, including paintings, manuscripts, coins, and clothes.[84]

KPJ's elder son C.S. Jayaswal, a Barrister at Patna High Court, also donated a few objects to the Museum: One big-sized brick obtained near Brahma Kund, Rajgir, three samples of Egyptian handiwork showing Cleopatra and two scenes were presented by him.[85] Five pieces of decorated pottery of Sindh (Mohenjo Daro), Reg. nos. 8180-8184, also found their way to the Museum.[86]

Cataloguing the Artefacts

One of the major contributions of KPJ was the initiative taken towards the preparation of the Museum's Catalogue. However, it could not be completed during his lifetime. By the end of 1934 the Museum had collected 7593 archaeological objects—sculptures, architectural pieces, metallic images, terracotta, pre-historic objects, inscriptions, seals and sealings, potteries and numerous varieties of minor antiquities. At this stage, KPJ, who was then the President of the Managing Committee of the Museum, thought it desirable to publish a catalogue of the antiquities of the Museum; and he placed a proposal for the same before the government on the 11 January 1935. It was readily approved by the Government. In October, the same year, Stella Kramrisch was commissioned to undertake this work. She submitted the catalogue of stone sculptures, metal images, terracottas and some minor antiquities sometime in March 1939. The catalogue was entrusted by the managing committee to A.P. Banerji-Sastri for scrutiny. On his report, the managing committee found it necessary that it needed to be revised. Accordingly, the catalogue, prepared by Kramrisch, was thoroughly revised by P.C. Manuk, A.P. Banerji-Sastri, Father J. Moran, J.H. Hill assisted by S.A. Shere, the then Curator, and A.C. Ghosh. The transcription of the inscriptions on the Kurkihara images, prepared by Shri A. Ghosh, the then Superintendent of Archaeological Survey of India, Mid-Eastern Circle, Patna (later on, Director-General of Archaeological Survey of India), was also added to it.

The final script of the catalogue was ready for the press by 1941. But for one reason or the other, it could not be sent for printing before 1953. In that year in August the script was entrusted to the Allahabad Law Journal Press Ltd. However, finally it was edited and published in 1965.[87]

KPJ contributed in some other ways as well. When Babu Shyamapada Misra, Modeller, took casts of interesting medieval sculptures and Gandhara images as well as some of the Buddhist reliefs and the headless Patna image identified by KPJ as one of the Śiśunāga kings,[88] on the suggestion of KPJ, an epigraphist peon went to Darbhanga district and took estampages of important inscriptions on sculptures at places called Habidih and Anḍrathorhi.[89] Some eight paper estampages were thus added to the Museum. Similar expeditions for collections of estampages belonging to the medieval age were obtained from different places in Bhagalpur and Darbhanga districts. KPJ studied and published them later in *JBORS*.[90]

Apart from making donations, KPJ was also making efforts to acquire antiquities. He obtained eighty coins for the Museum in 1934-35. From London, he purchased two ivory court scenes—one of the last Moghul Emperor and another of Ranjit Singh.[91] He also gave approval for the visit to the important site of Kauśāmbī (Allahabad district) and the officiating Curator Adhar Chandra Ghosh secured fine terracotta figurines, stone sculptures, large collection of beads, and some fine copper coins out of which one unique coin is of the Śuṅga king (Sugarajasya). KPJ took the photographer and curator of the Museum along on his visits to Ajanta, Ellora, Bhaja, Karle, Nasik and Elephanta caves.[92]

The Museum suffered a great setback by the sad death of KPJ, President, in August 1937. The managing committee's reports for the years 1935-36 and 1936-37 could not be issued in time on account of the death of the Curator and the President which occurred one after the other in the course of but little over a year.

Health Museum

One of the most interesting happenings was the exhibition of the Health Museum within the Patna Museum, which was organised by the Red Cross Society and inaugurated by no less a figure than Lady Stephenson, the wife of Lt. Governor, on the 12 November 1930. The exhibits were on view in the Museum in the Committee Room. The Health Museum had made some additions to their models and charts. Personnel of the Bihar and Orissa Public Health Department sat in the hall and explained the exhibits to the visitors. The exhibits were put under glass covers during the year 1933-34.[93] Its safe exhibits was an indication of its popularity.

The Health Museum was later allotted a separate room in the verandah to the north of the Geological Hall on the ground floor and was shifted from the Committee Room to the new room. By a resolution of the managing committee on 4 May 1933, this accommodation of the Health Museum was considered to be a temporary one until the office-bearers of the Health Museum could have a separate building of their own somewhere else.[94] The Health Museum was shifted from the Committee Room to the ground floor and was an attractive feature of the Museum.[95] It was given prime visibility.

Although the inventory of the exhibits at the Health Museum is not available, it seemed to have caught the imagination of the public in general and women in particular. It seems that the main purpose of organising the Health Museum was to spread awareness among the women particularly. It appeared a very attractive idea, something that connected the history of health to the then times, and could be seen as an issue of general interest. If on the one hand, the idea of getting important persons there lent the museum the much needed publicity, the act of holding an exhibition around health was an exercise in generating social goodwill, by bringing the 'present, the here and now', in conversation with history and it could also be seen as part of a social welfare exercise, whereby just to demonstrate that museumwallas were not unconcerned with the health of their immediate neighbourhood. It was thus a public relations exercise *par excellence.*

Patna University and KPJ

Another abiding institution of great repute with which KPJ worked for several years and in important capacities was the Patna

University. After his rejection by the University of Calcutta, this was his chance to work with the formal academia, and he grabbed it with both hands. In turn, Patna University did everything that it could to honour him, as if to underline with a sense of irony, the loss that the University of Calcutta had suffered by spurning him. However, before the conferment of the honorary Ph.D degree in 1936, KPJ had served Patna University in various capacities: as a member of the Senate and Syndicate, as a Reader, as a member of the Board of Examiners, and was also part of the Board of Research Studies etc. The Patna University, the first university in Bihar and the seventh oldest in the Indian subcontinent, was established in 1917. At that time, the jurisdiction of the University extended to Bihar, Orissa, and the Kingdom of Nepal. The bulk of the evidence for this section is drawn from the *Annual Reports of the Patna University* (hereafter *ARPU*).

Positions held by KPJ in the Patna University

KPJ made his debut in Patna University in 1918, when he was appointed as one of the additional members of the Faculty of Arts and a Reader in Indian Archaeology.[96] It was expected of the University Readers to deliver their lectures during the University session 1919-1920. Since the University was newly born, the Readers were devoted solely to research. Although it was hoped that the lectures would be attended by post-graduate students, greater stress was laid upon the publication of original lectures and direct promotion of research.[97] KPJ was the only elected member (elected on 4 November 1919) by the Senate to the Faculty of Law as a member for the year 1919-20.[98] The Faculty of Arts elected KPJ as one of the members of the Board of Studies of Archaeology.[99]During 1936-1937, he was elected as an additional Fellow-Member to the Faculty of Law.[100] During this period he was also appointed to the Faculty of Arts as a Fellow Member.[101]

The Faculty of Arts had elected KPJ as one of the seven members for the Board of Studies in Sanskrit and Pali and the Board of Studies in History, Ethnology, and Indian Archaeology for the year 1917-18.[102] In 1919-20, the same faculty elected him as the President of the Board of Studies of Sanskrit and Pali, and History Departments.[103] He was again appointed on the Board of Studies for Sanskrit and Pali for the period 1921-1922.[104].

KPJ also served Patna University as a member and convenor

of the Board of Examiners. For the year 1918-19, he was appointed the Examiner of Pali and History, up to the degree standard.[105] He was elected as the Convener of Sanskrit for the period 1918-1919 and one of the examiners of Indian Archaelogy.[106] In the subsequent year, he was promoted and appointed as an Examiner for Masters Examination in History, besides being one of the examiners of the History Honors courses.[107] He got Rs. 97 and 8 Annas, and Rs. 70 as remuneration for evaluating the scripts for M.A. and B.A. respectively.[108]

KPJ served Patna University as a member on various other committees. The Senate elected him as one of the members of the Board of Accounts and Library General Committee on the 4 November 1919 for the year 1919-20.[109] He served the Library General Committee till 1923 and that year he was also elected as one of the Members of Library Executive Committee.[110] He was also elected as a member of Printing Delegacy from the Faculty of Arts, elected by the Senate on 7 December 1918 for the year 1919-20 and he worked on the Committee till 1922.[111]

In 1936, a committee of five members, including KPJ, was formed to amend the Syndicate Resolution No. 100 of 13 August, 1932 to recognise the Title Examination of the Calcutta Sanskrit Association as equivalent to the Acharya examination of the Bihar Sanskrit Association.[112] In the same year, another Committee of the Syndicate was also formed to look into the matter of unemployment and the following issues: the teaching of Law in the universities, the teaching in commercial subjects, industrial and technical education, and the nature of research work to be done by the universities.[113]

On the basis of the suggestion given by the Director of Public Instruction, a committee was appointed to consider the steps to be taken considering the fact that hardly any candidate failed in the vernaculars as principal subjects at the I.A. (Intermediate of Arts) examination, making these subjects an easy option for candidates to the prejudice of the study of other subjects. A Committee, therefore, consisting of Messrs. F.R. Blair, Baldeva Sahay, S.M. Hafeez, K.P. Jayaswal and Hari Chand was appointed to go into the question and submit a report.[114] Regrettably, the Report, if any, has not been accessible.

In April 1936, the General Secretary of the Hindustani Academy wrote a letter to the Patna University intimating that the Academy was compiling a dictionary in Hindustani. In response to that the Syndicate constituted a Committee consisting of Messrs. F.R. Blair, Baldeva Sahay and S.M. Hafeez, and K.P. Jayaswal and Hari Chand to consider what steps needed to be taken in connection with the compilation of the Dictionary of words and idioms to be used in the basic Hindustani language.[115]

KPJ was one of the members of the Governing Body of Government Law College, Bankipur, nominated by the Faculty of Law. The College was established in July 1909, and was duly affiliated to the University of Calcutta. In 1917 it was transferred to the newly created Patna University. The College was a government institution and was under the control of the Director of Public Instruction, Bihar and Orissa.[116]

With his entry into the university system, KPJ proposed several reforms and suggestions and most of them were accepted. In 1918, it was proposed by KPJ that the courses of study in French, German, and Italian, History, Ethnology, and Indian Archaeology, Sanskrit and Pali, and Mathematics be recommended for provisional adoption and be circulated for opinion according to Resolution 17, Chapter IV of the Regulations.[117] KPJ also made an effort to democratise the foreign language studies and wrote a letter to the Vice-Chancellor, in which he suggested that some Indian members should be placed on the Board of Studies in foreign languages.[118] It was, perhaps, because of KPJ's intervention that an Indian, Hari Chand Sastri was elected as the member, of the French, Italian, and German Department by the Faculty of Arts on November 21 1919, besides The Rev. G.J. Dann as President and the others.[119] This was the first time an Indian was made a member in this particular Board.

KPJ had the opportunity of serving in the highest decision making bodies of the University — the Senate and the Syndicate. He was the first person who represented the BORS on the Senate of Patna University. He was unanimously elected on the 8 August 1919 and was on the Board from October 1, 1919 to September 1924.[120] Later on, he was also appointed—one among the fifteen members—by the Syndicate on the Central Board of the Senate.[121] He was elected from the Faculty of Arts to the Syndicate during the period 1936-1937.[122] In 1921, he fought elections to the Syndicate from the Senate, but lost.[123] However, he was nominated from the Senate to the Syndicate.

As a member of the highest decision making body, KPJ took part in several discussions and sometimes created debate and controversy in the meetings. When the question of separate curriculum for women was debated in the house and after amendment it was put before the House, KPJ was the only member who spoke against the motion. The motion was passed by 34 votes to 1.[124]

Women's Representation/Reservation to Senate

We are not too sure when the question of women's representation in the public institutions in India was debated and when exactly it came into force, but it was KPJ who raised the issue of reservation of women in the Senate of Patna University. He moved the proposal that the Senate recommend to the government that of the members nominated by government to the Senate at least three should be non-official ladies, domiciled in the Province.[125] In favour of his arguments, he said that the Province had Girls' schools and the question of higher education of women was also receiving consideration. It was, therefore, essential that educated women should be better represented on the Senate. The government could afford to allot three of the twenty-five seats reserved for nominations to non-official ladies. The issue was debated in the house and some of the members argued that the word *domiciled in the Province" be deleted and that "five" be substituted for "three"*. However, permission was not granted by the Senate. KPJ further explained his position on the issue, "proposal did not exclude either official ladies or ladies not domiciled in the Province. All that he contended was that non-official ladies domiciled in the Province should be nominated. More ladies might be nominated."[126] Some of the members were in favour of the postponement of the issue, and the motion that the Senate pass on to the next item of business was carried by seventeen votes to fifteen.[127]

Military Training

KPJ was in favour of imparting military training to the members of the university. When the proposal came to the Senate that the "Local Government be moved to make arrangements for the military training of the members of this University on lines similar to those provided for the members of the other Provincial Universities." It was also said that what had been done in some other Indian universities should also be done here and it is sure that if opportunities were offered a number of undergraduates [would] come forward."[128] KPJ seconded the motion by saying that the proposal had the support of the Syndicate. It seems the idea of military training was in the air in the immediate aftermath of the First World War, and KPJ did not want Patṇa University to lag behind others.

'Let them have the happiness of Learning their Language':

Another important and long debate was on the question of the vernacularisation of education and the new education policy. A number of arguments—in favour and against—were made during the deliberations and it was also argued that the proposal should be sent back to the department. However, KPJ spoke in favour of the motion (vernacularisation of education) and opposed the suggestion that it be sent back to the department and proposed for a definite time-limit for the implementation. He said, "The Faculty will not pass it and, after all, we are to decide the matter finally. It is more a question of policy than of any expert opinion of the Faculty. I had a talk with Mr. Fawcus on my return from France last year, and I had a talk in France with a number of savants who support this view of Mr. Justice Noor that we should preserve these languages; they have a wider significance than what is generally understood. Mundari, Oraon, and the allied languages cover large areas outside the Province. Apart from this fact, it is sheer injustice that the aborigines should not be allowed to learn their own language. If we pass the motion now, it will come into effect in 1942, so there is enough time. Therefore, I am beseeching the Senate that they should pass this amendment here and not shelve it. The injustice so long done to them will be prolonged by refusing the proposal."[129] And, finally he made an emotional appeal, "Let them have the happiness of learning their language."[130] The House was divided equally—31 voting for and 31 against the motion. By the casting vote of the Vice-Chancellor in favour of the motion, it was declared carried.[131]

A proposal was introduced in the Senate that teaching would be done in Hindi up to B.A. Honours and M.A. with effect from 1937-38 and the department would be separated from the Sanskrit department. KPJ supported the motion and said it was under the purview of the Principal and the Governing Body. The motion was put to vote and carried.[132]

It is clear from these significant interventions that KPJ, a practising multilingual scholar himself, was also a diehard liberal democrat on issues of education and language. He did not believe in any given hierarchy of languages and instantly recognised the joy people could feel at the opportunity of using their own languages. He was so prescient in his democratic vision. The sad part of the post-independence linguistic history is that the tribal languages supported by KPJ have not yet found any respectable status in India. Hindi, of course, has come a long way. Education remains the forte dominated largely by the upper-caste elite.

Building a Pool of Competent Resource Persons

As a member of the highest University body, KPJ took every opportunity to rope in competent persons in teaching positions. On his recommendations, a number of persons were appointed as Readers in the departments. The following gentlemen were appointed: Banaili, Reader in Indian Economics, and Sukhraj Rai, Reader in Indian Natural Science respectively for the session 1937-38; Mr. Manu Subedar, B.A. (Bom.), B.Sc. (Lond.), "Federal Finance"; Mr. Kamta Prasad M.Sc. (Cal.), B.A. (Cantab) "X-rays." Natuarlly, he defended his recommendations and explained why he was recommending certain names:

> Mr. Subedar had a distinguished career. He was a graduate with Honours of the London University in Economics, taking Public Finance as his special subject. He had been associated with the Calcutta University and the University of Bombay in the past as a Reader and a Prof. of Economics, and was, considered to be an expert in Federal Finance. He was, at the moment, advising the Chamber of Princes on that very subject. The Syndicate thought that the University should take interest in current topics and it would be quite a good subject to be dealt with before this University. He had much pleasure in moving the resolution, on behalf of the Syndicate, for the acceptance of the Senate...
>
> ...Mr. Kamta Prasad does not need any introduction to the Senate. He has been doing original work on allied subjects for a number of years and at present occupies the senior Professorship of the Science College. He would have been called upon by any other University to lecture on the subjects of his original research and I think we have done better in requesting him to lecture to us. If you approve of the

> subject and my proposal, it will give satisfaction to the whole province.[133]

All of his recommendations were accepted.

Acknowledging his contribution to Indology in general and his services to Patna University in particular, Patna University conferred on KPJ an Honorary Ph.D. on 26 November 1936.

Bharatiya Itihas Parishad (See also Appendix F)

KPJ's engagements with historical discussions and controversies found expression in his vision of establishing the Bharatiya Itihas Parishad. Although he had been writing against the colonial interpretation of India's ancient past since the first decade of the twentieth century, he was very unhappy with the fact that no efforts were made by any Indian to write a comprehensive history of India. He lamented thus,

> Till date the value of history has not been understood in our country. Because of that, there is no such text available, which presents the facts of the entire Hindu period before the country. I have approached some people to write such history in English, but no one has come forward to bear the expense of that. Although, there is no scarcity of funds for Mahatmaji (Gandhiji) and the other gentlemen for their public proposals, but for history, nobody wants to give a single penny. The reason for that is; that both the leaders and public do not think it necessary, they do not consider it a public work. The Cambridge University has been so concerned that it has written and printed Indian History after spending thousands of rupees, but what interest India has with its own history? There should have been hundreds of books about our own history, but there is not even a single text which is indigenously written.[134]

He implored the people,

> If some gentleman amongst you stands up with courage and spends some money for history-writing, then it is possible to write the history chronologically by establishing a group of historians. If you do not think it necessary, then the matter is finished; the world will go on. Every day there is the same morning and the same evening. Then, why not the Hindus could live without history? They are still living. Our ancestors have also said, 'काकोदपि जीवति चिरंच बलिच्चा भुक्ते'। In answer to that I have to say to the crows the opportunity like that will not come again. We will always be alive and picking up grains.[135]

In his capacity of the President of the History Section of the Annual Session of the Hindi Sahitya Sammelan in 1935 in Indore, KPJ explained why it was necessary to have our own school of history-writing,

> As of now, Indian history has been written by the foreign scholars only. For them, our history begins with the Alexander's victory over India. After reading these books in our schools and colleges, the children of Rama and Krishna have started considering their history as lies and non-respectable. There is a story in *Panchatantra* that a person was taking an animal on his shoulder. Several people on the way asked if he was carrying a dog on his shoulder, he threw away the animal. In our country, the people have started searching for their ear after continuously hearing that the crow had taken away their ear. If you want to undo this situation today, then you have to write the true texts of history and propagate them in the schools and colleges. I am not going to believe in my life that the history of India begins with the coming of Alexander or with the birth of the Buddha.[136]

KPJ's views were endorsed by Gandhi. In his general Presidential Speech, Gandhi said, "I have no hesitation in accepting whatever Jayaswalji has said."[137] The editor of *Veena* commented on the speech of KPJ, "The speech of Jayaswalji demonstrates his dedication to the letters. He has drawn attention to the lacunae in the field of history-writing in India."[138] However, he had a complaint: "The President of the *'Itihas Parishad'* (Sectional President, History, at Hindi Sahitya Sammelan, Indore, 1935) is thinking about the Comprehensive History of India, but is there any useful proposal about that?"[139] The complaint was addressed the very next year, when KPJ established Bharatiya Itihas Parishad in 1936.

During the last decade of his life, the association with two of his friends, Prof. Jayachandra Vidyalankar and Rahul Sankrityayan exerted a great influence on KPJ's views and activities. The former, a pupil of M.M. Gaurishankar Hirachand Ojha, came to Patna in 1927 as a lecturer in the Bihar Vidyapeeth. His work (in Hindi) on the geographical background of Indian History had attracted KPJ's attention. Prof. Vidyalankar had undertaken another comprehensive work on the history of India and had begun to consult KPJ about its problems and difficulties. Slowly and gradually, he became his regular apprentice and colleague and the two scholars consulted each other almost on every problem that either of them had to face for about ten years. Mr. Vidyalankar's work on Indian History was published in 1933 under the title *Bharatiya Itihas ki Ruparekha*. It covers the period from the earliest times to *circa* 200 A.D. Before publication, the whole manuscript was read by KPJ in July 1931 and revised in the light of his criticism. While this was being done, KPJ felt uneasy from time to time over the fact that work of that type and of such national utility was not being done in an organised manner. He recorded the opinion that, "Such a synthetic work had not been attempted before," and remarked that he himself should have engaged with it in a more substantial manner, but his life had been taken up by Hathigumpha Inscription!" He regretted that he was wasting his time over his practice at the Bar, but there was not much that could be done. Now that he had fulfilled most of his family obligations; his son and daughter whom he had sent abroad for study were due to return soon. So he decided to renounce his practice at the Bar and devote himself exclusively to such work by joining some university which might undertake to help him in organising it.

KPJ broached the subject again in his Presidential Address at the seventh All India Oriental Conference in Baroda. He had good response from many different quarters as his correspondence shows, but he could not see what was to be done with those promises. He was a scholar and not a practical man of affairs. He realised this and approached Babu Rajendra Prasad to help him in organising the work. On 31 of May 1936, Rajendra Babu came to his house and discussed the scheme with him and Mr. Jayachandra Vidyalankar. They decided to start what is known as the Bharatiya Itihasa Parishad.[140]

KPJ made a proposal about the writing of history of ancient India and sent it to Banaras Hindu University in 1935 for approval. In that proposal the period was taken from Vedic Period to the history of Bhoja. In the team of editors, there were three intellectuals: KPJ himself, Father Heras, and Hiranand Shastri. According to the proposal, the University had to bear some expenditure and the rest of the expenditure would be taken care of by KPJ himself. It was duly communicated that though the University of Calcutta was keen to take up this project, the offer was being made to the Banaras Hindu University because KPJ found himself to be close to that University.[141]

A close look at his speech in Baroda and the proposal of the

Itihas Parishad show that he visualised Indian history-writing in contrast to the colonial writing and also saw power play in history-writing. It is also interesting to see that although his plan was to write the history of the 'Hindu period', yet he realised that it could be written by any Indian. The periodisation was carefully done because in his opinion the period of Bhoja was a period of cultural revival. Till that time the Muslim invaders were restricted to the Gulf. The victory of the Muslims and the decline of the Hindus are virtually an indicator of a new era. Significantly, KPJ's vision of possible contributors to the project did not remain confined to 'Hindu' writers.

KPJ's vision of establishing the Indian school of historiography might not have been fulfilled during his lifetime because he left this world rather early. It is also clear that while arguing for an Indian historigraphical agenda he never really challenged the colonial school of periodisation. It is also obvious that he could not really challenge the basic premise of colonial periodisation into Hindu and Muslim periods, even if he envisioned a shift in the dates beyond the Gupta age (king Bhoja).

Hindi weekly *Pataliputra* (See detailed discussion in Chapter 3)

KPJ was truly a polyglot but he recognised the role of Hindi in all aspects of national reawakening. Apart from his numerous contributions in the highly respected and intellectually stimulating magazines which have already been discussed earlier (Chapter 2), KPJ's penchant for building and rearing institutions can also be seen in envisioning a popular weekly in Hindi, i.e., *Pataliputra*. This Hindi weekly *Pataliputra* was started in June 1914 and KPJ was appointed its founder-editor and served in the position for almost a year. KPJ mobilised a pool of renowned scholars to contribute to the weekly and he himself wrote several articles of historical interest. *Pataliputra* did pretty well during his brief tenure as its editor. According to the historians of Hindi journalism, it could not maintain its stature after he left.[142]

KPJ once considered a 'dangerous revolutionist' and the 'cleverest Indian', earned for himself a great name in the institutional history of Patna. He made remarkable contributions to the newly established institutions of Patna: BORS, Patna Museum, Patna University, etc., and dominated the intellectual scene in Patna. Politics was not his chosen profession, but he was instrumental in launching several initiatives that could challenge the power-knowledge combine that colonialism represented. He utilised every space provided by the colonial regime to refute the alien hegemony in the domain of historical interpretation. KPJ utilised them because he might have been aware of the role these institutions would play in consolidating the national consciousness: cleverness of KPJ was at work here!

Quite appropriately, the Government of Bihar established the Kashi Prasad Jayaswal Research Institute in his memory immediately after independence. The purpose of the Institute was to provide facilities for, and organise research in the different branches of knowledge relating to Indian civilisation such as History, Polity, Economics, Literature, and Languages including Linguistics, Religion, and Philosophy, Art, Industries, Epigraphy, Numismatics, Archaeology, Ethnology, Anthropology, and other allied subjects.[143] Remembering the contribution of KPJ, the Institute celebrated KPJ's birth centenary in 1981 and published *K.P. Jayaswal Commemoration Volume* in his memory. However, we hope that in near future, the Institute will publish more substantial research on the person and his oeuvre in whose memory the Institute was established.

NOTES

1. For historiographical details, Thapar, Romila, *Ancient Indian Social History*, Orient Longman, New Delhi, 1996, pp. 1-22, Sharma, R.S., *Rethinking India's Ancient Past*, Oxford University Press, New Delhi, 2009, pp. 55-63.
2. See, Chapter No. 2.
3. G.P. Ambastha, 'Dr. K.P. Jayaswal - A Memoir', *Hindu Polity*, 3rd Edition, Bangalore, 1943, pp. xxvii-xxviii.
4. For entire proceedings see, *JBORS*, Vol. I, Part I, Sept. 1915, pp. 133-57.
5. Ibid.
6. Ibid.
7. Ibid.
8. Ibid.
9. P.C. Manuk, 'Dr. K.P. Jayaswal–The Barrister and Man–A Character Sketch', *KPJCV*, p. 47.
10. Ambastha, op. cit. pp. xxvii-xxviii.
11. List of officers corrected up to 1921, *JBORS*, Vol. VII, March 1921 p. 2.

12. Annual Report of *BORS*, 1922, *JBORS*, Vol. VIII, p. 70.
13. *JBORS*, Vol. IX, 1923, pp. 142, 144-45.
14. *JBORS*, Vol. XIX, Part IV, December 1933, p. 419.
15. *JBORS*, vol. XXIII, Part III, September 1937, p. 382.
16. *JBORS*, Vol. XXIV, Part-I & II, March-June, 1938, pp. 74-75.
17. *JBORS*, Vol. VI, Part I, March 1920, p. 2.
18. There might have been personal engagements or professional conflicts with the other office-bearers, because Jadunath Sarkar did not appear in his either speech or writings except the speech at the sixth All India Oriental Conference in Patna in 1930.
19. *JBORS*, Vol. XXIII, Part I, March 1937, pp. 166-67.
20. *JBORS*, VOL. X, Part I-II, March-June, 1924, pp. 21-22.
    * For KPJ's position in the Society, see reports of the quarterly meetings and annual meetings of the Society in *JBORS*.
21. Meetings of the Council and Library Committee, Annual General Meeting, Lectures, Quarterly Meetings etc.
22. See, discussion on KPJ's edited work in the previous chapter on History.
23. The details of his writings are given in the bibliography and the nature, content and significance of his findings have already been discussed in the previous chapters.
24. Annual Presidential Address, *JBORS*, March 1919, Vol. V, Part I, p. 2.
25. Annual Presidential Address, *JBORS*, Vol. VI, Part I, March 1920 pp. 1-13, (such sentiments were reiterated in later years as well).
26. *JBORS*, Vol. X, Part I, II, March and June, 1924, pp. 1-20.
27. *JBORS*, June 1918, Vol. IV, Part II, pp. 498-99.
28. *JBORS*, Vol. XI, Part I, March 1925, p. 102
29. *JBORS*, Vol. XII, Part I, March 1926, p. 176-78.
30. *JBORS*, Vol. XIV, Part I. 1928, March 1928, p. 128 & 167.
31. *JBORS*, Vol. XVI, Part I, March 1930, p. 128.
32. *JBORS*, Vol. XIX, Part I-II, March-June 1933, p. 419.
33. *JBORS*, Vol. XII, Part I, March 1926, p. 47.
34. *JBORS*, Vol. V, Part III, September 1919, pp. 420-21.
35. *JBORS*, Vol. XV, Part I-II, March-June 1929, p. 663. For Presidential Speech see, *Proceedings and Transactions of the Sixth All India Oriental Conference*, BORS, Patna, 1930, pp. xxvi-xxxiii.
36. *JBORS*, Vol. XVII, Part III, September 1931, p. 468.
37. *JBORS*, Vol. XIX, Part III, September 1933, p. 352.
38. For Presidential Speech see, *Proceedings and Transactions of the Sixth All India Oriental Conference*, Oriental Institute, Baroda, 1935, pp. lix-lxxxii.
39. *JBORS*, Vol. XX, Part I, March 1934, p. 124.
40. *JBORS*, Vol. XXI, Part III, March 1935, p. 199.

41. V.H. Jackson proposed that Rule 2 of the Society's rules be amended so as to raise the number of Vice-Patrons from five to seven. KPJ, seconded the proposal, which was unanimously carried (March 1917, Vol. III, Part I, p. 166), Jayaswal called attention to Rule 24, which required the papers, submitted for the Journal to be submitted to the Sectional Committee for consideration. The Council resolved that the rule should be followed as far as practicable, in future (March 1918, Vol. IV, Part I), KPJ moved on behalf of the Council, that in Rule 4, after the word "Treasurer", in line 2, the word "a Librarian" be added; and that in lines 3 and 4, for the words "and Treasurer" be substituted the words "Treasurer and Librarian." Further that after Rule 23 the following Rule (to be numbered 23A) be added, viz., Librarian, 23A. The Librarian shall be elected at the AGM, and shall hold office for one year. He shall be in general charge of the Society's Library, and Convener of the Committee."The motion was duly seconded and adopted (*JBORS*, Vol. VIII, Part I, March 1922 p. 178).
42. *JBORS*, Vol. VI, Part I, March 1920, p. 166.
43. He took extra reprints of *Rājanīti Ratnākara*, the *History of India from 150 A.D. to 350 A.D.*, 'Coins of the Later Mauryas', see *JBORS*, , Vol. VI, Part IV, Dec. 1920 p. 582, Vol. XIX, Part I-II, Dec 1933, p. 241, Vol. XXI, Part I, March 1935, p. 87.
44. On KPJ's request Anagarika B. Govind of Sarnath, Banaras addressed the Annual meeting in 1937.
45. *JBORS*, Vol. V, Part I, March 1919, p. 154.
46. *JBORS*, Vol. XXIII, December 1937, two important obituary articles were written by Rajendra Prasad, 'Kashi Prasad Jayaswal', pp. 399-402 and P.C. Manuk, 'Dr. K.P. Jayaswal-the Barrister and Man–A Character Sketch', pp. 403-17).
47. *JBORS*, Vol. XXIX, Part I-II, March-June 1938, p. 3.
48. *Hindu Polity*, p. xxxvi.
49. Presidential Speech, Seventh All India Oriental Conference, Baroda, 1933 (Proceedings were published in 1935).
50. For the entire proceedings, see, *JBORS*, Vol. I, Part I, Sept. 1915, pp. 133-57.
51. For the list of Acquisitions see, P.L. Gupta, *Patna Museum Catalogue of Antiquities*, Patna, 1965.
52. Government Notification no. 1390-E, dated 28 February 1927, *ARPM* 1927, p. 1.
53. Government Notification no. 102-E., dated 11 May 1927, *ARPM* 1928, p. 1.
54. Government Notification no. 4187-E., dated 25 June 1928, *ARPM*, 1929, p. 1.
55. Government Notification no. 2729-E., dated 25 April 1929, *ARPM*,

1930, p. 1.

56. Government Notification no. 366-E., dated 18 June 1930, *ARPM*, 1931, p. 1.
57. Government of Bihar and Orissa Resolution no. 637-E., dated 3 February 1933, *ARPM*, 1935, p. 1.
58. Government Notification no. 4522-E., dated 10 December 1934, *ARPM*, 1935, p. 1.
59. Government Notification no. 1752-E., dated 2 April 1935, *ARPM*, 1936, p. 1.
60. *ARPM*, 1929, p. 16. Also see, *JBORS*, Vol. XV, Part I-II, p. 13.
61. Anderson, Benedict, *'Census, Map, Museum', in Imagined Community*, Verso, London, 1991.
62. I had the opportunity to see his houses at Kortghat in Mirzapur and Patna. For visual comparisons with the Patna Museum, see the picture of these houses and the Patna Museum in the Appendix C.
63. P.C. Manuk, op.cit., p. 52.
64. Ibid., p. 52.
65. For this Presidential Speech see, *Proceedings and Transactions of the Sixth All India Oriental Conference*, Oriental Institute, Baroda, 1933, pp. lix-lxxxii.
66. For details of these data see, *ARPM* from 1931 to 1938.
67. *ARPM*, 1930, p. 1.
68. Ibid.
69. Ibid., p. 2.
70. Ibid.
71. *ARPM*, 1932, p. 2.
72. Ibid.
73. *ARPM*, 1933, p. 2.
74. Ibid.
75. Ibid.
76. Ibid.
77. *ARPM*, 1934, p. 2.
78. *ARPM*, 1935, p. 2.
79. See, *ARPM*, 1931-1934.
80. *ARPM*, 1935. The article was published in the *Journal of the Indian Society of Oriental Art*, Volume II, No. 12, December 1934.
81. For number of acquisitions from the year ending 31 March 1918 to 31 March 1938, see, Appendix D. For KPJ's contributions, see, Appendix E.
82. *Rahul Vangmaya*, Vol. II, Part I, p. 673
83. *ARPM*, 1933, p. 4.
84. For Rahul's donations see, Annual Report from the year ending 31 March to 1938, and its appendices.
85. *ARPM*, 1934.

86. *ARPM*, 1936-37.
87. Gupta, P.L., *Patna Museum Catalogue of Antiquities*, Patna Museum, Patna, 1965.
88. *ARPM*, 1920, p. 3.
89. *ARPM*, 1924, p. 3.
90. *ARPM*, 1930, p. 6.
91. *ARPM* 1935.
92. *ARPM* 1935.
93. *ARPM*, 1932, p. 2.
94. *ARPM*, 1933, p. 2.
95. *ARPM*, 1934, p. 2.
96. *ARPU*, 1918, p. 128, also see, Syndicate's Annual Report for 1918-19, p. 386.
97. Ibid., p. 386.
98. *ARPU*, 1919-1920, p. 36.
99. Ibid., p. 42.
100. *ARPU*, 1936-1937, pp. 60-61.
101. Ibid., p. 136&190.
102. *ARPU*, 1917-1918, pp. 173-74.
103. *ARPU*, 1919-1920, pp. 40-41.
104. *ARPU*, 1921-1922, p. 99.
105. *ARPU*, 1917-1918, p. 161.
106. *ARPU*, 1919-1920 pp. 47-48.
107. *ARPU*, 1918-1919, pp. 293-95.
108. Ibid., p. 442.
109. *ARPU*, 1919-1920, pp. 52-53.
110. *ARPU*, 1921-1922, p. 7, *ARPM*, 1922-1923, p. 27 &104.
111. *ARPU*, 1919-1920, p. 54, *ARPM*, 1921-1922, p. 7.
112. *ARPU*, 1936-1937, p. 228.
113. Ibid., p. 273.
114. Ibid., p. 274.
115. Ibid., p. 287.
116. Ibid., p. 115.
117. *ARPU*, 1917-1918, pp. 178, 181, 204.
118. *ARPU*, 1917-1918, p. 143.
119. *ARPU*, 1919-1920, p. 40.
120. *ARPU*, 1919-1920, p. 28.
121. *ARPU*, 1936-37, p. 20.
122. Ibid., p. 61.
123. *ARPU*, 1921-1922, p. 4.
124. Ibid., pp. 24-25.
125. Ibid., p. 26.
126. Ibid., p. 27.
127. Ibid., pp. 26-27.

128. The proposal was moved by Sri Narayan Sahai, *ibid.*, p. 31.
129. *ARPU*, 1936-1937, p. 115.
130. Ibid., p. 118.
131. Ibid., p. 118.
132. Ibid., pp. 182-83.
133. Ibid., pp. 136-37.
134. Presidential Speech, *Itihas Parishad*, 24th Hindi Sahitya Sammelan, Indore, 20-23 April 1935; Source, *Veena*, May 1935, pp. 521-23.
135. Ibid.
136. Ibid.
137. *Veena*, May 1935, p. 530.
138. Ibid., p. 561.
139. Ibid., p. 561.
140. For the proposal, see Appendix F.
141. Baijnath Singh 'Vinod', 'Dr. Kashi Prasad Jayaswal', 'Veh din: Ve log, Janmashati Shradhanjal', *Nai Dhara*, 1981, pp.25-28.
142. Vajpeyi, Ambika Prasad, *'Hindi Patrakarita ka Sinhawalokan'*, in *Shri Venkateshwar Samachar Hirak Jayanti 1896-1956*, p. 1.
143. For the entire proceedings of the establishment of the Institute see, *K.P. Jayaswal Research Institute: An Introductory Glimpse*, by Dr Chittaranjan Prasad Sinha, KPJRI, Patna, 1985.

Conclusion

The overall writings and contributions of KPJ show the amazing diversity of a historian's skill crossing over within and beyond the discipline of history, the boundaries of which are not so tightly defined. KPJ made tremendous contributions as a numismatist, epigraphist, historian, linguist, journalist, and institution builder. In several ways he broke new grounds.

Born just four years before the birth of the Indian National Congress in 1885, KPJ lived for a little over half a century. The latter half of his lifetime was indeed marked by the hardening of the divide between the Muslims and the Hindus. The All India Muslim League and the Rashtriya Swayamsevak Sangh (RSS), standing for two different religion-centred nations were established in 1906 and 1925 respectively. The seeds of such a divide had been sown more than a century earlier in James Mill's *History* of British India which periodised the pre-British history of the sub-continent in religion-oriented terms – ancient = 'Hindu' and medieval = 'Muslim'.

How far can we regard KPJ as a 'nationalist' historian? If indeed he was a 'nationalist', what brand of nationalism did he reflect in his action and writings? Barring his initial infatuation for 'revolutionaries' during his stay in England—a legacy that he consciously disowned soon after his arrival in India, KPJ remained characteristically silent on the well-known landmarks of the trajectory of the Indian national movement. The partition of Bengal (1905), the establishment of the Muslim League (1906), Tilak's trial on the charges of sedition (1908), Gandhi's Champaran campaign (1917), the Rowlatt Bill and subsequent Jallianwala Bagh massacre (1919), the Non-Cooperation Movement Resolution (1920), the founding of the RSS (1925), the police assault on Lala Lajpat Rai when he was protesting against the Simon Commission (1928), launching of the Civil Disobedience Movement (1930), the execution of Bhagat Singh, Sukhdev and Rajguru (1931)—none of these seem to have ignited any 'nationalist' spirit in KPJ.

From the overall writings of KPJ, a few things are clearly visible: first, everything in ancient India was 'Hindu'/'Āryan', such as; 'Hindu' polity, 'Hindu' literature, 'Hindu' sculpture, 'Hindu' painting, 'Hindu' science, 'Hindu' language, 'Hindu' script, Sanskrit as the language of Rāma and Kṛṣṇa, and so on. Second, he did not at all move out of the tracks laid down by Western Indology, i.e., the periodisation of Indian history—ancient/Hindu, medieval/Muslim, and modern/British. He, however, differed from the Western Indologists only in his approach to India and tried to establish a distinctive and original character of the Indian civilisation even beyond the domains of religion and philosophy. Third, as far as Indian imperialism in ancient India was concerned, KPJ was trying to do for Southeast Asia and Nepal, what the Western Indologists did in the context of India. His approach to the history to these regions did not really differ much from Vincent Smith's approach to the history of ancient India.[1] Fourth, although KPJ was writing in opposition to colonial interpretation, he had no qualms in borrowing a number of symbols and similarities from the European world. Thus, for him Nalanda was the 'Oxford of Hindu India', and the Khudabaksh Oriental Library of Patna was the 'Bodleian of India'. Similarly, KPJ talks of a number of 'Hindu' heroes and compares them with Bismarck, Cromwell, Napoleon, etc. KPJ's writings on medieval history are almost negligible; only a short note on Chhatrasal and Shivaji and few articles on Mithila are available. He wrote nothing on the 'medieval' ('Muslim') and it generally remained dark for the 'Hindus', the veil of which could be lifted only under the impact of European science and scientific thoughts; KPJ in his journalistic writings and speeches of the *BORS* and at the Oriental Conference praised the British rule for their contributions to scientific and academic progress of India.

In KPJ's personal relations, we did not come across any instance, where he had any personal conflict with any Muslim. Not only that, in some of his early pieces of writing he was quite critical of the Hindu writers and fundamentalists and speaks of Hindu-Muslim equality.[2] On the other hand, we have evidence of his conflict with Mahavir Prasad Dwivedi and Ramachandra

Shukla and others. His discursive texts thus present to us a paradox. It would be more appropriate to say that he could not transcend the temporal and cultural framework laid down by such colonial historians of 'Muslim' India as H.M. Elliott and R. Orme, as well as the Brahmin scholarship prevailing in North India.

It is true that KPJ's understanding, methodology, theoretical framework, and some of the conclusions were criticised by the later generations of historians. However, the important point is: are the writings of KPJ to be dismissed as of no value, and as no substantial permanent contributions? This would be going to the other extreme. The systematic history of ancient Indian republics that he put before the learned world was not only the first in the field but has, to date, formed the main framework of later researchers: both Indian and foreign. The writings of U.N. Ghoshal and A.S. Altekar show their indebtedness to KPJ. His discussion on the constitutional significance of the coronation ceremonies is richly rewarding.

KPJ's writings, specially on polity, certainly gave a rude shock to those scholars and administrators who had assumed the existence of Oriental Despotism in India before the advent of the British rule and British constitutional institutions in the country. He stimulated research work into the political and constitutional fields of ancient Indian history: hitherto only studies in ancient Indian religion, philosophy, and art had received major attention. KPJ's contributions to the dynastic political history also are not negligible. While his main thesis of the existence of the Nāga-Vākaṭaka empire in North India may be rejected, there is no denying the fact that he pieced together stray references in epigraphs, literature and coins and showed, for the first time, the great part the Bhāra-Śivas and other Nāgas played in Indian history before the rise of the Guptas. He certainly succeeded in showing that the period between the extinction of the Kuṣāṇa and the Andhra dynasties and the rise of the imperial Gupta dynasty was not "one of the darkest in the whole range of Indian History", as Smith would have us believe. KPJ was the first Indian scholar who introduced *Mañjūśrī Mūlakalpa* as a book throwing important light on the political history of India, specially between the exit of the Guptas and the early history of the Pālas—a period that was also seen as 'dark' by Smith and his followers.

It is to be admitted that KPJ's writing, in the context of time, could be edifying. The national consciousness and pride about progress in the constitutional field in the past, seldom emphasised by scholars before, certainly served a useful purpose. As a the nationalist movement progressed and as slow steps were being taken in the direction of a more representative government in India, her ancient history was called upon by KPJ to show that she was fitted by her tradition for democracy and self-government.[3] He could even see the strains of federalism of the United States of America in the Yaudheya *gaṇarājya*. In order to prove his thesis, KPJ employed a large range of resources, but used them in the manner of a barrister trying to win a favourable judgment, emphasising every passage which tended to support his case.

KPJ was proud of the national heritage and the versatile genius of the Indian people in the bygone days. He was consistently condemning the foreign rulers of ancient days. Impartial Indian scholars have given some credit to and shown their appreciation of Kuṣāṇa contribution to the development of Indian religions and culture, art and literature, not only in this country but outside as well. To KPJ, however, Kuṣāṇa policy was "a policy of social tyranny and religious fanaticism, both actuated by political motives." He goes further and after indulging in specious arguments, concludes that "Kuṣāṇa rule destroyed them (the pre-Gupta Hindu temples)." He observed: The Śaka rule aimed at denationalising the Hindus. The social revolutions which the Śakas strove for with a calculated policy, was a scheme to depress the high and aristocratic, the custodians of national culture and the trustees of national liberty—the Brahmins and the Kshatriyas." Impartial critics of the Kuṣāṇa rule will not find enough evidence to credit or discredit the Kuṣāṇas with the alleged successful scheme to destroy the *Varṇāśrama Dharma* and Hinduism. Kadphises II and Vasudeva could not be accused of anti-Hinduism. But KPJ's main concern was to show the totally unacceptable character of all foreign rulers and theirs calculated policy to denationalise and enslave the nation. Probably he was transferring the attributes of the British rule in his days, as he saw them, to the Kuṣāṇas. And, as any movement against the British rule and for reassertion of Hindu ideas and cultural norms would be a nationalist movement, he saw in the rise of the Bhāraśiva-Nāgas and the growth of the Vākāṭaka power the fulfilment of national aspirations of the period (A.D. 150 to 350) against the degraded and tyrannical rule of the alien Śaka-Kuṣāṇas. He, therefore, wove a story from scattered slender threads, often of doubtful authenticity, of a national regeneration movement against the foreign rule, and tried to demonstrate the resounding success of the movement.

"The undertaking to deliver the country from such a national calamity was shouldered by Bhāra-Śivas on the Ganges... They undertook to execute and they successfully executed that national dance of destruction in the valley of Ganges", says KPJ. In order to enhance the so-called achievements of the Bhāra-Śivas, the enemy's —the Kuṣāṇa's—power is at first magnified, and then the success of the Bhāraśivas from humble beginnings against such a great power is admirably dramatised, "The greedy imperialism of the Kuṣāṇa was destroyed: the Hindu people were purged of deteriorated morals. And when the task was done the Bhāra-Śivas retired... They restored the Hindu imperial throne and the national civilisation and gave a new life to their country... they left their deeds and obliterated themselves."

In this entire construct of the Bhāraśiva-Vākaṭaka role in overthrowing the Śaka-Kuṣāṇa 'tyranny', the latter are clearly being seen as 'the other' and were also being demonised. This may well be seen as the resurgence of the Brahmanical/Hindu order against the Buddhists/*mlecchas*. Even if one is tempted to locate this episode in the contemporary milieu of India's national struggle against the modern day 'other' (read the British), it may have a very limited appeal—perhaps only for the Hindu nationalists. It is perhaps not a coincidence that KPJ's 'Āryāvarta' also remains confined to the present-day Hindi-heartland.

The limits of KPJ's alleged 'nationalist' bias are also visible in his strong defence of the *Varṇāśrama* system and the ritual-ridden Brahmanical religion. No wonder he gave, much importance to Khāravela than Aśoka, because the Ceṭi king, for him was a defender of the Brahmanical system. Caste of any king or dynasties was not important, if they were defenders of the *varṇāśamadharma*, "Samudragupta becomes a Hindu of Hindus... Candragupta the Kāraskara was the earliest Shivaji of India, or the second early Shivaji, the first being Candragupta Maurya. The powerful *Śudra* protectors of Hindu culture rivalled the race of Rāma and Parikshit in upholding orthodox rites, the cause of Brahmanism, the preservation of the cow, and the support of the sacred Sanskrit."[4] KPJ considered Aśoka as one of the greatest sons of India. However, because of his pro-Buddhist policy and KPJ's affection for the old system, Aśoka is not held in very high esteem by him. KPJ wrote,

> The Dharma is of course the particular Dharma of Aśoka which in the beginning he refrains from preaching in all its details. As a preparatory step in his propaganda of Buddhism, he preaches a set of morals which were common both to the Jains and Buddhists and in fact all dissenting sects and which generally by themselves were not antagonistic to the orthodox national ethics. *But in the last analysis they were destructive of the national religion.*[5]

During the last few decades, in the domain of history-writing, there has been a renewed attempt to exalt KPJ's views, and to impose on the medieval period of Indian history, what has been imposed by KPJ upon the post-Mauryan centuries. If the Śakas and Kuṣāṇas and numerous other 'foreign' rulers were villains in KPJ's paradigm of history, the 'Muslims' of the medieval period have been delineated in similar vein in the writings of the Hindu cultural nationalists. For them, the 'Islamic' millennium (from the seventh to the seventeenth centuries) was as much a 'Dark Age' as were the post-Mauryan centuries for KPJ specially in terms of the destruction of Hindu temples. For us, the construct of a 'Dark Age' of this sort can be no more than a myth. The perceptive observation made by D.D. Kosambi, though made in the context of the 'Golden Age', can be reproduced with a slight change for comprehending a 'Dark Age'—it can be looked for neither in India's past nor, hopefully, in its future.

> In the short span of nearly 40 years of his scholarly activities, KPJ had left us a large volume of original research material. Some may often wonder whether if he had waited a little more to evaluate his sources more critically, he could have bequeathed such varied and pioneering contributions. He was the original spade which removed the first earth from then almost virgin soil, and in this he was naturally a more enthusiastic pioneer than a careful meticulous researcher who waits long to examine his sources by all canons of scholarly criticism. KPJ appears to be in a hurry to place his ideas, some of them very original and exciting, before the learned people. As a clever advocate he was anxious to stress upon the arguments for his brief, and was not acting as a Judge who hears both sides and comes to his conclusions. But he was the first of a generation of historians having great historical responsibility in the colonial atmosphere.

The remarks of the two of KPJ's friends are remarkable in the context. Rajendra Prasad wrote, "It was an enigma how in the midst of his professional activities he found time to study the ancient records on stone and coin, in manuscripts and architecture. Many also wondered whether he loved law or ancient history more. I have no doubt in my mind that he was a historian by choice and interest and a lawyer by compulsion. His own inclinations and talents attracted him towards history but the demands of the flesh dragged him towards law courts and law reports."[6] Similarly, P.C. Manuk, a friend and a colleague at Bar, wrote, "Glancing through numerous obituary notices on Dr. Jayaswal, I found that there was but scanty reference to his professional career. That department of his activities had been submerged by the deservedly copious references to his brilliant achievements in the wider field of scholarly research, in other words to Jayaswal, 'the international', whose reputation had spread from China to Peru as a profound professional scholar of India's ancient languages, history, culture and laws."[7]

KPJ was a busy soul working with energy and drive matched only by the great leaders of the nation engaged in mounting a challenge to the colonial operations of power and knowledge. He was aware of his strengths and weaknesses: that he could be a good researcher, but not a political activist. He avoided any political conflict with the colonial regime; rather he supported it. KPJ was more interested in redefining terms of history-writing than his own practice. Even if he did not quit his practice at the Gandhian call, and even when he was severely ill, he was extremely happy to clad himself in *khadi* to watch the victory procession after Congress decided to form its ministry in Bihar.[8] So he was and remained an intellectual, but his life was that of a 'tapasvi' and 'satyagrahi'. Politics was not his chosen profession, but he was instrumental in launching several initiatives that could challenge the power-knowledge combine that colonialism represented. He sometimes grudged Gandhi the disproportionate attention (i.e. disproportionate to history-writing) he received, but he was his own little Gandhi, supporting small and big efforts at rewriting Indian history in English and Hindi, and popularised history.

Gandhi had once endorsed KPJ's appeal for history of India written by its own historians. Regrettably, however, KPJ's concept of such a venture did not go beyond the 'Hindu period' (from Vedic kings to the time of king Bhoja), which he saw as a period of 'cultural revival'. Juxtapose this to what KPJ called 'the victory of the Muslims and the decline of the Hindus is virtually an indicator of a new era.' Surely, such a history of India would not have satisfied Gandhi's vision of our nation. KPJ's numerous writings analysed here, appear to be focusing on the glories of India's past and crediting these glories to the 'Hindus'. Even if one cannot accuse KPJ of being a mere 'back to the glorious Vedic age' kind of an obscurantist, such an idea of India is, perhaps, closer to the vision of a fragmented nation rooted in its religious identity.

NOTES

1. For a detailed discussion about the Nationalist Historiography, see Chakrabarti, D.K., *Colonial Indology: Sociopolitics of the Ancient Indian Past*, Munshiram Manoharlal, New Delhi, 1997, pp. 207-42.
2. Kashi Prasad Jayaswal, 'Hindi Upanyas Lekhakon ko Ulhana', *Hindi Pradeep*, January 1899, reprinted in Abhishek Raushan, *Balkrishna Bhatt aur AAdhunuk Hindi Aalochana ka Aarambha*, Antika Prakashan, Gaziabad, 2009, pp. 213-15.
3. Basham A.L., 'Modern Historians of Ancient India' in *Studies in Indian History and Culture*, Calcutta, 1964, p. 222.
4. 'Historical Data in the Drama Kaumudī Mahotsava', *Annals of Bhandarkar Oriental Research Institute*, Vol. XII, 1930-1931, p. 56.
5. 'Places and People in Asoka's Inscriptions', *IA*, LXII, July 1933, pp. 81-82.
6. Rajendra Prasad, 'Kashi Prasad Jayaswal' *KPJCV*, p. 44.
7. P.C. Manuk, 'Dr. K.P. Jayaswal -The Barrister and Man–A Character Sketch', *KPJCV*, p. 46.
8. Ramdhari Singh 'Dinkar', 'Punyslok Jayaswalji', *KPJCV*, p. 18.

Bibliography

Writings of KPJ

Monographs

Hindu Polity, Patna, 1924, reprinted (3rd edition), Bangalore Printing and Publishing Co., Bangalore City, 1943.

Manu and Yājñavalkya, Patna, 1929, reprinted, Cosmo Publications, New Delhi, 2004.

History of India (150 A.D. to 350 A.D.), (Nāga-Vākaṭakā Imperial Period), Motilal Banarasi Das, Lahore 1933.

An Imperial History of India (700 B.C. to C. 770 A.D.), Lahore, 1934, reprinted, Eastern Book House, Patna, 1988.

Chronology and History of Nepal (600 B.C. to 880 A.D.), Patna, 1937, reprinted Bharati Prakashan, Varaṇasi, 1976

Edited Works

Rājanīti-Ratnākara of Chaṇḍeśvara, *JBORS*, Vol. X (IV), December 1924, Appendix, reprint, XXII (IV), December 1936, pp. 1-77.

Bhaṭṭa-Svāmin's *Commentary on Kauṭilya's Arthaśāstra*, (in six parts with A.P. Banerji-Sastri), (i) *JBORS*, XI (I) Appendix, March 1925, pp.1-24, (ii) XI (II), Appendix, June 1925, pp. 25-54, (iii) XI (III-IV), Appendix, September-December 1925, pp. 55-92, (iv) XII (I), Appendix, March 1926, pp. 93-130, (v) XII (II), Appendix, June 1926, pp. 131-68, (vi) Appendix, XII (III), September 1926, pp. 169-214.

Descriptive Catalogue of Manuscripts in Mithila, Vol. I., Smṛiti Manuscripts, (With A. Banerjee Sastri), *BORS*, Patna, 1927.

Descriptive Catalogue of Manuscripts in Mithila, Vol. II Literature, Prosody, *BORS*, Patna, 1933.

The Text of the Mañjūśrī Mūlakalpa (with Rahul Sankrityayan), published as Appendix to *the Imperial History of India*, pp. 1-75.

Adhyarddhaśataka of Mātṛceṭā, (with Rahul Sankrityayan), *JBORS*, Appendix, Vol. XXIII (IV), December 1937, Appendix, pp. i-vii, & 1-14.

Vigrahavyāvarttanī of Āchārya Nāgārjuna (with Rahul Sankrityayan), *JBORS*, Vol. XXIII (IV), December 1937, Appendix, pp. i-xi, 1-29, Appendix I, i-vii.

Translated Work

Lassen's History of Indian Commerce (Vikramāditya to Later Guptas), with A.P. Banerjee Shastri,), *JBORS*, X (III), September 1924, pp. 227-316.

Articles

Journal of the Bihar and Orissa Research Society

'Śaiśunāka and Maurya Chronology and the Date of Buddha's Nirvana', I (I), September 1915, pp. 67- 116.
'Republics in the Mahābhārata', I (II) December 1915, pp. 173-78.
'The Empire of Bindusara', II (I), March 1916, pp. 79- 83.
'Chronological Summary in the Puranic Chronicles and the Kali-Yuga Era', III (II), June 1917, pp. 246-62.
'Hathigumpha Inscription of the Emperor Khāravela (173 B.C.-160 B.C.)', III (IV), December 1917, pp. 425-72.
'Further Note on Hathigumpha Inscription', III (IV), December 1917, pp. 473- 507.
'The Bṛihadrath Chronology', IV (I), March 1918, pp. 26- 35.
'The Terms "Anusamyana", "Rājuka" and "Former Kings" in Aśoka's Inscription', IV (I), March 1918, pp. 36- 43.
'A Note on Hathigumpha Inscription (Elephant Ships)', IV (I), March 1918, pp. 96-98.
'Aśoka's Inscription II', IV (II), June 1918, pp. 144-47.
'Revised Notes on the Brahmin Empire', IV (III), September 1918, pp. 257-65.
'Importance of the Janibigha Inscription of the Year 83 of the Lakshmaṇa-Sena Era', IV (III), September 1918, pp. 266-72.
'Hathigumpha Inscription Revised from the Rock (with plates)', IV (IV), December 1918, pp. 364- 404.
'Statues of two Śaiśunāka Emperors (483-409 B.C.)', V (I), March 1919, pp. 88-106.
'Copper-Plates in Bhubneshwar Temple', V (II), June 1919, pp. 298-99.
'Chastana's Statue and the Date of Kanishka', V (IV), December 1919, p. 511
'Śaiśunāka Statue', V (IV), December 1919, pp. 512-49.
'Another Śaiśunāka Statue, (515 B.C.)', V (IV), December 1919, pp. 550-51.
'The Statue of Wema Kadphises and Kuṣāṇ Chronology', VI (I), March 1920, pp. 12-22.
'The Statue of Ajātaśatru-Kuṇika and a Discussion on the Origin of Brāhmi', VI (II), June 1920, pp. 173- 204.
'A Judgment of a Hindu Court in Sanskrit', VI (II), June 1920, pp. 246-58.

'The Unexplained Passage', VII (II-III)', June-September 1921, pp. 123-24.

'A Hindu Text on Painting', IX (I), March 1923, pp. 30-39.

'Contributions to the History of Mithila (King Nanya Deva of Mithila and an Inscription of His time)', IX (III-IV), September-December 1923, pp. 300-10.

'Contributions to the History of Mithila', X (I-II), March-June 1924, pp. 37-46.

'Hridaya Narayana of Mithila', X (I-II), March-June 1924, pp. 47-48.

'Brāhmi Seals Newly Discovered at Patna', X (III), September 1924, pp. 189-93.

'An Inscription of the Śuṅga Dynasty (with plate)', X (III), September 1924 pp. 202-08.

'The Rājanīti-Ratnākara by Chaṇḍeśvara', X (IV)' Appendix-a-i-1, December 1924.

'New light on Hindu Political Science Literature', XI (I), March 1925, pp. 66-70.

'Hathigumpha Inscription of the Emperor Khāravela (Correction)', XIII (III-IV), September-December 1927, pp. 221-46.

'The Śuṅga Inscription of Ayodhya', XIII (III-IV), September-December 1927, pp. 247-49.

'Search for Sanskrit and Prakrit MSS. in Bihar and Orissa', XIII (III-IV), September-December 1927, pp. i-xv.

'Revised Notes on the Brahmin Empire', XIV (I), March 1928, pp. 24-27.

'A Deed of Acquittance in Sanskrit', XIV (I), March 1928, pp. 63-64.

'Demetrios, Khāravela and the *Garga-Saṁhitā*', XIV (I), March 1928, pp. 127-28.

'Hathigumpha Notes', XIV (I), March 1928, pp. 150-51.

'Date of Vardhamāna', XIV (II), June 1928, p. 311.

'Historical Data in the *Garga-Saṁhitā* and the Brahmin Empire', XIV (III, September 1928, pp. 397-421.

'The Paris Manuscript of the *Garga-Saṁhitā*', XV (I-II), March-June 1929, pp. 129-33.

'On the Rule of Puṣyamitra Śuṅga', XV (III-IV), September-December 1929, pp. 583-84.

'An Important Brāhmi Inscription, Barli Stone (with plate)', XVI (I), March 1930, pp. 67-68.

'Problem of Śaka-Sātavāhana History', XVI (III-IV), September-December 1930, pp. 227-316.

'Purana Coin and the Date of the Mānava-Dharmaśāstra', XVII (IV), December 1931, p. 398.

'Kumārāmātya', XVII (IV), December 1931, p. 399.

'The Exact Data in the Reign of Aśoka', XVII (IV), December 1931, p. 400.

'Girdharpur Pillar Inscription', XVIII (I), March 1932, pp. 4-7.

'Śaka-Sātavāhana Problem', XVIII (I), March 1932, pp. 7-16.

'Chandra Gupta II (Vikramāditya) and his Predecessor', XVIII (I), March 1932, pp. 17-36.
'The Book on Political Science by 'Śikhara', Prime Minister of Chandra Gupta II', XVIII (I), March 1932, pp. 37-39.
'Chandra Gupta Maurya as 'Vir Varshal', XVIII (I), March 1932, p. 79.
'A Note on Certain Sanskrit Geographical and Ethnic Terms', XVIII (I), March 1932, pp. 97-98.
'The Yaunus of Purāṇas and the last Kuṣāṇa Emperor in India', XVIII (II), June 1932, pp. 201-06.
'A Passage in Samundra Gupta's Inscription at Allahabad and Gupta Coinage', XVIII (II), June 1932, pp. 207-11.
'The Kākās – their Location', XVIII (II), June 1932, pp. 212-13.
'A Note on 'Tikin' and 'Khasa' XVIII (II), June 1932, p. 225.
'Danta', a Weapon, XVIII (III-IV), September-December 1932, p. 391.
'History of India (c. 150 A.D. - 350 A.D. Nāga-Vākāṭaka Imperial Period)', XIX (I-II), March-June 1933, pp. 1-222.
'Appendix to the History of India, 150 A.D. to 350 A.D.', XIX (III), September 1933, pp. 289-318.
'Some Unpublished Seals', XX (I), March 1934, pp. 1-6.
'Six Unique Silver Coins of the Śuṅgas', XX (I), March 1934, pp. 7-9.
'Kandahā Inscription of King Narasimhadeva of Mithila (Oinwar Dynasty dated S. 1357)', XX (I), March 1934, pp. 15-19.
'Dating in Lakshmaṇa-sena Era', XX (I), March 1934, pp. 20-23.
'Early Signed Coins on India', XX (III-IV), September-December 1934, pp. 279-308.
'Early Signed Coins of India (Additions and Corrections)', XXI (III), September 1935, pp. 191-93.
'On Some Hindu Coins of Pre-Christian Centuries (With plates)', XXII (II), June 1936, p. 59.
'New Coins of Nāga-Vākāṭaka Period', XXII (II), June 1936, pp. 70-78.
'Rājgir (Maniar Math) Stone Image Inscription (with plate)', XXII (II), pp. 79-80, June 1936, pp. 79-80.
'An Unrecorded Muhammadan Invasion of Nepal (with Appendix)', XXII (II), June 1936, pp. 81-95.
'Nepal Chronicles on the Caste of the Guptas', XXII (II), June 1936, pp. 108-10.
'Chronology and History of Nepal (600 B.C. to 880 A.D.)', XXII (III), June 1936, p. 161.
'The Rājanīti-Ratnākara by Chaṇḍeśvara', XXII (IV), Appendix, December 1936, pp. 1-77.
'Branding Seals of the Second Century A.D. (with plates)', XXIII (I), March 1937, pp. 128-29.
'Jaina Image of Maurya Period', XXIII (I), March 1937, pp. 130-32.

'Numismatic Notes on Some Hindu Coins of Pre-Christian Centuries', XXIII (I), March 1937, pp. 148-49.

Indian Antiquary

'The Harappa Seals', XLII, July 1913, p. 203
'The Rock Edicts VI of Aśoka', XLII, November 1913, pp. 282-84.
'The Date of the Mūdrā-Rākshasa and the Identification of Malayaketu', XLII, October 1913, pp. 265-67.
'On the Origin of the Nārada-Smṛiti', XLII, December 1913, p. 306.
'Ethnic Origin of Tāmralipti', XLIII, April 1914, p. 64.
'Kauṭilya and the Arattas', XLIII, June 1914, p. 124.
'The Historical Position of Kalki and his Identification with Yaśodharman', XLVI, July 1917, pp. 145-53.
'Bandhu-bhṛitya of the Mūdrā-Rākshasa', XLVI, November 1917, p. 275.
'The Arthaśāstra Explains', XLVII, February 1918, pp. 50-56
'Vaishnava Worship and Buddhism', XLVII, March 1918, p. 84.
'The Week-days and Vikrama', XLVII, April 1918, p. 112.
'Date of Pāṇini and Kātyāyana', XLVII, May 1918, p. 138.
'Notes on Aśoka Inscriptions: The term Ashasu in Rock Edict XIII', XLVII, December 1918, p. 297.
'Identification of Some of the Post Andhrabhṛitya Rulers of the Puranic List', XLVII, December 1918, pp. 298-99.
'Śaka-Pārthiva', XLVIII, January 1919, p. 12.
'The Jogimara Cave Inscription', XLVIII, p. 131, July 1919, p. 131.
'A Seal of a Janapada', LVIII, July 1929, pp. 139-40.
'Evidence of an Aśokan Pillar at Bhuvanesvar in Orissa', LVIII, November 1929, pp. 218-19.
'Airkina and Sānchi', LXI, August 1932, pp. 159-60.
'The Vikramkhol Inscription', LXII, March 1933, pp. 58-60.
'Some Notes on Names in Hindu Geography', LXII, June 1933, p. 119.
'Places and People in Aśoka's Inscriptions', LXII, July 1933, pp. 121-33.
'Proclamation of Aśoka as a Buddhist and his Jambudvipa', LXII, September 1933, p. 167.

The Modern Review

'The Man in Turkey', Vol. X, August 1911, pp. 139-41.
'The Man in Turkey', Vol. X, October 1911, pp. 386-92.
'Ritual at Hindu Coronation: Their Constitutional Aspects', Vol. XI, January 1912, pp. 97-106.
'A Note on the Black Antelope and the Āryāvarta', Vol. XIII, March 1913, pp. 329-30.
'An Introduction to Hindu Polity', Vol. XIII, May 1913, pp. 535-41.
'An Introduction to Hindu Polity', Vol. XIII, June 1913, pp. 664-68.

'An Introduction to Hindu Polity', Vol. XIV, July 1913, pp. 77-83.
'An Introduction to Hindu Polity', Vol. XIV, August 1913, pp. 201-06.
'An Introduction to Hindu Polity', Vol. XIV, September 1913, pp. 288-91.
'Vikramāditya and Nahapana', Vol. XIV, December 1913, pp. 622-23.
'The Vikrama Era', Vol. XV, January 1914, pp. 98-99.
'Proclamation of Aśoka: With a Revised Translation', Vol. XVII, January 1915, pp. 75-85.
'The Discovery of the Source of the Nile by Ancient Hindus', Vol. XVII, April 1915, pp. 515-17.
'Political Cipher-Writing in Hindu India', Vol. XXII, December 1917, pp. 662-63.
'The Hindu Parliament under Hindu Monarchy', Vol. XXVII, February 1920, pp. 121-39.
'The Hindu Parliament: Paura and Janapada', Vol. XXVII, April 1920, pp. 466-68.
'University Examiners and Examinees related to them', Vol. XXX, October 1921, pp. 453-55.
'An Ancient Statue at Muttra', Vol. XXX, November 1921, pp. 611-14.
'Hindu Culture in Mesopotamia', Vol. XXX, December 1921, pp. 682-84.
'A Hindu Text on Painting', Vol. XXXIII, June 1923, pp. 732-35.
'An Inscription of Śuṅga Dynasty', Vol. XXXVI, October 1924, pp. 430-32.
'The Beginning of Old Hindi', Vol. XLII, July-Dec, 1927, pp. 270-72.
'Sanskrit Revival and King Bhoja's Art Criticism of Lyrical Poetry', XLIII, June 1928, p. 722.
'Origin of the Imperial Guptas', Vol. XLVI, November 1929, pp. 499-501.
'A Sandstone Head of the Gupta Period', Vol. XLVII, January 1930, pp. 26-27.
'Puran Singh the Sikh Poet (1881-1931)', Vol. L, August 1931, pp. 175-78.
'King Chhatrasal Champion of Hindu Independence, and Queen Kamalavati, the Devoted Wife', Vol. LI, May 1932, pp. 545-48.
'The Udaypur Temple of Malawa and its Builder', Vol. LI, June 1932, pp. 603-06.
'A Note on a Terracotta Ramayana Panel of Gupta Period, and on Shikhara Temples', Vol. LII, August 1932, pp. 148-50.
'King Udayāditya', Vol. LII, August 1932, pp. 171-78.
'Re-founders of the Imperial Hindu Throne', Vol. LII, November 1932, pp. 546-51.
'Buddha's Hermitage', Vol. LIII, February 1933, pp. 179-81.
'Neglect of Monuments', Vol. LIII, April 1933, pp. 385-91.
'Mahasthan (Bogra) Mauryan Inscription', Vol. LIII, May 1933, pp. 508-09.
'Mauryan Rocks-cut Hermitage at Barabar', Vol. LIII, May 1933, p. 705.
'Śiva Busts at Nachana (Ajaigarh State, C. I) Circa 320-350 A. D.', Vol. LIV, July 1933, p. 68.

'An Imperial History of India (600 B. C. to 770 A. D.)', Vol. LIV, August 1933, pp. 136-141.
'Hindu Scientist of Earthquake', Vol. LV, March 1934, pp. 310-11.
'A Coin of Daśarath Maurya', Vol. LV, May 1934, p. 516.
'Coins of Samprati Maurya', Vol. LV, May 1934, p. 647.
'Dr. Hiralal', Vol. LVI, July-December 1934, p. 319.
'Great Resolution', Vol. LXI, January 1937, p. 16.
'Lost Sanskrit Works Recovered from Tibet', Vo. LXI, February 1937, pp. 159-64.
'Self-Assertion of the Masses Inevitable', Vol. LXI, April 1937, pp. 387-88.
'Statues of Indian Scholars in Tibet', Vol. LXI, pp. 401-402, April 1937, pp. 401-02.
'The Discoverer', Vol. 61, 1937.

Epigraphia Indica

'The Ghosundi Stone Inscription', Vol. XVI, 1921-1922, pp. 25-27
'The Hathigumpha Inscription of Khāravela', Vol. XX, 1929-1930, pp. 71-89 (This article was written in association with R.D. Banerji).
'The Text of the Sohagaura Plate', Vol. XXII, 1933-1934, pp. 1-3.
'Shell Character Rock Inscription at Ci-Aruton (Java)', Vol. XXII, 1933-1934, pp. 4-5.

Journal of the Royal Asiatic Society of Great Britain and Ireland

'Some Coins of the Mauryas and Śuṅgas', No. 4, Oct., 1935, pp. 788-96.
'The Punch-Marked Coins: A Survival of the Indus Civilization', (14 June 1935).
'Mauryan Symbol', 1936.

Annals of Bhandarkar Oriental Research Institute

'Historical Data in the Drama Kaumudṣ Mahotsava', Vol. XII, 1930-1931, pp. 50-56.

Journal of the Indian Society of Oriental Art

'Nāgara and Vesara', Vol. I, no. 1, pp. 57-58, June 1933, pp. 57-58.
'Pataliputra Śiva-Pārvati Gold Plaque', Vol. II, 1934, p. 1.
'Metal Images of Kurkihar Monastery', Vol. II, 1934, pp. 70-82.
'Terracotta Dug Out at Patna', Vol. III, no. 2, December 1935, pp. 125-26.
'An Early Ivory', Vol. IV, no. 2, June 1936, pp. 75-82.

The Jaina Antiquary

'Oldest Jaina Images Discovered', Vol. III, 1937, pp. 17-18. (This article was originally published in *The Searchlight* on 20 February 1937.

Speeches

A Voussoir From Patna, *Proceeding and Transactions of the Second All India Oriental Conference*, Arch Stone, 1922, pp. 271-74.

Welcome Address, As President of the Reception Committee of the Sixth All India Oriental Conference, Patna, December 1930, *Proceedings and Transactions of the Sixth All India Oriental Conference*, Patna, 1933, pp. xxvi-xxxiii.

Presidential Address, Seventh All India Oriental Conference, December 1933, *Proceedings and Transactions of the Seventh All India Oriental Conference*, Oriental Institute, Baroda, 1935, pp. lix-lxxxii.

Presidential Address, XXV Session of the Numismatic Society of India, Mysore, 30 December 1935, Gupta, P.L., *Sixty Years of the Numismatic Society of India (1910-1971)*, History and Presidential Addresses, published on the occasion of the Diamond Jubilee, 1973, pp. 128-42.

Presidential Address, XXVI Session of the Numismatic Society of India, Udaipur, 13 November 1936, Gupta, P.L., *Sixty Years of the Numismatic Society of India (1910-1971)*, History and Presidential Addresses, published on the occasion of the Diamond Jubilee, 1973, pp. 143-48.

काशी प्रसाद जायसवाल के हिंदी लेखन एवं भाषण

हिंदीप्रदीप

'काशी नागरी प्रचारिणी सभा के प्रश्नों के उत्तर', जिल्द 21, सं. 5-6, जन.-फेब, 1898, पृ. 10-15।

'हिन्दी-उपन्यास लेखकों को उलहना', जनवरी, 1899।

'लंका और सिंहल', जिल्द, 23, सं 4-6, अप्रैल-जून, 1900, पृ. 26-30।

'वायु' और 'अग्नि' स्त्रीलिंग क्यों है?', जिल्द 25, संख्या 5-8, मई-अगस्त, 1903, पृ. 30-33।

सरस्वती

'भारत वर्ष की पुरानी इमारतें', भाग 3, सं. 3, मार्च 1900।

'स्वर्ण', भाग 4, सं. 6, जून 1903, पृ. 198-199।

'कवि-कीर्ति', भाग 4, सं. 2-3, फरवरी-मार्च 1903, पृ. 51-52।

'भाषा का महत्व', भाग 4, सं. 6, जून 1903, पृ. 209-211।

'उपन्यासकार और उनकी कृति', भाग 4, 1903, पृ. 440।

'जल-वर्षक वृक्ष', भाग 5, सं. 2, फरवरी 1904, पृ. 386-389।

'पंडितवर डॉ. एफ. रुडोल्फ़हॉर्नली', सी.आई.ई., भाग 4, सं. 10, अक्टूबर 1903, पृ. 337-45।

'मार कर लौट आने वाला अस्त्र', भाग 4, सं. 11, नवंबर 1903, पृ. 386-89।

'पठानी सिक्कों पर नागरी', भाग 5, सं. 11, नवंबर 1904, पृ. 380-85।

'बुधवर मिस्टर एफ़.एस.ग्राउस', सी.आई.ई., भाग 7, सं. 1, जनवरी 1906, पृ. 5-10।

'शेक्सपियर', भाग 8, सं. 2, फरवरी 1907, पृ. 70–71।
'श्रीयुत महेशचरण सिंह, बी.ए., एम.एस. (मास्टर ऑफ साइंस)', भाग 8, सं. 3, मार्च 1907, पृ. 119–22।
'परलोक-वासी मिस्टर जॉन बीम्स', भाग 8, सं. 4, अप्रैल 1907, पृ. 134–37।
'इंगलिस्तान क़ा बंक' (बैंक ऑफ इंग्लैंड), भाग 8, सं. 5, मई 1907, पृ. 202–05।
'लन्दन का क्यू नामक शाही बाग', भाग 8, सं. 7, जुलाई 1907, पृ. 287–89।
'चीन जापान में संस्कृत ग्रन्थ', भाग 8, सं. 10, अक्टूबर 1907, reprint अक्टूबर 1963, पृ. 372–76।
'इंग्लैंड की जातीय चित्रशाला', भाग 8, सं. 12, दिसम्बर 1907, पृ. 496–99।
'हमारा संवत और उसकी रक्षा', भाग 9, सं. 3, 135–137, मार्च 1908, पृ. 135–37।
'इंग्लैंड के देहात में महाराजा बनारस का कुआँ', भाग 9, सं. 7, जुलाई 1908, पृ. 299–302।
'योरोप और हमारे विचार', भाग 11, सं. 11, नवंबर 1910, पृ. 483–84।
'योरोप और हमारे विचार', भाग 12, सं. 1, जनवरी 1911, पृ. 36–37।
'मेरी यात्रा : हंगरी से तुर्क देश', भाग 13, सं. 1, जनवरी 1912, पृ. 1–5।
'मेरी यात्रा : हंगरी से तुर्क देश', भाग 13, सं. 3, मार्च 1912, पृ. 121–25।
'मेरी यात्रा : तुर्की – कुस्तुन्तुनिया की राह', भाग 13, सं. 5, मई 1912, पृ. 233–36।
'मेरी यात्रा : तुक्र राजधानी कांस्तान्तिनोपोल', भाग 13, सं. 7, जुलाई 1912, पृ. 345–55।

नागरी प्रचारिणी पत्रिका

'कौशाम्बी', 1900, पृ. 75–95।
'बुनेर के प्राचीन स्थानों का अनुसंधान', 1901, पृ. 150–68।
'पुरानी हिंदी का जन्मकाल', भाग 8, 1927, पृ. 219–27।
'कलिंग चक्रवर्ती महाराज खारवेल के शिलालेख का विवरण', भाग 8, 1927, पृ. 301–22।
'श्री खारवेल प्रशस्ति और जैन धर्म की प्राचीनता', भाग 10, 1929, पृ. 499–502।
'ज्योतिष ग्रन्थ गर्ग-संहिता में भारतीय इतिहास', भाग 10, 1929, पृ. 1–14।
'भारशिव राजवंश', भाग 13, पृ. 1–6, 1932, पृ. 1–6।
'प्रस्ताविक', हरिऔध अभिनन्दन ग्रन्थ, नागरी-प्रचारिणी सभा, आरा, 1936।

कविताएँ

'नर और नारायण'
'तथ्य गीता'
'अग्निगिरी का बेढब उलहना'
'देवों का भारत गीत'

काशी प्रसाद जायसवाल के भाषण

अध्यक्षीय भाषण, अखिल भारतीय हैहेय क्षत्रिय महासभा, जबलपुर, 1927.
अध्यक्षीय भाषण, प्रांतीय हिंदी साहित्य सम्मलेन भागलपुर, 21.10.1933, (देखें, बिहार की साहित्यिक प्रगति, बिहार-हिन्दी साहित्य-सम्मलेन, पटना, 1956, पृ. 245–56)।

अध्यक्षीय भाषण, इतिहास परिषद, अखिल भारतीय हिंदी साहित्य सम्मलेन, इंदौर, 20-23 अप्रैल, 1935, (देखें, वीणा, मई 1935, पृ. 521-23)।

पाटलिपुत्र में काशी प्रसाद जायसवाल के सम्पादकीय लेख

'हमारा परिचय', 27.6.1914, पृ. 3।
'रथयात्रा', 4.7.1914, पृ. 3।
'लार्ड हार्डिंग', 11.7.1914।
'लेडी हार्डिंग', 18.7.1914, पृ. 3।
'चांदी का वर्त्तमान सिक्का', 25.7.1914, पृ. 3।
'स्वर्गीय पण्डित बाल कृष्ण भट्ट', 1.8.1914, पृ. 3।
'युद्ध और हमारा कर्त्तव्य', 8.8.1914, पृ. 3।
'हमारा उत्साह', 15.8.1914, पृ. 3।
'युद्ध में भारत', 22.8.1914, पृ. 3।
'युद्ध में हमारा योग', 29.8.1914, पृ. 3।
'युद्ध को भारतीय युद्ध समझना चाहिए', 5.9.1914, पृ. 3।
'लम्बी युद्ध की तैयारी', 12.9.1914, पृ. 3।
'शत्रुओं की पराजय', 19 9.1914, पृ. 3।
'विजयदशमी', 26.9.1914, पृ. 3।
'फ्रांस में भारतीय सेना', 10.10.1914, पृ. 3।
'गाथा सत्तसई', 17.10.1914, पृ. 3।
'जर्मन जल-सेना', 24.10.1914, पृ. 3।
'न्यूट्रलाइज़्ड स्टेट्स अथवा उदासीन बनाए हुए राज्य', 31.10.1914, पृ. 3।
'अशोक की धर्म-लिपि', 7.11.1914, पृ. 3।
'रूम की भूल', 14.11.1914, पृ. 3।
'भारत में वीर पूजा', 21.11.1914, पृ. 3।
'स्विट्ज़रलैंड की स्थिति', 28.11.1914, पृ. 3।
'अरब के इस्लामी तीर्थ', 5.12.1914, पृ. 3।
'अशोक और भारतवर्ष', 12.12.1914, पृ. 3।
'गुरु गोविन्द सिंह की वर्षगांठ', 19.12.1914, पृ. 3।
'जातियों का गिरना और उठना', 26.12.1914, पृ. 3।
'कांग्रेस', 2.1.1915, पृ. 3।
'इंगलैंड और युद्ध', 9.1.1915, पृ. 3।
'मैथिल भाषा', 16.1.1915, पृ. 3।
'बिहार में 'कौंसिल' सभा', 23.1.1915, पृ. 3।
'देवोत्तर जायदाद', 30.1.1915, पृ. 3।
'भारत में महंगी', 13.2.1915, पृ. 3।

'कैथी या नागरी', 20.2.1915, पृ. 3।
'स्वर्गीय गोखले', 27.2.1915, पृ. 3।
'डारडनेल्स', 13.3.1915, पृ. 3।
'हमारा संवत', 20.3.1915, पृ. 3।
'हिन्दू विश्वविद्यालय', 27.3.1915, पृ. 3।
'महाकवि भास के नाटक', 3.4.1915, पृ. 3।
'प्रांतीय कौंसिल', 10.4.1915, पृ. 1।
'शिल्प शिक्षा की ज़रूरत', 24.4.1915, पृ. 3।

Unpublished Letters of KPJ (Bharat Kala Bhawan, Varanasi)

Book Reviews by KPJ

A.V. Ramanathan, *Administration of Criminal Justice in Ancient India*, *MR*, Vol. XIX, January-June 1916, p. 227.

D.B. Spooner, *The Zoroastrian Period of Indian History*, *JBORS*, Vol. II, Part I, March 1917, pp.97-104.

Rao Bahadur R. Narasimhachar's *Architecture and Sculpture in Mysore*, *IA*, Vol. XLVI, October 1917, p. 248.

Vijanpti Triveni, A Jaina Epistle, *IA*, XLVI, November 1917, p. 276.

Harabilas Sarda, *Maharana Sanga, The Hindupat* (Published by Scottish Mission Industries Company Limited, Ajmer, 1918), *MR*, Vol. XXIV, July-December 1918, pp.155-57.

S. Krishnaswami Aiyangar, *The Beginnings of South Indian History*, University of Madras, Madras 1932, *JBORS*, Vol. V.

Franklin Edgerton, *The Panchtantra Reconstructed* (two volumes), American Oriental Society, *JBORS*, Vol. XI, Part II, June 1924, p. 192.

Haraprasad Sastri (ed.) *Kirttilata by Vidyapati*, Oriental Press, Calcutta, 1331, Bengali year, *JBORS*, Vol. XIII, Parts III-IV, September-December 1927, pp. 296-300.

Rai Bahadur Hira Lal, *Catalogue of Sanskrit and Prakrit Manuscripts in the Central Provinces and Berar*, Nagpur 1926, *JBORS*, Vol. XIII, Parts III-IV, September-December 1927, pp.301-03.

P.L. Vaidya (ed.), *Jasahara-chariu*, Karanja Jain Publication Society, 1931, (Karanja Jain Sereis, No. 1), *JBORS*, Vol. XVII, Part IV, December 1931, p. 461.

P.P.S. Shastri (ed.), *The Mahābhārata - Southern Recension*, Madras 1931, *JBORS*, Vol. XVIII, Part I, March 1932, p. 99.

Jayachandra Vidyalankar, *Bharata-Bhumi aur Usake Nivasi* (Indian and her Inhabitants) with an introduction by Rai Bahadur Hira Lal, Punjab, *JBORS*, Vol. XVIII, Part I, March 1932, pp. 99-100.

R.D. Banerji, *History of Orissa: From the Earliest Times to the British Period*, Calcutta, 1930, *JBORS*, Vol. XVIII, Part I, March 1932, pp. 101-03.

Pandit Ramanaresh Tripathi (ed.), *Ghagh aur Bhaddari*, *JBORS*, Vol. XVIII, Part III, September 1932, p. 393.

Ganganath Jha, *Kavi-Rahasya*, *JBORS*, Vol. XVIII, Part III, September 1932, p. 393.

Syed Sulaiman Nadbi, *Arab aur Bharat ke Sambandh* (Intercourse between Arabia and India), *JBORS*, Vol. XVIII, Pt. III, September 1932, pp. 393-94.

Mr. A.A. Yusuf Ali, *Social and Economic Conditions of Medieval India* (in Hindi, 81 pages), published by Tara Chand, Secretary to the Academy, *JBORS*, Vol. XVIII, Part III, September 1932. p. 394.

MM. Gauri Shankar Ojha, *Madhya-kalin Bharatiya Samskriti*, *JBORS*, Vol. XVIII, Pt. III, September 1932, p. 394.

Prathiraja Rathaur, *Veli-Krisana-Rukamani-ri*, *JBORS*, Vol. XVIII, Part III, September 1932. p. 393-94.

Kanhaiya lal H. Vakil, *Rock-cut Temples around Bombay*, Taraporevala Sons & Co., Bombay, *JBORS*, Vol. XVIII, Part III, September 1932. p. 395.

Annual Bibliography of Indian Archaeology for the Year 1930, published with the aid of the Government of Netherlands and with the support of the Imperial Government of India, Kern Institute, Leyden, 1932, *JBORS*, Vol. XVIII, Part III, September 1932, p. 395-96.

V.S. Sukhthankar (ed.), *The Mahabharta Text*, Bhandarkar Oriental Research Institute, Poona, *JBORS*, Vol. XVIII, Pt. III, September 1932, p. 396.

B.D. Basu, *Rise of Christian Power in India*, 2nd edition, by the late published by Mr. R. Chatterji, Calcutta, 1931, *JBORS*, Vol. XVIII, Part III, September 1932. p. 396-97.

Chimanlal J. Shah, *Jainism in North India, 800 B.C. to A.D. 520*, Longmans, Green & Co., 1932, *JBORS*, Vol. XVIII, Part III, September 1932. p. 397.

Rev. H. Heras, *The Pallava Genealogy*, Indian Historical Research Institute, Bombay, 1931, *JBORS*, Vol. XVIII, Part III, September 1932. p. 398-99.

Hiralal Jain (ed.), *Savaya-dhamma-doha*, Berar, 1932, *JBORS*, Vol. XIX, Part III, September 1933, p. 345.

Hiralal Jain (ed.), *Naya-Kumara-Cariu*, Berar, 1932, *JBORS*, Vol. XIX, Part III, September 1933, p. 345-46.

C. Kunhan Raja (ed.), *The Rigvedanukramani of Madhavabhatta*, Madras, 1932, *JBORS*, Vol. XIX, Part III, September 1933, p. 346.

Robert Sewell, *The Historical Inscriptions of Southern India (collected till 1923) and Outlines of Political History*, Madras, 1932, *JBORS*, Vol. XIX, Part III, September 1933, p. 346.

Rao Bahadur S.K. Aiyangar, *Hindu Administrative Institutions in Southern India*, *JBORS*, Vol. XIX, Part III, September 1933, p. 346-47.

V.R. Ramachandra Dikshitar, *The Mauryan Polity*, Madras.

K.N. Sivaraja Pillai, *The Chronology of the Early Tamils*, 1932, *JBORS*, Vol. XIX, Part III, September 1933, p. 347.

Niharranjan Ray, *Brahmanical Gods in Berma*, Calcutta, 1932, *JBORS*, Vol. XIX, Part III, September 1933, pp. 347-48.

H.C. Raychaudhuri, *Studies in Indian Antiquities*, Calcutta, 1932, *JBORS*, Vol. XIX, Part III, September 1933, p. 348.

A.C. Woolner and Lakshman Sarup (tr.), *Trivandrum Plays of Bhāsa*, University of Punjab, 1930, *JBORS*, Vol. XIX, Part III, September 1933, p. 348.

V.S. Sukthankar and Shaikh Abdul Kadir (ed.), *Journal of the Bombay Branch of the Royal Asiatic Society*, April 1927, *JBORS*, Vol. XI, Part II, June 1925, pp. 196-97.

George M. Moraes, *The Kadamba Kula: A History of Ancient and Medieval Karnataka*, Bombay, 1931, *JBORS*, Vol. XVII, Part IV, December 1931, pp. 462-63.

Binoytosh Bhattacharya, *An Introduction to Buddhist Esoterism*, Oxford University Press, 1932, *JBORS*, Vol. XIX, Part III, September 1933, pp. 348-49.

MM. S. Kuppuswami Sastri, *A Primer of Indian Logic*, P. Varadachari & Co., Madras, 1932, *JBORS*, Vol. XIX, Part III, September 1933, pp. 349-50.

T.V. Ramachandra Dikshitar (ed.), *Vibhramaviveka of Mandana Misra*, Journal of Oriental Research, Madras 1932, *JBORS*, Vol. XIX, Part III, September 1933, p. 350.

J.C. Chatterji, *India's Outlook on Life*, Kailasa Press, New York City, 1931, *JBORS*, Vol. XIX, Part III, September 1933, p. 350.

Rai Bahadur Hira Lal, *Inscriptions in the Central Provinces and Berar*, Second Edition, a publication of the Central Provinces Government, *JBORS*, Vol. XIX, Part III, September 1933, pp. 350-51.

Nirmal Kumar Bose, *Canons of Orissan Architecture*, Calcutta, 1932, *JBORS*, Vol. XIX, Part III, September 1933, p. 351.

W. Norman Brown, *The Story of Kalaka*, Washington, 1933, *JBORS*, Vol. XIX, Part IV, December 1933, pp. 413-15.

P.V. Kane, *Katyayana-Smṛiti-Saroddhara*, Bombay, 1933, *JBORS*, Vol. XIX, Part IV, December 1933, p. 415.

Jatindra Mohan Chatterjee, *Gatha of Zarathushtra*, Navasari, 1933, *JBORS*, Vol. XIX, Part IV, December 1933, p. 416.

A.J. Bernet Kempers, *The Bronzes of Nalanda and Hindu-Javanese Art*, Leiden, 1933, *JBORS*, Vol. XIX, Part IV, December 1933, pp. 416-17.

Pandit Bisheswar Nath Renu, *History of the Rashtrakutas* Jodhpur, 1933, *JBORS*, Vol. XIX, Part IV, December 1933, pp. 417-18.

Buddhist Sutras in Hindi, Mahabodhi Sabha of Sarnath (Benares), *JBORS*, Vol. XXI, Part IV, December 1935, p. 251.

Rahula Sankritayayan, *Buddha's Life* (Hindi), Benares, *JBORS*, Vol. XXI, Part IV, December 1935, p. 251.

N.C. Mehta, *Bharartiya Chitrakala*, *JBORS*, Vol. XXI, Part IV, December 1935,

p. 252.

Ranjit Sitaram Pandit, *River of Kings (History of Kashmir)*, Allahabd, *JBORS*, Vol. XXI, Part IV, December 1935, p. 252.

Bimala Churn Law, *Mahavira: His Life and Teachings*, Luzac and Co., London, 1937, *JA*, 1937.

V.M. Shah (ed.) *Pauma Chariyam of Vimalasuri*, Surat, 1936, *JA*, 1937.

Writings on KPJ

Ambastha, G.P., 'Dr. K.P. Jayaswal – A Memoir', *Hindu Polity*, Third Edition, Bangalore City, 1943, pp. xxiii-xxxii.

Banerji-Sastri, A.P., 'Dr. K.P. Jayaswal – A Tribute' *Hindu Polity* (2nd Ed), The Bangalore Printing & Publishing Co., LTD, Bangalore City, 1943, pp. XXXII-XXXIV

Dikshitar, V.R. Ramachandra, 'Dr. K.P. Jayaswal – An Appreciation', *Hindu Polity* (2nd Ed), The Bangalore Printing & Publishing Co., LTD, Bangalore City, 1943, pp. XXXIV-XXXVI.

Dinkar, Ramdhari Singh, 'Punyashlok Jayaswalji' in Ramdhari Singh Dinkar, *Sansmaran aur Shraddhanjaliyan*, Udayachal, Rajendranagar, Patna, 1969, and *KPJCV*, KPJRI, 1981, pp. 13-22.

Diwakar (ed.), *Itihas-Purusha Dr. Kashi Prasad Jayaswal (Sansmaran aur Shraddhanjali)*, Drishti Prakashan, Navada, Bihar, 2003.

Dutt, Jayshree, 'Kashi Prasad jayaswal: Vakil jo Itihaskaar Bana', Saptahik Hindustan, 22-28 November, New Delhi, 1981, p. 39&53, 'Jayaswal Centenary Function', *The Indian Nation*, Patna, Nov. 27 & 28, 1981, p. 1.

Gangoly, O.C., 'A Note on Mr. Jayaswal Discovery of Two Saisunaga Statues' (?), *MR*, October 1919, pp. 419-24.

Jayaswal, Chaturbhuj Singh, 'Dr. Kashi Prasad Jayaswal: Bikhari Smritiyan', *Aaj*, Patna, 1 December, 1981 Patna, 1st December, 1981.

Jayaswal, Sushila, 'Mere Pujya Pita Shri Kashi Prasad Jayaswal', *KPJCV*, KPJRI, 1981, pp. 56-58.

Kesari, Arjun Das, 'Jayaswal: Ek Apritam Pratibha, Anokha Vyaktitv', Dharmyug, 15 November 1981, pp. 43-44.

Manuk, P.C., 'Dr. K.P. Jayaswal–The Barrister and Man–A Character Sketch', *JBORS*, Vol. XXIII, Part IV, 1937, pp. 403-17, Reprinted, *KPJCV*, KPJRI, 1981, pp. 46-53.

Pathak, Indira Kant, 'Bharatiy Itihas-Vidya ke Jyotidhar Dr. Kashi Prasad Jayaswal', KPJRI, Patna, 1987.

Prasad, Dr. Rajendra, 'Kashi Prasad Jayaswal', *JBORS*, Vol. XXIII, Part IV, 1937, pp. 399-402, Reprinted, *KPJCV*, KPJRI, 1981, pp. 44-45.

Ram, Dr. Rajendra, 'Life and Works of Kashi Prasad Jayaswal', *KPJCV*, KPJRI, 1981, pp. 59-72.

Roy, K.K., 'Mr. K.P. Jayaswal at the Oriental Conference', *MR*, May 1935, Vol. 55, pp. 424-28.

Sankritayayan, Rahul, 'Dr. Kashi Prasad Jayaswal', Vishal *Bharat*, September 1937, Reprinted, *KPJCV*, KPJRI, Patna, 1981, pp. 1-12.

Sankritayayan, Rahul, 'Dr. Kashi Prasad Jayaswal', JBORS, Vol. XXXVII, Reprinted, *KPJCV*, KPJRI, 1981, pp. 54-55.

Sankritayayan, Rahul, 'Dr. Kashi Prasad Jayaswal', *Rahul Vangmaya*, Vol. II, No. I, pp. 672-80.

Sen, Surendranath, 'Mr. Jayaswal discovery of two Śaiśunaga statues', *MR*, November 1919, p. 546.

Sinha, Dr. Sachchidananda, 'Kashi Prasad Jayaswal', *Some Eminent Bihar Contemporaries*, Himalaya Publication, Patna 1944, Reprinted, *KPJCV*, KPJRI, 1981, pp. 27-30.

Sinha, Dr. B.P., 'Kashi Prasad Jayaswal', *Historians and Historiography in Modern India*, ed. by S.P. Sen, Institute of Historical Studies, Calcutta, 1973, Reprinted, *KPJCV*, KPJRI, 1981, pp. 31-43.

Umashankar, 'Dr. Kashi Prasad Jayaswal' 1881-1937, *KPJCV*, KPJRI, 1981, pp. 23-26.

'Vinod' Baijnath Singh, 'Ve Din: Ve Log, Janmshati Shraddhanjali Dr. Kashi Prasad Jayaswal', *Nai Dhara*, November 1981, pp. 20-28.

Vinod, Bhagawan Chandra, *Dr. Kashi Prasad Jayaswal (Mahaan Jivan-Laghu Parichay)*, Bateshwar-Priya Shodh Sansthan, Madhepura, Bihar, 1983.

Verma, Mathura Prasad, *Jayaswal Jati Parichay*, H.K. Jayaswal Sabha, Prayag, 1978.

Verma, Mathura Prasad, Jayaswal, Mishrilal, *Vishwavikhyat Itihaskar Dr. Kashi Prasad Jayaswal*, H.K. Jayaswal Sabha, Prayag, 1985.

Viyogi, Mohanlal Mahato, 'Vidya Mahodadhi K.P. Jayaswal', in Mohanlal Mahato Viyogi, *Sapt- Suman*, Sahitya Nikunja, Saran 1935, pp. 141-48.

Viyogi, Mohanlal Mahato, 'Doctor Jayaswal', *Saraswati*, Oct. 1937, Part 38, No.4, pp. 330-40.

History-Sheet of Kashi Prasad Jayaswal, File No. 118c, File No. 137, Political Special, File No. 178/1914, File No. XIIIE-41/36, File Nos. 83, 2N-1 of 32, 42/102(1), 4036 P, 42/102(3) BSA.

Further Readings

Altekar, A.S., *State and Government in Ancient India*, Motilal Banarsidas, Delhi, 1996.

Basham, A.L., *The Wonder That Was India*, Picador, 3rd ed., 2004.

Basham, A.L., *Studies in Indian History and Culture*, Sambodhi Publications, Calcutta, 1964.

Bhandarkar, D.R., *Some Aspects of Ancient Hindu Polity*, Banaras Hindu University, 1929.

Blackburn, Stuart, Dalmia, Vasudha, *India's Literary History, Essays on Nineteenth Century*, second edition, Permanent Black, New Delhi, 2008.

Chakrabarti, Dilip K., *Colonial Indology: Socio politics of the Ancient Indian Past,* Munshiram Manoharlal, New Delhi, 1997.

Chandra, Bipan, *India's Struggle for Independence 1857-1947,* Viking, New Delhi, 1987.

Chatterjee, Partha, *Empire and Nation*, Permanent Black, Ranikhet, 2010.

Dalmia, Vasudha, *Nationalisation of Hindu Traditions: Bharatendu Harishchandra and Nineteenth-Century Banaras*, Oxford University Press, New Delhi, 1999.

Gautam, P.K., *One Hundred Years of Kauṭilya's Arthaśāstra,* Indian Institute for Defence Studies and Analysis, 2013

Ghoshal, U.N., *Studies in Indian History and Culture,* 2nd Rev. Edn, New Delhi: Orient Longman, 1965.

Gopal, S., & Thapar, Romila, *Problems of Historical Writings in India,* New Delhi, 1963.

Goyal, Shankar, *Recent Historiography of Ancient India,* Kusumanjali Prakashan, Jodhpur 1997.

Gupta, P.L., *Sixty Years of the Numismatic Society of India* (1910-71), History and Presidential Addresses, Banaras, 1973.

Gupta, P.L., *Patna Museum Catalogue of Antiquities,* Patna, 1965.

Gupta, P.L., *The Imperial Guptas*, Vishwavidyalaya Prakashan, Baranas, 1979.

Habib, Irfan, *Essays in Indian History: Towards a Marxist Perception*, Tulika, New Delhi 1995.

Habib, Irfan (ed.), *Religion in Indian History,* Tulika Books, New Delhi, 2007.

Harder, Hans, *Literature and Nationalist Ideology*, Social Science Press, New Delhi, 2008.

Jha, Jata Shankar, *Early Revolutionary Movements in Bihar,* KPJRI, Patna, 1977.

Jha, Jata Shankar, *K.P. Jayaswal Commemoration Volume*, KPJRI, Patna, 1981.

Kane, P.V., *History of Dharmaśāstra.*

Kosambi, D.D., An *Introduction to the Study of Indian History,* Popular Prakashan, Bombay, 2nd Revised edition, 1975.

Kruger, Horst (ed.), *Kunwar Mohammad Ashraf: An Indian Scholar and Revolutionary* (1903-1962), Delhi, 1960.

Lal, Vinay, *The History of History,* Oxford University Press, New Delhi, 2003.

Lahiri, Nayanjot, *Marshalling the Pasts Ancient India and its Modern Histories*, Ranikhet, 2012.

Mukherjee, Meenakshi, *An Indian for All Seasons: The Many Lives of R. C. Dutt,* Penguin Books, New Delhi, 2009.

Mishra, Girish and Pandey, Braj Kumar, *Sociology and Economics of Casteism in India: A Study of Bihar,* New Delhi, 1996.

Nehru, Jawaharlal, *An Autobiography*, 1936, Oxford University Press, New

Delhi.

Orsini, Francesca, *The Hindi Public Sphere*, 1920-1940, 3rd Ed., Oxford University Press, New Delhi, 2011.

Panda, Harihar, *Prof. H.C. Raychaudhuri*, ICHR, Northern Book Centre, Delhi, 2007.

Patel, Hitendra, *Communalism and Intelligentsia in Bihar*, 1870-1930, Orient Blackswan, New, Delhi, 2011.

Pathak,V.S., *Ancient Historians of India: A Study in Historical Biographies*, Asia Publishing House, Bombay 1966; 2nd Imp., Gorakhpur: Purva Sansthana, 1984.

Phillips, C.H., *Historians of India, Pakistan and Ceylon*, Oxford University Press & SOAS, 1961.

Puri, B.N., *Ancient Indian Historiography*, Atma Ram & Sons, Delhi, 1994.

Ramaswamy, Vijaya, & Sharma, Yogesh (eds.), *Biography as History: Indian Perspective*, Orient Blackswan, New Delhi, 2009.

Raychaudhuri, H.C., *Political History of Ancient India*, 6th ed. Calcutta, 1953.

Sinha, Sachchidanand, *Some Eminent Bihar Contemporaries*, Himalaya Publications, Patna, 1943.

Sarkar, Sumit, *Modern India 1885-1947*, Macmillan Delhi, 1983.

Sen, S.P. (ed.), *Historians and Historiography in Modern India*, Institute of Historical Studies, Calcutta, 1976.

Sharma, R.S. (ed.), *A Survey of Research in the Social and Economic History of India*, New Delhi, ICHR and Ajanta Press, 1986.

Sharma, R.S., *Rethinking India's Ancient Past*, Oxford University Press, New Delhi, 2009.

Sharma, R.S., *Political Ideas and Institutions in Ancient India*, Motilal Banarasidas, Delhi, Reprint, 2012.

Sharma, R.S., *India's Ancient Past*, OUP, New Delhi, 2005.

Sharma, R.S., *Sudras in Ancient India*, Motilal Banarasidas, Delhi, 1990.

Sharma R.S., *Material Culture and Social Formations in Ancient India*, Macmillan, Delhi, 1985.

Sharma, R.S., Jha, Vivekanand Jha, *Indian Society Historical Probings*, ICHR, New Delhi, 1974.

Shrivastava, S.K., *Jadunath Sarkar: The Historian at Work*, Anamika Publication, Delhi 1989.

Singh, Upinder, *The discovery of Ancient India*, Permanent Black, Delhi 2004.

Sinha, Chitaranjan, *K.P. Jayaswal Research Institute: An Introductory Glimpse*, KPJRI, Patna, 1985.

Thapar, Romila, *Aśoka and the Decline of the Mauryas*, 2nd ed., Oxford University Press, 1997.

Thapar, Romila, *Ancient Indian Social History* Some Interpretations, Orient Longman, Reprint, 1996.

Thapar, Romila, *Early India from Origins to AD 1300*, Penguin Books, 2003.

Thapar, Romila (ed.), *Recent Perspectives of Early Indian History*, 2nd ed.,

Popular Prakashan, Mumbai, 1998.
Thapar, Romila, *Cultural Pasts*, Oxford University Press, New Delhi, 2000.

Works in Hindi

शर्मा, रामविलास, *महावीर प्रसाद द्विवेदी और हिन्दी नवजागरण*, तृतीय संस्करण, राजकमल प्रकाशन, नई दिल्ली, 2010।

बच्चनए हरिवंश राय, *नीर का निर्माण फिर*, राजपाल एण्ड सन्स, नई दिल्ली, 1999।

तलवारए वीरभारत, *रस्साकशी : उन्नीसवीं सदी का नवजागरण और पश्चिमोत्तर प्रान्त*, द्वितीय संस्करण, सारांश प्रकाशन, नई दिल्ली, 2006।

शिशिर, कर्मेन्दु, *हिन्दी नवजागरण : वाद-विवाद और आधुनिक सन्दर्भ,* पहल, दिल्ली, 2012।

गौड़, हरप्रकाश, *सरस्वती और राष्ट्रीय जागरण,* नैशनल पब्लिशिंग हाउस, नई दिल्ली, 1983।

मिश्रा, शिवगोपाल, *राहुलजी के अज्ञात पत्र,* हिन्दुस्तानी एकेडेमी, इलाहाबाद, 2010।

व्यास, लक्ष्मीशंकर (सं.), *सभापतियों के भाषण, भाग 1*, हिन्दी साहित्य सम्मलेन, प्रयाग, इलाहाबाद, 1987।

शुक्ल, प्रेमनारायण, (सं.), *सभापतियों के भाषण, भाग 3*, हिन्दी साहित्य सम्मलेन, प्रयाग, इलाहाबाद, 1987।

मिश्र, विद्यानिवास, (सं.), *सभापतियों के भाषण, भाग 2*, हिन्दी साहित्य सम्मलेन, प्रयाग, इलाहाबाद, 2001।

तिवारी, गंगासागर, *हिन्दी साहित्य सम्मलेन का इतिहास*, द्वितीय खण्ड, हिन्दी साहित्य सम्मलेन, प्रयाग, इलाहाबाद, 2012।

शुक्ल, बच्चा, *हिन्दी साहित्य के विकास में सरस्वती का योगदान*, विशाल पब्लिकेशंस, पटना, 2004।

रौशन, अभिषेक, *बालकृष्ण भट्ट और आधुनिक हिन्दी आलोचना का आरम्भ*, अंतिका प्रकाशन, गाजियाबाद, 2009।

श्रीवास्तव, मुरलीधर, *हिन्दी के यूरोपीय विद्वान : व्यक्तित्व और कृतित्व*, बिहार हिंदी ग्रन्थ अकादमी, पटना, 1973।

मिश्र, विभूति, (सं.), *हिन्दी की विकास यात्रा और हिन्दी सेवी संस्थाएँ,* हिन्दी साहित्य सम्मलेन, प्रयाग, इलाहाबाद, 2011।

यायावर, भारत (सं.), *महावीर प्रसाद द्विवेदी रचनावली,* किताबघर, नई दिल्ली, 1995।

सिंह, ओम प्रकाश (सं.), *आचार्य रामचन्द्र शुक्ल ग्रंथावली*, प्रकाशन संस्थान, नई दिल्ली, 2007।

सांकृत्यायन, कमला (सं.), *राहुल वाङ्मय*, राधाकृष्ण प्रकाशन, नई दिल्ली, 1994।

मंगलमूर्ति (सं.), *शिवपूजन सहाय साहित्य-समग्र,* अनामिका पब्लिशर्स, नई दिल्ली, 2011।

पालीवाल, कृष्णदत्त (सं.), *मैथिलीशरण गुप्त ग्रंथावली,* वाणी प्रकाशन, नई दिल्ली, 2008।

नागर, शरद (सं.), *अमृत लाल नागर रचनावली,* राजपाल सन्स, नई दिल्ली, 1992।

राय, नंदकिशोर नवल (सं.) *दिनकर रचनावली,* लोकभारती प्रकाशन, इलाहाबाद, 2011।

शर्मा, सुरेश (सं.), *रामवृक्ष बेनीपुरी ग्रंथावली,* राधाकृष्ण प्रकाशन, नई दिल्ली, 1998।

श्रीधर, विजयदत्त (सं.), *भारतीय पत्रकारिता कोष,* वाणी प्रकाशन, नई दिल्ली, 2010।
लाल, श्रीकृष्ण (सं.), *हीरक जयंती : नागरी प्रचारिणी सभा,* नागरी प्रचारिणी सभा, वाराणसी, संवत 2011।
वर्मा, ब्रजशंकर, *बिहार की साहित्यिक प्रगति,* बिहार हिन्दी साहित्य सम्मलेन, पटना, 1956।
श्री वेंकटेश्वर समाचार (साप्ताहिक) हीरक जयंती, (दो खंडों में), 1956।

Journals, Weeklies & Reports

Annual Report of the Patna Museum
Annual Report of Patna University
Hind-Kesari
Hindi Pradeep
Journal of Bihar and Orissa Research Society
Journal of the Royal Asiatic Society
Journal of the Asiatic Society of Bengal
Journal of Indian Society of Oriental Art
Kalwar Kesari
Nagari Pracharini Patrika
Prajna Bharati
Pataliputra
Saraswati
The Epigraphia Indica
The Indian Antiquary
The Jaina Antiquary
The Calcutta Weekly Notes
The Calcutta Review
The Modern Review
The Proceedings of the All India Oriental Conference
The Express
The Beharee
Veena

Appendix A
KPJ: Life in Chronology

- 27 November 1881: Born in Jhalda in the Presidency of Bengal. Soon shifted to parental home in Mirzapur, United Provinces.
- 1895-1899: Education at London Mission School, Mirzapur.
- 1899: Joined Queen's College in Banaras, but soon gave up the college and joined his father's business.
- June, 1898: Debut in journalism as a contributor to *Hindi Pradeep*, a Hindi magazine published from Allahabad, United Provinces.
- 1900: Started contributing to other magazines. First article in *Nagari Pracharini Patrika*, a Hindi magazine published from Banaras, United Provinces.
- 1903: First article in *Saraswati*, a Hindi magazine published from Banaras, United Provinces. At that time *Saraswati* was the most prestigious Hindi journal.
- 1906: Appointed editor, *Kalwar Gazette*, a Hindi magazine published from Mirzapur, United Provinces.
- August 1906: Went to Lincoln's Inn, Oxford University, England, to study Law. Was in contact with the Indian revolutionaries living in England.
- 1909: At Oxford awarded the Davis Chinese Scholarship to study Chinese language.
- July 1910: Came back to India after acquiring the credentials of a Barrister-at-Law, a master's degree in Ancient History and certification in Chinese language. In India he was put under police surveillance.
- January 1911: Enrolled as a lawyer at the Calcutta High Court.
- 1912: Delivered a lecture on 'Hindu Rajyashastra' (Hindu polity) at the third Hindi Sahitya Sammelan, in Calcutta.
- 1913: The lecture at the Hindi Sahitya Sammelan was published as: 'An Introduction to Hindu Polity' in *Modern Review*, an academic magazine published in English from Calcutta.
- 1913: Was appointed lecturer in the University of Calcutta, but was rejected by the colonial government.
- 1913: Shifted to Patna.

- 1914: Enrolled for practice at the Patna High Court. Surveillance was lifted.
- 1914: Appointed editor of *Pataliputra,* a Hindi weekly published from Patna (resigned in 1915).
- 1915: Was founding member of BORS and Patna Museum. Both were established in this year.
- 1918: Appointed as Reader at Patna University, where he served in various capacities till his death in 1937.
- 1924: Appointed member of the Bodh-Gaya Temple Inquiry Committee.
- 1924: Publication of *Hindu Polity* as a monograph, KPJ's first book.
- 1927: Awarded the Baroda Golden Jubilee Prize from the Gaekwad rulers of Baroda.
- 1927: Appointed Member, Managing Committee, Patna Museum, and in the same year elevated to Officiating President. He was repeatedly made Officiating President till 1930 when he was appointed as President, which he remained till his death in 1937.
- 1930: Elected Chairman, Reception Committee, Sixth All India Oriental Conference, Patna. Elected General President of the Seventh All India Oriental Conference, Baroda, 1933.
- 1933: Elected President, Bhagalpur Hindi Prantiya Sammelan
- 1935: Elected President, Numismatic Society of India, Mysore. Re-elected President for subsequent year in Udaipur.
- 1935: Elected President of Bharatiya Itihas Parishad, All India Hindi Sahitya Sammelan, Indore.
- 1936: Delivered a lecture at the Royal Asiatic Society, London.
- 1936: Conferred Doctor of Philosophy by Patna University.
- 1936: The principal founder of the Bharatiya Itihas Parishad, emerging from the Itihas Parishad of the All India Hindi Sahitya Sammelan. It was to be a body of historians coming together to counter colonial writings on Indian history.
- 4 August 1937: Died after months of illness.

Sahu Mahadev Prasad, KPJ's Father

KPJ before leaving for England in 1906

KPJ before leaving for England in 1906

डा० काशीप्रसाद जायसवाल (सपरिवार, 1929 ई०)

A group of delegates to the VIth Oriental Conference, Patna, 1930 (with the President in the centre to the right of Sir Jivanji Jamshedji Modi)

His Excellency the Patron, the President, and the Members of the Reception Committee with some distinguished guests at Mr. Jayaswal's 'At Home'.

1st Row—His Excellency Sir Hugh Stephenson (centre), Mr. Hira Lal (to the right) and Sir Jivanji Modi (to the left),
2nd Row—Mr. Justice Mackpherson, Sir Md. Fakhruddin, Mr. Justice James, Mr. K. P. Jayaswal, Sir Courtney Terrell.
3rd Row—Mr. H. Lambert, Mr. H. E. Stapelton, Mr. G. E. Fawcus, Mr. M. Seth, Mr. P. C. Manuk, Rai Br. R. K. Jalan, Moulvi Md. Reyaz Hasan Khan, Mr. Sham Bahadur.

A Group Photo of the Delegates of Seventh Oriental Conference, Baroda 1933

A Group Photo of the Delegates of Seventh Oriental Conference (Hall), Baroda 1933

KPJ and his wife

KPJ's Last Journey – 4th August 1937

Eldest Son of KPJ's – Sri Chet Singh Jayaswal

KJP's Son Chaturbhuj Singh Jayaswal – 1990

Celebrating 100th Birth Anniversary of KPJ, the Government of India had issued Postal Stamp in his honour in 1981

Appendix B

सम्मान-पत्र

ओम्
बा खिदमते
जनाब काशी प्रसाद जायसवाल
एम ए (ओक्सन) बार-एट-लॉ
प्रेसीडेंट
ऑल इंडिया ओरीएन्टल कांफ्रेंस
तोहफा-ए-मुबारक
श्रीमान गुल्फी शहर बरोदें उड़ी सुवास
युग युग से अर्ज की थी यमुना नदी के पास
तकदीर में लिखा था ये शुभकार का होना
काबिल शख्स की कद्र पे इकरार का होना
शिक्षण को जा विलायत कामिल हो गए
प्रगटे हमारी जात में जौहर चमक गए
साहित्य पुष्पवादी के तुम पुष्पहार हो
दरबार सर के ताज हो बागो बहार हो
कोमल फूलों से गूथ के में काव्याहार को
नवरंग से चमन में लाया बहार को
बरसे कृपा की वृष्टि रखे हरा चमन को
निशदिन करे गुलों से क्षणगार में जीवन को
तकते रहेंगे तुमको बागो जहां के हर गुल
किस शोख में मुबारक देते है आज बुलबुल
मुख पे रहे प्रकाशित नीति वचन की ज्योति
बामे फलक से बरसे तुमपर कृपा की ज्योति
रहे वे सदा कृपालु तुम पर नसीब देवी
करते रहें दुआएं खीदमत में आके फिदवी
वादे बहार आकर खुशियां मना रही है
दख्जा दीला के आला खुशबो उड़ा रही है

नडीयाद नवनीत
26-12-1933

Appendix C

Photographs of KPJ's House and Patna Museum

Patna Museum

Main Gate of Mirzapur House

Main Structure of Mirzapur House

KPJ's Patna House in 1926

KPJ's Patna House in 1968

Appendix D

Acquisitions of Patna Museum

Acquisitions made by the Patna Museum from the year ending 31st March 1918 to 31st March 1938

1918: In the Archaeological section 114 pieces of sculpture including a magnificent statue of the Maurya period, have been collected. The Sati Stone from the Manbhum district and boundary stones from the Orissa States form an interesting feature of the collections. A special feature of the Museum is the collection of articles of the Stone Age and copper age and a few ancient ornaments and plates made of bronze discovered by Babu S.C. Roy, from ancient graves of Chhota Nagpur, locally attributed to a pre-Munda people whom tradition calls the Asurs. Forty-seven stone celts collected by the Hon'ble Mr. E.H.C. Walsh from the Santal Paraganas and the Darjeeling districts have been presented to the Museum besides two hundred stone celts from Ranchi district presented by Babu S.C. Roy from his own collection. Mr. C.W. Anderson of Chakradharpur has presented sixty-two stone celts and sixty one flakes and scrapers, besides pieces of the skull of what looks like a wild horse found in association with these celts, which were obtained by him from a stratum which points to the celts being Paleolithic in origin.

In the ethnological section, His Honor Sir E.A. Gait has presented a number of articles of ethnological interest collected by him, including an Andamanese bow and arrow, a Nicobarese devil-dodger, bark-cloth used by the Nicobarese. A number of articles in present and former use by the aborigines of Chhota Nagpur (including weapons and implements, household utensils, musical instruments, clothing and ornaments) have been collected by Babu S.C. Roy, and a collection of similar articles from the Tributary States of Orissa have received from Mr. Cobden-Ramsay.

In the section of mineralogy, specimen of different kinds of minerals quarried in this Province have been presented to the Museum by the Cape Copper Company, and several coal, mica and other mining companies.

~	1919	1920	1921	1922	1923	1924	1925	1926	1927	1928	1929	1930	1931	1932	1933	1934	1935	1936	1937	1938
Archaeology	885	1089	969	1966	273	775	39	2	255	19	135	20	62	266	680	45	242	157	209	35
Numismatics	291	316	43	3744	2721	1267	179	326	267	368	101	57	84	900	159	3049	248	26	2051	1411
Picture Gallery	10	28																		
Mineralogy		240																		
Wartrophies	16					24														3
Estampages		435	9	138	27	16	9	22	1	103	85	8	5	25	11	9	4		1	
Plaster of Paris Casts		36	20	9	18		2	11	23	22	1	3	3	3		1				
Photo Prints			163	40	24	30	25	23	2	61	67	44	48	90	51	96	76	191	145	61
Ethnological		44	53	4	13		27			1	5	4	9	19	2		57		6	
Art		5	13	13								53	52	57	153	35	24	22	46	60
Industrial		169	14									10								
Geological					52	2		193	300	65	153	9	190				255			
Art & Industrial					33	75	9	15	51	11	18									
Natural History							2				31	72	1	1	1	30	4	1	2	
Old Arms										9	4		51	3		1		1	4	
Arch. Mohenjodaro																			514	
Arch. Patna Sewerage	~	~	~	~	~	~	~	~	~	~	~	~	~	~	~	~	~	1028	~	~
coins - do -	~	~	~	~	~	~	~	~	~	~	~	~	~	~	~	~	~	71	~	~
Misc.	~	5	2	~	~	~	~	~	~	~	~	~	40	23	112	~	1	8	25	66

(Source: *Annual Reports of Patna Museum*)

Appendix E

Donations made by KPJ to the Patna Museum

- Tantra Manuscript, *ARPM*, 1920, p. 63.
- Pieces of Estampages of selected portion of Khāravela inscription (2nd C.B.C.) from Khandagiri, Bhuvaneswar, district Puri, *ARPM*, 1928, p. 46.
- Estampages of inscription from unknown place (2nd century B.C.), *ARPM*, 1928, p. 46.
- Asokan Rock Edict from Bhabra (3rd century B.C.), *ARPM*, 1928, p. 46.
- Dhauli Rock Edict of Aśoka (3rd century B.C.) from Dhauli, Bhuvaneswar, *ARPM*, 1928, p. 46.
- Mathura, Indian Museum, Khāravela, etc., from various places (1st century A.D.), *ARPM*, 1928, p. 46.
- Estampages of inscription in one piece from Khandagiri, Khāravela inscription (2nd century B.C.), *ARPM* 1928, p. 47.
- Casts of important portions of the inscriptions from Khāravela and Bodh Gaya railing, *ARPM* 1928, p. 68.
- Granite Arch Stone, measurement, length 2'-8 3/4", length of top are 2'-3"; length of bottom top upper portion of are 11", breadth of stone bottom portion 1'-5/8", breadth of stone upper portion 1'- 11/4". The Stone has of sets on three faces and the fourth face of the stone is projecting. The peculiar cut of the stone does not support the idea of the central key-stone. The stone certainly formed a portion of an arc of a circle. It is nicely polished. Three letters of the inner are Ko, Kau and Chu. Absence of letter in 3rd corner is significant (Pre-Maurya period, Dargah Arzani, Patna), *ARPM*, 1929, p. 18.
- Modern copper coins (7411-7414), *ARPM*, 1929, p. 28.
- Inscription on the statue of Wema (KuṃgḌa time), Mathura Museum, District Muttra, *ARPM*, 1929, p. 31.
- Brick, 13 1/8"x 11"x 3", broken at one end. It is a brick used in making a platform; well burnt (Maurya period, Jalamandir, Pawapuri, district

Patna, 9' below the present level at the north-east corner of the mandir), *ARPM*, 1930, p. 16.

- Brick, 12 14/16"x10"x 2 1/4" complete. It is a brick used in making platform; well burnt. It differs in measurement from the other brick; one end 13", another 12'6"? (Maurya period, Jalamandir, Pawapuri, Patna), *ARPM*, 1930, 16.
- Brick, 8 1/2 x 7 1/2 x 3 1/2, both sides rough with marks like letters (Gupta Age, Bhumra, Nagod State, Central India), *ARPM*, 1933, p. 53.
- Sri Raghav (coin, Obverse - Sri Raghav Chandra Pratabputra), *ARPM*, 1933, p. 54 (Jayaswal presented 3 bricks and one coin in the year ending 31st March 1933).
- A piece of sandstone coping?, a mortice hole below, 10 1/4 x 10 x 5 1/2 (Maurya period, Bhita, district Allahabad) *ARPM*, 1935, p. 16.
- 17. A piece of stone containing a relief figure of an elephant with the rider having fly whisk, much defaced, 10" x 7" x 3 1/4 (SuÙga period, Bhita, district Allahabad) *ARPM*, 1935, p. 16.
- A fragment of stone containing the head of a man in relief with tenon, 6 1/4" x 3 1/4 x 2 1/4 (Suṅga period, Bhita, district Allahabad) *ARPM*, 1935, p. 16.
- A terracotta bust of some human being, probably female but it is not clear, face much defaced, height 4 1/4" (Maurya period, Bhita, district Allahabad) *ARPM*, 1935, p. 16.
- A fragment of stone containing a.figure flying Gandharva, 9 1/2" x 4 1/2" x 3 1/2" (Gupta period, Bhita, district Allahabad) *ARPM*, 1935, p. 16.
- AR Punch-marked coin, obverse - (1) solar, (2) Taurine and crescent, (3) Three arched chaitya and crescent, Reverse-Indistinct, *ARPM*, 1935, p. 18.
- Handi pieces from Radhia, Champaran, Bihar, *ARPM*, 1935-38, p. 19.
- Brick Broken 12"x10" from the Stupa in front of the Balehara (Kolharia) pillar of Aśoka, Muzaffarpur, Bihar, *ARPM*, 1935-38, p. 27.
- Punch-marked coins, serial numbers 12552-52} E, *ARPM*, 1935-38, p. 105.
- Cast coin, 12655, *ARPM*, 1935-38, P.105.
- Post Card containing the autograph of V.A. Smith, size 4.5"x 3.5", London, *ARPM*, 1935-38, p. 133.
- Nepalese title deed on palm-leaf, two lines are written in Newari character, size 2'- 5.5"x 1.25", Nepal, *ARPM*, 1935-38, p. 133.
- One silver punch-marked coin from Jahanabad (of a lot of 85 coins discovered in a pot buried underground, other coins having been lost in the hands of the finder) was presented by K.P. Jayaswal, Esq., M.A. (Oxon.), Barrister-at-Law, President, Managing Committee, Patna Museum. (1935).

(Source: *Annual Reports of Patna Museum*)

Appendix F

Proposal for Bharatiya Itihas Parishad

1. It is proposed that a history of India (Hindu Period) will be prepared (the writer of which should be Indian), which should be considered authentic to their field and must be absolutely free from those faults, which is engrossed in the Cambridge History of Rapson and the History of Vincent Smith. The History of Vincent Smith has been becoming obsolete and there is a lack of uniformity in the Cambridge History and believes the beginning of the History of India from the time of the Buddha.
2. I want to start this history from Vedic Kings and finish it to the time of King Bhoja and his contemporaries because it is a period of cultural revival. Till that time the Muslim invaders were restricted to the gulf. The victory of the Muslims and the decline of the Hindus are virtually an indicator of a new era. Therefore, it should be understood that with King Bhoja there was end of the Hindu period.
3. The Hindu period should be in two parts: part one—From Vedas to the Bharashiva and, part two- From Vākāṭakas to the Bhoja.
   In each part, there will be 500 readable pages and 100 pages supplementary material including the plates. It is possible that in the second part there would be more than 100 pages. The size of the page will be similar to the Cambridge History.
4. The expected expenditure would be as follows;

a.	The honorarium to the writers, @ Rs. 10 per page	Rs. 10000
b.	The expenditure of printing of 1200 pages (1000 +200 pageIndex etc., @ Rs.3 per page including proof reading)	Rs. 36,000
c.	The expenditure on my house as the Editor (mainly the salary of the fellow scholar and tankan	Rs. 9000/-
d.	Extra to the expenditure of photo, which will be given from the contingency fund & mounting of the 2000 books	Rs. 4,000
e.	Misc.	Rs. 1,000
	Total	Rs. 60,000

5. Apart from roughly 60,000 expenditure, a publisher has promised me that if I become an Editor, then he has taken the responsibility to sponsor extra fund, along with the expenditure of item 2, 3, and 4. That is how, there will be a collection of extra money with me, through that we can sustain the expenditure of the honorarium and general contingencies, which should be around Rs. 15,000 to 20,000.
6. The following proposal is before the University:
   a. The name of the book should be on the name of the University, "The Banaras History of India".
   b. That should be considered as a publication of the Hindu University.
   c. The amount of Rs. 20,000 or 25,000 should be collected in the name of the University, for that I will give a agent to the Editor of the Hindi weekly *Ganga*, who would arrange this amount within a short period of time by only from 20 people and if he becomes failure in that then I will give it from my own pocket. If this amount of Rs. 20,000 or 25,000 is collected from the cooperation and in the name of the University, then the right of the ownership will be that of the University. But it will be in that ratio only because there will be more expenditure of the publisher in that.
   d. The University authorities must ponder over the above said issues, as much as possible, and I must be informed about their decision. I just want to say in this regard that the Pro Vice-Chancellor of the Calcutta University wants to think about my proposal. But because I have first of all informed the authorities of your University and I have relation with this University as a visiting Prof. that is why I think appropriate for consideration of this proposal for acceptance to Hindu University.
7. There will be group of three Editors along with me and I will be the chief Editor: 1. Shri K.P. Jayaswal, Chief Editor, 2. Dr. Hiranand Shastri, 3. Father Heras.
8. If it is necessary for the execution of the work, then there could be an Executive Committee, consisting of: 1. Principal Dhruva, 2. Dr. A.K. Kumaraswami, 3. Dr. Hirananda Shastri, 4. Father Heras, 5. K.P. Jayaswal.
9. The proposed history will be both political and cultural; the Editor will choose the articles and will give the uniformity to the history. The number of writers will be between 5 and 10.

(Source: Baijnath Singh 'Vinod', वे दिन : वे लोग, जन्मशती श्रद्धांजलि। 'डॉ. काशी प्रसाद जायसवाल', *Nai Dhara*, November 1981, pp. 20-28.)

Appendix G

KPJ's Personal Letters

13/1/13

Dear Mr Varhaspatya,

I wonder if the long letter I wrote to you from Mirzapur ever reached you.

I shall be very grateful if you could make time to work out the data I give in the next page and tell me the dates in "BC". I want it for my chronology.

Yours truly

Kashi Prasad Jayaswal

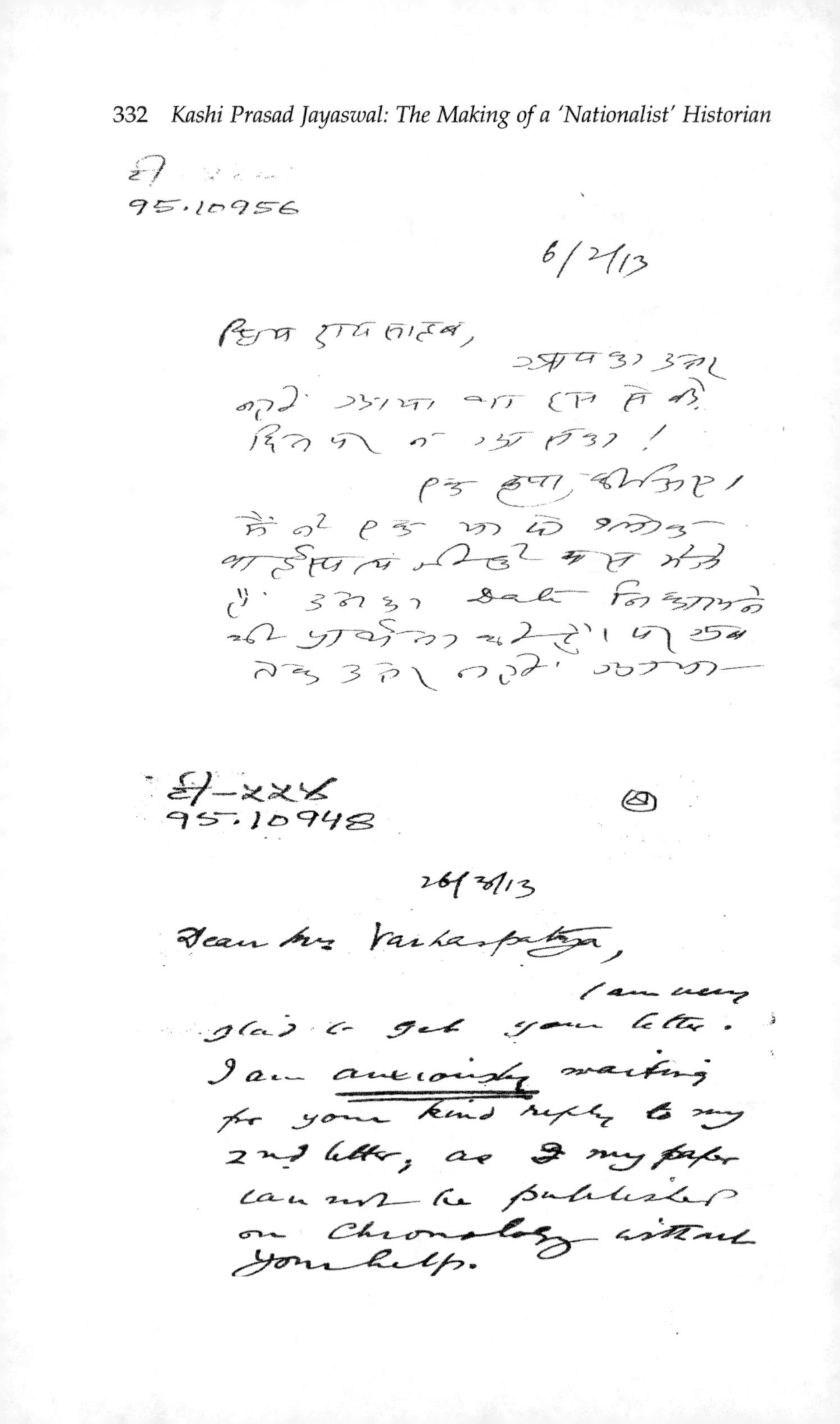

6/2/13

प्रिय राय साहब,

आपका उत्तर [illegible]

[illegible]

यह कृपा कीजिए।

मैं ने [illegible] Date निकालने [illegible]

(8)

26/2/13

Dear Mr Vachaspatya,

I am very glad to get your letter. I am anxiously waiting for your kind reply to my 2nd letter, as my paper can not be published on Chronology without your help.

डी - ५५६
१५.१०.४९

(10)

14/5

प्रियवर [illegible] साहब,

बहुत दिनों से पत्र नहीं आया। मैंने यह, अनुवाद से, ~~Indian~~ Review में [illegible] है। हिन्दी का मूल लेख [illegible] को उपयुक्त [illegible] ने लौटा दिया।

[illegible] के उत्तर नहीं दिया। कई महीने हो गए।

I hope you would find time to consider these data at an early ~~opportunity~~ date.

[illegible]

सन

=

॥

[illegible]
15.10955 Patna, 3-1-28

[illegible]

[illegible]

[illegible]

[illegible]

[illegible]

[illegible]

[illegible]

[illegible]

[illegible]

c/o B. Motilal B.L.
Vakil,
Flora Cottage
Monghyr
[illegible]

[illegible]
[illegible]
75.10947 ① [illegible] Patna, 7/6/36

[illegible]

[illegible]

[illegible]

[illegible]

[illegible]

[illegible]

[illegible]

[illegible]

[illegible] 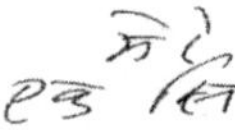 [illegible]

die struck. [illegible]

[illegible]

[illegible]

[illegible]

Index